AMERICA VOTES!

A Guide to Modern Election Law and Voting Rights

Benjamin E. Griffith, Editor

Section of State and Local Government Law

AMERICAN BAR ASSOCIATION
Defending Liberty
Pursuing Justice

Library of Congress Cataloging-in-Publication Data

America votes! : a guide to modern election law and voting rights / edited by Benjamin Griffith. --1st ed.
   p. cm.
 Includes index.
 ISBN 978-1-59031-972-7
 1. Election law--United States. 2. Elections--United States. I. Griffith, Benjamin E.

 KF4886.A86 2008
 342.73'07--dc22

                                                                2007050614

Contents

CHAPTER ONE

Lessons Learned from the 2000 and 2004 Presidential Elections   **1**

JOHN HARDIN YOUNG
SARA L. DUBOIS
RACHEL STEINBERG

CHAPTER FIVE

The Promise and Practice of Election Day Registration 65

STEVEN CARBÓ
BRENDA WRIGHT

CHAPTER SIX

Felon Disenfranchisement 91

JOHN C. KEENEY JR.

CHAPTER SEVEN

Section 5 and the Voting Rights Act Reauthorization and Amendments Act of 2006 105

ABIGAIL THERNSTROM

CHAPTER EIGHT

Reports of My Demise Have Been Overstated: Assessing the Constitutionality of the Recently Renewed Section 5 Preclearance Provision of the Voting Rights Act 129

KRISTEN CLARKE

CHAPTER NINE

Sections Two and Five as Amended by the Voting Rights Act Reauthorization and Amendments Act of 2006   147

BENJAMIN E. GRIFFITH
DAVID D. O'DONNELL

CHAPTER TEN

The Role of Demographic and Statistical Experts in Election Law Litigation   177

BENJAMIN E. GRIFFITH
DAVID O'DONNELL

CHAPTER ELEVEN

Government-Issued Photo Identification and Proof of Citizenship Requirements for Voters 201

JON M. GREENBAUM
JONAH H GOLDMAN

CHAPTER TWELVE

Function Follows Form: Voting Technology and the Law   241

STEPHEN ANSOLABEHERE
CHARLES STEWART III

CHAPTER THIRTEEN

The Growth of Early and Nonprecinct Place Balloting: When, Why, and Prospects for the Future   261

PAUL GRONKE
EVA GALANES-ROSENBAUM

CHAPTER FOURTEEN

Nuts and Bolts for Election Officials: Mississippi: A Case Study   281

LESLIE C. SCOTT

CHAPTER FIFTEEN

Election Challenges Involving Candidates for Federal Office   301

TOMMIE S. CARDIN
LESLIE C. SCOTT

CHAPTER SIXTEEN

Bailout Under the Voting Rights Act   319

J. GERALD HEBERT

CHAPTER SEVENTEEN

Help America Vote Act of 2002: Origins and Impact   335

LESLIE C. SCOTT

Foreword

RICHARD L. HASEN
*William H. Hannon Distinguished Professor
of Law, Loyola Law School, Los Angeles*

Disputes over the proper adoption, interpretation, and implementation of local, state, and federal election law are nothing new, nor is the American Bar Association's involvement in election law questions. As far back as 1972, the ABA House of Delegates passed a resolution urging states to allow college students to register to vote in the area where they attend school. Since then, the ABA, especially through its Standing Committee on Election Law, has published a number of useful publications on election law issues ranging from campaign financing to legislative redistricting to judicial elections. The House of Delegates also has taken positions on election law questions ranging from the proper role of ballot initiatives and referenda to voting rights for residents of the District of Columbia.

But public and professional attention to election law questions has greatly increased since the 2000 Florida election debacle, culminating in the United States Supreme Court's opinion in *Bush v. Gore,* which ended the recount of Florida's vote for president, thereby assuring that George W. Bush and not Al Gore would become the 43rd president of the United States. And the attention is not just of academic interest: Since 2000, the amount of election law litigation has skyrocketed, including (but not only) litigation related to the rules for conducting presidential elections in so-called "battleground states." Election law has become part of each candidate's political strategy, and in a highly polarized political atmosphere the stakes can be high indeed: The public's view of the fairness of the electoral process and the impartiality of the judiciary can be in the balance.

So for lawyers, policymakers, academics, and others with a keen interest in the fairness and integrity of the electoral process, this latest volume by the ABA Section of State & Local Government Law, cosponsored by the ABA Standing Committee on Election Law, comes at a most opportune time. Bringing together a diverse group of lawyers, academics, political scientists, and others, *America Votes! A Guide to Modern Election Law and Voting Rights* explores some of the major questions in the election law area, especially in voting rights and election administration. The chapters offer a nice blend of relevant background, theory, and advocacy on some of the most pressing current election law questions, including

- Does the U.S. Congress have the power to renew the "preclearance" and language assistance provisions of the Voting Rights Act, which Congress recently renewed for another 25 years? The question is likely to come before the U.S. Supreme Court within the next few years. If the Court strikes down these provisions, it could have a great effect on minority voting power in the United States.

- To what extent do either longstanding barriers to voting, such as felon disenfranchisement laws, or more recent election administration changes, such as laws requiring voters to provide photographic identification at the polls, violate the constitutional rights of voters? The photo identification question itself is currently under review by the Supreme Court.

- How will the increased use of absentee ballots and early voting procedures, along with changes in voting technology (such as the adoption of electronic voting) affect the way that ballots are cast and counted, and what legal issues do these voting procedures raise? The recent dispute regarding "undervotes" in the 2006 election for Florida's 13th Congressional District brought the issue back to national attention.

- How should courts handle difficult evidentiary questions that arise in the context of election law litigation?

- What are the appropriate standards for conducting recounts in elections, or for remedying other irregularities in election procedures?

To be sure, the 17 chapters in this volume will not provide the final word on these and other important yet controversial topics. Indeed, the authors of some of the chapters strongly disagree with the authors of other chapters. But for both the novice and the expert in election law, these chapters are useful, interesting, and provocative.

Acknowledgments

This book is a snapshot of America's voting and electoral practices, problems, and most current issues. *America Votes! A Guide to Modern Election Law and Voting Rights* evolved from a loosely organized election-law handbook into a timely publication covering a broad range of current issues and fundamental principles in the dynamic field of election law and voting rights.

From the outset, my intention was to bring together a group of nationally recognized scholars and litigators representing a rich diversity of perspectives. In a single publication our chapter authors have compiled a useful guide for election officials, state and local government personnel involved in election administration during the 2008 election cycle, and grass-roots level election workers, election observers, and poll workers. They have also created a practical tool for lawyers, advocates, and others in the legal profession with an interest in current developments, practices, and standards in the electoral process and participatory democracy. Moreover, this book is intended to be a teaching and learning aid for law school professors and students on the hottest topics in the administration, organization, and implementation of the vast body of law and regulations that govern elections and voting rights in this country.

Almost three years ago Marti Chumbler, a member of the Council of the Section of State & Local Government Law, casually asked me if a book on election law would be marketable. I took the bait. Reauthorization of the expiring preclearance and language-minority assistance provisions of the Voting Rights Act was about to come up on Congress's radar. Electronic voting, same-day registration, and voter identification were getting more and more traction in the news. Sure, a book on cutting-edge issues in election law and voting rights would be marketable.

But could it be written in time for the 2008 election cycle? Would it be useful to a broader segment than the relatively small fraternity of litigators who represent plaintiffs, defendants, and the Justice Department in litigation over vote dilution, redistricting, and minority electoral access and participation? Would it be helpful to election administrators and election officials? Would it be worthwhile reading for citizens interested in some of the hottest topics that will play out in the 2008 election cycle?

And would it be significant to the general public, that vast pluralistic collection of conservative, liberal, right-wing, left-wing, moderate, and uncommitted potential voters who will have the opportunity to exercise their fundamental right to vote and participate in the democratic process in November 2008?

These were serious challenges as I began contacting prospective authors, narrowing down potential subjects that could be treated in this kind of book. What our diverse group of authors created is more about checking the pulse of the electoral process in America as of 2008 than a purely academic analysis of election law. It is more than a sterile study of the political process as it has developed over the past two centuries and as it will unfold during this decade. And it is far more than a recap of the successful yet ongoing struggle for equal voting rights by those citizens eager to be a part of this work-in-progress we call Democracy.

This book is a frank, up-close-and-personal look at the issues I sincerely believe will play an outcome-determinative role in the elections of 2008 and beyond. It is a very generous slice of life, a serious evaluation of the current status of issues that even now are being litigated in the district courts and argued in the appellate courts and the United States Supreme Court. It also draws much of its energy from the left, right, and center of the political spectrum, creating a tension akin to a high-wire act without a net.

As editor and one of the contributing authors, I have many people to thank.

I wish to thank my good friend and colleague in the Section of State and Local Government Law, Mary Kay Klimesh, Chair of the Publications Oversight Board of the ABA Section of State & Local Government Law; the ABA Publishing team of Rick Paszkiet, Holly Hickey, and Rebecca Hicks-Zammit; and the Section's Executive Committee, all of whom energized me with their constant words of encouragement and guidance as we moved forward with the publication process.

I also wish to thank our Section's Director, Tamara Edmonds Askew, an attorney and ABA professional with seven years of experience in this Association, who embraced this publication project and has helped develop a series of CLE Election Law programs for the ABA Midyear Meeting in Los Angeles and the Annual Meeting in New York. I thank her predecessor, Jackie Baker, who served as our Section Director and was a devoted ABA professional for over 22 years before retiring in August 2007, as well as Leigh Stewart, our Section's former Administrator, who was always there to answer day-to-day questions about deadlines, procedure, and protocol.

I also thank the many cosponsors for this book, including the ABA's Standing Committee on Election Law and its Advisory Commission, members of which did triple double duty as authors, reviewers, and editorial assistants. My thanks also go to the Section of Individual Rights and Responsibilities (IR&R) for cosponsoring this book. I thank Constance Slaughter-Harvey, a fellow Mississippian and Margaret Brent Award winner, for graciously allowing the ABA to publish as the Preamble to this book her 2006 testimony before the Senate Judiciary Committee in support of reauthorization of key provisions of the Voting Rights Act. My thanks also go to the Section of Administrative Law and Regulatory Practice, the Commission on Racial Equality and Justice in the Legal Profession, and other entities that agreed to cosponsor and help publicize this book as it hit the shelves in February 2008.

This is a peer-reviewed publication. I want to thank Nadine Cohen, Mathias W. Delort, and Kenneth Tinkler for serving as peer reviewers during the final stages of the publication process. Their constructive criticisms, suggested revisions, and commentary on the 17 chapters helped improve the readability, sharpen the focus, and heighten the intellectual vigor of those chapters.

I also wish to thank a group of dedicated professionals who reviewed the chapter drafts and submitted their own commentaries on the usefulness, relevance, and value of this book. These include my colleagues and former adversaries, Armand Derfner and Laughlin McDonald, with whom I have had the privilege of litigating some of the voting rights issues dealt with in this book. Also included in this group are Bernie Grofman, a nationally recognized expert in the leading voting rights cases decided during the past three decades. Their generous comments that appear on the back cover of this book are sincerely appreciated.

Many members of the Standing Committee on Election Law contributed to this publication project in many helpful ways over the past two years, and I gratefully acknowledge their hard work, time, and effort. My special thanks to Jocelyn F. Benson, Professor at the Wayne State University Law School, and John C. Keeney of Hogan & Hartson's Washington, D.C., office, and also to Jack Young, Jenny Kim, Gigi Hyland, Pamela Gagel, Victoria Wu, and many others who gave unselfishly of their time to read over, critique, and help guide toward the final drafting stages every chapter in this book. Without their hands-on help, we would never have completed this project in such a relatively short period of time.

Above all, I thank the contributing authors for their diligence and commitment to this publication project. I also thank two nationally recognized election law experts, Robert D. Lenhard, Chairman of the Federal Election Commission, and Richard L. Hasen, the William H. Hannon Distinguished Professor of Law at Loyola Law School in Los Angeles, for preparing the book's Introduction and Foreword, respectively. Both labored through the draft manuscript and provided concise and very helpful observations for readers who begin this journey through the most current legal and political issues facing the electorate, the courts, and the nation on the eve of the 2008 Presidential Election.

—Benjamin E. Griffith

About the Editor

Benjamin E. Griffith is Chair of the ABA Section of State & Local Government Law, World Jurist Association's National President for the United States, and State Chair for the International Municipal Lawyers Association (IMLA). He focuses his civil practice on defense of state and local government entities and officials in litigation under the Voting Rights Act, election law, civil rights actions under 42 U.S.C. § 1983, public sector insurance coverage, insurance defense, and environmental law. He is an IMLA Local Government Fellow, recipient of the IMLA Distinguished Public Service Award, and a Fellow of the International Society of Barristers. Since 1994 he has been board-certified in Civil Trial Advocacy by the ABA-sanctioned National Board of Trial Advocacy. He is serving a second term on the ABA Standing Committee on Election Law, and serves on the Governmental Liability Committees of the ABA Litigation Section and the Tort Trial and Insurance Practice Section. He has been a member of Defense Research Institute's Governmental Liability Committee since 1983. He served as chair of IMLA's Counties and Special Municipal Districts Department, President of the National Association of County Civil Attorneys, Chair of the Mississippi Bar's Government Law Section, and President of the Mississippi Association of County Board Attorneys. He has written extensively on the subject of voting rights litigation and local government, with articles published in *The Urban Lawyer, Catholic University Law Review, Stetson University Law Review, The Mississippi Law Journal, The University of Arkansas at Little Rock Law Journal,* and other national journals and professional magazines. In May 1994 he was invited by Chairman Henry Hyde to testify before the House Judiciary Committee's Subcommittee on Civil Rights and the Constitution in Washington, D.C., as part of the Voting Rights Roundtable. He has authored and edited numerous publications in his field of practice, the most recent being "Reinforcing the Formidable Arsenal: Restoration of Purposeful Discrimination as Basis for Denial of Section 5 Preclearance Under the Voting Rights Act Reauthorization and Amendments Act of 2006," *University of Arkansas Law Review* (2007). He is editor of *Census 2000: Strategies and Considerations for State and Local Government* (ABA 2000); *Sexual Harassment in the Public Workplace* (ABA 2001); and *Handbook for County Board Attorneys* (Center for Governmental Technology 2004). He is a partner in the Cleveland, Mississippi, firm of Griffith & Griffith and earned his Juris Doctor from the University of Mississippi School of Law in 1975. He is listed in *Mid-South Superlawyers* 2006 and 2007, and was selected by his peers for inclusion in the 2007 and 2008 editions of *Best Lawyers in America* in the field of municipal law.

About the Contributors and Peer Reviewers

Stephen Ansolabehere is the Elting Morison Professor of Political Science at MIT. He was Co-Director of the Caltech-MIT Voting Technology Project from 2000 to 2004, and has written extensively on electoral politics and representation in the United States. His most recent book, *The End of Inequality* (Norton 2008), examines the history and consequences of *Baker v. Carr* and the Court's interventions to guarantee equal political representation. Since 1998 he has served as a member of the Board of Overseers of the American National Election Study; he is the Director and Principle Investigator of the Cooperative Congressional Election Study, and in 2007 he was inducted into the American Academy of Arts and Sciences.

Terry M. Ao is the Director of the census and voting programs for the Asian American Justice Center (AAJC). A national expert on decennial census and census policy matters, she cochairs the Leadership Conference on Civil Rights' Census Task Force with the National Association of Latino Elected & Appointed Officials (NALEO) and sits on the U.S. Department of Commerce's 2010 Census Advisory Committee as a permanent substitute advisor to the U.S. Secretary of Commerce. She has been consulted on matters pertaining to the privacy and confidentiality of census data, planning for the 2010 census and the American Community Survey, and other important issues. She is a leading expert on Section 203 of the Voting Rights Act, reauthorization of the Voting Rights Act, and election protection. In 2004 and 2006, the Lawyers' Committee for Civil Rights Under Law selected Ao to serve in a leadership capacity in its national Election Protection Program. Also in 2004, the Youth Vote Coalition honored her as one of 30 people under the age of 30 who are engaging young people in the electoral process. Ao was an Advisory Board Member to the Civil Rights Project at the University of California Berkeley's Voting Rights and Democratic Participation Project. In 2006, she published an article in *Alabama Law Review* discussing the impact of the immigration debate on the reauthorization of Section 203 of the Voting Rights Act, titled "When the Voting Rights Act Became

Un-American: The Misguided Vilification of Section 203." She has appeared before the national, ethnic, local, and regional media on her program areas. She has also been a featured speaker at many events, such as the National Asian Pacific American Conference on Law and Public Policy at Harvard University, the National NOW Conference, the National Asian Pacific American Bar Association National Convention, the Japanese American Citizens League and Organization of Chinese American Leadership Conference, the Congressional Black Caucus Foundation's Conference on the Voting Rights Act: Strengthening Diversity in Democracy, Yale University's Lessons from the Past, Prospects for the Future: Honoring the 40th Anniversary of the Voting Rights Act of 1965, and events coordinated by the Leadership Conference on Civil Rights. She has also provided staff briefings on Capitol Hill on issues of importance to the community. In 2003, Ao was counsel on the amicus curiae briefs filed in support of the University of Michigan in the landmark affirmative action cases of *Gratz v. Bollinger* and *Grutter v. Bollinger* before the U.S. Supreme Court. Her amicus work also includes assisting in the drafting of amicus briefs in both *Adarand v. Mineta* in the U.S. Supreme Court and *Grutter v. Bollinger* in the Sixth Circuit Court of Appeals. Ao received her juris doctor, cum laude, from American University Washington College of Law and her bachelor's degree in economics at the University of Chicago.

Jocelyn Friedrichs Benson joined the faculty of Wayne State University Law School as an Assistant Professor of Law in 2005, after serving as a law clerk to Judge Damon J. Keith on the United States Court of Appeals for the Sixth Circuit. She previously worked for the Democratic National Committee during the 2004 presidential election, organizing and developing an Election Protection program that trained and placed over 17,000 volunteer lawyers in precincts throughout the nation. She is currently serving as a member of the American Bar Association's Standing Committee on Election Law. Benson graduated magna cum laude from Wellesley College, where she was the first student to be elected to serve in the governing body for the town of Wellesley, the Town Meeting. She subsequently earned her master's in sociology as a Marshall Scholar at Oxford University in the United Kingdom, conducting research into the sociological implications of white supremacy and neo-Nazism. She received her J.D. from Harvard University Law School, where she was a general editor of the *Harvard Civil Rights-Civil Liberties Law Review*. During her time at Harvard Law, Benson also worked as the Voting Rights Policy Coordinator for the Harvard Civil Rights Project. She has also worked as a summer associate for voting rights and election law for the NAACP Legal Defense and Education Fund, as a legal assistant to Nina Totenberg at National Public Radio, and as an investigative journalist for the Southern Poverty Law Center in Montgomery, Alabama. Her published work includes "Election Fraud and the Initiative Process: A Study of the 2006 Michigan Civil Rights Initiative," *Fordham Urban Law Journal* (2007), "¡Su Voto

Es Su Voz! Incorporating Limited English Proficient Voters into American Democracy," *Boston College Law Review* (2007), and "Turning Lemons into Lemonade: Making *Georgia v. Ashcroft* the *Mobile v. Bolden* of 2007," *Harvard Civil Rights–Civil Liberties Law Review* (2004).

Steven Carbó has extensive experience in advancing civil rights, social justice, and community economic development at the federal, state, and community levels. He currently serves as a Senior Program Director in the Democracy Program at Dēmos: A Network for Ideas and Action, a national research and advocacy organization. The Democracy Program supports public policy changes that eliminate barriers to political participation, providing policy makers, activists, and election administrators with applied research, policy analysis, and organizing assistance. The Program's current policy agenda includes Election Day Registration, enhanced implementation of the National Voter Registration Act, redistricting reform, and other election reforms. Before joining Dēmos, Carbó worked in the public and nonprofit sectors in New York; Washington, D.C.; North Carolina; and Philadelphia. His varied professional experience has included work as Legislative Director for U.S. Rep. Nydia Velazquez, Special Counsel on Environmental Justice for U.S. Rep. José Serrano, and Legislative Staff Attorney with the Mexican American Legal Defense and Educational Fund. He has helped shape federal and state policies and programs on voting rights, fair employment, education, environmental justice, economic development, and affordable housing. He holds a J.D. and B.A. from the University of Pennsylvania.

Tommie S. Cardin is Practice Group Leader of the Public Law and Finance Group at Butler, Snow, O'Mara, Stevens & Cannada, PLLC. He concentrates his practice in the areas of administrative, environmental, and governmental law, including elections and voting rights issues. He is listed in the Government Relations section of *The Best Lawyers in America*. A member of the Mississippi Bar, Cardin is past chair of the Government Law Section. He also serves as a member of the Section of State & Local Government Law of the American Bar Association. He served as lead counsel to the Standing Joint Legislative Committee on Reapportionment and the Standing Joint Congressional Redistricting Committee during the state legislative and congressional redistricting in the State of Mississippi following the 2000 census. Cardin received his B.A., magna cum laude, from Mississippi State University in 1983. He received his J.D. from the University of Mississippi in 1986 and in 1986–87 served as a law clerk to the Honorable James L. Robertson, Justice, Mississippi Supreme Court. Cardin has served as an adjunct professor at Mississippi College School of Law, teaching a course on regulated industries. He also serves as a member of the Advisory Board of the John C. Stennis Institute of Government at Mississippi State University. He is a resident of Clinton, Mississippi, where he serves as a member of the Board of Trustees of the Clinton Public School District.

He is also an active member of Galloway Memorial United Methodist Church in Jackson, Mississippi, where he teaches an adult Sunday School class.

Kristen Clarke is a voting rights attorney based in Washington, D.C. Currently, she serves as Co-Director of the Political Participation Group at the NAACP Legal Defense and Educational Fund, Inc. (LDF). Prior to joining LDF, she worked for several years in the Civil Rights Division of the U.S. Department of Justice. Between 2000 and 2003, Clarke served as a trial attorney in the Voting Section of the Division where she handled enforcement efforts under the Voting Rights Act of 1965. She worked on major litigation concerning a state house redistricting plan, coordinated federal election monitoring efforts, helped develop Section 2 litigation, and handled numerous Section 5 preclearance matters. Between 2003 and 2006, Clarke worked as a Federal Prosecutor in the Criminal Section of the Division where she handled a range of police misconduct, hate crimes, human trafficking, and obstruction matters, and litigated these cases throughout the country. She received her A.B. from Harvard University and a J.D. from Columbia Law School, where she served as Editor in Chief of the *National Black Law Journal.* Her book, coedited with Dr. Manning Marable, *Seeking Higher Ground: The Hurricane Katrina Crisis, Race, and Public Policy Reader,* was published by Palgrave Macmillan in 2007.

Nadine Cohen was formerly staff attorney with the Lawyers' Committee for Civil Rights Under Law of the Boston Bar Association, and is now with Greater Boston Legal Services. She served as Director of the Fair Housing Project at the Boston Lawyers' Committee for Civil Rights for ten years, where she handled numerous housing discrimination cases in federal and state courts as well as administrative agencies, developed Boston's first private fair-housing testing project in 1987 and established a private bar panel to handle referrals of fair-housing cases, was involved with community groups in Boston to change the racially discriminatory lending practices of banks and mortgage companies, and achieved settlements that significantly increased mortgage lending to people of color in the greater Boston area. Cohen is involved in voting rights, education, employment, environmental justice, and other civil rights cases, in addition to housing discrimination cases. She was cocounsel in a major class action lawsuit against the Boston Housing Authority, involving the housing authority's failure to protect tenants of color in predominantly white developments from racial violence and harassment by white tenants, and has conducted numerous training programs on housing discrimination law and has presented at many national conferences. She was awarded a Wasserstein Public Interest Fellowship from Harvard University to counsel law students on careers in public interest law, is a past recipient of the Newton Human Rights Award for her commitment to human and civil rights, and has also been honored by the Boston Branch NAACP and other groups for her work on housing discrimination issues.

In 2000 she was honored by the National Lawyers' Committee, and was the 2001 honoree of the Boston Chapter of the National Lawyers Guild for her long-standing work in fair housing and civil rights cases.

Mathias W. Delort is an Associate Judge of the Circuit Court of Cook County in Chicago and was previously a partner with the Chicago office of Robbins, Schwartz, Nicholas, Lifton & Taylor, Ltd., specializing in local government and election law. He was named a Local Government Fellow by the International Municipal Lawyers Association and is the Editor in Chief of the Illinois Institute for Continuing Legal Education's *Election Law Handbook*.

Sara L. DuBois is the Director of Compliance for Sandler, Reiff & Young, PC, a nationally recognized election practice firm. She is responsible for managing the compliance activities for over one hundred political and nonprofit organizations. She has been a contributor to the ABA's *Voice of Experience*. She participated as a staff member for the 2004 Democratic National Convention. Prior to joining Sandler, Reiff & Young, PC, she spent a year in South America studying Chilean political structures at the Pontificia Universidad Católica. She is a cum laude graduate of Washington University in St. Louis with a B.A. in literature & history and Spanish, where she was an active member in the political and arts communities.

Eva Galanes-Rosenbaum (B.A. Reed College '06) is the Associate Director of the Early Voting Information Center at Reed College in Portland, Oregon. She studies convenience and nonprecinct voting in the United States and abroad. Galanes-Rosenbaum has coauthored a chapter in *Democracy in the States: Experiments in Elections Reform* (Brookings Institute Press, forthcoming 2008) and an article in the October 2007 issue of *PS: Political Science & Politics*. Several of her articles have gone to national conferences, including the Annual Meeting of the American Political Science Association. The Early Voting Information Center (http://www .earlyvoting.net) is a nonpartisan academic research center focusing on modes of casting ballots before Election Day and/or outside of the traditional precinct polling place. Galanes-Rosenbaum has been with the EVIC for three years and manages staff and research projects, in addition to writing grants, press releases, and articles. Her thesis research was in homegrown European nationalist terrorism. Galanes-Rosenbaum lives in Portland, Oregon, where she manages a cafe and designs knitting patterns. She plans to pursue her interests in European politics in the fall of 2008 via graduate school in the United Kingdom.

Jonah H Goldman is the Director of the National Campaign for Fair Elections in the Lawyers' Committee for Civil Rights Under Law's Voting Rights Project. He is responsible for implementing the Campaign's mission of developing policy and strategy to reform the administration of elections at the federal, state, and local level. In addition to his leadership in developing and implementing the Lawyers' Committee's voting policy reform priorities and his active role in the Voting Rights Project's litigation docket, he leads the legal program for the Election Protection Coalition, the nation's largest and most diverse nonpartisan voter protection program, and the National Network on Election Reform, a national coalition committed to meaningful election reform at the federal and state level. Goldman graduated with honors from Binghamton University and from Boston College Law School, where he received the John F. Cremens Award for outstanding work in clinical programs.

Jon M. Greenbaum has been the Director of the Voting Rights Project for the Lawyers' Committee for Civil Rights Under Law since 2003. He is responsible for overseeing all of the efforts of the Lawyers' Committee to enable citizens to fully participate in the electoral process. These efforts include ensuring that federal, state, and local authorities comply with the United States Constitution, the Voting Rights Act, the National Voter Registration Act, and state and local laws; leading the legal program for Election Protection, the nation's leading nonpartisan voter protection program; and pursuing statutory and administrative reforms that improve the electoral process for voters. From 1997 to 2003, Greenbaum worked in the Voting Section at the U.S. Department of Justice, where he enforced federal voting protections. Most notably, he successfully tried and settled cases that vindicated the rights of minority and language-minority voters under Sections 2 and 203 of the Voting Rights Act. From 1993 to 1996, Greenbaum was a litigation associate at the international law firm of Dewey Ballantine LLP. He graduated with honors from the University of California at Berkeley in 1989 and received his J.D. from the University of California at Los Angeles in 1993.

Paul Gronke (Ph.D. Michigan, '93, B.A. Chicago '82) is a Professor of Political Science at Reed College, Portland, Oregon. Gronke studies American politics and methodology, specializing in convenience and early voting, public opinion, congressional and presidential elections, and social science methodology. He has published a book, *The Electorate, The Campaign, and the Vote* (Michigan 2000) and scholarly articles in *American Journal of Political Science, Journal of Politics, Legislative Studies Quarterly, Public Opinion Quarterly, Electoral Studies, Political Research Quarterly,* and *American Politics Quarterly,* and has contributed chapters to edited volumes. Gronke's current research examines the phenomenon of "early voting," modes of balloting whereby voters can cast their ballots at a place and time other than at the polling place on Election Day. Gronke has also conducted research on trust in government, the media, and the military; presidential approval; congressional representation; and congressional elections. Gronke has written opinion pieces for a variety of newspapers, has served as a radio and television commentator, and participates in a number of political and election reform blogs. In 2005, Gronke established the Early Voting Information Center (http://earlyvoting.net) to study early voting and advocate for best practices in voting by mail and early voting systems. Gronke lives with his wife Karin Purdy and their four children in Portland, where he participates in and follows local politics.

Richard L. Hasen is the William H. Hannon Distinguished Professor of Law at Loyola Law School in Los Angeles. He holds a B.A. from the University of California at Berkeley and a J.D., M.A., and Ph.D. (political science) from the University of California at Los Angeles. After law school, Hasen clerked for the Honorable David R. Thompson of the United States Court of Appeals for the Ninth Circuit, and then worked as a civil appellate lawyer. From 1994 to 1997, Hasen taught at the Chicago-Kent College of Law. He joined Loyola's faculty in 1997 as a visiting professor and became a member of the full-time faculty in fall 1998. In 2005, he was named the William H. Hannon Distinguished Professor of Law. Hasen is a nationally recognized expert in election law and campaign finance regulation, is coauthor of a leading casebook on election law, and is coeditor of the quarterly peer-reviewed publication *Election Law Journal.* He is the author of more than three dozen articles on election law issues. In 2002, Hasen was named one of the 20 top lawyers in California under age 40 by the Los Angeles (and San Francisco) *Daily Journal* and one of the top 100 lawyers in California in 2005. Hasen also writes the widely read Election Law blog. His op-eds and commentaries have appeared in many publications, including the *New York Times, Washington Post, Los Angeles Times,* and *Slate.* His election law book, *The Supreme Court and Election Law: Judging Equality from Baker v. Carr to Bush v. Gore,* was published by NYU Press in 2003.

J. Gerald (Gerry) Hebert is a sole practitioner in Alexandria, Virginia, who specializes in election law and redistricting. Since 2004, he has been associated with the Campaign Legal Center in Washington, D.C., a nonprofit, nonpartisan campaign finance reform organization. He is presently Executive Director and Director of Litigation of that organization. From 1973 to 1994, Gerry served in the Department of Justice in many supervisory capacities, including Acting Chief, Deputy Chief, and Special Litigation Counsel in the Voting Section of the Civil Rights Division. He was lead attorney in numerous voting rights and redistricting lawsuits, several of which were ultimately decided by the U.S. Supreme Court. From 1995 to 2006, he taught courses on voting rights, election law, and campaign finance at Georgetown University Law Center. From 1999 to 2002, he served as General Counsel to IMPAC 2000, the National Redistricting Project for Congressional Democrats. He has authored a number of law journal articles and other publications on redistricting and the Voting Rights Act, including "Redistricting in the Post-2000 Era," *George Mason University Law Review,* and is coauthor of *The Realists' Guide to Redistricting,* published by the ABA's Section of Administrative Law and Regulatory Practice.

John C. (Jack) Keeney Jr. is a partner in the Washington, D.C., office of Hogan & Hartson LLP and Chair of the ABA Standing Committee on Election Law. His practice includes election law representation of candidates, political parties, corporations, and PACs, as well as a trial practice in complex litigation involving election laws, securities laws, fiduciary duties, legal malpractice, and the Foreign Corrupt Practices Act. He is also the long-time cochair of Hogan & Hartson's legal ethics committee, and formerly served as the partner in charge of the firm's award-winning pro bono Community Services Department. Keeney is a past president of the 84,000-member District of Columbia Bar and served in the ABA House of Delegates 2003–2005. He serves on the Advisory Committee on Procedures of the Court of Appeals for the D.C. Circuit and the Board of Directors of the Washington Lawyers Committee for Civil Rights and Urban Affairs. He is a cum laude graduate of Harvard Law School and received his undergraduate degree summa cum laude from the University of Notre Dame. He is listed in *Washington, D.C., Superlawyers 2007* and in *Washingtonian* magazine's "Top Lawyers in Washington, D.C."

Robert D. Lenhard is Chairman of the Federal Election Commission. He was an Associate General Counsel with the American Federation of State, County and Municipal Employees, AFL-CIO (AFSCME) from 1991 until he became a member of the Federal Election Commission. At AFSCME, he was responsible for legal issues related to federal and state election laws. His work included counseling the union on federal and state campaign finance issues, litigating enforcement actions before the FEC and state agencies, and providing training to field staff on federal and state election law issues. Prior to becoming an Associate General Counsel at AFSCME, Lenhard was an associate at the law firm of Kirschner, Weinberg & Dempsey, where he represented AFSCME and other labor unions. Prior to that, he worked for the United Mine Workers of America and the Amalgamated Clothing and Textile Workers Union. After graduating from law school, he worked as an associate at the Los Angeles law firm of Grace, Neumeyer & Otto. Lenhard is a 1981 graduate of the Johns Hopkins University, where he earned a B.A. with Honors, and a 1984 graduate of the University of California, Los Angeles, School of Law.

Karen K. Narasaki is the President and Executive Director of the Asian American Justice Center, a nonprofit, nonpartisan civil rights organization whose mission is to advance the human and civil rights of Asian Pacific Americans through advocacy, public policy, public education, and litigation. AAJC is affiliated with the Asian American Institute in Chicago, the Asian Pacific American Legal Center in Los Angeles, and the Asian Law Caucus in San Francisco. Before joining AAJC, Narasaki was the Washington, D.C., Representative for the Japanese American Citizens League. Prior to that she was a corporate attorney at Perkins Coie in Seattle. Before joining Perkins Coie, she served as a law clerk to Judge Harry Pregerson on the United States Court of Appeals for the Ninth Circuit in Los Angeles.

David D. O'Donnell maintains an active trial and appellate practice in the areas of labor and employment, civil rights, and complex commercial and voting rights litigation and serves as the attorney for Lafayette County, Mississippi. He is also a member of the adjunct faculty at the University of Mississippi School of Law, where he teaches courses in federal pretrial and trial practice. He is the author of "Wading into the Serbonian Bog of Vote Dilution Litigation Under Amended Section 2 of the Voting Rights Act: Making the Way Towards a Principled Approach to 'Racially Polarized Voting,'" *Mississippi Law Journal* (Winter 1995) and an insurance practice text, *Mississippi Automobile Insurance Law and Practice* (West 1997), a practice manual for lawyers and insurance claims professionals. After receiving his undergraduate degree from the School of International Service of The American University (Washington, D.C.), O'Donnell earned a J.D. degree from the University of Mississippi. While in law school, he was a member of the *Mississippi Law Journal* editorial staff serving as Research and Articles Editor. After law school, he received a two-year appointment (1985–1987) as a law clerk to United States District Judge Neal B. Biggers (Oxford, Mississippi). O'Donnell is a member of the Florida and Mississippi Bars and is active in a number of Bar organizations including the W. C. Keady American Inn of Court (President, 1993–96; Program Chair, 1996–present) and the Mississippi Board of Bar Admissions, Character and Fitness Committee (2002–present).

Leslie C. Scott is a member of the Public Law and Finance Group at Butler, Snow, O'Mara, Stevens & Cannada, PLLC. She concentrates her practice in the areas of civil rights defense, administrative law, government representation, and election law. She is a member of the Mississippi Bar and its Administrative Law Section. In 2003, she published "Encyclopedia of Mississippi Law, Election Law," in the *Encyclopedia of Mississippi Law,* New Practice Series. Scott has made presentations on various topics including the Mississippi College School of Law Election Law Seminar on Election Law and the Mississippi Bar Summer School for Lawyers on the Mississippi Administrative Procedures Act Reform. She is the former City Attorney for the City of Jackson, Mississippi, the former Mississippi Assistant Attorney General in charge of civil litigation, the former Mississippi Assistant Secretary of State for Business Services, and the former Mississippi Assistant Secretary of State for

Elections. In 2006, she served as an Adjunct Professor of Law at Mississippi College School of Law, teaching election law. Scott received her B.A., summa cum laude, from the University of Mississippi in 1979, and her J.D. from the University of Mississippi School of Law in 1981. While at the University of Mississippi Law School, she served on the Editorial Board for the *Mississippi Law Journal.* She serves on the Board of Directors of the Millsaps Arts and Lecture Series. She is also a member of the Mississippi Museum of Art, a volunteer at the Stewpot Community Services, and a member of the Advisory Board of Habitat for Humanity Metro-Jackson.

Rachel Steinberg is the Director of Regulatory Services at Sandler, Reiff & Young, P.C., a nationally recognized election practice firm. She is responsible for national, state, and local regulatory compliance for all of the firm's political and nonprofit clients. She has been a contributor to the ABA's *Voice of Experience.* She has an extensive resume in political campaigns on a national and local level. She is a cum laude graduate of Bryn Mawr College with a B.A. in political science, where she was a known Democratic leader on campus during the 2004 election cycle.

Charles Stewart III is Kenan Sahin Distinguished Professor and Head of the Political Science Department at the Massachusetts Institute of Technology. Stewart was an original member of the Caltech/MIT Voting Technology Project. As part of that project, he has written and spoken extensively on issue of voting technology in the United States. He has especially focused on the statistical estimation of voting machine performance, chronicling changes to the residual vote rate associated with various election reform efforts. This research has appeared in journals such as the *Journal of Politics, Election Law Journal,* and *The Policy Studies Journal,* in addition to collected volumes and special reports. Beyond his work on voting technologies, Stewart has published research on many aspects of U.S. congressional behavior and electoral politics. He received his Ph.D. in political science from Stanford University in 1985 and has taught American politics at MIT since that time.

Abigail Thernstrom is a senior fellow at the Manhattan Institute in New York, and the vice-chair of the U.S. Commission on Civil Rights. She was a member of the Massachusetts State Board of Education for more than a decade until her third term ended in November 2006. She also serves on the board of advisors of the U.S. Election Assistance Commission. She received her Ph.D. in 1975 from the Department of Government, Harvard University. In 2007 she and her husband, Harvard historian Stephan Thernstrom, along with James Q. Wilson, Martin Feldstein, and John Bolton, were the recipients of Bradley Foundation prizes for Outstanding Intellectual Achievement. Thernstrom and her husband are the coauthors *of No Excuses: Closing the Racial Gap in Learning* (Simon & Schuster, 2003), which has been awarded the 2007 Fordham Foundation prize for "for distinguished scholarship," and was named by both the *Los Angeles Times* and the *American School Board Journal* as one of the best books of 2003. They also collaborated on *America in Black and White: One Nation, Indivisible* (Simon & Schuster, 1997), which the *New York Times Book Review,* in its annual end-of-the-year issue, named as one of the notable books of 1997. They are the editors of *Beyond the Color Line: New Perspectives on Race and Ethnicity* (Hoover Institution, 2002). Their lengthy review of William G. Bowen and Derek Bok's much-noticed work, *The Shape of the River,* appeared in the June 1999 issue of the *UCLA Law Review.* Thernstrom's 1987 work, *Whose Votes Count? Affirmative Action and Minority Voting Rights* (Harvard University Press) won four awards, including the American Bar Association's Certificate of Merit and the Anisfield-Wolf prize for the best book on race and ethnicity. It was named the best policy studies book of that year by the Policy Studies Organization (an affiliate of the American Political Science Association), and won the Benchmark Book Award from the Center for Judicial Studies. Along with her husband, she also won the 2004 Peter Shaw Memorial Award given by the National Association of Scholars. She is currently completing a book titled *Voting Rights and Wrongs: The Elusive Quest for Racially Fair Elections,* and is working with her husband on another book with the tentative title of *Don't Call It Segregation: The Myth of Contemporary Apartheid.* She and two coauthors submitted an amicus brief in *Parents Involved in Community Schools v. Seattle,* challenging the constitutionality of Seattle's racial balancing plan. Her frequent media appearances have included *Fox News Sunday, Good Morning America,* and *This Week with George Stephanopoulos.* For some years, she was a stringer for *The Economist,* and continues to write for a variety of journals and newspapers, including the *Wall Street Journal,* the *Los Angeles Times,* the *New York Times,* and the (London) *Times Literary Supplement.* She serves on several boards, and from 1992 to 1997 was a member of the Aspen Institute's Domestic Strategy Group.

Kenneth A. Tinkler is an attorney in the Tampa office of Carlton Fields, P.A., where he is a member of the firm's Government Law and Consulting Practice Group. He is also a member of the firm's Real Estate & Finance Practice Group and the Energy Practice Group. He is board-certified in City, County, and Local Government Law by the Florida Bar and a member of the Executive Council of the Florida Bar's City, County, and Local Government Law Section. His practice focuses on a variety of government law issues including land use law and environmental permitting. Tinkler's experience includes representation of government agencies and officials, including county government and constitutional officers. He also has expertise in public records and sunshine law, government ethics, parliamentary procedure, Florida county home-rule charters, and election law, including Voting

Rights Act issues. Prior to joining Carlton Fields, Tinkler served as a Senior Assistant County Attorney for Hillsborough County, Florida. He received his J.D. from the University of Florida College of Law in 1997 and his B.A., cum laude, in political science from Boston University in 1994.

Brenda Wright is the Legal Director of the Democracy Program at Dēmos: A Network for Ideas and Action. She joined Dēmos in January 2007 with nearly two decades of experience in litigation, public education and advocacy on voting rights, campaign finance reform, and election reform issues. She directs Dēmos's litigation initiatives in the Democracy Program and participates in Dēmos's research and policy work on democracy issues. Before joining Dēmos, Wright served as Managing Attorney at the National Voting Rights Institute, which has worked in close partnership with Dēmos since 2005. She also served previously as Director of the Voting Rights Project at the Lawyers' Committee for Civil Rights Under Law in Washington, D.C. Her extensive trial and appellate experience in voting rights and campaign finance cases includes two arguments before the U.S. Supreme Court. Wright frequently testifies before Congress, federal agencies, and state legislatures and has authored numerous law review articles and other publications on voting rights, campaign finance reform, and other democracy issues. She is a member of the Board of Trustees of the Lawyers' Committee for Civil Rights Under Law and a member of the Advisory Boards of Common Cause Massachusetts and the Prison Policy Initiative. She received her law degree from Yale Law School and her B.A. from Bryn Mawr College.

John Hardin (Jack) Young has held senior positions in private practice, industry, and government. His primary areas of practice are administrative and regulatory law and litigation, complex dispute resolution, technology company development, and electoral process and recounts. He has represented clients in federal and state litigation across the United States. His offices include Past Chair, ABA Section of Administrative Law and Regulatory Practice; Life Fellow, American Bar Foundation; Board of Trustees, American Inns of Court Foundation (2004–2008); Founding Board Member, Temple Scholars program; Life Member, American Law Institute; ABA Board of Governors (2007–2010); Adjutant Professor, George Mason Law School (2003–2005); Special Counsel to the DNC & Co-Chair, National Lawyers Council (1996–2000); and Chair, American Inns of Court/Commercial Court of England Rule of Law Conference (2007). Young is the author of *Young's Federal Rules of Evidence* 8th ed. (West 2003); *Mastering Written Discovery* 4th ed. (with T. Zall, et al.; Lexis 2004); and *International Election Principles* (ABA 2008). He received his A.B. from Colgate (1970), J.D. from the University of Virginia (1973), and B.C.L. from Oxford University (1976).

[Editor's Note: More than twenty months ago, fellow Mississippian Constance Slaughter-Harvey testified before the Senate Judiciary Committee's Subcommittee on the Constitution, Civil Rights and Property Rights, eloquently summing up the continuing need for vigilance in the protection of an open and accessible electoral process for all Americans. A Margaret Brent Award recipient that same year, she spoke in support of key provisions of the Voting Rights Act Amendments. Her remarks set forth below reflect the passion and strength of a pioneer of the Civil Rights Movement. Her words serve as a resounding reminder that the struggle for electoral access, meaningful political participation and true diversity is an ongoing one. With Connie's permission, we give you this excerpt from her testimony as a fitting Preamble for *America Votes!*]

Preamble

Excerpts from the Testimony of Constance Slaughter-Harvey
Former State Election Official, Lawyer and Long-term
Resident of Forest, Mississippi
Before the Senate Committee on the Judiciary Subcommittee on the
Constitution, Civil Rights and Property Rights
"The Continuing Need for Federal Examiners and Observers
to Ensure Electoral Integrity"
Hearing on S. 2703 Federal Observer Provisions
July 10, 2006

During my twelve years (1984–1996) as Assistant Secretary of State for Elections, my staff and I coordinated Election Day activities and worked with election officials on the municipal, county, state, and federal levels. During my tenure, I established procedures for conducting professional, open, and honest elections throughout the state. I helped implement an annual training program for local election administrators and organized voter registration conferences throughout the state. Our administration also took the federal observer provisions of the [Voting Rights] Act seriously and sought to avail ourselves of the protections afforded by the Act when appropriate. To this end, I developed Election Day complaint forms that could be used by voters or officials to document specific voting-related complaints. Our office not only received complaints from voters, but also from local and state officials. These complaints varied in range and scope. Some reported that officials selectively refused to provide voters with assistance they needed to cast their ballots while others reported illegal purges and outright denial of a ballot to a qualified voter. Often, when these problems occurred, voters were not provided any explanation or justification for the denial.

When our office received complaints regarding potential problems likely to emerge during an election, we contacted local officials and attempted to resolve the problems. In addition, we also worked closely with officials at the U.S. Department of Justice and, when appropriate, formally requested that federal observers be deployed to a particular area. Our efforts helped open dialogue between federal and local officials to try and identify ways to resolve problems prior to Election Day. Often, officials from the federal government would apprise local officials about the requirements of the Voting Rights Act and secured commitments from these officials that elections would be conducted accordingly. In one instance, observers were sent to monitor elections because of reports indicating that local law enforcement officers were intimidating minority voters by stationing themselves at polls in prior elections.

In particular, Sunflower [Mississippi] residents alleged that law enforcement officers were arresting voters at the polls for traffic violations and other minor offenses. Others alleged that the sheriff and local deputies were aggressively searching for individuals with outstanding warrants at polling sites. Federal observers were deployed, in part, to monitor for unwarranted police presence at polling sites and to help restore voter confidence in the electoral process.

During a recent election, poll workers at a majority African-American precinct failed to offer affidavits to voters without proper identification. However, the presence of federal observers helped correct the problem to ensure that all eligible voters were ultimately able to cast their ballots. (Interview with Reubin Smith, Registered Voter and Volunteer Poll Watcher in Clarksdale, Mississippi (July 7, 2006).)

Nine counties in Mississippi are required to make their election-related materials available in the Choctaw language. Federal observer deployment has helped bring greater levels of encouragement among many of these voters who require effective language assistance to cast their ballots. Indeed, these bilingual observers have served as "eyes and ears" over the process, ensuring that local officials carry out a smooth language assistance program. In many of these communities, Choctaw voters have extended great appreciation to federal observers as this oversight had a measurable impact on voter confidence and turnout levels. Among the numerous complaints received, some included concerns about potential tampering with absentee ballots, candidates' names omitted from ballots, and intimidating poll watchers who prevented concerned voters from investigating these potential improprieties. This election also illustrates the value of the federal observer program, as monitors could have provided sufficient documentation of these problems to help in efforts to seek post-electoral relief.

In addition to the accounts provided above, I also recall receiving a range of complaints from voters about intimidating behavior at the polls including:

- Use of video cameras to intimidate Black voters in Noxubee and Lowndes Counties, Mississippi
- Black voters required to provide Social Security Numbers in order to cast their ballots in Hinds County, Mississippi

- Election Official refusing to pick up and count absentee ballots from a local post office in Warren County, Mississippi
- A Black incumbent's name excluded from ballots during a 1991 Hinds County election
- Voting machine problems, misalignment of ballots, and absentee balloting problems during a hotly contested election in Coahoma County
- White men wearing dark sunglasses and beige trench coats intimidating Black voters by demanding that Black voters provide their names and addresses and documenting this information in notebooks

John Walker testified about the role that federal observers play in the State of Mississippi. Walker noted that the observer role is key given varying interpretations of state and federal election law among different layers of government. In particular, he observed that the Voting Rights Act and threat of litigation "are the levees that keep the repression from raining back and running back into Mississippi."

Brenda Wright, the managing attorney and director of the nationwide litigation program for the National Voting Rights Institute in Boston, Massachusetts, testified that Section 5's continuing success in curtailing legislation and practices which disenfranchise minority voters is inextricably linked to the importance and strengthening of the federal examiner and observer systems. Wright noted that "most jurisdictions believe only certain things need to be submitted [for preclearance], such as redistricting plans" and noted that "there are a lot of voting changes that have not been submitted." The observer program provides one vehicle that can be used to "catch" those non-compliant jurisdictions in order to ensure compliance with the preclearance provisions of the Act.

Congress has the authority to renew the expiring federal observer provisions of the Voting Rights Act. The extensive record that has been compiled provides evidence of continuing discrimination in covered jurisdictions. So long as such discrimination exists, there is the possibility that problems might emerge that would inhibit minority voters' access to the ballot box. The federal observer program has helped provide an effective means of oversight in this regard to help ensure that all voters will be able to freely cast their ballots and have those ballots counted.

Although the Voting Rights Act does not permit federal observers to interfere with the conduct of the election, the Department of Justice retains the authority to stop discriminatory action as it occurs and has effectively used this authority in the State of Mississippi. Moreover, the mere presence of neutral third-party observers inside polling places has the prophylactic effect of deterring impermissible and illegal conduct among hostile voters and local officials on Election Day.

Introduction

ROBERT D. LENHARD
Chairman, Federal Election Commission

Elections are the means by which a free people choose the individuals who will govern on their behalf. The legitimacy of the democratic form of government turns on the fairness and accuracy of its elections. I am not sure there has been a time in recent history when the fairness and accuracy of American elections has been as broadly questioned as in the past decade. Issues of how polling places and voting machines are allocated, how ballots are designed and counted, and who can vote and what they must do to prove their eligibility to vote have moved out of the stale meetings of election boards and the random academic papers and onto the front pages of our newspapers and form the foundations of symposiums and angry blogs.

This struggle over how best to conduct our elections is not necessarily bad. If the end product of this examination and debate is a better system, a more reliable system, a system that more accurately reflects the will of the People, then the time spent sorting through these problems will have been time well spent. This handbook has been constructed in that hope. It is designed to provide election officials, state and local government personnel involved in election administration, lawyers, academics, and advocates with current thinking and experience of experts in the field.

For those looking to understand recent developments, this handbook will be of immense help. John Hardin Young, Sara L. DuBois, and Rachel Steinberg bring a practitioner's eye to issues raised in the 2000 and 2004 elections. Tommie S. Cardin and Leslie C. Scott provide a roadmap for those interested in the various federal and state laws that govern election challenges for candidates for federal office.

Given the importance of the Voting Rights Act and its recent reauthorization, this handbook addresses many aspects of the Act. Benjamin E. Griffith and David D. O'Donnell discuss the Voting Rights Act Reauthorization and Amendments Act of 2006 (VRARA) and provide background on its key provisions. J. Gerald Hebert focuses on the bailout provisions of the Act, which allow a jurisdiction to exempt itself from Section 5's requirement that any change in voting practices or procedures be reviewed and precleared by the Attorney General or the District Court for the District of Columbia. Additionally, the use of demographic and statistical evidence is an essential part of any successful litigation in prosecuting and defending vote dilution cases under Section 2 of the Voting Rights Act. Griffith and O'Donnell provide a cogent analysis of developments in this area of the law with an eye toward the process of redistricting after the 2010 census.

While this handbook is helpful in understanding and analyzing recent developments, it is even more useful as a guide to comprehending the current fault lines and future issues in election law.

The next year will see the federal judiciary weighing in on many of the most important election law provisions. The courts will soon rule on the constitutionality of a key provision of the VRARA. Articles by Kristen Clarke and Abigail Thernstrom analyze the constitutional questions raised by the Section 5 preclearance provision of the Act. These articles are especially relevant given that the litigation in *Northwest Austin Municipal Utility District Number One v. Gonzales* may ultimately make it to the Supreme Court's docket.

The Supreme Court will also be hearing a challenge to Indiana's voter identification law this term in two companion cases: *Crawford v. Marion County Election Board* and *Indiana Democratic Party v. Rokita*. An article by Jonah Goldman and Jon Greenbaum confronts the issues that underlie those cases.

With the demographic changes facing America, issues concerning voting by individuals who are not proficient in English will only grow. Jocelyn Friedrichs Benson provides a concise history of the evolution of the language-assistance provisions in the Voting Rights Act, its current operation, and possible areas of expansion of assistance to voters in the future. Terry M. Ao and Karen K. Narasaki add to this discussion by giving concrete advice to jurisdictions in how best to provide language assistance to their citizens.

In addition, greater public attention is now directed to felon and ex-felon disenfranchisement as the result of litigation and Florida Governor Charlie Crist's efforts to change his state's disenfranchisement rules. John C. Keeney Jr.'s article provides a good overview of the legal landscape concerning felon voting rights, which will become increasingly relevant as the discussion in Florida proceeds.

This handbook also discusses the nitty-gritty of election administration practices. The issue of voting technology has been a hot topic of legislative action, media attention, and academic research since the 2000 election. Stephen Ansolabehere and Charles Stewart III help illuminate this discussion by chronicling the history of voting technologies as well as the relationship between voting technology and election law. This is one of the most important issues affecting voter confidence and their analysis frames the issues well, highlighting successes as well as problems that remain. In light of the decentralized system of U.S. election administration, the articles by Leslie C. Scott and Jocelyn Benson provide important discussions of the various roles played by the many different entities involved. Steven Carbó and Brenda Wright address the movement toward Election Day registration and its effect on raising voter participation. Additionally, as documented by Paul Gronke and Eva Galanes-Rosenbaum, early voting has become increasingly common, and the trend may ultimately require changes in candidates' campaign strategies.

Public attention and litigation of election law and voting issues will only increase as we approach the 2008 election. Whether one is a lawyer or an interested member of the public, this handbook will prove a useful accompaniment and will help shed light on these important issues.

CHAPTER ONE

LESSONS LEARNED FROM THE 2000 AND 2004 PRESIDENTIAL ELECTIONS

JOHN HARDIN YOUNG*
SARA L. DUBOIS**
RACHEL STEINBERG***

I. Introduction

The 2000 and 2004 elections are controversial. It is fair to say that not everyone agrees on what happened in those elections, let alone why; that is the nature of highly political controversies. This chapter presents one view based on a review of what appears to be a consensus by the majority of the authors who have written books particularly on the 2000 election.[1] The significance of this chapter is to demonstrate that both elections were far from perfect and that there are many lessons to be learned from them, some of which we describe in this chapter.

The Supreme Court in *Bush* v. *Gore* declared: "Having once granted the right to vote on equal terms, the State may not, by later arbitrary and disparate treatment, value one person's vote over that of another."[2] The story of the 2000 and 2004 elections is about how the electoral process failed to avoid arbitrary and disparate treatment and in the end damaged the faith in a fair electoral system. Biased chief election officials, impediments to voting, long lines, and inefficient, and possibly inaccurate, means to count the vote have led to a crisis in confidence. The 2000 election showcased holes in the system, which officials could exploit and voters could slip through. As an underinformed public met an underprepared system, alarm bells that the system was ailing were sounded and many were left feeling that their vote did not count. Legislation, such as the Help America Vote Act (discussed

* J.D. University of Virginia, B.C.L. Oxford University; Sandler, Reiff & Young, P.C.
** B.A. Washington University in St. Louis; Director of Compliance, Sandler, Reiff & Young, P.C.
*** B.A. Bryn Mawr College; Director of Regulatory Services, Sandler, Reiff & Young, P.C.

in Section III, *infra*), has caused as many problems as it seeks to cure, particularly in encouraging the expenditure of federal funds for voting machines that cannot be verified as accurate. The 2004 election, particularly in Ohio, indicated that the buck does not stop with improving election technology; nonpartisan election officials and voters need more education to ensure that no one's vote is discounted, invalidated, or altered, in any way. The study of the 2000 and 2004 elections shows that reform within the American electoral process is an ongoing process, but the elections can also be taken as lessons in how to improve and correct past mistakes. It may take several more elections before the public has confidence in that process.

II. The 2000 Election

A. TOO CLOSE TO CALL

While other presidential elections have remained undecided long after the polls closed, never in American history has that uncertainty lasted as long as it did in 2000. For 36 days following Election Day, Americans watched and waited as the race for votes continued—this time not on the campaign trail or at the polls, but in courts and county canvassing boards. On December 12, 2000, George W. Bush was finally declared the winner and the uncertainty of the close race was resolved, at least officially. Yet the faith in the American electoral process had lost something, its fairness and effectiveness called into serious question.

What happened in the 2000 presidential election that caused such controversy and disenchantment? First, the neck-and-neck presidential race exaggerated the undemocratic peculiarities of the electoral college system. Second, a series of problems at the polls occurred on Election Day as a result of questionable election practices, lack of foresight by election officials, and technical problems at the polls. These Election Day issues received extra attention because of the close nature of the race, especially in pivotal states like Florida. Third, major media blunders—prematurely calling the election not once, but twice—on Election Day further undermined the election. Fourth, the lack of statewide precedent and administrative regulations for recounts in Florida, and federally, led to accusations of partisanship in a contentious and confusing recount process that concluded with a controversial ruling in the United States Supreme Court. Finally, the Supreme Court's decision to focus on the "safe harbor" provision (3 U.S.C. §5) left many Americans left feeling that concerns about timeliness weakened the chances for fairness and accuracy in this fundamental process.

B. CLOSE RACE IN A WINNER-TAKE-ALL SYSTEM

With the economy strong and the president at term limit, the 2000 election was open for anything to happen. It was clear from the beginning that the race for the presidency was going to be tight, determined in close contests in a handful of battleground states. America was split nearly evenly along partisan lines, half sticking with Democrats who had stewarded the country to a budget surplus during Bill Clinton's eight years in office, half looking to Republicans as a moral saving grace in the face of the ethical laxness they saw epitomized by Clinton's numerous sexual and financial scandals. Independent "swing voters" were to be the key to electoral success, and shifting dynamics among women, the middle class, Latinos, and African Americans made them the voters to watch. Gunning toward the same sliver at the center of the political spectrum, both sides, as well as a host of interest groups, raised and spent record amounts of money on advertising and campaigning.

Emerging as early frontrunners in their respective parties, Vice President Al Gore Jr. and Texas Governor George W. Bush spent the majority of the general election campaign in a neck-and-neck race. From the time of nomination, Bush and Gore jockeyed for position in a close and volatile race. Their respective national party conventions gave them each a boost—first Bush, then Gore. Gaffes, like Bush's verbal slipups and Gore's embellishments, later cost them ground, giving the other candidate a slight edge. Ralph Nader's relative success as a third-party candidate intensified the competition; the race was so close at the end that both sides could not help but pay heed to the Green Party candidate, prompting Gore to reach out to Nader supporters while Republicans encouraged voting for Nader in hopes of splitting the "left" vote. These factors, combined with impressive voter-registration efforts giving way to high voter turnout on Election Day, meant that the 2000 presidential race was a fight to the finish. By November 6, Bush and Gore were in a dead heat.[3]

As results on Election Day came in, the nonbattleground states went as expected into the Gore and Bush categories. Bush took the South, the upper Midwest, Ohio, Indiana, and the Rocky Mountain states; Gore carried Pennsylvania and most of the Northeast, most of the Northwest, and the Pacific Coast states. As Election Night wound down, there were three states that remained to be decided: New Mexico, Oregon, and Florida. Gore held a slight lead in the popular vote; the decisive electoral vote, however, was still up in the air. By the next morning, Gore had won 260 electoral votes and Bush had won 246;[4] 270 electoral votes were needed to win so it was still either candidate's game. Mathematically, the election would have to come down to Florida's 25 electoral votes. All eyes soon turned to Florida, and, though no one knew it at the time, they would remain there until the election was resolved weeks later.

While Gore eventually won the popular vote by a margin of over 500,000 votes,[5] the election came down to the electoral vote. The state-by-state winner-take-all system ultimately hinged on one state, Florida, whose 25 electoral votes turned on a few hundred votes, out of over six million cast in the state. For many Americans, seeing a presidential election—the country's most important election—be determined by less than one half of 1 percent of the vote in Florida—less than one five-thousandth of 1 percent of the vote nationwide[6]—was very unsettling. For many, the 2000 election threatened values at the core of American democracy, namely, the notion that every person was equal under the law, and so was every vote.

C. PROBLEMS AT THE POLLS ON ELECTION DAY

Questionable polling-day occurrences further magnified flaws in the American voting system. Across the country, confusion, whether on the part of the voters or the poll workers, prevented voters from casting their ballot for their desired candidate. A significant issue was who could vote. Rightly and wrongly, innocently and intentionally, some voters were told that they were not on the rolls while others were allowed into the polling booths. Some people averred their eligibility and were permitted to vote; many were turned away. Democrats alleged discrimination, Republicans railed against voter fraud.

Some of the most pronounced charges and countercharges came out of St. Louis, Missouri, where there was widespread confusion at the polls. Massive voter-roll purges—the inactive voter list increased by more than 25-fold, from approximately 2,000 people in 1996 to over 54,000 people in 2000[7]—and scant communication about the purge resulted in chaos and confusion about who was eligible to vote. Thousands of St. Louis residents showed up on Election Day only to be informed by poll workers that they were not on the active voter list and thus not eligible to cast a ballot. Many of these people went home without having voted. Others protested and sought to prove their eligibility. Again, there were obstacles. Voter eligibility could be verified in one of two ways—and neither went smoothly. For one, a poll worker could call an elections board staff member who could confirm whether the elections board had a record of the voter. Alternatively, the voter in question could physically go to the city elections board to request a hard copy of his or her voting eligibility. The St. Louis elections board, though, had not anticipated dealing with these problems, and especially not on this scale. It had only one phone line open to verify calls about thousands of voters, and staffers were similarly unable to process the influx of voters who came in person to verify their eligibility to vote.[8] Long waits at the elections board ultimately left thousands standing in line when the polls closed, never casting a ballot. According to subsequent audits, the vast majority of these voters had been erroneously removed from the rolls; as many as 96 percent of the voters purged from the rolls between 1996 and 2000 were registered to vote, according to some findings.[9] Controversy continued when a local judge, presented with evidence of persistent problems and long lines into the evening, ruled that poll hours be extended past the 7:00 PM deadline. This led to outcry by Republicans, who alleged that state Democrats, a significant majority of the St. Louis voting population, were being unfairly and illegally given more time to vote. An appeals judge ordered the polls closed at 7:45 PM.

In Florida, significant concerns regarding who could cast a ballot were raised. Florida law prevented (and continues to do so) from voting any person who is convicted of a felony until his or her civil rights are restored (i.e., the prison term and/or parole are completed).[10] In preparation of the voter registration rolls prior to Election Day, though, state election officials instructed some local Florida jurisdictions to remove a voter from the rolls if the last name and first four letters of the person's first name of a registered voter matched the name of a felon. Some local authorities were further instructed that if a match was made in this manner, other information, such as race, gender, or address, did not have to match in order for the name to be removed from the rolls.[11] In this way thousands of Florida voters were erroneously purged from the voting rolls and, thus, told they could not vote on Election Day. This practice disenfranchised many Floridians in an election where every vote would ultimately affect the outcome. Charges were lodged by the NAACP, which claimed that African Americans and other minority groups, who lean heavily Democratic, were systematically disenfranchised in Florida. They and other civil rights groups claimed that police checkpoints were set up around some polling places to intimidate African American voters, while Spanish-speaking voters were disenfranchised when their bilingual translators were wrongly told they could not accompany the voter into the polling booth.[12] The groups alleged, furthermore, that many of the ballots never counted by hand came from predominantly African American precincts.

Elsewhere in Florida, problems occurred once voters were allowed inside the polling booths, where complicated ballot designs led to confusion over who voters were actually voting for when they cast their ballots. In Palm Beach County, a region with a large elderly population that tends to lean heavily Democratic, the results were called into question when significant numbers of ballots were cast for Reform Party candidate Pat Buchanan, whose name appeared adjacent to Al Gore's on the confusing "butterfly" ballot. Other Palm Beach butterfly ballots were disqualified for having multiple votes being cast for one position ("overvotes"). In Duval County, too, there were problems with overvotes, likely the result of poor ballot design: The ballot ran presidential candidates over several pages, with instructions to "vote every page." Many contended that these ballots did not reflect voters' actual intent, but rather signified mistakes made by voters faced with ballots they did not understand.

In other Florida counties, "undervotes," wherein a punch-card ballot registered negligible or no mark for a candidate, were the issue. These ballots were a particular point of contention during the recount. The Bush team contended that the ballots represented nonvotes by voters who were actively abstaining from casting a presidential ballot. Conversely, Gore's lawyers argued that the undervotes were intended to be an affirmative vote for a candidate, but the faulty punch-card machinery had failed to mark the ballot accordingly.

Throughout the country, and particularly in Florida, accusations and counter-accusations regarding voter discrimination, voter fraud, and voter intimidation, as well as confusing ballot layout, undereducated voters, underprepared poll workers, and machine error, severely undermined confidence that all Americans' votes were being counted fairly and accurately. Few, if any, resources had been spent to educate poll workers and voters on how to handle ballots and what their rights were on Election Day. The systems in place for removing voters from the rolls and notifying them thereof were crude; systems for dealing with Election Day problems, like unexpected long lines in St. Louis, were similarly lacking. Lack of preparation by election officials and political parties allowed faulty systems to prevail, distorting the electoral process with overvotes and undervotes.

D. WHEN THE MEDIA MAKES THE NEWS

On top of these hurdles in the structure and process of the election, there was the media. Confident—to a fault, as it would turn out—in its polling technology and consultants, and eager to be the first with a big story, the media ignored precautions and leapt to pronouncements. At 7:50 PM Eastern Standard Time, the networks all called Florida for Gore,[13] based on projections from the Voter News Service (VNS), which was conducting national exit polls.[14] Two hours later, they were forced to retract this projection, prompted by ever-dwindling margins in polling information and by on-air challenges from Bush's chief political consultant, Karl Rove.[15] By 10 PM, Florida was back in the "undecided" column, and the presidency back up for grabs. Four hours later, the polls, which had been showing Bush ahead by a slight lead, registered a jump that put Bush ahead by a margin of 50,000 votes.[16] Worried that other networks, seeing the same information that they were seeing, would upstage them with an earlier call, the networks were on edge. When Fox News called Florida, and thus the national election, for Bush at approximately 2:16 AM EST, the other networks quickly fell in line: first NBC, then CBS, and finally ABC at 2:20 AM.[17] Trusting the network projections, Gore called Bush to concede. Just before he was to make his public concession, however, his advisers alerted him that the Florida returns were still too close to call. Again, the networks had jumped the gun. Gore called Bush to retract the concession, and he sent out his campaign manager, Bill Daley, to explain to the audience gathered in Nashville that he would not be conceding at this time. By 4 AM on November 8, the networks had again retracted their calling of Florida and the election, and Florida was again deemed "undecided."

Aside from causing confusion and suspense, many believed that the media's premature conclusions adversely affected the election itself. First, by calling Florida for Bush, and thus prompting Gore's private concession to Bush, an image of Gore's defeat was created. During the recount process, this last image of a Bush victory over Gore made the process seem more like a sore loser's griping, and thus made the public less sympathetic to his contestations.[18] Some contend, furthermore, that the media's early call of Florida for Gore may have discouraged people from voting in the western Panhandle region of the state, which is part of the central time zone so the polls close later than in the rest of the state.[19] Though it is unlikely that the media calling the state minutes before the polls closed in a region where turnout is typically slim had any significant effect on the outcome of the election, it may have added to the spirit of disappointment in an overeager, irresponsible media on election night. The discovery a few weeks after the election that John Ellis, who ran the "decision desk" at Fox News, was also a first cousin of the Bushes, and that they had been in frequent communication on Election Night, further bruised public confidence in a reliable and independent media.[20]

E. LACK OF ESTABLISHED STANDARDS LEADS TO CONTENTIOUS RECOUNT

By November 8, one thing was clear: With the margin of victory at less than half a percent of total votes cast, Florida law required an automatic recount.[21] What was not clear was everything else. While recounts are not uncommon for elections—in Florida and elsewhere[22]—Florida had no precedent of statewide recounts, especially not for the election of the president, and neither did the federal court system. The Florida election machinery, along with the legal teams of Bush and Gore, would have to navigate uncharted waters, and they would have to do it fast. Following federal law, all state electors would meet to cast their votes on December 18,[23] so whatever was to be decided, whatever was to be done, arguably had to happen in a little over a month. This was the one parameter defining the process of protests and contests that followed; the rest was a matter of legal strategy, audience, and chance.

First, a machine recount was carried out, narrowing the margin slightly but not proving conclusive. The next step was a manual recount in four counties: Palm Beach, Broward, Volusia, and Miami-Dade. These recounts would prove to be a contentious issue, bogged in questions about the scope of and standards for recounting ballots. The manual recount meant that canvassing boards had to determine voter intent on punch-card and butterfly ballots. A flurry of claims and counterclaims were filed in Florida courts, and both sides began debating overvotes and so-called "hanging," "pregnant," and "dimpled" chads on punch-card ballots.[24] Separate from the candidates, individual groups filed suits contesting the Palm Beach County butterfly ballots, on the basis that the ballot layout was confusing.[25] Other petitions were also filed that challenged the standards, and lack thereof, for determining voter intent within and across Florida counties.[26] How could an official tell if the partially punched chads signified a voter's intention of casting a vote or were merely the result of being handled roughly?[27]

At the same time, another set of cases—these challenging the very constitutionality of the recounts—were also being filed and fought in Florida courts. These cases sought to determine whether a full manual recount was constitutionally justified. The ultimate battle came down to a Democratic strategy of counting as many votes as possible in the four Democratic counties slated for a manual recount versus a Republican strategy of preventing a full manual recount therein.[28] Beneath all this, the Bush camp drew a key advantage from having fellow Republicans at the head of the state and thus at the head of the election administration in Florida. Given the absolute time deadline, preventing a full manual recount could be accomplished merely by causing delays in the process.[29] Republican Secretary of State Katherine Harris was given wide discretion to fashion administrative procedures. Harris, who was also cochair of Bush's campaign committee in Florida, was able to use her position to create requirements for authorizing recounts and their results that served the Bush team strategy.[30] Even if the procedures proposed by Harris were successfully challenged in the state supreme court, they were able to add delays to the recount. On November 11 and 13, Harris rejected requests that the deadline for certification of election and recount results be extended. Lawyers for Bush and Gore and interested parties subsequently filed numerous lawsuits in the state and federal courts, seeking to prevent or permit counts and certifications, seeking access to ballots, and seeking to challenge the legal validity of absentee ballots in some counties.[31] As cases came up from circuit courts, the Florida Supreme Court ruled repeatedly to permit full manual recounts.

As the deadline neared, questions of what court had what authority to rule intensified. On November 26, Harris certified election results of the Florida vote, which gave Bush a 537-vote victory over Gore, after a state Supreme Court deadline passed.[32] This count excluded results from Palm Beach County, which finished its manual recount two hours after the deadline. The Gore team feverishly contested these results, as the Bush camp began planning its transition to office. Maneuvering continued as numerous cases were heard and decided in circuit courts, the Florida State Supreme Court, and the United States Supreme Court. On December 8, a divided Florida Supreme Court overturned a circuit court decision that Harris's certification should stand despite excluding significant numbers of presidential undervotes, and ordered manual recounts in all counties with significant numbers of these undervotes.[33] Bush appealed the decision and sought an injunction to stop the recount. The following day, the U.S. Supreme Court agreed to hear arguments, halting the recounts in the meantime. Commentators were surprised that the United States Supreme Court would choose to hear and, ultimately, to decide a political contest, as turned out to be the case.[34] On December 12, however, the U.S. Supreme Court handed down a 5–4 decision in *Bush v. Gore* in favor of Bush, citing concerns that a lack of consistent standards across counties raised equal protection issues. Harris's November 26 certification results would stand. The next day, December 13, Gore again offered his concession and the Bush team declared victory.

F. TIME PICKS A SIDE

In the usual statewide recount, there is sufficient time to set standards, to develop a record, to examine ballots, and to have a decision maker rule on challenges to counted and uncounted ballots. For example, statewide recounts for governor were held in Virginia in 1989 and Maryland in 1994; other statewide recounts have occurred in Ohio in 1990 for attorney general and Nevada in 1998 for a U.S. Senate race. In none of the recounts was the legitimacy of the ultimate winner seriously questioned.

No such luxury existed in 2000 in Florida. Time was always a factor. Even as manual counting was being conducted under a system for review of challenged ballots by a single judge, who could and invariably would develop a single standard, the United States Supreme Court called "time." The Supreme Court, with little to support its decision, set midnight, December 12, 2000, as the last moment a recount could be performed. The Court's rationale was that Florida should be allowed to avail itself of the safe harbor rules found in 3 U.S.C. §5 that prevent challenges in Congress to timely submitted slates of electors. The Court opted for this statutory presumption over the search for accuracy in the vote. The Court, moreover, may have caused the time crunch earlier, by not initially granting certiorari in *Palm Beach County v. Harris*[35] and then by limiting its initial review in *Bush v. Palm Beach County Canvassing Bd.*[36] to not include the issues ultimately addressed in *Bush v. Gore*. At that time, the lawyers for Bush requested that the Court determine "[w]hether the use of arbitrary, standardless and selective manual recounts violated the Constitution," albeit under the 14th Amendment (the third question in Bush's writ for certiorari). Three weeks later, the Court in deciding other issues raised by Bush's lawyers answered, as a practical matter, this question—but with no time left to undertake a recount.

Direct confrontation of the issue of a "standardless" recount sooner may have provided the Florida courts and the county canvassing boards time to undertake a court-supervised count to which uniform standards would apply. The net result of the Court's decisions was to let Bush's slight lead remain. On December 18, 2000, electors met in state capitols across the country and officially gave Bush the electoral majority to make him the 43rd president of the United States. When he was sworn in on January 20, 2001, George Walker Bush took over a nation that was not only divided on the vote, but disenchanted with it.

III. The 2004 Election

Following the 2000 election, there were hopes that the egregious errors that had occurred could be erased, or at least improved. Numerous laws were passed and systems set in place to prevent the electoral process and voters from going through a crisis such as occurred in 2000 in Florida. Unfortunately, and to the further detriment of the voting process in America, there were still major problems in 2004, either new and unexpected or unimproved from four years earlier. These problems are best quantified by focusing on the 2004 election in Ohio. By studying the electoral climate leading up to and during the 2004 election, the causes of the issues and the lessons to be learned can best be analyzed.

A. LEARNING FROM OUR PAST?

In the wake of the 2000 presidential election, Americans expressed their strong disillusionment with the Electoral College,[37] with the media as a reliable and independent source of information, and, overall, with the apparent partisanship of the judiciary (including, and especially, the United States Supreme Court); the notion of "one person, one vote" was tainted. In response to these criticisms, Congress passed several pieces of reform legislation, most notably the Help America Vote Act of 2002 (HAVA),[38] as well as the Bipartisan Campaign Finance Reform Act of 2002.[39] Among other objectives, HAVA sought to preclude the problems at the polls of Election Day 2000, which had shaken confidence that election results accurately reflected voters' decisions. Lawmakers sought to address the controversies like those in Missouri, where concerns about voter fraud faced off with charges of disenfranchisement, and in Florida, where many blamed structural problems like ballot design and faulty voting machines for obscuring the election process. Instead, HAVA would institute a provisional ballot system and would require better voting technology so that subsequent elections would hopefully run smoothly and accurately.

HAVA was signed into law on October 29, 2002. The law states that its purpose is to—

> establish a program to provide funds to States to replace punch card voting systems, to establish the Election Assistance Commission to assist in the administration of Federal elections and to otherwise provide assistance with the administration of certain Federal election laws and programs, [and] to establish minimum election administration standards for States and units of local government with responsibility for the administration of Federal elections.[40]

HAVA promised to provide funding to states that submitted proposals to improve their federal election systems. This was especially interpreted and applied to physical voting systems, in an attempt to eliminate issues with punch cards or other techniques that make reading votes difficult; the law required the states to update their voting equipment, and to provide instructions to voters and poll workers on how to use the voting equipment. The law also required states to overhaul their systems in any areas they found lacking, whether it was accessibility to polling places, computerized voter registration, voter identification at the polls, and the availability of the opportunity to cast provisional ballots. HAVA created an Election Assistance Commission (EAC) to oversee these reforms. The EAC consisted of four commissioners, two Democrats and two Republicans, and would submit annual reports to Congress. The Commission would also oversee the timeline created to implement the election changes in HAVA.

HAVA was the government's response to the problems of 2000. It was anticipated that with this, many past problems for voters and Election Day would be eliminated. The plans submitted by states centered on the technology and equipment of voting, and replacing antiquated systems with electronic voting systems came to be the main focus and main use of the HAVA initiatives. However, it became evident that this action was too little, and there was much more to the voting system problems than equipment replacement.

Leading up to the 2004 election, there was some speculation that all might not go smoothly despite the efforts of HAVA. Some of this was based on the belief that there was a failure to utilize HAVA money to its full extent and without political fallout and debate impeding its implementation, while some of this skepticism was based on stories coming out of Ohio. Secretary of State Kenneth Blackwell, cochair of the Ohio Bush-Cheney reelection campaign, who maintained political aspirations,[41] supposedly attempted to reject thousands of voter registrations[42] because they were not printed on heavy enough paper. Further, in 2003, Walden O'Dell, the CEO of Diebold, the main provider of voting machines in Ohio, announced that he had been a top fundraiser for George W. Bush—raising the public perception of a conflict of interest.[43] These events, even with the passage of HAVA, clearly did nothing to soothe fears of future potential problems and controversy for Election Day.

B. ELECTION DAY 2004: LONG LINES AND CONFUSION

The political climate was filled with tension as November 2004 drew closer. Not only were candidates engaged in fierce battles over issues not prevalent in 2000—such as the events of September 11, 2001, and who was to blame, the war in Iraq, weapons of mass destruction, and domestic issues such as gay marriage—but there were also underlying concerns over how to prevent another Florida 2000 voting debacle. Politically, the 2000 election had intensified the partisan division in America. Republicans believed George W. Bush clearly won the 2000 election, while Democrats believed, and in some cases continued to criticize the decision that ended the Florida recount,[44] that Al Gore had truly won Florida, justly making him president of the United States.

Election Day 2004, in fact, started smoothly—its record turnout was being applauded, and exit polls seemed to indicate a lack of problems. However, as the results and complaints poured in, and discrepancies between the exit polls and the actual results became clear, it was apparent that something had gone seriously wrong. Investigations after Election Day revealed much. A consulting firm, Sproul & Associates, hired by the Republican National Committee, came under investigation for altering voter registrations in six swing states.[45] Voting machines malfunctioned in New Mexico. An electronic voting machine in Columbus, Ohio, added 3,893 votes to George W. Bush's vote count, though there were only 800 voters in the precinct (luckily, this was caught on Election Day by a poll official).[46] Similar problems with electronic voting machines, such as voters not being able to understand how to use them, occurred throughout the country, with no paper trail to make up for lost or incorrect data. Further, although HAVA made replacing machines one of its main goals, Congress provided too little money and minimal standards, leaving many machines unreplaced—including 70 percent of Ohio's machines, which are still punch card and faulty in nature.[47]

It became clear that the voting problems were the worst in Ohio on November 2, 2004. In hindsight, it appears that there were indicators that all might not go well, and that the speculation had merit. Ohio Secretary of State Blackwell was noticeably and vocally partial towards the reelection of George W. Bush. Not only did Blackwell chair the reelection campaign, but he sought to negate registrations for petty details. He actively allowed the purging of voting lists,[48] and many voters were removed unnecessarily, and thus stripped of their right to vote. Further, too many election officials and vote counters in Ohio are partisan, and this is certain to have played a part in skepticism of the credibility of official vote counts in the state. Whether conspiracy or not, inadvertent or purposeful, there certainly were many problems or rumored problems that favored the Bush side, likely causing many voters of all political views to be distrustful of the strength and nonpartisanship of the election process.

First-hand stories and some studies indicate that precincts with a large population of African Americans were hit especially hard in Ohio on Election Day. In fact, many more African American voters than white voters reported experiencing problems at the polls (52 percent versus 25 percent).[49] First, there were exorbitant and unnecessary lengths of lines to vote in certain areas of Ohio. It was later discovered that the longest lines were found in predominantly urban African American communities, although long lines were also found in rural or college communities. This was mostly the result of a lack of the proper number of voting machines to accommodate the people registered in precincts in Ohio.[50] For example, in Franklin County (Columbus), the board of elections estimated that it would need 5,000 machines to handle the amount of voters registered. However, only 2,866 machines were provided.[51] Lines were prominent elsewhere throughout the state as well; lack of adequate numbers of machines was also reported in Cincinnati and Toledo, and on college campuses; Republican and Democratic election officials both acknowledge this issue.[52] What is alarming about this is that high voter turnout in all

Ohio precincts was not unexpected; on October 29, 2004, Blackwell stated that the expected turnout was 72 percent—there was in fact 70 percent.[53] Ohio should have been better prepared for its turnout in light of this information.

In addition, precinct borders and polling places were changed without proper notification to residents; people arrived at one polling place to be told to go to another, and then would arrive at this place to be told to go back or somewhere else.[54] Many gave up and went home.[55] From the various confusions and lines on Election Day, it is estimated that, for example, 5,000 to 15,000 Columbus voters went home in frustration without casting a vote.[56]

Another voting hurdle in Ohio was the identification requirements. Also experienced mainly by African American voters, identification at polls was requested without proper legal support for these demands. The law in Ohio previously stated that only newly registered voters are required to show identification (this law changed as of June 1, 2006, to require all voters to show identification at the polls).[57] While only 7 percent of the voters on November 2 were new, 37 percent of the total voting population was asked for identification, and 47 percent of African Americans were asked.[58] Many voters were thus turned away for not having what was supposedly required, when in actuality they should have been allowed to vote.

Other problems included voter intimidation and the misuse of provisional ballots, mainly perpetuated by poorly trained poll workers or election officials. One precinct in Cleveland reported low turnout, based on a rumor spread around the neighborhood that a voter who had outstanding parking tickets, warrants, or child support payments would be arrested while attempting to vote.[59] Similar warnings were also rumored to take place elsewhere.

Determining the election results was further hindered by the amount of provisional votes cast. Provisional ballots, encouraged by HAVA, allow a voter who is otherwise prevented from voting to cast a ballot that will later be counted if proven legitimate. There were reports that voters were not offered provisional ballots, that locations ran out of them, or that they were not handled properly.[60] One of the main problems was confusion by poll workers and election officials over the law of when provisional ballots can be cast, and therefore given to a voter who claims a right to one. This stems from the unique interpretation by Secretary Blackwell of the state law governing the use of provisional ballots under Ohio Revised Code § 3505.181. He ruled that voters must cast provisional ballots not only in the county but the exact precinct where they are from for the ballots to be considered.[61] However, one of the main reasons for the casting of these ballots was confusion over voters' polling places; this interpretation of the law negated the provisional ballot system created to help voters who were in danger of being disenfranchised because of unexpected problems on Election Day. In total, 23 percent of provisional ballots in Ohio were disqualified.[62] Clearly, provisional ballot laws were not fully understood by election officials, and thus yet another obstacle was presented to prevent legitimately registered voters from having an opportunity to cast a vote.

C. WHAT OHIO TAUGHT US: PROPOSALS FOR IMPROVEMENT

As November 2, 2004, came to a close, there was still no official presidential winner declared. People in Ohio were still in line voting as late as 3 AM, and it became apparent that with such a close race, the national presidential result would come down to what happened there. However, a state with such importance encountered too many problems to make its results official in a timely manner. In the days and weeks following November 2, the discrepancies and stories from Ohio made some citizens, groups, and politicians argue for an official recount, which was ultimately conducted, although amid accusations of improper and illegal management (in fact, three recount officials were criminally charged with rigging the recount).[63] There were public hearings held by the Ohio Election Protection Coalition on November 13 and 15[64] featuring sworn first-person testimony from voters, poll workers, precinct judges, and legal sources about the difficulties faced in Ohio on Election Day, often skewed towards poor or minority areas.[65] The election was ultimately certified in Ohio in early December, and on an official recount it was confirmed that Bush won Ohio by a margin of approximately 119,000 votes.[66] Investigations found that allegations of fraud and misallocation of votes from Kerry to Bush in Ohio were for the most part unfounded.[67]

While many scholars and lawyers, including those from John Kerry's camp,[68] report that it is unlikely that the final result of George W. Bush for president would have changed in Ohio even with recounts and provisional ballots adding several thousand more votes, the results were close, and this was coupled with mass numbers of voters feeling disenfranchised or extremely disillusioned with the process on Election Day itself. Additionally, when data was collected after the election, it became apparent that many problems stemmed from a lack of proper election procedure education for poll workers and a partisan bias of election officials.[69] All of these issues led the country to believe that the electoral process was in trouble and unreliable.

The 2004 election, exemplified at its worst with Ohio, indicated many issues that make it clear the election system in America is in need of improvement. First, HAVA was not entirely successful. While it was utilized to update antiquated voting technology, congressional money was not enough to complete this task and that little amount was not utilized well; meanwhile, HAVA did little else for the election system. States interpreted a need for new voting machines as their main issue, rather than looking at other areas in need of improvement. However, the experience of Ohio should teach the country several lessons for reform in the future. Federal money should go into election education—both voter education on procedures and education and training for poll workers. Clearly, simply updating voting machines with technology was not adequate, and the 2004 problems had a lot in common with 2000. Again, thousands of votes were almost or actually lost from malfunctions or a lack of educated poll workers to help with the use of machines or provisional ballots. Education would also prevent some of the issues that disenfranchised voters on Election Day, such as intimidation, identification, confusion over polling places, long lines, and improper use of voting machines and ballots. Voters should know what is required of them and what is illegal. Additionally, steps should be taken to ensure the proper conduct for registrations. Mainly, it appears that the politicization of this process as well as other aspects of voting and election officials should be removed. Finally, states should learn from the positive experiences of other states. It may even be fruitful to employ more uniform voting systems on a national level, which would help with issues of funding, providing adequate resources, and allowing for and encouraging more voting participation. These suggestions for reform will be addressed further in the following section.[70]

IV. Lessons from the 2000 and 2004 Elections

A. THE 2000 ELECTION

The 2000 presidential election raised concerns about the fairness of the American electoral process. The 2004 election did nothing to alleviate those concerns. In both elections, the right to vote was being mismanaged. After the passage of HAVA in 2002, confidence would return to the voting process, and our democracy would not have to weather another electoral crisis. The promise did not materialize in the 2004 elections.

The 2000 Florida election controversy was avoidable. It could have been avoided if state or county officials had carefully reviewed the way the presidential ballots were designed. It could have been avoided if governmental and political party officials had undertaken to educate voters and polling officials on the ballot and machines on which the ballot was to be voted.

Despite apparent years of work by the State Association of Supervisors of Elections, machines were not upgraded, and flaws in the voting process persisted. Neither the Democratic Party nor the Gore-Lieberman campaign seemed to be aware of the importance of what was to happen on Election Day in three Democratic "must win" punch-card counties. The local Palm Beach election official most directly concerned, Teresa LePore, did realize that a problem existed with the instructions to "vote every page" when applied to the vote for presidential electors that spilled over to multiple pages. The Palm Beach butterfly ballot was designed to avoid the problem of spreading presidential electors over several pages (the so-called caterpillar ballot used in Duval County contained the "vote every page" instruction while spreading presidential electors over more than one page). The Palm Beach ballot was published before Election Day. No one objected to the ballot as confusing to elderly or other voters. No one saw a need to prepare, or to take extraordinary efforts to teach voters not to confuse two candidates closely placed on the ballot—one of whom many wanted to vote for and one who had expressed views anathema to their religious and historical beliefs. When the problem came to the attention of state and national campaigns on Election Day, many individuals had already voted.

The Florida state recount process fared no better. No uniform state standards existed to inform local canvassing boards how to interpret the "intent of the voter." Intercounty variations in the accuracy of vote totals, and the alarming rate of undervotes and overvotes, existed through the state. The lack of sufficiently precise standards gave the United States Supreme Court reason to ultimately end any manual recount.[71] No amount of legal strategy would have overcome this fatal flaw in the law. Similarly, the lack of standards led the United States Supreme Court to warn the Florida Supreme Court that it could not provide the necessary gloss on the term "intent of the voter" without the risk of violating the United States Constitution, Article II, § 1, Clause 2, or the 1886 Electoral Count Act, 3 U.S.C. § 5. The Florida Supreme Court never provided the standard to be applied.

The lack of standards in the Florida election laws, coupled with a history of local canvassing boards acting with wide discretion and the lack of direction from the state Supreme Court, made it improbable that the outcome would be anything other than to let Bush's slight lead remain. Without standards, the competing legal arguments were nothing but choices among flawed approaches.

While Florida in 2000 was not the first time a "tied" election required a recount, the enormous impact of such a small number of votes demonstrated the need to revise the nation's voting system. Curative steps have included the acceptance of new technology with the replacement of punch cards and other unreliable processes. State recount and contest statutes still need to establish comprehensive procedures, transparent standards, and fully accountable systems. These changes, however, will not improve the process unless the core principle of a democratic election, namely the right to vote, is protected. The lesson from the 2000 election is that a comprehensive infrastructure must exist to ensure that all registered voters are afforded the right to vote and know how to vote the ballot particular to their precinct. In each state, problems associated with registering and voting must be identified and corrected. Through training, preparation, and dissemination of voter rights information, one of the problems from 2000—lack of voter education—can be addressed. When problems in the precincts arise, means must exist to solve them effectively and efficiently. The goal is to ensure that the ballots cast reflect the voters' intent. The large number of undervotes and overvotes shows the frailty of the 2000 Florida voting machines. In response and with the encouragement of HAVA, many states quickly embraced touch-screen voting machines. These devices were thought to be the panacea. Proponents claimed that they were reliable, accurate, easier on the eye, multilingual, and more accessible to handicapped voters. The 2004 election proved that problems persist.

Bush v. Gore leaves a legacy by forcing states to look to the creation of administrative standards and uniform enforcement. The Court's decision may provide the final spark to the realization of the goals of the 1965 Voting Rights Act of transparent, uniform, and open voting processes. Uniformity in the administration of the election laws has always been a problem. States have had difficulty in ensuring that local boards and registrars followed the law. *Bush v. Gore* requires not only a uniform standard but uniform rights to how one's vote is cast, counted, and, where necessary, recounted. Voting machines that do not permit a full audit of the vote tally raise constitutional concerns—particularly if disparate processes are used in a state where some machines create a paper trail and others do not.

B. THE 2004 ELECTION

The presidential election of 2004 was no improvement over its predecessor. The 2000 election recount involved butterfly ballots, hanging chads, clueless election officials "eyeballing" ballots, a very ambitious and politically connected secretary of state, a lack of statewide standards, lawyers everywhere, and numerous court decisions that left more questions than answers. In 2004, long lines replaced the butterfly ballot, election officials still had problems administering the process when they excluded thousands of voters from the registration rolls, new voting machines proved fallible and unreliable, a very ambitious secretary of state (this time in Ohio) was in charge, and statewide standards failed to appear. The only saving grace to the 2004 election was that it was not close enough to change the results in the Electoral College.

Between the 2000 and 2004 elections, under HAVA, Congress appropriated billions of dollars to improve voting machinery, mandated statewide registered voter lists, expanded the right to cast a provisional ballot, and authorized requiring an ID before a person could vote. But the system has not improved. Problems still existed in the administration of elections in 2004.

C. THE CONTINUED NEED FOR REFORM

A significant part of the problem with the 2000 and 2004 elections is found in the local nature of the process. Elections are run and managed on the precinct level, where training is marginal and help almost nonexistent. New machines are mandated, but sufficient training is not. County and city electoral boards are generally understaffed, undertrained in modern technology, and unable to deal with the influx of new registrations.

The 2000 and 2004 elections show that

- Elections at all levels warrant a solid centralized processes managed by professional administrators.

- State laws need a complete overhaul from registration to recounts.
- State and local officials in 2004 need to recognize that they jumped too quickly into the electronic voting machine briar patch.[72]
- Too many eligible voters were turned away from the polls.[73]
- Voting by provisional ballot and requiring the voter to later confirm his or her right to vote are not the answer; rather they are solid evidence of an election process that has run out of control, especially given that more than two-thirds of those voting by provisional ballot were entitled to cast an Election Day ballot.
- Early voting and no-fault absentee voting need to be expanded to alleviate long lines and conflicts on Election Day.
- States should decertify voting equipment that does not meet the highest standards for security, accuracy, and auditability.

Unless strong standards and centralized nonpolitical administration are put in place, with greater access for qualified voters, the 2000 and 2004 presidential election problems will become the rule rather than the exception.

Notes

1. *See, e.g.,* JEFFREY TOOBIN, TOO CLOSE TO CALL (2001); JAKE TAPPER, DOWN AND DIRTY: THE PLOT TO STEAL THE PRESIDENCY (2001); RICHARD A. POSNER, BREAKING THE DEADLOCK: THE 2000 ELECTION, THE CONSTITUTION AND THE COURTS (2001).

2. Bush v. Gore, 531 U.S. 98, 104–105 (2000) *citing* Harper v. Virginia Bd. of Election, 383 U.S. 663 (1966).

3. *See, e.g., Hard-Fought Election Stays Close to the End* (ABC News television broadcast Nov. 6, 2000) (*available at* http://abcnews.go.com/images/pdf/836a20Tracking20.pdf).

4. *See CNN Breaking News: Election 2000: Curtis Gans of the Committee for Study of American Electorate Discusses Voter Turnout* (CNN television broadcast Nov. 8, 2000) (transcript available at http://transcripts.cnn.com/TRANSCRIPTS/0011/08/bn.08.html).

5. *See* EILEEN J. CANAVAN & R. BRYAN WHITENER, FEDERAL ELECTIONS COMMISSION, 2000 PRESIDENTIAL POPULAR VOTE SUMMARY FOR ALL CANDIDATES LISTED ON AT LEAST ONE STATE BALLOT, FEDERAL ELECTIONS 2000 (2001) [hereinafter 2000 PRESIDENTIAL POPULAR VOTE SUMMARY], *available at* http://www.fec.gov/pubrec/fe2000/prespop.htm.

6. *See* Nancy Gibbs et al., *Standoff! The Wildest Election in History*, TIME, Nov. 20, 2000, at 28.

7. *See* Kelly Anthony, Testimony at the Elections Assistance Commission Public Hearing (June 3, 2004) (transcript available at http://www.eac.gov/News/meetings/060304/pres7-060304).

8. *Id.*

9. *Id.*

10. FLA. CONST. art. VI, §4(a).

11. *See* Anthony, *supra* note 7.

12. *See NewsHour with Jim Lehrer: Voting Rights* (PBS television broadcast Dec. 15, 2000).

13. *See* Mattie J. Germer, *The Road to the Presidency: A Timeline of the 2000 Presidential Campaign*, created for the Institute of Politics' Campaign for President: The Managers Look at 2000 Conference (2001), at 119.

14. *See* DAVID A. KAPLAN, THE ACCIDENTAL PRESIDENT: HOW 413 LAWYERS, 9 SUPREME COURT JUSTICES, AND 5,963,110 FLORIDIANS (GIVE OR TAKE A FEW) LANDED GEORGE W. BUSH IN THE WHITE HOUSE 10–11 (2001).

15. *Id.*

16. KAPLAN, *supra* note 14, at 12.

17. *Id.*

18. *Id.* at 18.

19. *See* SCOTT BENNETT, POLITICS AND PUBLIC ADMINISTRATION GROUP, DEPT. OF THE PARLIAMENTARY LIBRARY, PARLIAMENT OF AUSTRALIA, CURRENT ISSUES BRIEF NO. 9 2000–01, US PRESIDENTIAL ELECTION 2000, at 10–11 (2001).

20. KAPLAN, *supra* note 14, at 10.

21. FLA. STAT. § 102.141 (2000).

22. David E. Cardwell, *Thirty-Six Days in Florida: From the Election Law Analyst's Chair*, STATE & LOCAL L. NEWS (ABA Section of State and Local Government Law), Spring 2001, at 15.

23. 3 U.S.C. § 7.

24. Mitchell W. Berger & Candice D. Tobin, *Election 2000: The Law of Tied Presidential Elections*, 26 NOVA L. REV. 647 (2002).

25. Fladell v. Palm Beach County Canvassing Board, 772 So. 2d 1240 (Fla. 2000).

26. Cardwell, *supra* note 22.

27. *See* Timothy Downs, *Recounts: Reality, Myths and the Florida Experience*, STATE & LOCAL L. NEWS (ABA Section of State and Local Government Law), Spring 2001, at 5, 18 (Downs, an election lawyer specializing in recounts, makes the argument that the Bush team created and propagated this "myth" that determining voter intent on punch-card ballots is difficult and subjective. In fact, establishing voter intent is actually a clear and easy process, which employs a standard with ample precedent.).

28. *Id. See also* Stephen Murdoch, *Bush v. Gore Revisited*, WASH. LAW., Apr. 2003.

29. Downs, *supra* note 27.

30. *Id.* at 18.

31. Berger & Tobin, *supra* note 24.

32. *See How We Got Here: A Timeline of the Florida Recount*, CNN.COM, Dec. 13, 2000, http://archives.cnn.com/2000/ALLPOLITICS/stories/12/13/got.here/index.html.

33. Gore v. Harris, 772 So. 2d 270 (2000).

34. *See, e.g.*, Cardwell, *supra* note 22, at 16–17.

35. Palm Beach County v. Harris, 772 So. 2d. 1220 (Fla. 2000).

36. Bush v. Palm Beach County Canvassing Bd., 531 U.S. 1004 (2001).

37. *See, e.g.*, Yuval Rosenberg and Victoria Scanlan Stafanakos, *Building a Better Election*, NEWSWEEK, Nov. 20, 2000, at 20. *See also* Howard Fineman et al., *A Whiff of Victory . . . But Now It's War*, NEWSWEEK, Nov. 20, 2000, at 10. In a *Newsweek* poll conducted shortly after

the 2000 presidential election, 57 percent of voters answered that they wanted to get rid of the Electoral College, compared to 33 percent who said they did not.

38. Help America Vote Act of 2002, Pub. L. No. 107-252, 107th Cong.

39. B. Partisan Campaign Finance Reform Act, Pub. L. No. 107-155, 107th Cong. (2002).

40. Help America Vote Act of 2002, *supra* note 38.

41. Bob Fritakis & Harvey Wasserman, *Hearings on Ohio Voting Put 2004 Election in Doubt*, COLUMBUS FREE PRESS, Nov. 18, 2004.

42. Nancy Gibbs, *The Morning After*, TIME, Nov. 1, 2004.

43. *E-Voting: Is the Fix In?*, CBSNEWS.COM, Aug. 8, 2004.

44. Bush v. Gore, 531 U.S. 98 (2000).

45. Mark Krispin Miller & Jared Imus, *Team Bush Paid Millions to Nathan Sproul—and Tried to Hide It*, BALTIMORE CHRONICLE, July 13, 2005.

46. Adam Liptak, *Voting Problems in Ohio Set Off an Alarm*, N.Y. TIMES, Nov. 7, 2004.

47. Michael Powell & Peter Slevin, *Several Factors Contributed to "Lost" Voters in Ohio*, WASH. POST, Dec. 15, 2004, at A1.

48. Robert F. Kennedy, Jr., *Was the 2004 Election Stolen?*, ROLLINGSTONE.COM, June 1, 2006.

49. *Executive Summary*, in DEMOCRACY AT RISK: THE 2004 ELECTION IN OHIO §II, at 4 (2005).

50. STATUS REPORT OF THE HOUSE JUDICIARY DEMOCRATIC STAFF, 109TH CONG., PRESERVING DEMOCRACY: WHAT WENT WRONG IN OHIO (2005).

51. *Id.*

52. *See* Powell & Slevin, *supra* note 47.

53. *See* Liptak, *supra* note 46.

54. Julie Andreeff Jensen, *Ohio Election Protection Summary*, in DEMOCRACY AT RISK: THE 2004 ELECTION IN OHIO §X, at 3 (2005).

55. *See* Fritikas & Wasserman, *supra* note 41.

56. *See* Powell & Slevin, *supra* note 47.

57. *See* OHIO REV. CODE §3505.18(A) (2006) *amending* 1991 Ohio H.B. 182 (1991).

58. Diane Feldman & Cornell Belcher, *Voting Experience Survey*, in DEMOCRACY AT RISK: THE 2004 ELECTION IN OHIO §III, at 4 (2005).

59. *See* Jensen, *supra* note 54, at 4.

60. *See id.* at 5.

61. *See* Powell & Slevin, *supra* note 47.

62. *Id.*

63. M. R. Kropko, *Prosecutor: Ohio County Rigged Recount*, CBSNEWS.COM, Jan. 19, 2007.

64. *See* Fritikas & Wasserman, *supra* note 41.

65. *See* Liptak, *supra* note 46.

66. James Dao & Albert Salvato, *As Questions Keep Coming, Ohio Certifies Its Vote Count*, N.Y. TIMES, Dec. 6, 2004.

67. *See Executive Summary*, *supra* note 49, at 10.

68. *See Powell & Slevin*, *supra* note 47.

69. *See* Jensen, *supra* note 54, at 5.

70. *See generally* Dan Eggen & Jo Becker, *A Lot of Traffic, but Little Trouble at the Polls*, WASH. POST, Nov. 3, 2004, at A1; David Corn, *A Stolen Election?*, NATION, Nov. 29, 2004; Josh Schwartz, *Glitch Found in Ohio Counting*, N.Y. TIMES, Nov. 6, 2004; Tracy Warren & John Hardin Young, *Election Reforms Mean More Than Replacing Machines*, CAMPAIGNS & ELECTIONS, Sept. 2003.

71. Bush v. Gore, 531 U.S. 98 (2000).

72. *See* John Hardin Young, The 2008 Election Is Heading Towards a Meltdown That May Surpass Florida in 2000, ADMIN. REG. L. NEWS, 10 (Fall 2006), describing continuing issues affecting the electoral process. Voting machines present unique challenges because of the challenges to their accuracy, and there is some evidence, at least anecdotally, of lost or miscounted votes. Recent elections have raised significant concerns about the security and reliability of electronic machines, including weak security controls, system design flaws, inadequate system version control, inadequate security and ballot testing, incorrect system configuration, poor security management, and vague and incomplete standards and training. Ballot definition files (which tell the voting machine software how to display ballot information, interpret a voter's "touch," and record the tally) are constantly being questioned. Localities, moreover, are not open to double-checking ballot images that are printed from touch-screen machines (Florida 2004) or, in some states, reviewing and rerunning optical scan ballots even in the face of evidence of problems (Virginia 2005). In early and absentee voting, an additional concern is raised by the need to ensure the security and accountability of all ballots received (e.g., have all the ballots been counted?). Auditable processes for voting and vote counting are clearly needed, according to the author.

73. Some were in the wrong precinct, some were not on the registered voter lists because of administrative mix-ups, and some did not have the correct form of identification. Plus, many do not have the time to waste in line for hours.

CHAPTER TWO

THE LANGUAGE ASSISTANCE PROVISIONS OF THE VOTING RIGHTS ACT AND THE 2006 REAUTHORIZATION

JOCELYN FRIEDRICHS BENSON*

I. Introduction

Sections 203 and 4(f)4 of the Voting Rights Act (VRA)[1] are the federal government's most significant attempt to date to ensure that certain citizens with limited English proficiency have some accommodations in casting their ballots. The provisions originated in 1975 amendments to the VRA, after congressional hearings concluded that certain citizens with limited English proficiency were effectively excluded from participation in the electoral process as a result of poor educational opportunities, high illiteracy rates, and low voting participation.[2] To remedy this and promote the political participation of these historically underrepresented groups, Sections 203 and 4(f)4 required that jurisdictions provide translated election materials or bilingual poll workers if a significant number of Latino, Asian American, Native American, or Alaskan Native citizens living in those jurisdictions suffer from high rates of illiteracy.[3]

When the provisions were added to the VRA, congressional leaders held the optimistic hope that the sociological factors that created the need for language accommodations would eventually diminish. As such, the most significant aspects of the provisions were intended to expire in 1982, after seven years.[4] But in the face of consistent data indicating that language-minority citizens covered by the provision continued to suffer from high rates of illiteracy and poor access to both educational and electoral opportunities, Congress extended and renewed Section 203 for ten years in 1982,[5] 15 years in 1992,[6] and most recently, in 2006, for 25 years.[7]

---

*Assistant Professor of Law, Wayne State University Law School; J.D. Harvard Law School; M. Phil. Oxford University; B.A. Wellesley College; Member, ABA Standing Committee on Election Law.

Today, under the coverage formula of Section 203, language assistance is afforded to voters of the following descents: Hispanic, Chinese, Filipino, Japanese, Korean, Vietnamese, American Indian, and Native Alaskan.[8] In addition, if any covered state or political subdivision can show a federal district court that "the illiteracy rate of the applicable language minority group . . . is equal to or less than the national illiteracy rate," it can receive a declaratory judgment exempting it from coverage.[9] As of July 22, 2002, the most current coverage calculation until 2010, over 335 jurisdictions were covered under Sections 203 or 4(f)4: 220 jurisdictions required to provide language assistance in Spanish and about 115 required to provide assistance to Asian Americans, Alaskan Natives, or Native Americans.[10] The U.S. Department of Justice (DOJ), which monitors coverage compliance, typically requires covered jurisdictions to provide translated written materials, such as ballots, voter registration forms, and voting instructions;[11] oral assistance such as interpreters and bilingual poll workers;[12] and publicity regarding the elections and availability of bilingual assistance,[13] such as signs at polling sites and announcements in community media.[14] The DOJ also encourages covered jurisdictions to work with local community groups to ensure that the accommodations are tailored to the needs of the community.[15]

The following analysis reviews the congressional decisions to extend and renew Section 203, including its most recent renewal in 2006. It also discusses its effectiveness and usefulness in American political law. In particular, it examines the events leading to Congress's most recent decision to extend the provision for an additional 25 years, and outlines the various arguments surrounding its controversial 2006 renewal. It concludes with a look to the future, and attempts to identify the ongoing relevance of the protections afforded by the federal law and the role states and localities must play to ensure its efficacy.

II. The Development of Sections 203 and 4(f)4 of the Voting Rights Act

Sections 203 and 4(f)4 were an expansion of another provision of the VRA, Section 4(e), which was enacted in 1965.[16] Section 4(e) prohibits discrimination against persons who, due to poor educational opportunities, are not proficient in the English language,[17] but is traditionally interpreted to apply solely to citizens from Puerto Rico.

In 1975,[18] Congress engaged in an extensive debate over whether to broaden the scope of the VRA to protect other language minorities.[19] A coalition of several civil rights constituency groups testified before judiciary committees in both houses and presented overwhelming evidence of the educational disparities, low turnout rates, and discriminatory barriers to voting endured by Hispanics, Asian Americans, American Indians, and Alaska Natives.[20] After concluding that limited English proficiency was a serious barrier to political participation for these groups,[21] both houses voted to add Sections 203 and 4(f)4 to the Voting Rights Act.[22]

The coverage formula for Section (4)(f)4 applied only to jurisdictions that on November 1, 1972, failed to provide translated election materials to any language-minority groups that comprised over 5 percent of the voting-age citizen population on that date.[23] Section 203 was intended to provide similar protections but incorporated a flexible coverage formula, linked first to the decennial census conducted by the U.S. Census Bureau and now to the American Community Survey, and set to evolve with the size and literacy levels of language minority communities.[24]

At first, Section 203 mandated language assistance only to states and smaller jurisdictions where the voting-age citizen population of a single language minority was greater than 5 percent, provided the illiteracy rate of the citizens in the jurisdiction was higher than the national illiteracy rate.[25] Though it was set to expire in ten years, it was renewed in 1982 for an additional ten years after testimony from a multitude of community groups[26] documenting the continued need for the provisions[27] and noting the impact of the protections in increasing the electoral participation of the covered language minorities.[28] In particular, the House and Senate reports cited surveys conducted in 1976 and 1980 that indicated a strong link between providing bilingual registration and voting materials and oral assistance at the polls and increased voter participation among members of the Latino community,[29] emphasizing the benefits of these materials for elderly voters who had lower levels of English proficiency.[30]

Ten years later, Congress reviewed evidence from various Asian American community groups. The evidence emphasized both the effectiveness of the provision in boosting the electoral engagement of Asian American citizens and the gaps in coverage that led to the exclusion of many Asian communities from protections in the provision. In 1992, the only jurisdictions required under Section 203 to provide language assistance for Asian Americans were in Hawaii and San Francisco, California.[31] Excluded from coverage were several major cities, including Los Angeles and New York. In addition, data cited in congressional reports point to exit polls of Asian American voters in Los Angeles and New York expressing an overwhelming desire for translated materials—approximately 80 percent of those surveyed in both cities agreed that bilingual ballots would provide significant help in the voting process, and stated that they would vote more often if bilingual assistance were provided.[32] To address these gaps in coverage, Congress voted to amend Section 203 to also cover jurisdictions with at least 10,000 voting-age citizens of a single language minority already covered under the provision.[33] Immediately as a result of the amendment, ten counties in New York, California, and Hawaii were included and specifically required to provide ballots, voting materials, and language assistance in Asian languages.[34]

Congress renewed Section 203, as amended in 1992, in its 2006 passage of the Fannie Lou Hamer, Rosa Parks, and Coretta Scott King Voting Rights Act Reauthorization and Amendments Act,[35] after additional congressional hearings revealed an ongoing need for its protections.[36] The sole amendment to the provision came from a suggestion from a coalition of civil rights community groups who requested that coverage calculations be based not on the decennial U.S. Census Bureau census, but on data provided from the American Community Survey, collected every five years. The amendment ensures that the coverage formula for Section 203 is narrowly tailored to the language-minority communities that Congress sought to protect.

III. The 2006 Reauthorization of Section 203

Since their enactment in 1975, the language protections of the Voting Rights Act have ensured that government has played a direct and pivotal role in promoting political participation and a responsive, inclusive government. Latino citizens living in areas covered by Section 203 were 4.4 percent more likely to vote in 1996 and 2000 than Latino citizens living in noncovered areas.[37] In one Arizona county, the number of Native Americans registered to vote grew 165 percent between 1972 and 1980.[38] Turnout among Native Americans in Navajo County, Arizona, increased by 120 percent between 1972 and 1990.[39]

This increased participation has also led to an increase in the number of elected officials from the accommodated communities—the executive director of the Asian American Legal Defense and Education Fund (AALDEF) testified before Congress in 2005 that a recent increase in elected officials of Asian descent was directly attributable to Section 203 requirements and accommodations[40]—and better responsiveness from government entities.[41]

These results have not come without controversy. Congress weighed several arguments extensively during its deliberations over whether to reauthorize Sections 4(f)4 and 203 in 2006, both in hearings and on the House and Senate floor.[42] Critics of the provisions cited concerns ranging from the practical—arguing that the measure is unnecessary and that the costs of compliance exceed what the government should be expected to provide to accommodate any voters—to the symbolic—suggesting that the provision "Balkanizes America,"[43] reduces incentives for citizens to learn English, and "degrades the idea of citizenship."[44]

Opponents offered testimony citing low dropout rates among Asian immigrant groups as evidence that the educational disparities that led to the need for the materials no longer exist.[45] Other testimony emphasized what opponents saw as a ratio of high costs of compliance to low usage of the materials, pointing to a 1997 report by the Federal General Accounting Office that Los Angeles County spent just over $1 million to provide election materials during the 1996 election, while places like King County, Washington, reported that after it printed 3,600 Chinese-language ballots only 24 people requested them for a September 2002 primary election.[46]

And during the hearings, Rep. Peter King (R-NY) circulated a letter signed by 56 members of Congress that was reportedly drafted by ProEnglish, an advocacy organization that explicitly advocates for English-only laws, and that included a handful of anecdotes from newspaper articles about the supposed high costs of compliance and the failure of targeted citizens to use the materials.[47]

But the weight of statistics showed that translated materials and other accommodations were still needed and heavily utilized. A report by the Pew Hispanic Center cited in congressional testimony revealed that despite gains since 1975, only 47 percent of eligible Hispanics participated in the November 2004 election, compared to 67 percent of whites and 60 percent of African Americans.[48] Survey data from 2002 also showed that nearly a quarter (23 percent) of registered Latino voters identify Spanish as their primary language and indicate that they speak little or no English,[49] while a 2004 survey found that 47 percent of Southeast Asian Americans said they had limited English proficiency, and over one-third of all respondents needed some form of language assistance in order to vote.[50] And according to AALDEF's 2004 exit poll of 11,000 Asian American voters, almost one-third of all respondents needed some form of language assistance in order to vote, and the greatest beneficiaries of language assistance (46 percent) were first-time voters.[51]

The most extensive empirical data supplied to Congress revealed that for many covered jurisdictions, costs of compliance were relatively minimal. Researchers Jim Tucker and Rodolfo Espino surveyed 361 of 810 jurisdictions covered under the language protections to, among other things, collect data on compliance costs.[52] Their research revealed not only that 71 percent of the responding jurisdictions believed that federal language assistance provisions should remain in effect for public elections, but that the price of compliance was modest. Specifically, their 2005 study of election officials in the 31 states covered by Section 203 revealed that a majority of covered jurisdictions incurred no additional costs for either oral or written language assistance, with most of the remaining jurisdictions incurring additional expenses of less than 1.5 percent for oral language assistance and less than 3 percent for written language assistance.[53]

Symbolic arguments of either the immense importance or the disastrous effects of the language protections also abounded at the 2006 hearings. Linda Chavez, president of One Nation Indivisible, suggested in testimony to the House Judiciary Constitutional Subcommittee that Section 203 "Balkanizes" America, and stressed that "America should be unified and the government should be encouraging citizens to be fluent in English."[54] K. C. McAlpin, executive director of ProEnglish, also testified before the House Committee that bilingual ballots undermine our national unity.[55]

Rep. Jose Serrano of New York rebuffed the argument, noting that he had "never met any immigrant, much less one who became a citizen, who did not want to learn English or understand that learning English is their key to the American dream."[56] Testimony from Rebecca Vigil-Giron, secretary of state for New Mexico and past president of the National Association of Secretaries of State, similarly supported the language protections of the Voting Rights Act, stating they were the "legal foundation" of her administration's ability to protect the voting rights of Americans with limited English proficiency and to incorporate these citizens into American democracy.[57] Margaret Fung of AALDEF also testified that "At the most fundamental level, translated ballots . . . have enabled Asian American voters to exercise their right to vote independently and privately,"[58] while Juan Cartagena, general counsel of the Community Service Society, emphasized simply that the "rights we are advocating for today are the rights of citizens of this country to full and fair access to the franchise."[59]

A. AMENDMENTS AND OTHER ATTEMPTS TO WEAKEN SECTION 203 IN 2006

Despite the testimony documenting the continuing importance and relevance of the provisions, there were several attempts to repeal or limit the enforcement of Section 203 in particular throughout the reauthorization process.[60] In May 2006, during the House Judiciary Committee markup of the entire reauthorization bill, Rep. King proposed two amendments—one to abolish the provision entirely, and another that would limit its renewal to six years, as opposed to the 25-year renewal that all other expiring provisions received in the proposed legislation.[61] King argued that reauthorizing Section 203 would contradict "immigration law because English is a condition for naturalization."[62] The chairman of the House Judiciary Committee, Rep. F. James Sensenbrenner, emphasized in response that it was the "failure" of the American public education system that was partially to blame for not preparing all citizens to speak English proficiently.[63] The removal of Section 203, Sensenbrenner believed, would "close the door" to opportunities for these citizens to understand the ballot and participate in the electoral process.[64] Both King amendments failed committee votes and were not included in the markup legislation.[65] King also proposed an identical version of his amendment to strike Section 203 from the reauthorization altogether on the House floor in July 2006, which similarly failed in a full vote of 238–185.[66]

A backhanded attempt to do away with Section 203 occurred when Rep. Clifford Stearns, a Republican from Florida, proposed an amendment to the Science, State, Justice, Commerce, and Related Agencies Appropriations Act of 2007 to eliminate funding for the DOJ to enforce the language accommodation provisions of the Voting Rights Act.[67] Without appropriated enforcement funds, language assistance under the Voting Rights Act would be virtually nonexistent.[68] The Stearns amendment was ultimately defeated in a floor vote of 254–167.[69]

B. OTHER ATTEMPTS TO MODIFY SECTION 203

Congress also considered various proposals to modify Section 203 during the reauthorization process. Three specific changes were considered at the behest of a coalition of top civil rights organizations, academics, advocates, and litigators: (1) lowering the numerical trigger for coverage in jurisdictions from 10,000 to 7,500; (2) changing the basis for Section 203 determinations from the decennial long-form survey under the U.S. Census Bureau to the American Community Survey; and (3) requiring Section 203 determinations to be made every five years instead of every ten years, beginning in 2010.[70]

While the latter two changes were added to the reauthorized Section 203 without much fanfare, efforts to lower the numerical trigger for coverage faced stiff opposition. Congress had previously amended Section 203 to include jurisdictions where over 10,000 citizens were of limited English proficiency and members of a single language-minority group, extending coverage to several Latino and Asian populations in dense urban environments. In 2006, civil rights advocates testified before House and Senate committees that lowering this numerical trigger to 7,500 would extend coverage to at least 77,900 voters,[71] including many of Southeast Asian descent. In particular, Margaret Fung, executive director of the Asian American Legal Defense and Education Fund, offered specific testimony documenting the need for coverage to Southeast Asian communities,[72] and Juan Cartagena of the Community Service Society submitted similar testimony discussing the benefits that a lowered numerical threshold would provide for smaller Latino communities.[73] The issue failed to garner much support among congressional leaders and never moved beyond committee discussions.[74]

Finally, there was some debate over whether citizen-created recall petitions and ballot initiatives were "election materials" requiring translation under Section 203. This controversy emerged from a decision by the U.S. Court of Appeals for the Ninth Circuit.[75] The *Padilla* opinion held that Section 203 did not apply to citizen-initiated recall and initiative petitions because they were not election materials provided by the government. Though there was no formal amendment to Section 203 addressing this issue, the House committee report on the legislation included language explicitly noting that private citizens were not covered by the provision, reasoning that "[t]o impose Section 203's requirements on private citizens whose actions are outside governmentally administered voting systems would have the effect of penalizing private citizens for injuries caused by States."[76]

IV. Sections 203 and 4(f)4 in Action: Issues of Compliance and Efficacy

As the United States citizenry becomes increasingly racially and culturally diverse, with Latino citizens and citizens of Asian descent among the country's fastest growing populations,[77] the issue of federally mandated language accommodations in the electoral arena will continue to be a relevant ongoing discussion. And at the heart of this discussion will be the question of whether the existing assistance provisions in Sections 203 and 4(f)4 meet Congress's goals of reducing barriers to the electoral process for language-minority citizens who have not had adequate access to educational opportunities that would enable them to learn English.

Coverage under Sections 203 and 4(f)4 typically means only that the state or local jurisdiction must fund and provide election materials and assistance in the language of the applicable minority group.[78] Apart from that loose mandate, covered jurisdictions are given a great deal of discretion as to how to comply with the provision,[79] but are expected to take reasonable steps to provide materials and assistance in a way that allows members of the covered language group to be informed of and participate in election activities.[80] Jurisdictions may opt, though are not required, to use trained interpreters at poll sites[81] and may "target" their assistance to certain areas or precincts for coverage.[82]

Noncompliance is an ongoing problem with covered jurisdictions, partially as a result of these flexible guidelines and inconsistent monitoring by the DOJ.[83] Nearly 20 percent of the jurisdictions responding to the 2005 Tucker and Espino survey admitted that they did not provide any translated written or oral language materials, despite requirements under federal law. Just over 57 percent of the 336 respondent covered jurisdictions also did not have any full-time workers who were fluent in the covered language. And although the DOJ regulations require that covered jurisdictions have direct contact with the language-minority group organizations to ensure language assistance programs are effective, only 37.3 percent (120 jurisdictions) reported that they regularly consulted with community organizations or individuals from the covered language groups about providing election assistance in those languages.[84]

Where there is compliance, several nonprofit monitoring groups have found written materials to be poorly or incorrectly translated,[85] and oral language assistance to be unavailable or nonexistent.[86] Where bilingual interpreters are provided, they are sometimes poorly trained[87] or speak the wrong language or dialect: Mandarin interpreters are offered where voters speak Cantonese, or Korean interpreters are provided where most voters are of Chinese descent.[88] In Queens, New York, during the general election of 2000, Chinese-language ballots were translated incorrectly at six voting sites, so that Democratic candidates were labeled as Republican, and Republican candidates were labeled as Democratic.[89]

And discriminatory remarks made at polling locations in covered jurisdictions continue to be a problem. In 2004, election monitors from the Asian American Legal Defense and Education Fund observed that "several white voters at a poll site in Jackson Heights, Queens, N.Y. yelled at Asian Americans, saying: 'You all are turning this country into a third-world waste dump!'"[90] A study of the 2006 elections revealed similar anecdotes.[91] Compounding these issues is the fact that until very recently, the DOJ has been slow to investigate issues of poor compliance or noncompliance.[92] Further, the high evidentiary requirements of private causes of action under the Voting Rights Act often deter private litigants or community groups from pursuing litigation.[93]

Apart from poor compliance or noncompliance, other inadequacies of the language accommodation provided in Section 203 surround its coverage formula—namely, which language groups get coverage, and how many language-minority citizens must be present in order to trigger coverage. The fact that Section 203 defines "language minority" to include only Latino, Asian American, Alaska Native, and American Indian citizens leads to the exclusion of several other groups that face similar discriminatory barriers, such as Haitian Americans and Arab Americans.[94] The numerical trigger, which calculates coverage based on the number of language-minority citizens in one group, as opposed to collectively, also leads to problems for Asian American citizens. Because citizens of Asian descent speak a variety of languages and dialects, there may collectively be over 5 percent or 10,000 voting-age citizens of Asian descent in a particular jurisdiction, but Section 203 coverage will be triggered only if a single language group, such as citizens of Korean or Japanese descent, independently meets the numerical threshold.[95] As a result, following the 2000 census coverage determinations there were several localities with large Asian American populations that were not covered under Section 203's "individual language" calculation.[96]

These issues—the lack of compliance, the problems with how coverage is determined, and the many citizens with limited English proficiency who do not receive any accommodation under Sections 4(f)4 or 203—raise some concerns about the efficacy of Section 203 as the primary accommodation in electoral politics for citizens with limited English proficiency. This analysis suggests that language accommodations are a concept that is welcome and needed in American democracy, but emphasizes that additional work and tinkering is needed to ensure that the provisions do in fact accomplish Congress's goal of reducing language barriers to the political process that these communities face.

V. Conclusion

The language assistance provisions of the Voting Rights Act have played a pivotal role in fulfilling the constitutional promise of one person, one vote. While many language minority voters are proficient in English, most still require or benefit from some level of assistance in casting a vote based on an independent and educated decision. It is because of these provisions that language minority citizens are able to fairly and fully exercise their right to vote, thus helping to ensure that our American democracy is truly participatory and representative.

Notes

1. 42 U.S.C § 1971.

2. Voting Rights Act Amendments of 1975, Pub. L. No. 94-73 (1975); *see also* H.R. REP. NO. 94-196, at 17 (1975).

3. *Id.* Section 203 as codified states in part that:

(a) . . . The Congress finds that, through the use of various practices and procedures, citizens of language minorities have been effectively excluded from participation in the electoral process. Among other factors, the denial of the right to vote of such minority group citizens is ordinarily directly related to the unequal educational opportunities afforded them, resulting in high illiteracy and low voting participation. The Congress declares that, in order to enforce the guarantees of the fourteenth and fifteenth amendments to the United States, it is necessary to eliminate such discrimination by prohibiting these practices, and by prescribing other remedial devices.

(b) (1) Generally. Before August 6, 2007, no covered State or political subdivision shall provide voting materials only in the English language.

(2) Covered States and political subdivisions. (A) Generally. A State or political subdivision is a covered State or political subdivision for the purposes of this subsection if the Director of the Census determines, based on census data, that—(i) (I) more than 5 percent of the citizens of voting age of such State or political subdivision are members of a single language minority and are limited-English proficient; (II) more than 10,000 of the citizens of voting age of such political subdivision are members of a single language minority and are limited-English proficient; or (III) in the case of a political subdivision that contains all or any part of an Indian reservation, more than 5 percent of the American Indian or Alaska Native citizens of voting age within the Indian reservation are members of a single language minority and are limited-English proficient; and (ii) the illiteracy rate of the citizens in the language minority as a group is higher than the national illiteracy rate.

4. Voting Rights Act Amendments of 1975, Pub. L. No. 94-73 (1975).

5. Voting Rights Act Amendments of 1982, Pub. L. No. 97-205 (1982).

6. Voting Rights Language Assistance Act of 1992, Pub. L. No. 102-344 (1992).

7. Fannie Lou Hamer, Rosa Parks, and Coretta Scott King Voting Rights Act Reauthorization and Amendments Act of 2006, Pub. L. 109-246 (2006).

8. *Id.* Two years after the completion of each decennial census, the director of the Bureau of the Census publishes a revised list of areas covered under Section 203. For the most recent list of covered areas, see Voting Rights Act Amendments of 1992, Determinations Under Section 203, 67 Fed. Reg. 48,871, 48,871–77 (July 26, 2002).

9. 42 U.S.C. § 1973aa-1a(d) (2000).

10. Voting Rights Act Amendments of 1992, Determinations Under Section 203, 67 Fed. Reg. 48,871–77 (July 26, 2002). The next coverage calculation will occur in 2010, and every five years after that.

11. 28 C.F.R. §§ 55.15, 55.19.

12. *Id.* §§ 55.18, 55.20. Sometimes assistance must be provided in more than one dialect of the language. For instance, although there is one written form of Chinese, there are several spoken dialects, like Cantonese, Mandarin, and Toisanese. *Id.*

13. *Id.* § 55.20.

14. Of those polled, over 51 percent of Asian American voters got their news about politics and community issues from the ethnic press. AALDEF Asian American Vote 2004 Report 12 (2004).

15. 28 C.F.R. § 55.20.

16. In addition to Section 203, Section 4(f)4, codified as 42 U.S.C. § 1973b(f)(4) (2000), provides permanent protections for certain language minorities. The language-minority requirements of Section 4(f)(4) and Section 203(c) are essentially identical; however, Section 203(c) provides for a changing determination of coverage based on census data whereas protections provided by Section 4(f)(4) are limited to language minorities present and recorded prior to the Nov. 1, 1972, election. *See* 28 C.F.R. § 55.8 (2006) (discussing the relationship between Sections 4(f)(4) and 203(c)); 28 C.F.R. § 55.5 (discussing the coverage formula pursuant to Section 4(f)(4)).

17. 42 U.S.C. § 1973b(e) (1982) ("1. Congress hereby declares that to secure the rights under the fourteenth amendment of persons educated in American-flag schools in which the predominant classroom language was other than English, it is necessary to prohibit the States from conditioning the right to vote of such persons on ability to read, write, understand, or interpret any matter in the English language. 2. No person who demonstrates that he has successfully completed the sixth primary grade in a public school in, or a private school accredited by, any State or territory, the District of Columbia, or the Commonwealth of Puerto Rico in which the predominant classroom language was other than English, shall be denied the right to vote in any Federal, State, or local election because of his inability to read, write, understand, or interpret any matter in the English language.").

18. Voting Rights Act Amendments of 1975, § 203, Pub. L. No. 94-73 (1975).

19. *Id.* § 207 (codified as amended at 1973aa-1a(e)).

20. *See* Rodolfo de la Garza and Louis DeSipio, *Regulating the Electoral Process, Save the Baby, Change the Bathwater, and Scrub the Tub: Latino Electoral Participation After Seventeen Years of Voting Rights Act Coverage,* 71 Tex. L. Rev. 1479, 1482–84 (recounting testimony describing methods employed to exclude minority language voters from the voting booth); *id.* at 1492 ("In the testimony before Congress in both 1975 and 1982, Latino leaders offered many examples of the conscious exclusion of Mexican Americans from the vote. Techniques reminiscent of the pre-VRA South spiced the testimony.").

21. H.R. Rep. No. 94-296, at 22 (1975) ("The definition of those groups included in language minorities was determined on the basis of the evidence of voting discrimination."); S. Rep. No. 94-295, at 25 (1975) ("The extensive record . . . is filled with examples of the barriers to registration and voting that language minority citizens encounter in the electoral process. Testimony was received regarding inadequate numbers of minority registration personnel, uncooperative registrars, and the disproportionate effect of purging laws on non-english-speaking citizens because of language barriers.").

22. *See, e.g.,* H.R. Rep. No. 94-296, at 16–25 (1975); S. Rep. No. 94-295, at 24–28 (1975); 121 Cong. Rec. 13, at 16,246–47 (1975).

23. 28 C.F.R. § 55.5 ("Section 4(f)(4) applies to any State or political subdivision in which (1) Over five percent of the voting age citizens were, on November 1, 1972, members of a single language minority group, (2) Registration and election materials were provided only in English on November 1, 1972, and (3) Fewer than 50 percent of the voting-age citizens were registered to vote or voted in the 1972 Presidential election."). Jurisdictions covered under Section 4(f)4 are also required to submit any changes to their accommodations for language minorities to the Attorney General for preclearance. *See* 28 C.F.R. § 55.2(d).

24. Specifically, a jurisdiction is covered under Section 203 if the director of the Census Bureau determines that two criteria are met. First, the limited-English-proficient citizens, or citizens who speak English "less than very well," who are of voting age in a single language group must: (a) number more than 10,000; (b) comprise more than five percent of all citizens of voting age; or (c) comprise more than five percent of all American Indians of a single language group residing on an Indian reservation. Second, the illiteracy rate of the language minority citizens must exceed the national illiteracy rate.

25. *See* 42 U.S.C. § 1973 aa-1a(2)(A)(ii) (2000).

26. The Senate heard from groups such as the Mexican American Legal Defense and Educational Fund, the League of United Latin American Citizens, Chinese for Affirmative Action, the National Congress of American Indians, and various state officials, who all spoke in favor of Section 203. S. Rep. No. 97-205, at 65–66 (1982). The House Judiciary Committee Report cited similar testimony from the Southwest Voter Registration Education Project, the Mexican American Equal Rights Project, the Texas Labor Council for Latin American Advancement, the National Congress of American Indians, Chinese for Affirmative Action, and the Mexican American Legal Defense Fund. H.R. Rep. No. 97-227, at 27 n.85 (1981).

27. Henry Der, executive director of Chinese for Affirmative Action, delivered particularly compelling testimony to the House Committee. According to the House Committee report, Der's testimony "pointed out that persons who oppose these provisions 'do not understand the discriminatory experiences that Chinese Americans have had to suffer and which have made it difficult for Chinese Americans, particularly the elderly, to learn English." H.R. Rep. No. 97-227, at 27 (1981) (citing Testimony of Henry Der, House Judiciary Committee Hearings, June 10, 1981).

28. *Id.* Testimony from David Dunbar, general counsel for the National Congress of American Indians, for example, emphasized the positive effects of Section 203 in the American Indian community: "The provision of oral language assistance in the electoral process is of particular importance to American Indian communities." *Id.*

29. H.R. Rep. No. 97-227, at 27 (1981). According to a survey conducted by the Mexican American Legal Defense Fund and the Southwest Voter Registration and Education Project, 23 percent of surveyed Latino voters received assistance from a bilingual poll worker and 32 percent said they would be less likely to vote if Spanish language assistance were not available. S. Rep. No. 97-205, at 66 (1982).

30. S. Rep. No. 97-205, at 66 (1982) ("Among those who participated in the survey [by MALDEF and SVREP] who are between 18 and 25, 6 out of 100 persons speak only Spanish. Among those over 65, 34 persons, or more than 33 percent, speak only Spanish.").

31. H.R. Rep. No. 102-655, at 7 (1992); S. Rep. No. 102-315, at 17 (1992) ("After 1982 reauthorization, no Asian American community outside of Hawaii qualified for assistance. Under the 1990 census, only Chinese Americans in San Francisco County would qualify on the mainland.").

32. H.R. Rep. No. 102-655, at 7 (1992); *see also* S. Rep. No. 102-315, at 12 (1992) ("In New York City, for example, four out of five voters surveyed in that city's Chinatown had language difficulties. These voters stated that they would vote more often if bilingual assistance were provided. In Queens County, N.Y., four out of every five limited English proficient Asian-American voters indicated they would vote more if bilingual assistance were provided.").

33. H.R. Rep. No. 102-655, at 4 (1992) ("During the period from 1982 until the present, the need for a numerical benchmark became clear, so that jurisdictions with large language minority populations that do not meet the 5 percent trigger would be covered under Section 203. With a 10,000 person benchmark, 38 additional language minority communities will receive assistance."); S. Rep. No. 102-315, at 16–17 (1992) ("[A]n alternative, numerical trigger for section 203 coverage-jurisdictions with over 10,000 language minority citizens of voting age will be required to provide language assistance in the applicable minority language. According to 1990 census data, the addition of a 10,000 citizen benchmark coverage trigger will make the right to vote a reality for over 860,000 language minority citizens in the United States in 34 counties.").

34. Implementation of the Provisions of the Voting Rights Act Regarding Language Minority Groups, 28 C.F.R. pt. 55, app. (2005). The counties and languages included Alameda County, Cal. (Chinese); Los Angeles County, Cal. (Chinese, Filipino, Japanese, Vietnamese); Orange County, Cal. (Vietnamese); San Francisco County, Cal. (Chinese); Honolulu County, Haw. (Filipino, Japanese); Kauai County, Haw. (Filipino); Maui County, Haw. (Filipino); Kings County, N.Y. (Chinese); New York County, N.Y. (Chinese); and Queens County, N.Y. (Chinese).

35. Fannie Lou Hamer, Rosa Parks, and Coretta Scott King Voting Rights Act Reauthorization and Amendments Act of 2006, Pub. L. 109-246 (2006).

36. *See, e.g.,* Testimony of Margaret Fung, Executive Director of the Asian American Legal Defense Fund, Oversight Hearing on the Voting Rights Act: Section 203—Bilingual Election Requirements (Part I) (Nov. 8, 2005), *available at* http://judiciary.house.gov/oversight.aspx?ID=204.

37. Michael Jones-Correa, *Language Provisions Under the Voting Rights Act: How Effective Are They?* 86 Soc. Sci. Q. 549, 558 (Sept. 2005).

38. H. Rep. No. 102-655, at 6–7, *reprinted in* 1992 U.S.C.C.A.N. 770–71; S. Rep. No. 102-315, at 12; *S. 2236 Hearings,* S. Hrg. 102-1066, at 181–89 (1992) (statement of Navajo Nation Vice-President Marshall Plummer).

39. *Id.*

40. Testimony of Margaret Fung, *supra* note 36 ("In New York City, the municipality with the nation's largest Asian American population, the first Asian American, John Liu, was elected to the New York City Council in 2001. Jimmy Meng was elected the first Asian American member of the N.Y. State Assembly in 2004. Both Liu and Meng were elected in Queens County, one of three counties in New York City covered by section 203. In California, the state with the largest Asian American population, there were no Asian Americans

serving on the state legislature in 1990, and now, there are nine. In Houston, Texas, the first Vietnamese American, Hubert Vo, was elected to the state legislature in 2004, within years after Vietnamese language assistance was required in Harris County under Section 203."); *see also* Testimony of Eugene Lee, Asian Pacific American Legal Center, Before the Natl. Comm. on the Voting Rights Act, Western Regional Hearing (Sept. 27, 2005) *at* http:// www.votingrightsact.org/hearings/pdfs/eugene_lee.pdf ("One factor in [the recent electoral success of Asian Americans] has been Section 203 language assistance allowing limited English proficient voters (or voters who speak English less than very well) to fully exercise their right to vote. . . . [E]very county in California that is covered under Section 203 for an Asian language has at least one APIA legislator from a district in such county.").

41.   *See* de la Garza & DeSipio, *supra* note 20, at 1505 ("[Section 203] has offered Latinos the option to elect co-ethnics to office. The [Latino National Political Survey (LNPS)] offers several measures of the degree to which Latinos feel government officials are responsive, how the presence of a co-ethnic on the ballot influences their decision about whether to vote and for whom to vote, and how useful bilingual election materials are to voters. Overwhelmingly, LNPS respondents believe that they were treated fairly by the last public official with whom they interacted. Also, . . . large majorities of those who did report interaction [with their elected representatives] find that both Latino and non-Latino public officials treat them fairly. Surprisingly, perceptions of governmental fairness are even stronger among Spanish speakers.").

42.   For a detailed and first-hand account of the reauthorization proceedings, see James Tucker, *The Politics of Persuasion: Passage of The Voting Rights Act Reauthorization Act of 2006*, 33 NOTRE DAME J. LEGIS. 205 (2007).

43.   Testimony of Linda Chavez, President of One Nation Indivisible, Oversight Hearing on the Voting Rights Act: Section 203—Bilingual Election Requirements (Part I), at 1 (Nov. 8, 2005) *available at* http://www.judiciary.house.gov/OversightTestimony.aspx?ID=510.

44.   *See, e.g.,* John J. Miller, "English Is Broken Here," POL'Y REV. (Sept.–Oct. 1996), *available at* http://www.hoover.org/publications/policyreview/3574512.html ("Allowing voters to cast foreign-language ballots degrades the idea of citizenship.").

45.   Testimony of K.C. McAlpin, Executive Director of ProEnglish, Oversight Hearing on the Voting Rights Act: Section 203—Bilingual Election Requirements (Part II), (Nov. 9, 2005) *available at* http://judiciary.house.gov/media/pdfs/mcalpin110905.pdf.

46.   *Id.*

47.   Tucker, *supra* note 42.

48.   Testimony of Juan Cartagena, General Counsel to the Community Service Society in New York City, Oversight Hearing on the Voting Rights Act: Section 203—Bilingual Election Requirements (Part II), at 1 (Nov. 9, 2005) *available at* http://judiciary.house.gov/media/pdfs/cartagena110905.pdf.

49.   *Id.* at 6.

50.   Testimony of Margaret Fung, *supra* note 36, at 6.

51.   *Id.* at 5.

52.   JAMES TUCKER & RODOLFO ESPINO, MINORITY LANGUAGE ASSISTANCE PRACTICES IN PUBLIC ELECTIONS (2005). Tucker and Espino contacted all 810 jurisdictions covered under Sections 4(f)4 and 203. Of those jurisdictions, 361 responded fully to the survey and were included in the report.

53. *Id.* at ch. 6. The study also noted that many responding jurisdictions claimed they were unable to identify the costs, if any, of their language assistance programs because they did not "track such costs in their budgets, or because the costs are included in expenses they would have to incur anyway."

54. Testimony of Linda Chavez, *supra* note 43, at 1.

55. Testimony of K. C. McAlpin, *supra* note 45, at 9.

56. Terry Ao, *When the Voting Rights Act Became Un-American: The Misguided Vilification of Section 203,* 58 ALA. L. REV. 377, 390 (2007) (citing 152 CONG. REC. H5173 (daily ed. July 13, 2006) (statement of Rep. Serrano)).

57. Testimony of Rebecca Vigil-Giron, Secretary of State for New Mexico, Oversight Hearing on the Voting Rights Act: Section 203—Bilingual Election Requirements (Part I), at 1 (Nov. 8, 2005) *available at* http://www.judiciary.house.gov/OversightTestimony .aspx?ID=511.

58. Testimony of Margaret Fung, *supra* note 36, at 4.

59. Testimony of Juan Cartagena, *supra* note 48, at 4.

60. For further discussion on the 2006 reauthorization efforts surrounding Section 203 of the Voting Rights Act, see generally Tucker, *supra* note 42, and Ao, *supra* note 56.

61. H.R. REP. NO. 109-478, at 85–86.

62. Tucker, *supra* note 42, at 238.

63. *Id.* at 238 n.334.

64. *Id.*

65. The vote on the first amendment to strike the reauthorization of Section 203 failed by a vote of 26 to 9. The second amendment, which would have seen Section 203 expire in six years, failed by a vote of 25 to 10. *See* Ao, *supra* note 56, at 384.

66. 152 CONG. REC. H5205–06 (daily ed. July 13, 2006) (Roll Call Vote No. 372).

67. The amendment provided that "[n]one of the funds made available in this Act may be used to carry out any provision of section 203 of the Voting Rights Act of 1965." *See* Science, State, Justice, Commerce, and Related Agencies Appropriations Act for FY 2007, H.R.1145, 109th Cong. (2006) (amendment to H.R. 5672).

68. *See* Ao, *supra* note 56, at 385 ("The measure was designed to kill language assistance even before the renewal vote."); Tucker, *supra* note 42, at 248 (noting that "Representative King acknowledged [to the press] that the Amendment was a backdoor attempt to eliminate the language assistance provisions.").

69. 152 CONG. REC. H4774–75 (daily ed. June 28, 2006) (Roll Call Vote No. 340).

70. *See generally* Testimony of Margaret Fung, *supra* note 36; Testimony of Juan Cartagena, *supra* note 48.

71. Testimony of Margaret Fung, *supra* note 36, at 5.

72. Testimony of Margaret Fung, *supra* note 36, at 6 ("The current formula of section 203 still excludes a large sector of the Southeast Asian community, which includes Americans from Vietnam, Cambodia and Laos. Many came to the United States as refugees after the Vietnam War or are the children of refugees. They number over 1.8 million and have become U.S. citizens at rates higher than the national average. Southeast Asian American communities have high levels of limited English proficiency and low levels of educational attainment, which are the very characteristics of the citizens that Congress intended to protect under section 203.").

73. Testimony of Juan Cartagena, *supra* note 48, at 28.

74. Tucker, *supra* note 42, at 238–39 (describing the failed efforts to lower the numerical trigger as a "casualty" of the reauthorization process).

75. Padilla v. Lever, 429 F.3d 910 (2006) (en banc).

76. H. Rep. No. 109-478, at 59.

77. *See generally* U.S. Census Bureau, We the People: Hispanics in the United States (Dec. 2004); Hyon B. Shin & Rosalind Bruno, *Language Use and English-Speaking Ability: 2000,* at 2 (Series C2KBR-29, U.S. Census Bureau 2003).

78. *See generally* 28 C.F.R. §§ 55.18–55.20 (2006). Jurisdictions covered under Section 4(f)4 must also submit any changes to their election laws to the Justice Department for pre-clearance. *See* 28 C.F.R. § 55.8(b).

79. 28 C.F.R. §§ 55.14(c), 55.11 (2006) (discussing the discretion granted to jurisdictions covered under Section 203). *See also* 28 C.F.R. § 55.14(c) ("It is the responsibility of the jurisdiction to determine what actions by it are required for compliance" with Section 203); 28 C.F.R. § 55.11 (2006) ("It is the responsibility of covered jurisdictions to determine what languages, forms of languages, or dialects will be effective.").

80. 28 C.F.R. § 55.2 (b)(1), (2)(2006).

81. 28 C.F.R. §§ 55.18, 55.20 (2006).

82. 28 C.F.R. § 55.17 (2006) ("a targeting system will normally fulfill the Act's minority language requirements if it is designed and implemented in such a way that language minority group members who need minority language materials and assistance receive them").

83. Tucker and Espino, *supra* note 52.

84. *Id.* Several other publications detail noncompliance with the language assistance provisions. *See, e.g.,* Glenn D. Magpantay, *Asian American Access to the Vote: The Language Assistance Provisions (Section 203) of the Voting Rights Act and Beyond,* 11 Asian L.J. 31 (May 2004) (providing a detailed description of the lack of compliance among covered jurisdictions); National Asian Pacific American Legal Consortium, Access to Democracy: Language Assistance and Section 203 of the Voting Rights Act (2000); AALDEF, Asian American Access to Democracy in the NYC 2001 Elections: An Assessment of the NYC Board of Elections Compliance with the Language Assistance Provisions of the Voting Rights Act (2002); AALDEF, Asian American Access to Democracy in the 2003 Elections in NYC: An Assessment of the New York City Board of Elections Compliance with the Language Assistance Provisions of the Voting Rights Act 10 (2004).

85. *See* Magpantay, *supra* note 84, at 41–42.

86. *See, e.g.,* Kathy Feng, Keith Aoki & Bryan Ikegami, *Voting Matters: APIAs, Latinas/ os, and Post-2000 Redistricting in California,* 81 Or. L. Rev. 849, 867 (Winter 2002) ("A recurrent problem has been English-speaking and reading ability and the availability of multilingual voting materials and multilingual poll workers to answer questions."); Glenn D. Magpantay, *Two Steps Forward, One Step Back, and a Side Step: Asian Americans and the Federal Help America Vote Act,* 10 Asian Pac. Am. L.J. 31, 38, n.64 (2005) ("During both the 2000 NYC Primary Elections, twenty-nine Election Districts at sixteen sites were missing specific Chinese language materials, and in the General Elections, forty Election Districts at eighteen sites were missing specific Chinese language materials."); Keith Aoki, *A Tale of Three Cities: Thoughts on Asian American Electoral Power,* 8 UCLA Asian Pac. Am. 1, 5 (2002) (describing

an incident where the Asian American Legal Defense and Education Fund asked the New York City Board of Elections to provide ballots with the candidates' names translated into Chinese. "Election officials initially refused to supply the bilingual ballots, claiming there was insufficient room for translations of the names. AALDEF obtained a U.S. Department of Justice ruling that such noncompliance was in violation of the VRA because, 'a candidate's name is one of the most important items of information sought by voters when casting a ballot.'").

87. Barry H. Weinberg & Lyn Utrecht, *Symposium, Problems in America's Polling Places: How They Can Be Stopped,* 11 TEMP. POL. & CIV. RTS. L. REV. 401, 422 (Spring 2002) ("Even after the Voting Rights Act was amended in 1975 to require that areas designated under a formula must provide information and ballots in languages other than English, inadequate training of polling place workers continued to disadvantage minority language voters."); Magpantay, *infra* note 90, at 6 (noting that in 2004, "[p]oorly trained and inefficient poll workers caused chaos in several poll sites.").

88. Magpantay, *Asian American Access to the Vote, supra* note 86, at 39 ("In the 2004 elections, a Chinese American voter who asked for assistance was directed to a Korean interpreter." (citing AALDEF, 2003 ELECTIONS IN NYC, *supra* note 84, at 10)).

89. Glenn D. Magpantay, Editorial, *Letter to the Editor,* N.Y. TIMES, Jan. 1, 2001, at A12.

90. Glenn D. Magpantay & Nancy W. Yu, *Asian Americans and Reauthorization of the Voting Rights Act,* 19 NAT'L BLACK L.J. 1, 4 (2005).

91. AALDEF, THE ASIAN AMERICAN VOTE IN THE 2006 MIDTERM ELECTIONS (2007), *available at* http://www.aaldef.org/docs/AALDEF2006ExitPollReportMay2007.pdf

92. Magpantay, *Two Steps Forward, supra* note 86, at 31 ("Section 203 is primarily enforced by the Department of Justice so voters are relegated to report violations solely to the Department. It is in the Department's discretion whether and how to act on these complaints.").

93. *Id.* ("The Voting Rights Act has its own private right of action, but litigating under the Act can sometimes be prohibitively expensive."). *See also id.* n.73 ("Lawsuits under the Voting Rights Act require detailed and widespread evidence of voting barriers. Such barriers must be reported by location (e.g., neighborhood, county), poll site and election.").

94. *See* JOCELYN BENSON, LANGUAGE PROTECTIONS FOR ALL? VOTING RIGHTS ACT REAUTHORIZATION OF 2006: PERSPECTIVES ON DEMOCRACY, PARTICIPATION AND POWER (Ana Henderson ed., 2007).

95. April Chung, *Noncitizen Voting Rights and Alternatives: A Path Toward Greater Asian Pacific American and Latino Political Participation,* 4 ASIAN PAC. AM. L.J. 163, 170–71 ("APAs have had difficulty qualifying as language minorities under Section 203. Where APAs may comprise five percent of the voting age population, the composition of the APA community may include a number of language minorities, each falling short of the five percent threshold.").

96. Magpantay, *Two Steps Forward, supra* note 86, at 53 (Localities not covered under Section 203 with large Asian American populations post 2000: Los Angeles, Cal.: Khmer, Thai, Samoan; Honolulu, Haw.: Korean and Filipino; Bergen, N.J.: Korean; Middlesex, N.J.: Chinese; Boston, Mass.: Chinese; Dorchester, Mass.: Vietnamese; Lowell, Mass.: Khmer; Philadelphia, Pa.: Chinese. In addition, though currently only five Asian and Pacific Islander languages are covered (Japanese, Chinese, Vietnamese, Filipino, and Hawaiian), there are "at least seventeen Asian ethnic groups and eight Pacific Islander ethnic groups in the United States.").

CHAPTER THREE

MEETING THE DEMAND OF A GROWING LANGUAGE-MINORITY VOTING POPULATE

KAREN K. NARASAKI*
TERRY M. AO**

I. Introduction

America is a rapidly changing and dynamic nation, with many minority communities driving this growth.[1] Part of this growth can also be attributed to immigration.[2] The rising diversity of America's populace has resulted in more voices participating in the political debate, with many racial and ethnic groups seeing an overall increase in civic engagement.[3] Despite this increase across the board, however, disparities still exist between racial and ethnic groups.[4] The registration and turnout rates for Asian Americans and Latinos is more than 20 percentage points lower than that of whites, a difference that cannot be explained only by immigration.[5] Language barriers play a role in some of the disparities that we see. In 2000, 47 million persons spoke a language other than English at home.[6] Almost half of these language minorities had difficulty speaking English and are classified as Limited English Proficient (LEP).[7]

There is a need to address these changing demographics of America, particularly the increase of LEP citizens. The strong protections found in the Voting Rights Act for language minorities have shown to increase voter participation for the affected groups when properly implemented. This chapter will outline some best practices that have been successful in meeting the demand for assistance to language-minority voters. These best practices can be implemented by those jurisdictions covered by the Voting Rights Act, as well as other jurisdictions that choose to provide language assistance to their constituents.

---

* Yale University; UCLA School of Law; President and Executive Director of the Asian American Justice Center.

** J.D. American University Washington College of Law; B.A. University of Chicago; director of census and voting programs for the Asian American Justice Center.

II. Voting Rights Act Protections for Language-Minority Voters

LEP voters often experience a major barrier when confronted by the daunting election process in America: the inability to speak or read English very well. This is the single greatest hurdle that many language minorities must overcome in exercising their right to vote. Although many language minorities were born in this country or came here at a very young age, some have trouble speaking English fluently because of a substandard education, which did not afford them the opportunity to learn English in school. Other language minorities immigrated to this country and have not had adequate learning opportunities to become fluent in English. Additionally, some come from countries with no democratic systems and find voting to be a very overwhelming experience.

Many language minorities, particularly those who are also racial minorities, face discrimination when attempting to exercise their right to vote. Discrimination at the polls can manifest in different ways, including hostile and unwelcoming environments or the outright denial of the right to vote. LEP citizens can have difficulty understanding complex voting materials and procedures and are often denied needed assistance at the polls. While many of these voters understand that voting is the most important tool Americans have to influence government policies that affect every aspect of their lives—from taxes, to education, to health care—these barriers can depress their participation in the process.

Language-minority voters are afforded some protection under the Voting Rights Act (VRA). Section 203, which is discussed in further detail in Chapter 2, "The Language Assistance Provisions of the Voting Rights Act and the 2006 Reauthorization," requires jurisdictions that meet the act's threshold to provide language assistance to their voters in the covered languages. After discrimination has occurred due to a voter's membership in a language-minority group, Section 2 can be used to require the provision of language assistance to the injured community. These two sections of the VRA can be used in tandem to break down barriers for language-minority voters.

A. SECTION 203

As detailed in Chapter 2, Congress recognized that certain minority citizens who did not speak English proficiently and who had experienced historical discrimination were also being systematically disenfranchised. Congress broadened the protections of the VRA on their behalf by enacting Section 203 during the 1975 reauthorization of the VRA.[8] In particular, Congress sought to protect the voting rights of Latinos, Asian Americans, American Indians, and Alaska Natives, finding that

> [T]hrough the use of various practices and procedures, citizens of [the four covered groups] have been effectively excluded from participation in the electoral process. Among other factors, the denial of the right to vote of such minority group citizens

is ordinarily directly related to the unequal educational opportunities afforded them resulting in high illiteracy and low voting participation.[9]

Congress has limited Section 203 protections to these four language groups because it has continually found that they have faced and continue to face significant voting discrimination because of their race and ethnicity. Other language groups have not been included because Congress has not found evidence that they experienced similar sustained difficulties because of their race and ethnicity in voting.[10] In enacting Section 203, Congress intended to remedy racial discrimination in the voting process, education, and other facets of life that result in the disenfranchisement of language minorities of the four covered language groups.

Section 203 requires covered jurisdictions to provide language assistance during the electoral process, thereby removing the language barrier to voting for the covered language minorities. Chapter 2 details how a jurisdiction becomes covered by Section 203. Once covered, the jurisdiction is obligated to provide "any registration or voting notices, forms, instructions, assistance, or other materials or information relating to the electoral process, including ballots" in the covered language as well as in English.[11] Guidelines issued by the U.S. Department of Justice (DOJ) clarify that Section 203 compliance requires materials and assistance be provided in a way "designed to allow members of applicable language minority groups to be effectively informed of and participate effectively in voting-connected activities" throughout all stages of the electoral process.[12]

When effective language assistance has been provided, Section 203 has been successful in increasing the civic engagement of Latino, Asian American, American Indian, and Alaska Native citizens, resulting in higher voter registration and turnout levels.[13] Increases in voter registration and turnout can be directly linked to Section 203 compliance.

The efficacy of Section 203 can be seen in Harris County, Texas. After entering into a Memorandum of Agreement with the DOJ after noncompliance, Harris County saw the doubling of Vietnamese voter turnout, which resulted in the first Vietnamese candidate in history being elected to the Texas legislature, and doing so by defeating the incumbent chair of the Appropriations Committee.[14] The increased civic engagement of these groups has also led to increased political representation by candidates of choice. In recent years, more than 5,200 Latinos and almost 350 Asian Americans have been elected to office.[15] Additionally, Native American candidates, who have traditionally been unrepresented, are being elected to local school boards, county commissions, and state legislatures in ever-increasing numbers.[16]

B. SECTION 2 PROTECTION FOR LANGUAGE MINORITIES

While Section 203 has been able to break down the language barriers for Asian American, Latino, American Indian, and Alaska Native voters in certain jurisdictions, many language-minority voters still face language barriers at the polls. Voters of uncovered language groups have not benefited from Section 203.[17] LEP voters of the covered language groups in jurisdictions that do not meet the threshold for Section 203 coverage have also not benefited from Section 203. Section 2 of the Voting Rights Act provides another measure of protection for all language minorities by prohibiting any voting standard, practice, or procedure that results in the denial or abridgement of the right of any citizen to vote on account of race, color, or membership in a language-minority group.

Section 2 has been used on behalf of language-minority voters whose language was not covered under Section 203, such as the successful lawsuit DOJ brought on behalf of Arab American voters in Hamtramck, Michigan.[18] In 1999, an organization called "Citizens for Better Hamtramck" in Hamtramck challenged voters (including Bengali Americans) who "looked" Arab, had dark skin, or had Arab- or Muslim-sounding names. Voters were pulled from voting lines and forced to show passports or citizenship papers before they could vote. Some were asked to take an oath of allegiance even though they had appropriate citizenship documentation. No white voters were challenged. The city entered into an agreement with DOJ that required the city to appoint at least two Arab Americans or one Arab American and one Bengali American election inspector to provide language assistance for each of the 19 polling places where these illegal challenges occurred.

Section 2 is also used to require language assistance for communities whose population has not yet become large enough to meet the Section 203 thresholds. Recently, DOJ brought a Section 2 case against the City of Boston on behalf of Chinese- and Vietnamese-speaking voters.[19] While the City of Boston was required under Section 203 to provide language assistance to Spanish speakers, the Chinese and Vietnamese populations did not meet the Section 203 threshold. However, DOJ's investigation found that the city discriminated against LEP Latino and Asian American voters and denied them an equal opportunity to participate in the political process and elect candidates of their choice. DOJ found that poll workers treated LEP Latino and Asian American voters disrespectfully; refused to permit them to be assisted by a person of their choice; improperly influenced, coerced, or ignored their ballot choices; failed to make available multilingual personnel to provide effective assistance and information; and refused or failed to provide them with provisional ballots.[20] DOJ and Boston came to an agreement that included the additional provision of language assistance to Chinese and Vietnamese voters.

III. Meeting the Demand for an Increased Need to Serve Language-Minority Voters

Lessons can be learned from jurisdictions' experiences in complying with Section 203. Jurisdictions that have legal obligations under the VRA should continually work to improve their language assistance program and implement best practices into their program. Those jurisdictions who fail to comply with their legal obligations (as outlined in Chapter 2) must begin implementing these steps to satisfy the Section 203 requirements. Jurisdictions that are not legally obligated to provide language assistance but who have sizable LEP populations should investigate proactively implementing some of these best practices to address the growing language needs of their communities.

The Asian American Justice Center (AAJC), its affiliates—the Asian American Institute (in Chicago), the Asian Law Caucus (in San Francisco) and the Asian Pacific American Legal Center (in Los Angeles)—and its Community Partners, among other groups across the country, have been actively working with election officials on Section 203 compliance, conducting poll monitoring to ensure compliance on Election Day, and educating Asian American and other voters about their rights.[21] Using Los Angeles County's experience with Section 203 as a case study (in addition to the lessons learned from the work of AAJC and its affiliates during the 2004 elections, which are reported in *Sound Barriers: Asian Americans and Language Access in Election 2004*[22]), jurisdictions can design a language-assistance plan that addresses both the voters' needs and the jurisdictions' constraints.

A. LOS ANGELES COUNTY'S COMPLIANCE WITH SECTION 203 OF THE VRA

As the largest and most diverse election jurisdiction in the United States, Los Angeles County is a particularly instructive jurisdiction. Los Angeles County is required under Section 203 to provide voter assistance in six languages, Spanish, Chinese, Korean, Vietnamese, Tagalog, and Japanese, and has implemented one of the most comprehensive language assistance programs in the country.[23]

Multilingual poll workers play a crucial role in providing this assistance, and L.A. County determines the need for such poll workers by looking at several factors. First, it follows the legal requirement of looking at U.S. Census data on LEP voters within the jurisdiction.[24] L.A. County targets all precincts with multilingual poll workers where at least one percent of the population is LEP in any one language.[25] It then considers the number of previous requests for multilingual mailings from voters in each precinct, records kept by poll workers that note how many times they were asked for multilingual services in previous elections, and the advice of community-based organizations (CBOs).[26] Based on this data, precincts are added to the target list.[27] For high-priority Chinese-language precincts, the county conducts a mail survey among Chinese voters on file to determine which precincts need Mandarin or Cantonese dialect speakers.[28]

Once the need for multilingual poll workers is determined, L.A. County begins its recruitment. To tackle this issue, the county started the Pollworker/Recruiter Program during the 1998 election season to hire activists to recruit multilingual poll workers from their own communities. These recruiters attend and organize community events (sometimes with the help of CBOs), where they distribute poll worker applications.[29] On Election Day, the recruiters call the polls early in the morning to make sure that the poll workers have arrived and send replacements if necessary.[30] The county also uses a student poll worker program to hire high school and college students, thereby widening the pool of potential multilingual workers. To create a further incentive for individuals to apply, it increased poll worker pay in May 2006 from $55 to $80 for clerks and from $75 to $100 for supervisors.[31]

An important component of recruitment is retaining individuals who have worked the polls in the past. To aid with retention issues, the county holds focus groups after Election Day to review issues that poll workers faced. A few of these sessions are targeted specifically to multilingual poll workers and the unique issues they face in helping LEP voters. L.A. County also holds a ceremony honoring multilingual poll workers to show that their work does not go unacknowledged.[32]

In order to promote voter outreach, the Los Angeles County Registrar-Recorder/County Clerk invites community leaders, CBOs, city clerks, political party representatives, and other interested individuals to attend Community Voter Outreach Committee meetings.[33] The committee is used to create a partnership between the county and the CBOs to provide better services to voters with special needs and communicating important election issues, such as provisional ballots, transliteration, and touch-screen voting.[34] In 1998, Asian American and Pacific Islander CBOs advocated for transliteration of candidate names. Local CBOs assist the county in the review process. In addition, candidates and their representatives, community organizations, and members of the media are invited to provide feedback for transliteration during review periods.[35]

The county also uses services such as multilingual hotlines to work toward reaching voters and potential voters in minority language communities. In the past, the county has sent translated voter registration cards to Korean grocery stores and dry cleaning establishments, and included Spanish-language voter registration cards in La Opinion newspaper.[36] The secretary of state's office also maintains a Web site for multilingual voters.[37]

B. BEST PRACTICES FOR LANGUAGE ASSISTANCE

Language assistance can be viewed in terms of direct assistance (written or oral assistance) and indirect assistance (promotion, outreach, and education about voter's rights, the voting process, and the existence of language assistance for voters). Ideally, jurisdictions would implement steps to provide all these types of assistance. As costs can be a concern, however, jurisdictions should at a minimum work to ensure that some of these steps are taken, particularly those related to the promotion, outreach, and education of voters and oral assistance.

1. Written Language Assistance. Written language assistance can encompass many different types of translated materials. The most obvious, of course, are translated ballots or sample ballots. Jurisdictions can also create translated voter guides, multilingual instruction cards/videos, or other instructional pieces. Jurisdictions that may be concerned about the costs of printing can utilize voting technology by translating electronic ballots.

Regardless of what type of written language assistance is offered, jurisdictions must ensure a high quality of translation. Counties should evaluate their election materials to provide the best possible translations so that LEP voters can be accurately informed about election procedures, instructions, candidates, and issues. The quality of the translation should be checked both by the county and a panel of community experts to ensure that translations are accurate and easy to read at an appropriate level of education.[38]

The Los Angeles County Registrar of Voters solicits input from voters and translation experts within the community to evaluate the quality of translation prior to materials being printed and distributed. Additionally, the county created a glossary of accepted translations for commonly used election terms to standardize future translations. Jurisdictions should also explore the development of a joint translation program whereby CBOs assist in translation and back-translation work and receive a stipend for such work. Finally, local election officials should hire local vendors for translation services in order to make translations more relevant to the voters in that particular jurisdiction.

2. *Oral Language Assistance.* Oral language assistance is a very effective and cost-effective method of assisting LEP voters. A jurisdiction must hire a sufficient number of poll workers to staff polling sites on Election Day. It costs jurisdictions no additional funds to hire multilingual poll workers to serve this function. They need to increase recruitment of multilingual poll workers across the board. They should develop a plan for recruitment with consultation from CBOs that includes ethnic media outreach and targeted recruitment efforts. Jurisdictions should also conduct outreach to high school and college students to work as poll workers. Not only does this serve the purpose of increasing the pool of available poll workers, it also introduces younger potential voters to the election process.

Jurisdictions should ensure a high quality of multilingual assistance by recruiting multilingual poll workers who are fully proficient in both English and their Section 203 language. Difficulties in communication among poll workers can result in delays in the voting process or misunderstandings on how to handle problem situations.

Once the jurisdiction has a sizable pool of multilingual poll workers, it is imperative that the jurisdiction dispatch the multilingual poll workers in a fashion that maximizes their utility and skill. Jurisdictions must refine and prioritize multilingual poll worker assignments based on need. Particular emphasis needs to be placed on areas where there is a significant community presence for providing multilingual assistance, such as locations that have a prevalence of ethnic community centers, nonprofit organizations, churches, and ethnic-focused businesses.

The use of a more comprehensive method for targeting is recommended. Instead of relying solely on a surname dictionary to determine language-minority population density, place of birth within a household can be employed to enhance and clarify targeting. Finally, the jurisdiction should provide a listing of poll sites with the number of allocated multilingual poll workers against actual multilingual poll workers present with an explanation for any discrepancies that are found on the official roster.

The county should take proactive measures to maintain a multilingual poll worker database by conducting continuous outreach and recruitment, and by supplementing the current pool of multilingual poll workers with possible volunteers for upcoming elections. An ongoing program should be developed that maintains communication with the current pool of poll workers in the form of an informational periodical (such as an electronic or hard-copy newsletter) that provides continuing education on the election process and topics of election law.

Oral language assistance is paramount for languages that are historically unwritten, particularly American Indian and Alaska Native languages. In addition to the steps outlined above, jurisdictions with sizable language populations of a historically unwritten language should take further steps to ensure that assistance is provided to the voters. Since there is no written language to translate, the jurisdictions should instead produce videos in the language explaining the voting process, ballot, voters' rights, and any other materials. These videos could be available both online for voters to access prior to the election and at polling sites where the video could be looped and played throughout the day.

3. Promotion, Outreach, and Education. Providing written and oral language assistance will be pointless if the jurisdictions do not ensure that voters are aware that they can receive such assistance. The development and implementation of innovative strategies and tactics beyond traditional mainstream outreach methods is encouraged as a means of reaching as many voters as possible. Jurisdictions must work to promote their language assistance by outreach to the impacted communities through the communities' means of communications. Jurisdictions should work with ethnic media to get its message across to the community. Not only is this more cost-effective than advertising in mainstream media, it is also more effective in actually reaching the necessary communities. Ethnic media can also be utilized to recruit poll workers. Using ethnic media ensures that more multilingual persons are recruited for poll worker positions and that more LEP persons become aware of the available language assistance on Election Day.

Jurisdictions should look to increase voter education outreach in conjunction with CBOs and use community events to promote, conduct outreach for, and educate language-minority voters. Increasing voter education in language-minority communities will streamline the voting process and decrease voting time.

An LEP voter outreach program should include multilingual workshops to provide election and voting-related information to community social service and civic organizations, with ethnic media present.

Such a program can also benefit from participation by county election officials at community events to conduct voter registration drives and answer election-related questions from language minorities; an extensive mailing to registered voters with ethnic-specific surnames to inform them of available language assistance; and the distribution of information to community service organizations and media regarding the election process, availability of language assistance, and rights of voters.

4. *Role of Local Community-Based Organizations.* Local CBOs can play a very important role in a successful language assistance program. They can assist with poll worker recruitment, poll site identification, community outreach, and poll monitoring on Election Day. Jurisdictions need to work with local CBOs year-round to develop relationships—not just during their ramp-ups for elections. CBOs play a different role than the jurisdiction and help facilitate the jurisdiction's efforts. As trusted leaders, CBOs already have the trust of people in their communities, and they understand the culture and barriers. Similarly, local CBOs will have contacts with the ethnic media in their communities, which the jurisdictions can take advantage of through the relationships built with local CBOs.

5. *Pre-Election Day and Election Day Activities.* Effective language assistance occurs throughout the entire election process and not just on Election Day. Another step that must be taken prior to Election Day is adequate poll worker training. Poll workers must be thoroughly trained about voting laws so they can properly and efficiently run polling sites and assist voters. Poll workers must be knowledgeable about Section 203 of the VRA and its requirements and obligations; about provisions of the Help America Vote Act; and about any subsequent election reform legislation, including the proper use of provisional ballots, ID requirements applicable in their jurisdiction, and rules for third-party assistance when voting (Section 208 of the VRA).

In particular, poll workers need to be trained about the importance of language assistance to LEP voters, the need to actively assist voters with language and other barriers, what role the multilingual poll worker should play, and how to ensure sensitive and nondiscriminatory treatment of language-minority voters. The training should incorporate live training sessions and a demonstration of proper setup of poll sites with appropriate language materials. Poll workers should be tested on the importance of providing multilingual assistance in trainings. Local elections officials need to develop trainings and handouts for multilingual poll workers that emphasize their particular role, commonly encountered problems, and how to best serve the public.

On Election Day, it is important that the jurisdiction ensures that the hard work it has put into language assistance is realized. Each jurisdiction must implement a troubleshooter program that addresses and, if necessary, removes problematic poll workers. Once a complaint has been registered through the hotline or any other reporting mechanism, a troubleshooter should be dispatched to the polling site to investigate the claim. If the troubleshooter deems the poll worker's attitude to be entrenched, the problematic poll worker should be removed from the polling site and not allowed to work as a poll worker for the following two years. The same process should hold for complaints that arise after Election Day. Once the two-year ban has passed, the problematic poll worker should be required to receive special cultural sensitivity training and pass a test on cultural sensitivity prior to being allowed back as a poll worker.

Additionally, language assistance at the polling sites must be accessible to LEP voters. Multilingual materials must be allocated to all polling sites and in sufficient quantities. This will require an understanding of the demographics of precincts in order to know what constitutes a sufficient quantity for each polling site. Jurisdictions must mandate that multilingual materials be displayed in an easily accessible and visible manner. For example, multilingual materials can be color-coded so that all materials in a particular language are printed in a particular color. Jurisdictions should require the supervisor at the polling site to periodically check that multilingual materials are sufficiently stocked as well as easily accessible and visible.

Oral assistance must also be accessible. Jurisdictions should require clear identification of languages spoken by poll workers to increase the efficiency in processing voters. To make multilingual workers more conspicuous to LEP voters, the county can encourage multilingual poll workers to wear badges indicating language fluency that are enlarged in size, text, and otherwise distinct from those of English-only speakers. Additionally, the jurisdiction should have a system in place to ensure the appropriate placement of poll workers. For example, designated people should call the poll sites early in the morning to make sure that the poll workers have arrived, and if not, arrange for a replacement to be sent out to ensure that enough multilingual poll workers are available.

IV. Conclusion

Jurisdictions must always be conscientious of their language-minority populations and their impact on elections. In addition to complying with federal obligations to provide language assistance, whether under Section 203 or Section 2 of the VRA, jurisdictions must also be cognizant about complying with any applicable state law requirements for language assistance.[39] For example, in California, any voter who is not a resident of a county required under Section 203 to provide ballots in languages other than English has the right to access a facsimile copy of the ballot with ballot measures and instructions printed in Spanish and to facsimile copies in other languages if a significant and substantial need is found by the election official.[40] Minority-language sample ballots must be posted in polling sites where 3 percent or more of the voting age citizens lack sufficient English skills to vote without assistance, or when citizens or organizations provide information supporting a need for assistance.[41] In New Jersey, at least two multilingual sample ballots must be provided for covered election districts, and multilingual sample ballots must be sent out to voters. In addition, two additional election district board members who are Latino in origin and fluent in Spanish must be appointed in districts where Spanish is the primary language for 10 percent or more of the registered voters in the election district.[42]

Jurisdictions should also be mindful of the interaction between language assistance requirements under Section 203 or Section 2 and other areas of election law and election reform proposals. These sections must be considered while a jurisdiction implements existing election laws. For example, under the Help America Vote Act, jurisdictions must provide accessible voting machines. Any accessible voting machine that is provided under the act must also comply with Section 203 or Section 2 if applicable and provide language access. Section 203 and Section 2 may also affect a jurisdiction's deliberation on election reform proposals. For example, when considering proposals for all-mail elections, jurisdictions should give consideration to how it would fully comply with Section 203.

Concrete steps can and should be taken by jurisdictions to provide language assistance to its growing pool of diverse voters. The population of those who speak a language other than English at home is growing, as is the population of LEP persons. Jurisdictions need to recognize the growing need to provide language assistance to these voters. Jurisdictions required under law to provide language assistance must be particularly diligent in ensuring that steps are taken to fully comply with their legal obligations. Jurisdictions who are not currently required by law to provide language assistance should consider implementing at least some of these steps on a voluntary basis in order to meet the needs of their community. These steps are simply good election administration best practices and will ensure that elections run more smoothly. That they also lead America closer to fulfilling her promise of democracy is all the more reason they should be taken.

Notes

1. The largest census-to-census population increase in American history occurred between 1990 and 2000. U.S. CENSUS BUREAU, CENSUS 2000 BRIEF, POPULATION CHANGE AND DISTRIBUTION 1 (Apr. 2001). The growth in minority communities has led to significant minority communities spread out across each region. Nearly one in every 10 of the nation's 3,141 counties is a majority-minority county, which means it has a population that is more than 50

percent minority, for a national total of 303 majority-minority counties. Press Release, U.S. Census Bureau, More Than 300 Counties Now "Majority-Minority" (Aug. 9, 2007), *available at* http://www.census.gov/Press-Release/www/releases/archives/population/010482.html.

2. The foreign-born population increased by over 50 percent between 1990 and 2000. While more than half of the foreign-born population lived in three states (California, New York, and Texas), the foreign-born population in North Carolina, Georgia, and Nevada grew by 200 percent or more. There were significant increases in foreign-born populations in all four regions of the country, with the South experiencing the largest increase. U.S. CENSUS BUREAU, CENSUS 2000 BRIEF, THE FOREIGN-BORN POPULATION 2–5 (DEC. 2003).

3. Voter registration and turnout for the November 2004 elections were the highest since 1992. A total of 142 million citizens registered to vote and 126 million citizens turned out to vote, a record high for a presidential year. U.S. CENSUS BUREAU, VOTING AND REGISTRATION IN THE ELECTION OF NOVEMBER 2004, POPULATION CHARACTERISTICS 1–2 (Mar. 2006).

4. The voter registration rate for whites was 75 percent, with African Americans trailing at 69 percent and Latinos and Asian Americans significantly behind at 58 percent and 52 percent respectively. Voter turnout rates were similar, with 67 percent of white voters turning out, and only 60 percent of African Americans, 47 percent of Latinos, and 44 percent of Asian Americans doing so. *Id.* at 7.

5. The voter registration and turnout data cited refer to the rates for the citizen, voting-age population for the respective groups. Taking immigration into account would actually produce even lower figures for racial and ethnic minority groups. For example, looking at the turnout rate of both citizen and noncitizen Asian American and Latino voting-age persons in November 2004 shows a much lower rate of 28 percent of the population. *Id.*

6. This represents a 47 percent increase from 1990. U.S. CENSUS BUREAU, CENSUS 2000 BRIEF, LANGUAGE USE AND ENGLISH-SPEAKING ABILITY 2 (Oct. 2003).

7. *Id.* The current definition of LEP is persons who speak English less than very well. The Census Bureau has determined that most respondents overestimate their English proficiency and therefore, those who answer other than "very well" are deemed LEP. *See* H.R. REP. NO. 102-655, at 8, reprinted in 1992 U.S.C.C.A.N. 772. The Census Bureau noted that research showed that those who reported speaking a non-English language at home and speaking English "very well" performed as well on tests using English written materials as English-only speakers. However, those who reported speaking a non-English language at home and responded as speaking English "well," "not well," and "not at all" performed worse on the test. The Census Bureau believed that those respondents could be labeled as LEP and that "they may require materials and instructions in another language in order to vote or secure basic services." *See* U.S. Census Bureau, Language Use and Linguistic Isolation: Historical Data and Methodological Issues (Feb. 12, 2001) (paper prepared for the session on Language Differences and Linguistic Isolation at the FCSM Statistical Policy Seminar, Bethesda, Md., Nov. 8–9, 2000).

8. H.R. REP. NO. 109-478, at 9–10 (2006) ("In doing so, Congress 'documented a systematic pattern of voting discrimination and exclusion against minority group citizens who are from environments in which the dominant language is other than English,' and '[b]ased on the extensive evidentiary record demonstrating the prevalence of voting discrimination and high illiteracy rates among language minorities, the [relevant] Subcommittee acted to

broaden its special coverage to new geographic areas in order to ensure protection of the voting rights of language minority citizens.'") (footnote omitted) (quoting H.R. REP. No. 94-196, at 7, 16 (1975)). In 1975, Congress also enacted Section 4(f)(4) in response to its finding of pervasive voting discrimination against citizens of language minorities that was national in scope. Recognizing that these language-minority citizens came from environments with non-English dominant languages and that these citizens have been denied equal educational opportunities, Congress found that English-only elections excluded language-minority citizens from participating in the electoral process, which were aggravated by acts of physical, economic, and political intimidation in many areas of the country. Section 4(f)(4) has its own trigger formula that included redefining "test or device" within the Section 5/preclearance context to include English-only elections. This means that jurisdictions covered by Section 4(f)(4) must get preclearance, or prior approval, from the Department of Justice or the U.S. District Court of the District of Columbia prior to implementation of any voting changes. Additionally, Section 4(f)(4) jurisdictions are required to provide the same language assistance as required under Section 203 for their covered languages. 42 U.S.C. § 1973b(f) (2006). In this chapter, reference to Section 203 implies a reference to Section 4(f)(4). That is, the recommendations on how to comply with Section 203 also apply to compliance with Section 4(f)(4).

9. 42 U.S.C. § 1973aa-1a(a) (2006).

10. 42 U.S.C. § 1973aa-1a(a); S. REP. No. 94-295, at 31.

11. *Id.* § 1973aa-1a(c). Of course, when the covered language is oral or unwritten, then the covered jurisdiction is required only to furnish oral instructions, assistance, or other information relating to registration and voting. *Id.*

12. Implementation of the Provisions of the Voting Rights Act Regarding Language Minority Groups, 28 C.F.R. § 55.2 (1999).

13. H.R. REP. No. 109-478, at 18–19. For example, the House Committee report notes that the number of registered Latino voters grew from 7.6 million in 2000 to 9 million in 2004 and, in certain cases, Native American voter turnout has increased by more than "50 to 150 percent." *Id.* at 19–20.

14. *Id.* at 19.

15. *Id.*

16. *Id.* at 20.

17. Other language groups have not been included in the Section 203 framework because Congress has not found evidence that they experienced similar sustained difficulties because of their race and ethnicity in voting. 42 U.S.C. § 1973aa-1a(a); S. REP. No. 94-295, at 31.

18. United States v. City of Hamtramck (E.D. Mich. 2000).

19. United States v. City of Boston (D. Mass. 2005). DOJ also brought a Section 203 enforcement claim against the City of Boston for noncompliance in providing language assistance in Spanish.

20. Complaint, United States v. City of Boston (D. Mass. 2005), at http://www.usdoj .gov/crt/voting/sec_203/documents/boston_comp.htm.

21. ASIAN AMERICAN JUSTICE CENTER, VOTING IN THE ASIAN PACIFIC AMERICAN COMMUNITY: ASSERTING OUR RIGHTS, ASSERTING OUR VOICE (2004).

22. Asian American Justice Center, Sound Barriers: Asian Americans and Language Access in Election 2004 (2005), http://www.advancingequality.org/files/sound_barriers.pdf.

23. Conny McCormack, The National Commission on the Voting Rights Act (2005), http://www.votingrightsact.org/hearings/pdfs/mccormack.pdf, at 1.

24. *Id.* at 2.

25. County of Los Angeles, Registrar-Recorder/County Clerk, Voters with Specific Needs "Best Practices" Manual 3 (2001), http://www.lavote.net/Voter/Multilingual/Pdfs/Voter_Need_Manual.pdf (hereinafter Voter Need Manual).

26. McCormack, *supra* note 23, at 2.

27. *Id.* at 3.

28. Voter Need Manual, *supra* note 25, at 12.

29. *Id.* at 14.

30. *Id.* at 15.

31. Troy Anderson, *County Short on Poll Workers; Supervisors Bump Up Pay to Lure Staff for June 6,* Election Admin. Res. Center (2006), *available at* http://earc.berkeley.edu/news/2006/May/CountyShort.php.

32. Voter Need Manual, *supra* note 25, at 16.

33. *Id.* at 18.

34. *Id.*

35. *Id.* at 7.

36. *Id.* at iv–v.

37. California Secretary of State, Multilingual Voters Services, http://www.sos.ca.gov/elections/elections_multi.htm.

38. The reading level should be decided at the local level based on U.S. Census and local data for the particular language group.

39. There may be overlap between state and federal obligations in some jurisdictions, while others will be subject only to federal obligations and still others subject only to state laws. Each jurisdiction should be cognizant about what laws apply with respect to language assistance to voters. In 2004, 35 states included some legal requirements to assist language minority voters. These provisions ranged from those that provide voters who cannot read or write the ability to receive assistance from a person of their choosing, except for their employer or union representative, to translated ballots and written materials in counties or municipalities that reach a certain threshold that is not linked to the federal statutes. The ACLU has prepared a grid of state laws addressing language assistance that can be found at http://www.votingrights.org/resources/downloads/State%20Language%20Assistance%20Grid.doc.

40. *Id.*

41. *Id.*

42. *Id.*

CHAPTER FOUR

VOTER PROTECTION ON ELECTION DAY: HOW THE GOVERNMENT, POLL WORKERS, POLITICAL PARTIES, AND NONPARTISAN ADVOCATES CAN WORK TOGETHER TO ENSURE SMOOTH ELECTION ADMINISTRATION

JOCELYN FRIEDRICHS BENSON*

I. Introduction

Across the United States on Election Day multiple entities, from poll workers to candidates, voters to volunteers, election administrators to challengers, interact to shape the course of an election. Each has a specific role to play in ensuring that the day goes well, and each operates under the basic principle of working to ensure that the electoral outcome reflects the desires of a majority of voters.

When these entities fail to perform or interact well, however, their failures can lead to eligible voters being wrongfully removed from registration lists or otherwise being turned away from the polls. They can also lead to votes being cast but not counted, due to a variety of reasons. These failures are exacerbated when they lead to disparities on the state and local level with how elections are administered, to the effect that where voters live and seek to cast their ballot may have a direct effect on whether their vote is counted.[1]

At the most basic level, this lack of uniformity threatens the ability of our electoral system to achieve the level of equality that is at the core of the fundamental principle of one person, one vote. Several empirical studies have also concluded that

---

* J.D. Harvard Law School; M. Phil. Oxford University, B.A. Wellesley College; Assistant Professor of Law, Wayne State University Law School; member, ABA Standing Committee on Election Law.

when inequalities exist on Election Day—problems such as ballot spoilage, inaccurate voting lists, long lines, intimidation tactics, and the like—they often have a disparate impact on poor voters or voters of color. For example, in 2001, a study by the House Committee on Government Reform found that voters in low-income, high-minority congressional districts throughout the country were *three times* more likely to have their votes for president discarded than those in more affluent, low-minority districts.[2] Others note that precinct variations in spoiled ballot rates are strongly correlated with the percent of black and Hispanic registered voters in a particular precinct, suggesting that the more minorities residing in a precinct, the greater the percent of uncounted ballots.[3]

This analysis reviews the role of four particular entities in the election administration process: the government, the poll worker, political parties and candidates, and nonpartisan voter advocacy groups and individuals. In addition to briefly discussing the general responsibilities of each entity before, during, and after an election day, this chapter suggests several guidelines and standards which if implemented together could create a baseline of uniformity to counteract some of the variations that challenge the reality of the one person, one vote principle. At the center of the following discussion are also two presumptions. One is the basic standard of equality as articulated in the central principle of *one person, one vote*. The second is that the voter is sovereign most truly on Election Day, and every policy and all practices implemented on that day must consider voters and their experiences as paramount.

II. The Role of the Government

Government actors are able to play perhaps the most powerful and influential role in ensuring that voters are protected on Election Day. In addition to the legal mandates and protections that bolster the federal government's oversight position, states are charged with the power to ensure that elections are administered properly while local jurisdictions have the final responsibility in keeping the machine running smoothly. Elections work best when all three levels of government are working in sync to promote participation and integrity, and similarly elections are most likely to fail to go smoothly when these entities are unable to function together and in tandem with one another.

The primary role of the federal government lies in protecting the principles of equal access through the enforcement of statutes like the Voting Rights Act[4] and providing funding to ensure that states are able to meet the principles established in laws such as the Help America Vote Act[5] and the National Voter Registration Act.[6] To that end, the main responsibility of the federal government with regard to elections is to fully enforce all existing federal statutory protections and fully fund any existing statutory mandates. In addition, it is important to recognize the statutory and constitutional authority that the federal government has in this regard—including the power to send federal observers to localities to investigate and monitor election administration on the state and local level, and the resources to enable states with limited access to financial capital to update and improve their election machinery and other technology.

The nexus of election administration is state government.[7] Article I, Section 4 of the Constitution explicitly grants states the authority of regulating the "times, places and manner of holding elections" for federal officers.[8] This authority has evolved to give states the role of first responder and primary agent for ensuring that elections go smoothly, voters are protected, votes are counted, and outcomes are accurate. To that end, the primary role of states lies conceptually in maintaining accurate voter registration lists, and ensuring that voting is accessible and that all votes cast are counted.

This preeminent role of the states in administering elections has, however, led commentators to describe it as a complicated and "horrifying mish-mash of self-serving behavior."[9] A multitude of task forces and nonprofit good-government organizations have published numerous studies offering suggestions and proposals for more uniform standards of state-based election administration.[10] Some propose that state governments should take necessary steps to ensure that all voters are properly identified at the polls, though there is debate over whether a simple signature match or a more onerous requirement is necessary.[11] Most encourage state governments to make it a priority to protect the voter and ensure the voting process is open and accessible.[12]

Yet there are three specific areas where state oversight is particularly crucial. One is the importance of each state developing uniform rules for casting and counting ballots, including provisional ballots. This requirement is particularly important in the post-*Bush v. Gore*[13] era of election administration, where the Equal Protection Clause of the U.S. Constitution has been interpreted to require equal methods for counting ballots across a state.[14] Similarly, state governments should make certain that there is parity among localities receiving funding and technological support, and should be responsible for ensuring that all machines function properly throughout the state.[15] Finally, state governments should actively assist localities in the recruitment and training of poll workers to ensure that throughout the state, polling sites are fully staffed and each poll worker has equal access to information and support.

Local jurisdictions also play a very important role in administering elections. The administration role may be vested in individual professionals, through clerks, registrars, judges, or supervisors, or among several people in the form of election boards or commissions. Though they all function within the framework of state statutes and regulations, many localities have great responsibility over how elections are conducted, including voting equipment to be used, ballot design, and voter identification requirements at polling places.[16]

The most important role of a local government election authority is to conduct the organized and seamless administration of elections. Jurisdictions can best achieve this in working with state governments and other localities to share resources and best practices, including the crucial task of recruiting and training poll workers. To the extent that they are able to, local jurisdictions should also ensure that voting equipment is adequately apportioned throughout the jurisdiction and should seek to effectively administer all of the state and federal mandates. Jurisdictions must also ensure that any problems that do occur on Election Day are quickly resolved or adequately prevented in the future, and this is simplified where localities are able to openly communicate with state and federal authorities regarding any problems during or after an election.

III. The Role of the Poll Worker

Poll workers serve in the front lines on Election Day. In addition to protecting the integrity of the ballots that are cast, their most significant role lies in providing an efficient and positive experience for citizens arriving to vote. To that end, there are three general and somewhat universal guidelines that should be encouraged—at either the state, local, or, perhaps through statutory offers of funding, at the federal level—for poll workers. They must ensure that the rights of all voters are protected and respected, they must be sensitive to any special needs of individual voters, and they must also be familiar with the technology of all voting machinery and prepared to address any potential breakdowns that may occur.

First and foremost, poll workers should be aware of and respectful of the rights of voters, as defined under state and federal law. Most of these rights are typically enumerated under state law, but generally include the right of voters to cast a ballot if they are in line at a polling place at the proper time, and the right to cast a ballot in private and free from intimidation. There are also specific rights governing the casting of provisional ballots, which vary state to state, and it is incumbent on every poll worker to be familiar with when a voter who does not appear to be registered or otherwise entitled to vote also has a right to cast a provisional ballot. In addition, as many states develop a number of new identification requirements for voters, it is crucial for poll workers to be intimately familiar with all forms of identification that are legally acceptable and the procedures to be followed when a voter does not have legal identification. For example, under Indiana law, voters who do not present proper identification on Election Day may vote using a provisional ballot, while in Michigan, voters without identification may still vote with a regular ballot provided they sign an affidavit attesting to their identity.[17] In addition, in 2006 the Advancement Project published lists of "10 Things Every Poll Worker Should Know" for poll workers in Philadelphia, Baltimore, Detroit, Ohio, and Florida.[18] Such lists are helpful in ensuring that poll workers are sufficiently aware of the rights of voters in their state and are prepared to respect them.

Secondly, poll workers must be sensitive to the unique needs of each voter. As the country grows increasingly diverse, it is essential for poll workers to treat each voter with respect and ensure that individuals of all backgrounds enjoy equal access to the ballot box. Similarly, poll workers must be prepared to assist voters with disabilities in an open and nonpejorative manner. In July 2007, the U.S. Election Assistance Commission issued a report titled "Successful Practices for Poll Worker Recruitment, Training, and Retention."[19] The manual specifically recommended sensitivity training for poll workers, noting the importance of promoting accessibility for disabled voters and emphasizing that poll workers "respond well to sensitivity training, and appreciate the tips offered to ensure that all voters have a positive voting experience."[20]

To this end, several nonpartisan constituency organizations offer recommendations to increase the sensitivity of poll workers to the special needs of individual voters. The National Federation of the Blind lists 12 "courtesy rules" for poll workers, including "You don't need to raise your voice or address me as if I were a child," "Don't ask my spouse questions about what I want or need, ask me directly," and "I use a long white cane or guide dog for travel; please do not feel that it is necessary to move things out of my way."[21] The organization recommends that poll worker training include interaction with blind individuals who are able to demonstrate "the appropriate way to interact with the blind."[22]

States have also adopted their own procedures for ensuring poll workers are culturally sensitive; for example, California trains its poll workers to respect differences and "wait—recognize—listen":

- *Wait*—Slow down the instinctive reaction to launch into a quick response. Wait first to process the question, then formulate a reasoned, respectful response.
- *Recognize*—Poll workers must focus on how to recognize other people's feelings and anticipate their needs and be sensitive, accommodating, and courteous in assisting them.
- *Listen*—Poll workers must listen before speaking in order to understand exactly what the voter is feeling, seeing, needing, and trying to say/communicate. It is most important to remember to put automatic assumptions aside in order not to stereotype and to better hear and understand a voter's responses.[23]

A third general requirement is for poll workers to be adept at addressing any technological issues that may arise on Election Day, and be prepared to troubleshoot any potential problems related to voting machines and other possible breakdowns.

Adequate and effective training to ensure that poll workers are technologically proficient becomes increasingly crucial as several states and jurisdictions transition to electronic voting machines. It is also equally important for poll workers to be prepared to fix any minor problems with the machines, including machines designed for voters with physical disabilities.

While this may appear to be a somewhat obvious recommendation, the importance of technological aptitude is often not emphasized to poll workers during training sessions. A recent report noted that in Philadelphia in 2006, training for poll workers lasted "only 17 minutes," while only seven minutes were spent on explaining the set-up and operation of voting machines.[24] In addition, as the *Washington Post* noted in 2006, "many poll workers are well into their retirement years, and the technology changes can be daunting for some of those who didn't grow up using computers."[25] As such, some jurisdictions may find it reasonable to target recruitment efforts toward individuals who are accustomed to using computers. Whatever the method, it is crucial that poll workers arrive at their polling place on Election Day prepared to handle any technological crises that may arise.

IV. The Role of Political Parties and Candidates

Since the election of 2000, both the Democratic and Republican parties have increased their efforts to place their own monitors—often lawyers—at polling places on Election Day. And while most states and jurisdictions permit qualified political parties and candidates to designate poll watchers at each polling place and central counting station, there are three general guidelines that parties or campaigns should adhere to in sending representatives to the polls.

First, and most importantly, state law or regulations should instruct party or campaign representatives at the polls to interact with the voter inside the polling place only as an advocate or otherwise provide only innocuous assistance. They may not harass or otherwise intimidate any voter, or attempt to influence the content of an individual's vote. Any indication that they are doing so must be addressed swiftly, the action ceased, and the challenger removed from the polling place. Second, the numbers of poll watchers at each location should be limited to avoid undue crowding. Third, parties or candidates designating poll watchers should be prohibited from targeting certain polling locations or voters based on any pernicious affiliation of voters in the jurisdiction, particularly race, language status, or age.

The importance of the above three guidelines is illustrated in the 2004 case of *Spencer v. Pugh*,[26] in which the U.S. Supreme Court addressed the permissibility of an Ohio law that permitted political parties to place observers in polling sites on Election Day.[27] The case arose in part after the Hamilton County Republican Party filed a request for over 600 challengers to be "physically present in the polling places in order to challenge voters' eligibility to vote" on Election Day 2004.[28] Two-thirds of these challengers were to be sent to predominantly African American pre-cincts,[29] leading to claims that "African American voters will be intimidated; racial tension will rise and African American voters will be blocked from exercising their right to vote" on Election Day.[30]

On November 1, 2004, the District Court for the Southern District of Ohio granted a temporary restraining order and preliminary injunction against the place-ment of challengers in polling places as permitted under the state law.[31] Of primary concern to the district court was the poor training of potential challengers and their lack of experience, which, combined with the dearth of legal guidelines setting the parameters for their duties, created "an extraordinary and potentially disastrous risk of intimidation and delay."[32] The Sixth Circuit rejected this analysis on appeal a few hours later.[33] The court recognized the lower court's finding that allowing challengers in polling places without proper guidelines and parameters could lead to the "enormous risk of chaos, delay, intimidation, and pandemonium."[34] But Judge Rogers weighed the "strong public interest in allowing every registered voter to vote freely" against the "strong public interest in permitting legitimate statutory processes to operate to preclude voting by those who are not entitled to vote," and concluded that the latter interest was more compelling.[35] The U.S. Supreme Court agreed with Judge Rogers, noting a "faith" that voter deception and intimidation would not occur, and that "the elected officials and numerous election volunteers on the ground will carry out their responsibilities in a way that will enable qualified voters to cast their ballots."[36]

V. The Role of the Nonpartisan Voter Advocate

In addition to an increase in the number of partisan election observers or chal-lengers in the polls since the 2000 election, several nonpartisan groups have orga-nized volunteers to serve as voter protectors or advocates in the polls on Election Day. These organizations also vary in purpose. Some, such as a group founded by Harvard Law students called Just Democracy, focused on placing nonpartisan law students and attorneys in polling places to ensure that the rights of voters were protected. Others, including the NAACP, People for the American Way, and the Advancement Project formed an Election Protection coalition in 2004 and 2006 to encourage early voting and the use of absentee ballots, coordinate comprehensive legal field programs, work with local election officials, and develop legal responses to problems on and before Election Day, and to place volunteers to serve either as Election Day poll monitors in targeted precincts or to provide live voter assistance via a toll-free national hotline. In addition, groups like the Asian American Legal Defense and Education Fund (AALDEF) recruit several local polling-place observers to conduct exit polls of voters of Asian descent and collect information on intimi-dating acts targeting voters.

The work of these organizations can serve as guidance for establishing standards to which nonpartisan voter advocates should adhere. For example, voter advocates should be permitted to observe all official acts and records used at the polling places, and should be instructed to present all objections and challenges directly to the Election Day officials. They should ensure that protections of the Voting Rights Act are met, and be available to assist voters in asserting their rights throughout the voting process.

But perhaps the most unique and important role that these groups can play is to develop a record and report of any instances of irregularity at the polling location, including improper challenges to voters and any failures of the political process. Groups like AALDEF have, in recent years, illustrated the value of this role. Under the leadership of Margaret Fung and Glenn Magpantay, the group has placed advocates in polling locations during several recent federal elections, and has observed and recorded irregularities that inform subsequent successful legal actions and investigations by the U.S. Department of Justice. Through work such as this, nonpartisan voter advocates function almost entirely to serve the voter both on Election Day and in the future through the collection of information that can shine a light onto problems voters experience at the polls and help prevent the problems from reoccurring in the future.

VI. Conclusion

The above analysis offers a brief glimpse in to the roles that four major entities—the government, poll workers, political parties, and nonpartisan voter advocates—play on Election Day. Each is responsible for promoting and protecting the right to vote, and each is able to contribute in a unique way to ensuring the smooth administration of an election. If these entities are able to work together, but independently, towards this common goal, the voter, and democracy, reap the rewards.

Notes

1. *See, e.g.,* Stewart v. Blackwell, 444 F.3d 843 (2006) (determining the disparities in the accuracy of voting machines to be so great as to violate the Equal Protection Clause); Christopher Edley, Jr., et al., *Harvard Civil Rights Project, Democracy Spoiled: National, State, and County Disparities in Disenfranchisement Through Uncounted Ballots* 8 (2002) (finding significant disparities in ballot spoilage rates in the general election of November 2000).

2. SPECIAL INVESTIGATIONS DIVISION, COMMITTEE ON GOVERNMENT REFORM, U.S. HOUSE OF REPRESENTATIVES, INCOME AND RACIAL DISPARITIES IN THE UNDERCOUNT IN THE 2000 PRESIDENTIAL ELECTION (July 2001).

3. Edley, *supra* note 1; Bruce E. Hansen, A Precinct-Level Demographic Analysis of Double-Punching in the Palm Beach Presidential Vote (Nov. 12, 2000), (unpublished manuscript, *available at* http://www.ssc.wisc.edu/~bhansen/vote/vote.html); *see also* Michael C. Herron and Jasjeet S. Sekhon, *Overvoting and Representation: An Examination of Overvoted Presidential Ballots in Broward and Miami-Dade Counties,* 22 ELECTORAL STUDIES 21 (Sept. 14, 2001), *available at* http://elections.berkeley.edu/election2000/HerronSekhon.pdf.

4. 42 U.S.C. §§ 1973–1973e (2006).

5. Help America Vote Act of 2002, Pub. L. No. 107–252, 116 Stat. 1666 (codified in sections of 2.5, 10, 36, and 42 U.S.C.)

6. National Voter Registration Act of 1993, Pub. L. No. 103–31, 107 Stat. 77 (codified at 42 U.S.C. §§ 1973gg–10 (2006)).

7. Note, *Toward a Greater State Role in Election Administration,* 118 HARV. L. REV. 2314, 2323 (describing election administration as "almost entirely a state creature," emphasizing that states "administer federal elections through widely varying systems, with minimal federal regulation and even less federal financial support").

8. U.S. CONST. art. I, § 4. *See also* Storer v. Brown, 415 U.S. 724, 730 (1974) ("States have evolved comprehensive, and in many respects complex, election codes regulating in most substantial ways . . . the time, place, and manner of holding primary and general elections, the registration of voters, and the selection and qualification of candidates.").

9. *Toward a Greater State Role, supra* note 7, at 2316. *See also* Jeanne Richman & Robert R. Outis, *State Control of Election Administration, in* ISSUES OF ELECTORAL REFORM 117, 118 (Richard J. Carlson ed., 1974) ("[E]very state exercises some responsibility for the conduct of elections, but the method and degree of control vary widely.").

10. *See, e.g.,* NATIONAL TASK FORCE ON ELECTION REFORM, ELECTION 2004: REVIEW AND RECOMMENDATIONS BY THE NATION'S ELECTION ADMINISTRATORS (2005), *available at* http://www.electioncenter.org/documents/Task%20Force%20Final%20PDF.pdf; U.S. Election Assistance Commission, *Successful Practices for Poll Worker Recruitment, Training, and Retention* (2007), *available at* http://www.eac.gov/election/quick-start-management-guides; U.S. Commission on Federal Election Reform, *Building Confidence in U.S. Elections* (Sept. 2005), *available at* http://www.american.edu/ia/cfer/report/full_report.pdf.

11. *See* U.S. Commission on Federal Election Reform, *supra* note 10 at 18–21.

12. *See e.g., Id.* at 47, NATIONAL TASK FORCE ON ELECTION REFORM. *supra* note 10 at 1.

13. Bush v. Gore, 531 U.S. 98 (2000).

14. *Id.* at 104 (finding that under the Equal Protection Clause, "the right to vote as the legislature has prescribed is fundamental; and one source of its fundamental nature lies in the equal weight accorded to each vote and the equal dignity owed to each voter.")

15. *See generally* Stewart v. Blackwell, 444 F.3d. 843 (6th Cir. 2006) (applying the Equal Protection analysis in *Bush v. Gore* to require parity among election machinery and technology within a state).

16. One of the most elaborate local government election offices is in Miami-Dade County, Fla. The county's election department has over 65 employees responsible for voter registration, election support, absentee ballots, and voter fraud. *See* David Leahy, *Running an*

Election and the Work of the Elections Office, in COUNTING VOTES: LESSONS FROM THE 2000 PRESIDENTIAL ELECTION IN FLORIDA 61, 61–62 (Robert P. Watson ed., 2004).

17. *Compare* IND. CODE § 3–5–2–40.5 *with* MICH. COMP. LAWS § 168.523.

18. *See* Advancement Project, Voter Protection, http://www.advancementproject.org/ourwork/power-and-democracy/voter-protection/tools-training-materials.php.

19. U.S. Election Assistance Commission, *supra* note 10.

20. *Id.* at 121.

21. National Federation of the Blind, Nonvisual Election Technology Training Curriculum, http://www.nfb.org/nfb/training_poll_workers.asp?SnID=2.

22. *Id.*

23. California Department of State, "Poll Worker Training Guidelines" (2006). *Available at* http://www.sos.ca.gov/elections/poll_worker_training_guidelines_final_draft1.pdf.

24. ADVANCEMENT PROJECT, PLIGHT OF THE POLL WORKER: EFFORTS TO IMPROVE TRAINING AND SUPPORT FOR POLL WORKERS IN OHIO, PENNSYLVANIA, MARYLAND, FLORIDA, AND MICHIGAN, http://projectvote.org/fileadmin/ProjectVote/Publications/Plight_of_the_Poll_Worker-Advancement_Project.pdf, at 4 (also noting that in Philadelphia, "poll workers may elect, but are not required, to view a 30-minute video on how to use the voting machines").

25. Christian Davenport, *More Poll Workers Recruited, but Training Proves Daunting,* WASH. POST, Nov. 2, 2006, at A1; *available at* http://www.washingtonpost.com/wp-dyn/content/article/2006/11/01/AR2006110103212.html.

26. Spencer v. Pugh, 543 U.S. 1301 (2004).

27. *See* OHIO REV. CODE § 3505.20 ("Any person offering to vote may be challenged at the polling place by any challenger, any elector then lawfully in the polling place, or by any judge or clerk of elections"); OHIO REV. CODE ANN. § 3505.21 ("At any primary, special, or general election, any political party supporting candidates to be voted upon at such election and any group of five or more candidates may appoint to any of the polling places . . . one person, a qualified elector, who shall serve as challenger for such party or such candidates during the casting of the ballots . . .").

28. Spencer v. Blackwell, 347 F. Supp. 2d 528, 530 (2004).

29. *Id.* (also noting that "evidence presented at the hearing reflects that 14% of new voters in a majority white location will face a challenger . . . but 97% of new voters in a majority African-American voting location will see such a challenger.").

30. *Id.*

31. *Id.*

32. *Id.* at 535.

33. *See* Spencer v. Blackwell, 388 F.3d 547 (2004).

34. *Id.* at 550.

35. *Id.* at 551.

36. Spencer v. Pugh, 543 U.S. at 1303.

CHAPTER FIVE

THE PROMISE AND PRACTICE
OF ELECTION DAY REGISTRATION

STEVEN CARBÓ*
BRENDA WRIGHT**

I. Introduction

Although advances in technology in recent decades have greatly streamlined the process for adding newly registered voters to the rolls, many states continue to adhere to restrictive preelection registration deadlines that require voters to register up to 30 days before any given election. In many cases, these deadlines may not have changed for 35 years or more.[1] Because of such registration deadlines, eligible citizens may find themselves disfranchised on Election Day because a voter registration application may have gone astray, or elections staff may have erred in entering the registration information, or the voter may have failed to update registration after moving, or the voter simply may have been unaware of the registration deadline.[2]

Election Day Registration (EDR), which allows eligible voters to register and cast a ballot on Election Day, is a reform that reduces the unnecessary disfranchisement of eligible voters that may be caused by arbitrary registration deadlines. For many years, six states (Idaho, Maine, Minnesota, New Hampshire, Wisconsin, and Wyoming)[3] have offered EDR, and since the 2004 presidential election, two additional states—Montana and Iowa—have joined their ranks, while a third, North Carolina, has enacted an analogous measure[4] allowing Same Day Registration[5] at early voting sites. As a result of these recent changes, the 2008 presidential election may see unprecedented use of EDR by American voters.

This chapter provides an overview of the policy and practice of EDR. It first briefly examines the evolution of voter registration deadlines in the United States

---

*Senior Program Director, Democracy Program, Dēmos: A Network for Ideas & Action.
**Legal Director, Democracy Program, Dēmos: A Network for Ideas & Action.

(Part II). It then canvasses how EDR proposals have gained increasing interest in statehouses and in Congress in recent decades, beginning with the adoption of EDR in several states in the 1970s (Part III). The chapter next reviews the evidence on how EDR affects voter participation and turnout, both generally and with respect to specific demographic groups (Part IV). Finally, it assesses the impact of EDR on election administration by reviewing the experience of states that have adopted EDR (Part V). This examination establishes that EDR, when properly implemented, benefits the democratic process by boosting participation, particularly among groups that have had lower propensities to register and vote, and that states with a long history of EDR implementation report positive outcomes for election administration overall.

II. A Short History of Voter Registration in the United States

Although many Americans take it for granted that advance registration is a requirement for voting, most states had no voter registration requirements prior to the 1870s. Eligibility was determined at the polls on Election Day.[6] As the electorate expanded through immigration and the 15th Amendment's enfranchisement of former slaves, so too did calls for stricter controls on the registration and voting process. The majority of states adopted registration requirements between the 1870s and World War I,[7] and by 1929 all but three states required registration prior to an election.[8]

Historian Alexander Keyssar has described the mixed motives behind the move to preelection registration: "Registration laws . . . emerged in the nineteenth century as a means of keeping track of voters and preventing fraud; they also served—and often were intended to serve—as a means of keeping African American, working-class, immigrant, and poor voters from the polls."[9] States varied widely on the details of their registration requirements such as the deadline for voter registration, the locations at which registration was offered, whether and how often reregistration was required, and how a change in residence affected registration. One state might provide only two days during the year on which voters must appear in person to establish their qualifications to register;[10] another might require citizens to renew their registrations annually;[11] while others might make registration relatively easy by charging the election officials themselves with the primary responsibility of identifying eligible citizens and placing their names on the registry.[12] Often, the new registration requirements applied only to residents of the largest cities in the state, where immigrant and poor populations were concentrated.[13] Legislative choices about these details were shaped by cross-currents involving partisan aims; class, race, and ethnic prejudice; machine politics; and sincere good-government goals;[14] but there is widespread agreement that, whatever the motives, the institution of restrictive preelection registration requirements contributed to substantial reductions in voter participation and turnout among eligible voters in the United States.[15]

While state courts addressed a variety of legal challenges to registration laws during the late 19th and early 20th century, and occasionally invalidated them under state constitutional provisions guaranteeing the right of suffrage,[16] the federal courts played little role in such challenges until much later. Rejecting a constitutional challenge to a Maryland law regulating voter registration, the Supreme Court in 1904 declared that "the Federal Constitution does not confer the right of suffrage upon any one, and the conditions under which that right is to be exercised are matters for the states alone to prescribe."[17] As late as 1965, the Supreme Court summarily affirmed a lower court decision that applied much the same reasoning to uphold another Maryland law that imposed onerous durational residency requirements for voter registration.[18]

Congress, not the federal courts, took the first step to address restrictive registration deadlines. Five years after the landmark Voting Rights Act of 1965,[19] which created powerful federal protections against racial discrimination in registration and voting, Congress turned its attention to the burden imposed by "'archaic statutory limitations'" such as lengthy registration closing periods.[20] In the Voting Rights Act Amendments of 1970, Congress eliminated durational residency requirements for voting in presidential and vice-presidential elections and required states to allow registration for such elections up to 30 days before the election.[21]

Discussing the justifications for Congress's action, one court stated:

> Thus it is clear that the key to increasing participation in the democratic process lies in making registration available during crucial periods of voter interest on a relatively liberal basis, and that the imposition by states of requirements that bear no reasonable relationship to a compelling legitimate state interest will have the effect of disenfranchising many qualified members of the electorate and denying them the right to vote, which is one of the fundamental and precious rights of a United States citizen.[22]

The Supreme Court upheld Congress's authority to impose these liberalized registration requirements for federal elections in *Oregon v. Mitchell*.[23]

Two years later, in *Dunn v. Blumstein*,[24] the Supreme Court finally declared that onerous state-law requirements concerning the timing of voter eligibility could violate 14th Amendment guarantees, relying in part on Congress's findings accompanying the Voting Rights Act Amendments of 1970. *Dunn v. Blumstein* specifically involved a durational residency requirement; Tennessee required a would-be voter to have been a resident of the state for one year and a resident of the county for three months in order to register to vote in state elections. The Court held that durational residency requirements for voting were subject to strict constitutional scrutiny, and that none of Tennessee's proffered justifications—deterring fraud, assuring that voters are knowledgeable about issues, and serving administrative needs—were sufficient to sustain such a lengthy waiting time prior to registration.[25] The Court noted that 30 days appeared to be a sufficient period for carrying out administrative tasks necessary to verify residency, especially in light of the fact that Tennessee allowed general registration up to 30 days prior to an election.[26]

Although *Dunn v. Blumstein* did not directly address the constitutionality of registration closing deadlines, its analysis strongly suggested that the Court would view 30 days as the maximum registration cutoff that could be justified.[27] Nevertheless, in 1973 the Supreme Court upheld 50-day registration closing deadlines in Arizona and Georgia, holding that each state had made an adequate showing that the longer closing dates were required to accommodate specific needs of election administration in those states.[28] Today, many states still close registration up to 30 days before an election,[29] even though, as discussed below, the continuing administrative justifications for such lengthy cutoff periods are tenuous at best. The Supreme Court has not again addressed the constitutionality of registration deadlines in the three and a half decades since its 1973 decisions.

The question of whether lengthy preelection registration deadlines violate the Constitution is, however, separate from the question of whether they reflect sound policy.[30] In the 1970s, a number of states sought to address declining turnout and expand the participation of eligible citizens by easing their registration requirements. These reforms included enactment of EDR in several states.[31] The experience of those states confirms that EDR boosts voter turnout, a matter discussed in more detail in Part IV, *infra*. The next section describes three "waves" of EDR reform since 1970 and where these reform efforts stand today.

III. The Revival of Election Day Registration: From the 1970s to the Present

Five states adopted EDR in the early to mid-1970s: Maine (1973), Minnesota (1974), Wisconsin (1976), Oregon (1976), and Ohio (1977). The specific motivations for EDR's enactment in Maine, Wisconsin, and Minnesota have variously been attributed to a national Democratic campaign to boost turnout among the party's base voters or, alternatively, to homegrown desires for consistent, statewide voter registration rules and procedures.[32] The administration of EDR on Election Day also differed among these three states. In Minnesota and Wisconsin, EDR was available at all polling sites. In Maine, as in Minnesota and Wisconsin, all voters had the option of registering on Election Day, but the location for registration differed depending on local administrators' discretion. Maine's larger cities required Election Day registrants to present themselves first at the local registrar's office to register and then proceed to their polling place to vote, while smaller jurisdictions allowed registration directly at the polling place.[33]

EDR was short-lived in Ohio. The legislature adopted EDR in early 1977, but voters subsequently rejected EDR through a constitutional amendment approved in November 1977. The ballot initiative proposing the constitutional amendment was led by a group of disaffected Ohio legislators, who voiced fears of increased voter fraud, and was backed by Secretary of State Ted Brown. The constitutional change required individuals to be registered 30 days prior to an election.[34]

EDR met with a similar fate in Oregon; it was repealed by a 1985 ballot initiative. The impetus for the ballot measure was a political controversy involving Indian guru Bhagwan Shree Rajneesh and the self-styled utopian community that he and his disciples established near the village of Antelope, Oregon, in 1981. The Rajneesh disciples' successful capture of majority control of the local government, the registration of homeless individuals newly arrived from out of state, and fears of expanded political influence sparked a nativist backlash and repeal of Oregon's EDR statute.[35]

The successful enactment of EDR in several states in the 1970s and its positive effect on voter turnout encouraged President Jimmy Carter to propose a national EDR program.[36] Despite White House leadership and large Democratic majorities in both houses of Congress, the resultant legislation was not adopted.[37] Incumbency protection and fear of the unknown new voter apparently outweighed political interest in expanding democratic participation. According to President Carter,

> The conservatives, Democrats and Republicans alike, almost to a person opposed this legislation. I was taken aback that many of the liberal and moderate members of the Congress also opposed any increase in voter registration. . . . The key [source of resistance was] "incumbency." Incumbent members of the Congress don't want to see additional unpredictable voters registered. . . . [T]his is the single most important obstacle to increasing participation on election day.[38]

The next generation of EDR enactment would not come for another 15 years, when EDR was adopted in Idaho, New Hampshire, and Wyoming. Providing the occasion for this reform were the political negotiations surrounding congressional consideration of the National Voter Registration Act (NVRA) in 1993. Senate Republican leaders, who historically opposed registration reform, proposed that particular states could avoid NVRA coverage if they quickly enacted EDR.[39] The proposal was accepted by the sponsors of the legislation and incorporated into the text of the statute that was ultimately passed by Congress and signed into law by President Bill Clinton.[40] Wyoming, Idaho, and New Hampshire took advantage of the NVRA exemption, enacting EDR into law in 1993, 1994, and 1995, respectively.[41]

Many states again began seriously considering EDR in the wake of the flawed 2000 presidential election. The intense public scrutiny engendered by the close contest between Vice President Al Gore and Governor George Bush exposed deep flaws in the administration of U.S. elections. Up to three million Americans were deprived of an opportunity to cast a ballot in 2000 because of voter registration problems and flawed voter registries.[42] Many had believed themselves to be registered to vote, only to find at the polls that their names had not made it to the rolls and that they could not vote. Public policy organizations such as Dēmos began championing EDR as a solution to many of these registration problems.[43] With EDR, qualified voters who on Election Day found that their names were omitted from the voter rolls could readily register and vote at the polls, thus avoiding the vote denial that resulted from wrongful or mistaken voter purges in states such as Florida leading up to November 2000.

In the years following the 2000 election, EDR was proposed in 34 of the 43 states that still barred voting by those not registered in advance of the election.[44] In 2002, EDR advocates organized EDR ballot initiatives in California and Colorado; both measures were rejected by the voters.[45] The Connecticut state legislature voted to approve EDR in 2003, only to see the EDR proposal vetoed by then-Governor John Rowland. The governor cited concerns about voter fraud in his veto message.[46]

It was in Montana that EDR was to see its first post-2000 success. The legislature passed and the governor signed into law an EDR provision in 2005.[47] Although the Montana variant of EDR does not allow for registration at the polls (residents may register and vote at the offices of county election administrators after the close of the voter registration deadline (30 days before election), including on Election Day), it likely contributed to an appreciable increase in voter participation in the landmark 2006 election.[48] Registration gains were most pronounced among young people and in counties with large college student populations. The three counties where registrations spiked most—Missoula, Gallatin, and Yellowstone Counties—are home to University of Montana or Montana State University campuses. Montanans between the ages of 18 and 25 comprised more than a third of the approximately 9,200 individuals who registered to vote under Montana's new statute between October 7, 2006, and November 7, 2006.[49]

Legislative campaigns for EDR gained steam in over a dozen states in 2007.[50] With a confluence of factors (determined political leadership, focused grassroots advocacy, a cohesive lobbying campaign, expert support from national organizations, and the support of state election officials), EDR was enacted in Iowa, and Same Day Registration was enacted in North Carolina.[51] Eligible citizens may now register at early voting site up to three days before an election in North Carolina. Iowa began allowing registration on election day at all polling places in January 2008.

Interest in EDR has also increased at the federal level. Rep. Keith Ellison (D-MN) introduced a national EDR bill in 2007, taking up a concept that previously had been championed by his predecessor, Martin Sabo (D-MN).[52] A hearing on EDR was convened in the House of Representatives on November 9, 2007.[53] Sen.

Hillary Clinton and Rep. Stephanie Tubbs Jones incorporated EDR in their proposed Count Every Vote Act, an omnibus election reform plan for correcting many of the shortcomings witnessed in recent elections.[54] EDR also had been proposed in various forms in previous recent Congresses. These proposals, introduced by Democrats, have failed to move beyond the committee stage of consideration chiefly because of political partisanship and stated Republican concerns about ballot security. Other reservations include fear of inordinately complex election administration with EDR and political risk to incumbent legislators.[55] We assess how EDR affects issues of voting integrity and election administration by examining the experience of existing EDR states in Part V, *infra,* after first turning to a discussion of the impact of EDR on voter participation.

IV. Election Day Registration and Increased Voter Turnout

Healthy democracies aspire to high rates of voter participation and turnout, yet even the more optimistic estimates of U.S. voter turnout show that nearly 40 percent of eligible voters failed to vote in the last presidential election.[56] The United States, in addition, typically lags far behind other advanced democracies in turnout among eligible voters.[57] Moreover, those who do participate at high rates in the United States differ significantly from nonparticipants in terms of their socioeconomic profile: they have, on average, higher incomes and more education, and are more likely to be older and white.[58] These persistent disparities challenge the goal of a representative democracy, because they make it difficult to assume that the interests and needs of nonvoters will be adequately reflected in the choices of those who do participate.

There is no single factor that can be assigned exclusive blame for low voter participation,[59] and no silver bullet that will ensure that our nation has consistent high levels of turnout. But, as the evidence assessed below indicates, there is little doubt that restrictive preelection registration deadlines are a deterrent to participation for many voters, and that EDR is a reform that boosts voter turnout.

The role of registration requirements in depressing rates of voter participation after their widespread adoption in the late 19th and early 20th centuries has already been described. But even though some of the most burdensome features of those laws, such as literacy tests, poll taxes, and annual reregistration requirements, have long been eliminated, the requirement of preelection registration itself still plays a role in deterring full participation. Some of the reasons for this are summarized by Wolfinger and Rosenstone:

> Registration raises the costs of voting. Citizens must first perform a separate task that lacks the immediate gratification characterizing other forms of political expression (such as voting). Registration is usually more difficult than voting, often

involving more obscure information and a longer journey at a less convenient time, to complete a more complicated procedure. Moreover, it must usually be done before interest in the campaign has reached its peak.[60]

Indeed, polls indicate that the percentage of people giving "quite a lot" of thought to U.S. presidential elections rises dramatically in the final four weeks prior to the election, just at the time when registration no longer is possible in approximately half the states.[61] Moreover, the deterrent effects of registration requirements are compounded in the United States because, unlike in most other democracies, the government does not assume primary responsibility for assuring that eligible citizens are registered, but generally leaves the burden of securing registration on the individual.[62]

Registration requirements may affect participation not only because of their effect on would-be voters, but also because of their effect in structuring the mobilizing efforts of candidates and political parties. Preelection registration deadlines raise the cost of mobilizing those not already registered, because those individuals must first be encouraged to overcome the hurdle of registration weeks before the election and then mobilized to turn out on Election Day. Preelection registration deadlines are thus a disincentive for campaigns to focus on efforts to expand the electorate, especially in the final weeks of an election—precisely the time when less politically engaged citizens might otherwise become interested in the campaign.[63]

All these considerations suggest that EDR should boost voter turnout, and the available evidence bears this out. A typical summary of the social science literature states "[t]he evidence on whether EDR augments the electorate is remarkably clear and consistent. Studies finding positive and significant turnout impacts are too numerous to list."[64] EDR states as a group have turnout rates that are generally 10 to 12 percentage points higher than states without EDR.[65] Academic studies have concluded that a significant part of this difference is directly attributable to the availability of EDR in these states, with EDR increasing turnout by 3 to 6 percentage points depending on the states included in the study and the models used for isolating the effect of EDR.[66] Studies examining the likely impact of EDR in states such as New York and California that have somewhat different demographic profiles than the earlier EDR states have predicted higher turnout gains of 8.6 and 9.2 percentage points, respectively, if EDR were to be adopted.[67]

A related question is whether the adoption of EDR, in addition to increasing overall turnout, can help to make the electorate more representative of the American population as a whole. That question is more contested among social scientists than the question of whether EDR enhances turnout overall, but there is increasing evidence that some traditionally low-turnout groups benefit disproportionately from EDR. Several studies have found that younger citizens, those who move frequently, and other groups with historically lower turnout are particularly likely to benefit from EDR.[68] State-specific studies also predict larger-than-average turnout increases among groups with historically lower participation rates. For example, a study analyzing the impact of EDR in New York predicts that overall turnout would rise by 8.6 percentage points, but that turnout would increase 12.3 points among 18-to-25-year-olds, 9.8 points among those with a grade school education or less, 11 points among Latinos, 8.7 points among African Americans, and 10.1 points among those who have lived at their current address for less than six months.[69] A similar study on the impact of EDR in Iowa predicts an overall turnout gain of 4.9 percentage points, but a gain of 10.7 points among 18-to-25-year-olds, 8.8 points for those who have moved in last six months, 9.5 points for Latinos, and 6.6 points for African Americans.[70]

That being said, different studies analyzing how registration reforms such as EDR affect turnout sometimes appear engaged in a debate about whether the glass is half empty or half full. Some emphasize that registration reforms alone are not likely to bring about universal participation nor entirely erase socioeconomic disparities in turnout. They point out that even when registration is easy, those who lack a sense of political engagement and motivation to vote will remain unlikely to participate.[71] Others emphasize instead the measurable increase in turnout attributable to reforms such as EDR, and point out that mobilization campaigns are more likely to spur participation among disaffected groups when registration barriers are minimized.[72]

The authors of this chapter hold with the glass-half-full perspective. Projected turnout gains from adoption of EDR translate into millions of additional voters casting ballots nationwide, an extraordinarily valuable accomplishment regardless of whether it eliminates all causes of depressed turnout among eligible Americans. Moreover, the experience of EDR states shows that adoption of EDR itself can encourage political parties and grassroots organizers to adopt the very mobilization and outreach tactics that may be further prerequisites to expanded participation.[73]

V. Impact of Election Day Registration on Election Administration

While its proponents trumpet the potential for expanding voter turnout, EDR detractors raise concerns about voter fraud, expense, and the burden of administering registration at the polls on Election Day. A review of the experiences of EDR states and various studies of EDR is illuminating. The data show that EDR can be introduced without threatening the integrity of elections, driving up election costs, or inducing nightmares for voters and poll workers.

A. DOES EDR LEAD TO VOTER FRAUD?

The most extensive data on the extent of voter fraud in EDR states has been compiled by Lorraine Minnite, a political scientist at Barnard College and Senior Fellow at Dēmos. Her research shows that fears of voter fraud are overstated and unfounded in both EDR and non-EDR states. After an analysis of the incidence of voter fraud from 1992 to 2002 in 12 states that collectively represent about half of the electorate; an extensive Nexis search on reported voter fraud incidents throughout the United States; a survey of academic literature, government documents, congressional testimony and reports, law journal articles, and a wide variety of other sources on election administration; and an in-depth review of some of the highest-profile cases of real or alleged fraud, Minnite concluded that voter fraud was very rare in the 12 states examined.[74]

In a more recent analysis of data from 2002–2005 that focused specifically on states with EDR, Minnite again found very little evidence of voter fraud. Her review of nearly 4,000 news accounts netted one case of confirmed voter impersonation at the polls—a 17-year-old New Hampshire high student who shares his father's name cast his father's ballot in the 2004 Republican presidential primary.[75] An aggressive new Justice Department initiative against voter fraud led to prosecutions in only one EDR state, Wisconsin. Of 14 Milwaukee residents charged with double voting or casting ballots while disfranchised for felony convictions, five resulted in convictions (for felon voting).[76] And early returns from a survey of 252 prosecutorial jurisdictions in the EDR states turned up two fraud investigations in Minnesota. Charges against four of the 11 individuals suspected of committing fraud were dismissed; the remaining seven received warning letters.[77]

The report suggests several reasons why EDR does not facilitate voter fraud, and may in fact deter it. First, EDR is conducted in person, under the eyes and authority of election officials.[78] According to Minnesota Secretary of State Mark Ritchie,

> EDR is much more secure because you have the person right in front of you—not a postcard in the mail. That is a no-brainer. We [Minnesota] have 33 years of experience with this.[79]

Second, EDR states require registrants to substantiate their residence and identity at the time of registration. A broad range of documents is accepted (only Idaho requires Election Day registrants to produce photo identification).[80] And third, list maintenance and postelection audits adopted by some EDR states add an additional level of identity verification for persons registering at the polls.[81]

Minnite's findings on the security of EDR elections are corroborated by a 2007 Dēmos survey of 49 elections clerks in six EDR states.[82] The vast majority of respondents rated current fraud-prevention measures sufficient to protect the integrity of elections.[83]

The introduction of computerized statewide registration systems as required by the Help America Vote Act of 2002 (HAVA) also can help reassure policy makers concerned about the security of elections run with EDR. As of January 1, 2006, Congress required that all states implement a centralized, interactive, computerized statewide registration system.[84] This mandate was intended to improve the accuracy of voter lists and help avoid incidents of duly registered voters being turned away from the polls on Election Day because their names were omitted from voter registries, as documented in the 2000 election.

The integration of county registration databases into one computer file can help safeguard against the possibility, however rare, of multiple registrations and double voting in several jurisdictions. Security is particularly enhanced where election administrators have ready electronic access to computerized state registration lists at the polls on Election Day, and where registration and voting information can be inputted and accessed in "real time." It should be noted that Idaho, Maine, Minnesota, New Hampshire, Wisconsin, and Wyoming each implemented EDR before the advent of computerized voter registration databases and HAVA mandates. Each has administered secure elections even without the benefit of these technological innovations.

B. EDR AND ELECTION ADMINISTRATION

According to election officials with long-standing experience in administering registration at polling places, EDR can be managed efficiently by application of several commonsense measures.[85] Advance planning, voter education, and staff training are most relevant. A sound estimation of anticipated voter turnout on Election Day allows for adequate deployment of poll workers qualified to process same-day registrations on that day.

Milwaukee, Wisconsin, one of the largest EDR jurisdictions in the nation, assigns registrars to each of its 335 wards in peak election years. It also assigns new registrants to voting areas separate from those assigned to preregistered voters to avoid long lines and voter frustration. When voters arrive at the polls, a "greeter" approaches and directs them to the appropriate area, depending on whether they already are registered or are seeking to register at the polling place. Election officials observe that they have prevented excessive congestion, even in metropolitan locations, by structuring the physical environment of the polling place in this way. New Hampshire and Maine respond to potential staffing problems by assigning an additional election judge to each polling site on Election Day.[86]

Public education is another component of successful EDR systems. Maine and Minnesota make considerable efforts to advise their citizens about the process of voter registration and the mechanics of voting. Milwaukee election officials publicize information on how EDR works on television and radio, and on billboards. They also seek to avoid Election Day confusion through advance notice of lists of identification accepted for voter registration.[87]

Poll worker training is the third element of successful EDR systems. Poll workers, election clerks, and registrars must all be fully versed in state registration and voting regulations. For example, Maine requires that all its clerks and registrars receive such training every two years.[88] Wyoming provides 1.5 days of training for every poll worker two weeks before each election. And all election workers in Minnesota receive at least two hours of training every two years.[89]

C. THE IMPACT OF EDR ON REDUCING NEED FOR PROVISIONAL BALLOTS

Another EDR benefit frequently cited by election officials is that it nearly obviates the need for provisional balloting. Under the Help America Vote Act, voters whose names do not appear on the voter rolls on Election Day but who believe themselves to be registered to vote cannot be turned away without being given the opportunity to cast a ballot. They must be issued a provisional ballot.[90] Election authorities thereafter comb their registration records to determine if an error was made and such individuals were indeed duly registered, and whether the provisional ballots should be counted, under prevailing state law, and added to election tallies.[91]

The process of investigating the validity of provisional votes can be laborious and time-consuming. Over 1.9 million provisional ballots were cast in the 2004 general election.[92] Much of this strain on election administrators is avoided with EDR. Individuals who find themselves left off the voter rolls simply reregister at the polls and cast a regular ballot. Questions about an individual's eligibility can be resolved at the time of registration. According to the county clerk in Anoka County, Minnesota,

> [Election Day Registration] provides us with the most up-to-date information on the voter. . . . It assures that individuals are voting for offices and districts where they live on Election Day and it eliminates the need for provisional ballots because we can resolve any voter registration issues that day.[93]

Even more importantly, EDR avoids the disappointing results with provisional ballots experienced by many voters since provisional balloting was implemented nationwide in 2004: Over one in three of the nearly 2 million provisional ballots cast were not counted in the 2004 presidential election. Thirteen states each rejected over 10,000 provisional ballots; 23 states each counted less than 50 percent of provisional ballots.[94]

D. EDR AND ELECTION COSTS

Policy makers frequently ask how EDR affects the overall cost of election administration. Accurate calculation of the incremental expense of registering voters at polling places on Election Day is difficult, given inadequate record keeping and the fact that EDR costs are embedded in state, county, and municipal budgets. Nevertheless, election officials in EDR states do not report substantially higher election administration costs because of EDR.[95]

Where identified by EDR election clerks in Dēmos's 2007 survey,[96] the marginal costs of EDR mainly involved the training and deployment of additional staff—more poll workers or election judges on Election Day, and/or more clerical workers in the postelection period to add the new names and data to the permanent voter rolls.

The deputy clerk of a mid-sized New Hampshire city reported that EDR required one or two extra registrars per polling place (at $15 an hour or $125 a day). The clerk of one of Maine's largest jurisdictions figured that Election Day Registration costed $39,000. In a New Hampshire community of 23,000 people, the city clerk estimated the postelection cost at about $1,700—or 10 hours a week of service over 14 weeks on the part of a worker earning $12 an hour. In Idaho, the elections administrator of a county with a population of about 50,000 projected one or two extra persons working full-time for a week and a half. A Wisconsin official in a municipality of about 70,000 spoke of spending about $5,000 on temporary workers to process EDR registrants after the November 2006 election.[97]

The additional expenses reported in some EDR states may simply replace other costs that would otherwise be incurred if registration were not available on Election Day. In non-EDR states, data entry for new registrations before Election Day often requires hiring temporary workers or paying overtime to in-house staff, particularly when last-minute registrations pour in at the close of preelection deadlines. The same work goes on in EDR states, except that it is undertaken after the election and without the time pressures that can cause data entry errors. A Minnesota election administrator observed that EDR may be the more cost-effective alternative. Election judges who administer voter registration on Election Day are paid less than the in-house staff that handles voter registration throughout the year.[98]

EDR can also lead to more efficient election administration. An Idaho elections director who has worked on elections both before and since EDR was enacted in her state has found voter lists to be more accurate with EDR. Trained elections staff can carefully process voter registration applications submitted on Election Day without the frenzy associated with the close of voter registration periods. Before EDR, her county had to borrow staff from other county offices when a crush of voter registration applications arrived on the registration deadline. The temporary staff's inexperience in inputting voter information showed. Many errors were made in the preparation of voter lists used on Election Day. Eligible voters whose names could not be found there lost their opportunity to cast a ballot.[99]

EDR's reduction of the costs and delays involved in handling provisional ballots should figure in EDR cost assessments. As has been noted, EDR reduces the need for provisional ballots, which require separate and potentially time-consuming examination and handling during the vote counting process. Incremental costs associated with EDR may therefore be offset by the reduced need for provisional ballots in EDR states.

E. RESULTS OF 2007 DĒMOS SURVEY OF ELECTION ADMINISTRATORS IN EDR STATES

Debates about the efficacy of implementing EDR are to be expected when policy makers and election administrators are called on to consider adoption of EDR. In this context, the experience of local election clerks in the six states with a long track record of administering EDR is particularly instructive. Dēmos initiated a survey of 49 election officials in Idaho, Maine, Minnesota, New Hampshire, Wisconsin, and Wyoming over several months in 2007. The administrators were representative of election leaders across the six states. Targeted jurisdictions ranged in size from 520,000 to fewer than 600 residents; several had significant student populations. The survey addressed EDR's costs, administrative burdens, and security.[100]

Clerks reported that the incidental expense of administering EDR was minimal. Where costs rise, they typically involve the expense of deploying an extra poll worker at each precinct to handle registration, although this may be offset by reduced costs for pre-deadline processing.[101] The elections clerk in Portland, Maine, one of the larger EDR jurisdictions, saw a slight rise in election costs, but found it to be outweighed by the benefits of allowing more city residents to participate in local elections. In her words, "it is a little more expensive, but it's worth it."[102]

The six states also appear to handle registrations on Election Day without disrupting the voting process. Most such registrants are directed to a separate area for processing voter registration applications, and thereafter join all other voters in line to receive a ballot.[103] A minority of those surveyed reported that administering registrations at the polls can complicate Election Day operations. But most were quick to add that these challenges are more than outweighed by the benefit to voters.[104]

Finally, the election clerks confirmed the overall security of EDR elections, consistent with the results documented in voter fraud studies.[105] The vast majority reported that current fraud-prevention measures are sufficient to protect the integrity of their elections. Security measures may include proof of identity and residency requirements for persons registering for the first time on Election Day, address confirmation mailings via nonforwardable postcards to EDR registrants after Election Day, criminal penalties for committing voter fraud, and the use of statewide voter registration databases to prevent multiple registrations.[106] An election administrator in a populous Minnesota jurisdiction noted that he has never seen an organized attempt at mass voter fraud in his 22 years on the job.[107] A Maine legislator attested to her state's record of secure elections at a legislative hearing in Connecticut: As of April 2007, no substantiated case of voter fraud due to EDR had ever been reported in Maine.[108]

VI. Conclusion

For proponents of widespread and inclusive voter participation, the 21st century may be a time to go back to the future. Just as the adoption of restrictive preelection registration deadlines constricted the participation of the eligible electorate in the late 19th and early 20th centuries, so may the return to EDR help expand it in our time. EDR is a proven reform that increases participation, reduces many of the polling-place problems that have plagued the past several election cycles, and has been successfully administered without fraud for over 30 years. Its more widespread adoption may be expected to bring hundreds of thousands of new voters to the polls in future elections. Although no one reform will end the phenomenon of nonvoting, states that wish to make voting as accessible and widespread as possible should embrace EDR as an important step to a more inclusive democracy.

Notes

1. Michigan, for example, adopted its 30-day registration deadline in 1973. *See* MICH. COMP. LAWS ANN. § 168.497 (historical note). Mississippi has imposed a 30-day deadline since 1972, when a federal court struck down the state's previous four-month preelection registration deadline. *See* Ferguson v. Williams, 343 F. Supp. 654 (N.D. Miss. 1972); *see* MISS. CODE ANN. § 23-15-11 (setting forth current 30-day deadline). Louisiana's current 30-day advance registration requirement appears to date at least back to 1942, *see* LA. REV. STAT. ANN. § 18:135, Op. Att'y Gen. 1942-44, p. 490.

2. Indeed, a study by the Caltech-MIT Voting Technology Project estimates that between 1.5 and 3 million votes were lost in the disputed 2000 presidential election because of problems with the voter registration process. CALTECH-MIT VOTING TECHNOLOGY PROJECT, VOTING: WHAT IS, WHAT COULD BE 8 (July 2001). As two former secretaries of state have noted, "Election officials hate having to tell a citizen who has waited for hours on line that he or she is not on the list and cannot vote. On Nov. 7 [2006], this happened over and over again in non-EDR states, but rarely happened in Maine, New Hampshire, Minnesota, Wisconsin, Wyoming, Idaho and Montana." Miles S. Rapoport & Mike Cooney, *Citizens Count with Election Day Registration, reprinted in* DĒMOS, VOTERS WIN WITH ELECTION DAY REGISTRATION: A SNAPSHOT OF ELECTION 2006 (2007) [hereinafter VOTERS WIN WITH ELECTION DAY REGISTRATION], http://www.demos.org/pubs/voters%20Win.pdf.

3. IDAHO CODE ANN. § 34-408A; 21-A ME. REV. STAT. ANN. tit. 21-A, § 122.4; MINN. STAT. § 201.061; N.H. REV. STAT. ANN. § 654:7-a; WIS. STAT. § 6.55; WYO. STAT. ANN. § 22-3-103. In addition, Rhode Island allow Connecticut and EDR at the voter's city or town hall solely for elections for president and vice president. CONN. GEN. STAT. § 9-158(c) and R.I. GEN. LAWS § 17-1-3. Maine's EDR program requires election-day registrations to be accepted at the registrar's office, and does not specifically require registration to be made available at each polling place, *see* ME. REV. STAT. ANN. tit. 21-A § 122.4; but in practice, about 80 percent of polling places in Maine allow polling place registration (source: interview with Maine Secretary of State office, Oct. 26, 2007).

States that allow EDR generally maintain a cutoff or closing date for applications from persons other than those registering on Election Day. For example, in Maine, mail-in or third-party applications must be received 21 days before the election in order for the applicant's name to appear on the voter roll for that election; an individual not registered by that date must either register in person at the registrar's office or at the polling place on Election Day. ME. REV. STAT. ANN. tit. 21-A, § 121.1-A.

4. Iowa Code §48A.7A; Mont. Code Ann. §13-2-304; N.C. Gen. Stat. §163-82.6(c). Montana's version of EDR does not allow registration at polling places, but instead allows citizens to register and vote at the offices of county election administrators after the close of the voter registration deadline (30 days before the election), including on Election Day.

5. The terms "Election Day Registration" and "Same Day Registration" are sometimes used interchangeably, but there may be differences between the policies. "Same Day Registration" is the broader term because it encompasses systems that allow voters to register and vote on the same day, even if—as in the case of North Carolina—that opportunity is provided only at early voting sites, and not on Election Day itself. Idaho, Iowa, Maine, Minnesota, Montana, Wisconsin, and Wyoming allow voters to register and vote on Election Day itself, and can more accurately be referred to as EDR states. This article generally refers to EDR as the preferred policy option that offers the greatest opportunity for surmounting the barriers posed by preelection registration deadlines.

6. Alexander Keyssar, The Right to Vote: The Contested History of Democracy in the United States 151 (2000) [hereafter Keyssar]. A few states had begun imposing registration requirements earlier in the 19th century; Massachusetts was the first, with a law enacted in 1801. *Id.* at 152.

7. *Id.*

8. Frances Fox Piven & Richard A. Cloward, Why Americans Don't Vote 88 (1988) [hereafter Piven & Cloward].

9. Keyssar, *supra* note 6, at 312. According to one review of the literature, "Historians of voting in the United States generally agree that registration requirements were instituted at least as much 'to shape the social character of the eligible electorate' as to control fraud[.]" Stephen Knack & James White, *Election-Day Registration and Turnout Inequality,* 22(1) Pol. Behavior 29, 29 (2000) [hereafter Knack & White] (quoting Paul Kleppner, Who Voted? 9(1982)); *see also* J. Morgan Kousser, The Shaping of Southern Politics: Suffrage Restriction and the Establishment of the One-Party South, 1880–1910 (1974).

10. *See* People v. Hoffman, 116 Ill. 587, 5 N.E. 596, 613 (Ill. 1886) (describing 1885 Illinois voter registration law).

11. State v. Butts, 31 Kan. 537 (1884) (describing 1879 Kansas voter registration law).

12. Piven & Cloward, *supra* note 8, at 90. As Piven and Cloward observe, many of the registration systems initially adopted by states were "nonpersonal" systems that "placed the burden of compiling lists of eligible voters on town or county officials." *Id.* Such registration laws were far less onerous than the systems of "personal registration" that later became the norm, requiring voters to present themselves at specific times and places for registration. *Id.*

13. *Id.*

14. Keyssar, *supra* note 6, at 152–62; Piven & Cloward, *supra* note 8, at 89–94.

15. *See* Keyssar, *supra* note 6, at 158; Piven & Cloward, *supra* note 8, at 94.

16. One of the earliest such cases was Dells v. Kennedy, 49 Wis. 555, 6 N.W. 246 (Wis. 1880). In 1864, Wisconsin enacted a registry law requiring advance voter registration in cities of over 25,000 inhabitants. As described in the dissenting opinion, 6 N.W. at 381, the 1864 law included an exception for eligible voters who could prove by affidavit on election day that they had been unable to appear before the registrar on the day provided for

correcting errors to the published list of voters. An 1879 law eliminated this exception, and barred voting by anyone not on the register, unless the person had first become a resident of the election district after the registration closing date. The Wisconsin Supreme Court struck down the 1879 registry law, holding that the legislature could not deny the right to vote to a citizen otherwise eligible to vote under the qualifications set forth in the Wisconsin Constitution, solely because, through no fault of his own, the voter was unable to appear in person prior to the election to correct the published list. The "vice" of the law, the court said, was that

> [T]he law disfranchises a constitutionally qualified elector, without his default or negligence, and makes no exception in his favor, and provides no method, chance or opportunity for him to make proof of his qualifications on the day of election, the only time, perchance, when he could possibly do so. This law undertakes to do what no law can do, and that is to deprive a person of an absolute right without his laches, default, negligence or consent; and, in order to exercise and enjoy it, to require him to accomplish an impossibility.

Dells v. Kennedy, 6 N.W. at 247. In effect, the Wisconsin Supreme Court established a state constitutional right for a voter to establish his qualifications on election day, at least if he could present a valid excuse for not establishing his qualifications in the prescribed manner prior to the election. *See also* State *ex rel.* Stearns v. Connor, 22 Neb. 265, 34 N.W. 499 (1887) (Nebraska registry law violated Nebraska Constitution by providing only four days during which voters must appear in person and establish their qualifications to register, and allowing no exception for eligible voters who were unable to appear on one of the four registration days); Daggett v. Hudson, 43 Ohio St. 548, 3 N.E. 538 (1885) (Ohio law allowing registration only seven days during the year, and providing no exception for eligible voters unable to appear on those days, violated Ohio Constitution).

17. Pope v. Williams, 193 U.S. 621, 633 (1904). The Pope Court acknowledged that the U.S. Constitution prohibited "discrimination . . . between individuals" in state elections, *id.* at 632, and that the right to vote for members of Congress was not derived solely from state law, *id.* at 633, but regarded the details of state registration laws as otherwise outside the purview of the federal courts. The doctrine that the 14th Amendment conferred no direct right to vote in state elections had already been established in cases such as Minor v. Happersett, 88 U.S. 162, 21 Wall. 162 (1874), in which the Court held that denial of the vote to women did not violate the 14th Amendment.

18. Drueding v. Devlin, 380 U.S. 125 (1965).

19. P.L. No. 89-110, 79 Stat. 445 (codified as amended at 424 S.C. §§ 1971, 1973–1973bb-1).

20. Bishop v. Lomenzo, 350 F. Supp. 576, 586 (E.D.N.Y. 1972) (three-judge court) (quoting Sen. Barry Goldwater).

21. 42 U.S.C. § 1973aa-1(c); (d).

22. *Bishop,* 350 F. Supp at 584–85.

23. Oregon v. Mitchell, 400 U.S. 112 (1970).

24. Dunn v. Blumstein, 405 U.S. 330 (1972).

25. *Id.* at 336–37, 345–58.

26. *Id.* at 342, 347–49.

27. *See* Ferguson v. Williams, 343 F. Supp. 654 (N.D. Miss. 1972) (striking down Mississippi's four-month preelection registration deadline and imposing 30-day deadline as interim measure, citing *Dunn*); *cf. In re* Opinion of Justices of Supreme Judicial Court, 303 A.2d 452 (Me. 1973) (holding that under *Dunn*'s analysis even a 30-day residency requirement for voting would violate the 14th Amendment, because Maine did not require 30 days to process registrations).

28. Marston v. Lewis, 410 U.S. 679 (1973); Burns v. Fortson, 410 U.S. 686 (1973).

29. Last day to register in states that do not allow election-day or same-day registration: Alabama, 11 days before election, Ala. Code § 17-3-50(a); Alaska, 30 days before election, Alaska Stat. § 15.07.070; Arizona, 29 days before election, Ariz. Rev. Stat. § 16-120; Arkansas, 30 days before election, Ark. Code. Ann. § 7-5-201; California, 15 days before election, Cal. Elec. Code § 2107(a); Colorado, 29 days before election, Colo. Rev. Stat. § 1-2-201; Connecticut, 7 days before election, Conn. Gen. Stat. § 9-17(a), but may register on election day to vote for President and Vice-President, Conn. Gen. Stat. § 9-158c; Delaware, 20 days before election, Del. Code Ann. tit. 15, § 2011; District of Columbia, 30 days before election, D.C. Code Ann. § 1-1001.07(g)(1); Florida, 29 days before election, Fla. Stat. ch. 97–109; Georgia, fifth Monday before election, Ga. Code Ann. § 21-2-224(a); Hawaii, 30 days before election, Haw. Rev. Stat. §§ 11-16(a), 11-24(a); Illinois, 28 days before election, 10 Ill. Comp. Stat. 5/4-6, 5/5-5, 5/5-17, 5/6-29; Indiana, 29 days before election, Ind. Code §§ 3-7-33-3, 3-7-33-4; Kansas, 15 days before election, Kan. Stat. Ann. § 25-2311; Kentucky, 28 days before election, Ky. Rev. Stat. Ann. § 116.045(2); Louisiana, 30 days before election, La. Rev. Stat. Ann. § 18:135; Maryland, 21 days before election, Md. Code Ann., Elec. Law § 3-302(a); Massachusetts, 20 days before election, Mass. Gen. Laws ch. 51, § 26; Michigan, 30 days before election, Mich. Comp. Laws Ann. § 168.497, 168.500d; Mississippi, 30 days before election, Miss. Code Ann. §§ 23-15-11, 23-15-47; Missouri, fourth Wednesday before election, Mo. Rev. Stat. § 115.135(1); Nebraska, second Friday preceding election at office of the election commissioner or county clerk, Neb. Rev. Stat. § 32-302, third Friday preceding election for other sources, §§ 32-306, 32-308, 32-321; Nevada, fifth Sunday preceding the election by mail, third Tuesday preceding the election in person, Nev. Rev. Stat. § 293.560; New Jersey, 21 days before election, N.J. Stat. Ann. § 19:31-6; New Mexico, 28 days before election, N.M. Stat. Ann. § 1-4-8; New York, 25 days before election, N.Y. Elec. Law § 5-210; Ohio, 30 days before election, Ohio Rev. Code Ann. § 3503.01; Oklahoma, 25 days before election, Okla. Stat. tit. 26, § 4-110.1; Oregon, 21 days before election, Or. Rev. Stat. § 247.025; Pennsylvania, 30 days before election, 25 Pa. Cons. Stat. § 1326; Rhode Island, 30 days before election, but may register on election day to vote for president and vice president, R.I. Gen. Laws § 17-1-3; South Carolina, 30 days before election, S.C. Code Ann. § 7-5-150; South Dakota, postmarked 30 days before election, or received 15 days before election, S.D. Codified Laws § 12-4-5; Tennessee, 30 days before election, Tenn. Code Ann. § 2-2-109; Texas, 30 days before election, Tex. Elec. Code Ann. § 13.143; Utah, 30 days before election to be eligible for early voting (until 14 days before election), 1953 Utah Laws 20A-2-102.5, 15 days before election to be eligible for election-day voting, 1953 Utah Laws 20A-2-201; Vermont, the Wednesday preceding election, Vt. Stat. Ann. tit. 17, § 2144; Virginia, 29 days

before election, Va. Code Ann. § 24.2-414; Washington, 30 days before election, Wash. Rev. Code § 29A.08.140, or 15 days if applying in person, § 29A.08.145; West Virginia, 21 days before election, W. Va. Code § 3-2-6.

As noted above, eight states now allow EDR (Idaho, Iowa, Maine, Minnesota, Montana, New Hampshire, Wisconsin, and Wyoming), and North Carolina allows same-day registration at early voting sites until three days prior to the election. *See* sources at notes 3 & 4, *supra*. North Dakota does not require registration as a condition of voting. N.D. Cent. Code § 16.1-01-04(1) (list of voter qualifications does not include registration); N.D. Cent. Code § 16.1-01-05.1 (procedure for adding or transferring voter names when voter moves to different precinct "may not be used to require the registration of electors").

30. In 2004, groups mounted a constitutional challenge to Connecticut's 14-day preelection registration deadline, arguing that the burden of lengthy preelection deadlines can no longer be justified by the needs of election administration or as anti-fraud measures. The challenge was unsuccessful, although this was no doubt influenced by Connecticut's decision to reduce the deadline to seven days, the shortest of any state that required preelection registration, while the case was under litigation. ACORN v. Bysiewicz, 413 F. Supp. 2d 119 (D. Conn. 2005). Plaintiffs in Florida have mounted a somewhat narrower challenge to Florida's 29-day preelection deadline, arguing that Florida's refusal to allow a grace period for a voter to correct a deficient voter registration application that is rejected after the deadline places an unconstitutional burden on the right to vote. The district court denied the state's motion to dismiss, observing that "Defendants have not presented this Court with any justification for the state's legislative judgment that a twenty-nine day cutoff, without a grace period, is necessary to achieve the state's legitimate goals." Diaz v. Cobb, 475 F. Supp. 2d 1270, 1277 (S.D. Fla. 2007). The case remains pending.

31. *See* Keyssar, *supra* note 6, at 312.

32. Political scientists Craig Leonard Brians and Bernard Grofman attribute the adoption of EDR by Maine, Minnesota, and Wisconsin within a three-year period in large part to a national Democratic Party campaign for EDR and mail-in voter registration. Democrats aimed to boost turnout voting among people of color, the poor, and urban residents, according to these researchers. Craig Leonard Brians & Bernard Grofman, *When Registration Barriers Fall, Who Votes? An Empirical Test of a Rational Choice Model*, 99 Pub. Choice 161, 169 (1999) [hereinafter Brians & Grofman 1999]. In contrast, Joan Growe, who served as Minnesota secretary of state from 1974 to 1998 and sat in the state legislature when EDR legislation was adopted, does not recall any external political push for EDR. She ties EDR's enactment to a desire among Minnesota policymakers for consistent statewide voter registration procedures. Different Minnesota counties previously had maintained their own unique systems. Preregistration was not required in some smaller jurisdictions; voters merely signed in at the polls on Election Day. Other jurisdictions required that individuals register to vote 30 days before an election. Telephone interview with Joan Growe, former Minnesota Secretary of State, Minneapolis, MN (Oct. 24, 2007). In Maine, after the state's Supreme Judicial Court held that a proposed 30-day durational residency requirement for voting was unnecessarily lengthy and would be unconstitutional, the legislature responded by establishing EDR. *In re* Opinion of Justices of Supreme Judicial Court, 303 A.2d 452 (Me. 1973); *see*

ELIMINATING BARRIERS TO VOTING: ELECTION DAY REGISTRATION 19 (report on Nov. 30, 2001, conference cosponsored by Brennan Center for Justice at N.Y.U. School of Law & Dēmos) [hereafter ELIMINATING BARRIERS TO VOTING], http://www.demos.org/pubs/EDR_report_113001.pdf.

33. Stephen Knack, *Election-Day Registration: The Second Wave,* 29(1) AM. POL. Q. 65, 68 (2001) [hereafter Knack 2001]. Currently, about 80 percent of polling places in Maine allow polling place registration, while the remaining jurisdictions still require voters who wish to register on Election Day to do so at the local registrar's office before proceeding to their assigned polling place to cast a ballot. See note 3, *supra.*

34. Knack 2001, *supra* note 33, at 67 n.1; POLICY MATTERS OHIO, ELECTION DAY REGISTRATION: EXPANDING THE OHIO VOTE 5 (July 2003), http://www.policymattersohio.org/pdf/EDR_report .pdf.

35. Knack 2001, *supra* note 33, at 67 n.1.

36. See *infra* Part IV for a discussion of EDR and increased voter turnout.

37. Universal Voter Registration Act of 1977, S. 1072, 95th Cong. (1977), H.R. 5400, 95th Cong. (1977).

38. FRANCES FOX PIVEN & RICHARD A. CLOWARD, WHY AMERICANS STILL DON'T VOTE 188 (2000) (citing Harvard/ABC News Symposium (1984:27)).

39. Telephone interview with Lloyd Leonard, Senior Director, League of Woman Voters, Washington, DC (Oct. 25, 2007). States were variously opposed to the NVRA because of federalism concerns, resistance to offering voter registration at state departments of motor vehicles, and the need to standardize intrastate election administration among counties, towns, and other localities. Telephone interview with Jim Dickson, Vice President, Government Affairs, American Association of People with Disabilities, Washington, DC (Oct. 24, 2007).

40. Pub. L. No. 103-31 (codified at 42 U.S.C § 1973gg) 107 Stat. 77. Sec. 4(b)(2) of the NVRA provides that the statute will not apply to states that do not require registration or that allow voters to register to vote at polling places at the time of voting for in a general election for federal office. 42 U.S.C. §§ 1973gg–2(b). *See generally* IDAHO CODE ANN. § 34-408A; N.H. REV. STAT. ANN. § 654:7-a; WYO. STAT. ANN. § 22-3-103.

41. IDAHO CODE ANN. § 34-408A; N.H. REV. STAT. ANN. § 654:7-a; WYO. STAT. ANN. § 22-3-103. The impact of EDR on turnout in these states and in others is discussed in Part IV, *infra.*

42. CALTECH-MIT VOTING TECHNOLOGY PROJECT, VOTING: WHAT IS, WHAT COULD BE 8 (July 2001).

43. *See, e.g.,* ELIMINATING BARRIERS TO VOTING, *supra* note 32.

44. Alaska, Arizona, California, Colorado, Connecticut, Florida, Georgia, Hawaii, Illinois, Indiana, Iowa, Louisiana, Maryland, Massachusetts, Michigan, Missouri, Montana, Nebraska, Nevada, New Jersey, New Mexico, New York, Ohio, Oklahoma, Oregon, North Carolina, Pennsylvania, South Carolina, South Dakota, Tennessee, Texas, Utah, Vermont and Washington. As noted earlier, six states already allowed EDR as of 2000, while a seventh, North Dakota, had no statewide registration requirement (and still does not). N.D. CENT. CODE §§ 16.1-01-04(1), 16.1-01-05.1.

45. California Election Day Voter Registration Initiative (2002); Colorado Voter Initiative (2002).

46. Letter from Connecticut Governor John G. Rowland to Connecticut Secretary of State Susan Bysiewicz (July 9, 2003) (on file with Dēmos).

47. MONT. CODE ANN. § 13-2-304.

48. Turnout among eligible Montana voters increased by more than 8 and 4 percentage points from the previous two midterm elections, respectively (2002, 1998). U.S. Election Project, *2006 Voting-Age and Voting-Eligible Population Estimates; 2002 Voting-Age and Voting-Eligible Population Estimates and Voter Turnout; 1998 Voting Age and Voting Eligible Population Estimates and Voter Turnout, available at* http://elections.gmu.edu/voter_turnout.htm.

49. E-mails from Bowen Greenwood, Press Secretary, Montana Secretary of State Brad Johnson, to Regina Eaton, Deputy Director, Democracy Program, Dēmos: A Network for Ideas & Action (Sept. 6, 2007, 19:16 PST); e-mail from Bowen Greenwood, Press Secretary, Montana Secretary of State Brad Johnson, to Steve Carbó, Senior program Director, Dēmos: A Network of Ideas & Action (Sept. 17, 2007, 10:27 EXST) (on file with Dēmos). Montana previously closed voter reistration 30 days before an election. The state now allows continued voter registration throughout most of the 30-day period leading up to an election (voter registration closes from Noon to 5 p.m. on the day before an election) and on election day itself (on file with Dēmos).

50. California, Connecticut, Hawaii, Illinois, Iowa, Massachusetts, Nevada, New Mexico, North Carolina, Oregon, Utah, Vermont, and Washington.

51. IOWA CODE § 48A.7A; N.C. GEN. STAT. § 163-82.6(c). *See* Steven Carbó, DĒMOS: A NETWORK FOR IDEAS & ACTION, ANATOMY OF A SUCCESSFUL CAMPAIGN FOR ELECTION DAY REGISTRATION IN IOWA (Winer 2008) *at* http://www.demos.org/pubs/iowaanatomy.pdf; DĒMOS: A NETWORK FOR IDEAS & ACTION, THE ENACTMENT OF SAME DAY REGISTRATION IN NORTH CAROLINA (forthcoming Feb. 2008) for discussions of the enactment of EDR/SDR legislation in those two states.

52. H.R. 2457, 110th Cong. (2007).

53. Oversight Hearing on Election Day Registration and Provisional Voting: Before the Subcommittee on Elections, 110th Cong. (Nov. 9, 2007), *available at* http://ch.house.gov/indep.php?option=com_content&task=view&id-349.

54. S. 804, 110th Cong. (2007); H.R. 1381, 110th Cong. (2007).

55. *Supra* note 53; Veronica Gillespie, Democratic Elections Counsel, Senate Committee on Rules and Administration, Washington, DC (Oct. 23, 2007).

56. U.S. Election Project, *2004 Voting-Age and Voting-Eligible Population Estimates and Voter Turnout, available at* http://elections.gmu.edu/Voter_Turnout_2004.htm. Professor Michael McDonald of George Mason University calculates higher U.S. voter turnout rates than those generated by many other sources because he has developed measurements that seek to adjust for noneligible segments of the electorate such as noncitizens and prison populations. *See* U.S. Election Project, Presidential Turnout Rates for Voting-Age Population (VAP) and Voting-Eligible Population (VEP) (graph), *available at* http://elections.gmu.edu/turnout_rates_graph.htm.

57. PIVEN & CLOWARD, *supra* note 8, at 4–5, KEYSSAR, *supra* note 6, at 320; Robert A. Jackson, Robert D. Brown & Gerald C. Wright, *Registration, Turnout and the Electoral Representativeness of U.S. State Electorates,* 26(3) AM. POL. Q. 259, 260 (1998) [hereafter Jackson, Brown & Wright].

58. *Id.; see also* SIDNEY VERBA, KAY LEHMAN SCHLOZMAN & HENRY E. BRADY, VOICE AND INEQUALITY: CIVIC VOLUNTARISM IN AMERICAN POLITICS 233, 522–24 (1995).

59. The question of declining voter turnout in the United States is "one of the most intensively studied issues in political science," Knack 2001, *supra* note 33, at 65. It is of course beyond the scope of this chapter to address this vast literature. Registration barriers are but one piece of the puzzle.

60. RAYMOND E. WOLFINGER & STEVEN J. ROSENSTONE, WHO VOTES? (1980) (footnote omitted).

61. The Gallup Poll, *The Nine Weeks of Election 2000* (cited in VOTERS WIN WITH ELECTION DAY REGISTRATION, *supra* note 2, at n.13).

62. PIVEN & CLOWARD, *supra* note 8, at 17–18. For example, in the United Kingdom, "registration officers either send a form to every residential address or conduct a door-to-door canvass." John Mark Hansen, Task Force on the Federal Election System, *Voter Registration 3, in* TO ASSURE PRIDE AND CONFIDENCE IN THE ELECTORAL PROCESS (Task Force Reports to Accompany the Report of the National Commission on Election Reform) (July 2001), http://webstorage3 .mcpa.virginia.edu/commissions/comm_2001_taskforce.pdf. The National Voter Registration Act of 1993 (NVRA) took a partial step toward more active government responsibility for registration in the United States by requiring that states must treat an application for a driver's license as an application for voter registration (unless the applicant declines), 42 U.S.C. § 1973gg-3, and that states must offer voter registration at public assistance offices, offices providing disability services, and other agencies. 42 U.S.C. § 1973gg-5. However, for agencies more likely to be used by low-income persons, such as public assistance agencies, the NVRA did not require the same type of integrated registration as is provided to driver's license applicants, instead requiring that a mail-in voter registration application be provided along with the public assistance application. *Id.* This seemingly subtle difference has made compliance with voter registration responsibilities at public assistance agencies less reliable, and indeed many states have largely ignored those responsibilities in recent years, hampering the NVRA's goal of decreasing long-standing socioeconomic disparities in voter registration in the United States. *See* Brian Kevanaugh, Lucy Mayo, Steve Carbó, and Mike Slater, TEN YEARS LATER, A PROMISE UNFULFILLED: THE NATIONAL VOTER REGISTRATION ACT IN PUBLIC ASSISTANCE AGENCIES, 1995–2005 (Sept. 2005), *available at* http://www.demos.org/pubs/NVRA91305.pdf.

63. For a detailed discussion of how restrictions on the franchise can shape the strategies of political parties and other political actors in ways that reinforce participation disparities in the electorate, *see, e.g.,* PIVEN & CLOWARD, *supra* note 8, at 17–18, 103–12.

64. Knack & White, *supra* note 9, at 30 (emphasis omitted); *see also* R. MICHAEL ALVAREZ & JONATHAN NAGLER, DĒMOS: A NETWORK OF IDEAS & ACTION, ELECTION DAY VOTER REGISTRATION IN IOWA 4 (2007) [hereafter ALVAREZ & NAGLER], http://demos.org/pubs/iowa.pdf ("One of the more robust conclusions in the study of turnout for the last 35 years has been that making the registration and voting process easier will increase turnout among eligible voters.").

65. *See, e.g.,* VOTERS WIN WITH ELECTION-DAY REGISTRATION, *supra* note 2, at 1.

66. Knack 2001, *supra* note 33; Knack & White, *supra* note 9; Craig L. Brians & Bernard Grofman, *Election Day Registration's Effect on U.S. Voter Turnout,* 82(1) SOC. SCI. Q. 171 (Mar. 2001); Mark J. Fenster, *The Impact of Allowing Day of Registration Voting on Turnout in U.S. Elections from 1960 to 1992,* 22(1) AM. POL. Q. 74 (1994). *But see* James D. King & Rodney A.

Wambeam, *Impact of Election Day Registration on Voter Turnout: A Quasi-Experimental Analysis,* 14 Pol'y Stud. Rev. 263 (1995/96) (finding little turnout increase). King and Wambeam's selection of "control" states (that is, states that did not enact significant registration reforms prior to 1994) to compare with EDR states raises questions. For example, Michigan was paired as a control with Minnesota, although Michigan implemented a "motor-voter" registration program prior to 1990. *See* Knack 2001, *supra* note 33, at n.7.

67. R. Michael Alvarez, Jonathan Nagler & Catherine H. Wilson, Dēmos: A Network of Ideas & Action, Making Voting Easier: Election Day Registration in New York 1 (2004) [hereafter Alvarez, Nagler, & Wilson], http://www.demos.org/pubs/EDR%20 -%20NY%20report%20b&w%20_%20Aug%202004.pdf; R. Michael Alvarez & Stephen Ansolabehere, Dēmos: A Network of Ideas & Action, California Votes: The Promise of Election Day Registration 13 (2002), http://www.demos.org/pubs/california_votes.pdf).

68. R. Michael Alvarez, Stephen Ansolabehere & Catherine Wilson, *Election Day Voter Registration in the United States: How One-Step Voting Can Change the Composition of the American Electorate* 16 (Caltech-MIT Voting Technology Project Working Paper, 2002) [hereafter Alvarez, Ansolabehere, & Wilson], *available at* http://vote.caltech.edu/media/documents/ wps/vtp_wp5.pdf (estimating that if EDR had been implemented nationally for the 2000 election, overall turnout would have increased by about 8 percentage points, with traditionally underrepresented groups showing the highest gains in registration); Knack & White, *supra* note 9 (EDR improves turnout for youth and geographically mobile); Jackson, Brown & Wright, *supra* note 57, at 268 ("restrictive registration closing dates present a greater hurdle to the poor than to the rich and, similarly, to the less educated than to the highly educated"); Benjamin Highton, *Easy Registration and Voter Turnout,* 59(2) J. Pol. 565 (1997) (states with EDR or with no registration requirement have reduced education-based disparities in turnout compared to states that do not have EDR, although EDR does not eliminate the effect of educational level on turnout); *see also* Mary Fitzgerald, *Easier Voting Methods Boost Youth Turnout* (Circle Working Paper, 2003) [hereafter Fitzgerald] (EDR increases youth turnout by 14 percentage points in presidential elections; youth are much more likely to be contacted by a political party in EDR states than in non-EDR states), *available at* http://www.youngvoterstrategies.org/index.php?tg=fileman&idx=get&inl=1& id=1&gr=Y&path=Research&file=Easy+Voting+Methods+Boost+Youth+Turnout.pdf; *but see* Brians & Grofman 1999, *supra* note 32 (EDR benefits middle-income voters more than upper-income or low-income voters); Adam Berinsky, *The Perverse Consequences of Electoral Reform in the United States,* 33 Am. Pol. Res. 471 (2005) [hereafter Berinsky], *available at* http://apr.sagepub.com/cgi/reprint/33/4/471.pdf (literature review of studies assessing impact of electoral reforms including EDR, arguing that reforms do not eliminate existing turnout disparities, and some may exacerbate them).

69. Alvarez, Nagler & Wilson, *supra* note 67, at 1.

70. Alvarez & Nagler, *supra* note 64, at 1.

71. Brians & Grofman 1999, *supra* note 32; Berinsky, *supra* note 68.

72. Alvarez, Ansolabehere & Wilson, *supra* note 68; Jackson, Brown & Wright, *supra* note 57; Piven & Cloward, *supra* note 8, at 18–23.

73. Eliminating Barriers to Voting, *supra* note 32, at 9–10 ("Activists in states with EDR have mounted extremely successful voter mobilization drives among targeted constituencies,

precisely because they could capitalize on the excitement of the last days of the election and draw previously unregistered voters to the polls"; *see also id.* at 15–17); Fitzgerald, *supra* note 68, at 14 ("[Y]oung citizens are more likely to be contacted by a political party in states with election day registration by an estimated 11 percentage points in presidential elections, and by an estimated 18 percentage points in midterm congressional elections.").

The role of mobilization efforts in maximizing the impact of EDR also makes it difficult to project a clear-cut partisan effect for EDR. Although it is sometimes assumed that any reform that lowers barriers to voting will automatically bring more Democrats to the polls, the reality is more complicated. While the 2006 U.S. Senate election in Montana went to Democrat Jon Tester by 3,500 votes, in an election where approximately 4,000 people registered on election day and turnout increased greatly in college communities, EDR also was responsible for the registration of over 1,400 people on Election Day 2006 in Laramie County, Wyoming, which is home to the Warren Air Force Base and 4,440 base employees, service members, and their families. *See* Voters Win with Election Day Registration, *supra* note 2, at 6 & n.7; e-mails from Bowen Greenwood, *supra* note 49. Clearly, much depends on which party or candidate campaign decides to adapt its strategies to take advantage of EDR in a given election. Academic studies of EDR also have not projected consistent partisan impacts. *See, e.g.,* Knack & White, *supra* note 9, at 41 (observing that EDR most strongly increases turnout among young and mobile voters, who are not as reliably Democratic as other low-turnout groups).

74. David Callahan & Lorraine Minnite, Dēmos: A Network for Ideas & Action, Securing the Vote: An Analysis of Election Fraud (2003), http://www.demos.org/pub111.cfm; Lorraine Minnite, Dēmos: A Network for Ideas & Action, An Analysis of Voter Fraud in the United States (Sept. 2007), http://www.demos.org/pubs/analysis.pdf.

75. Lorraine Minnite, Dēmos: A Network for Ideas & Action, Election Day Registration: A Study of Voter Fraud Allegations and Findings on Voter Roll Security 2 (2007), http://www.demos.org/pubs/EDR%20VF.pdf. Minnite's research and analysis were derived from her forthcoming book on voter fraud in contemporary American elections.

76. *Id.* at 2.

77. *Id.*

78. *Id.* at 4.

79. *Id.*, citing May 10, 2007, e-mail communication with the author.

80. *Id.* at 4, n. 15.

81. *Id.*

82. Dēmos: A Network for Ideas & Action, Election Day Registration: A Ground Level View (Nov. 2007), http://www.demos.org/pubs/EDR%20clerks.pdf. See *infra* Part IV. F. for discussion of election clerks survey.

83. *Id.* Just one of 49 respondents suggested a link between EDR and an increased likelihood of vote fraud. This official—the clerk of a Wisconsin town of fewer than 9,000 people—was also unique in expressing emphatic opposition to EDR. By contrast, the great majority of respondents rated current fraud-prevention measures sufficient to protect the integrity of elections. This was the prevailing view in large and small jurisdictions, and also in college communities, including one Idaho city where, in 2006, some 5,000 out of a total 26,000–27,000 voters used EDR.

84. Help America Vote Act of 2002, Pub. L. No. 107-252, § 303, 42 U.S.C. § 15483.

85. Hearing on H.B. 2415, S.B. 342 before the Joint Committee on Election Laws, 183rd General Court (MA. 2003) (Statement of Dēmos: A Network for Ideas & Action) *available at* http://www.edmos_usa.org/pubs/EDR_Massachusetts_testimony_for_July_24_2003.pdf (citing remarks by Julie Flynn, Deputy Secretary of State, Maine; Joan Growe, former Minnesota Secretary of State; and Julietta Henry, Executive Director, City of Milwaukee Board of Election, at Dēmos/Brennan Center for Justice conference, "Eliminating Barriers to Voting: Election Day Registration," New York, NY, Nov. 30, 2001).

86. *Id*. at 5.

87. *Id*.

88. Me. Rev. Stat. Ann. tit. 21-A, § 101.9.

89. Telephone interview with Peggy L. Nighswonger, Elections Director, Cheyenne, Wyo. (Oct. 24, 2007); telephone interview with Patty O'Conner, Taxpayer Services Director, Blue Earth County, Minn. (Oct. 25, 2007).

90. Help America Vote Act, supra note 84, § 302, 42 U.S.C. § 15482.

91. *Id*.

92. Kimball W. Brace & Dr. Michael P. McDonald, Election Data Services, Inc., *2004 Election Day Survery* (2005), (submitted to the U.S. Election Assistance Commission), *available at* http://www.eac.gov/clearinghouse/docs/eds2004/2004-electionday-survey).

93. Electionline.org, Election-Day Registration: A Case Study 8 (Feb. 2007) (citing interview with Rachel Smith, Anoka County Clerk), http://www.electionline.org/Portals/1/Publications/FINAL%20EDR%20pdf.pdf.

94. Scott Novakowski, Dēmos: A Network for Ideas & Action, A Fallible "Fail-Safe": An Analysis of Provisional Ballot Problems in the 2006 Election 4 (Nov. 2007), http://www.demos.org/pubs/failsafereport.pdf (citing Kimball W. Brace & Dr. Michael P. McDonald, Election Data Services, Inc., *supra* note 92).

95. Election Day Registration: A Ground Level View, *supra* note 82; Hearing on H.B. 2415 S.B. 342, *supra* note 85.

96. Election Day Registration: A Ground Level View, *supra* note 82.

97. *Id*. at 3.

98. *Id*.

99. Telephone interview with Deedie Beard, Supervisor, Kootenai County Elections Department, Coeur d'Alene, ID (Oct. 26, 2007).

100. *See* Election Day Registration: A Ground Level View, *supra* note 82. Dēmos included jurisdictions with college campuses in its 2007 survey because EDR detractors often raise security concerns about the votes of students who register on Election Day. They question whether students' campus addresses meet relevant residency requirements.

101. *Id*. at 3.

102. *Id*.

103. *Id*. at 2.

104. *Id*.

105. See sources cited in Part V.A., *supra* notes 74, 75.

106. *See, e.g.,* Idaho Code Ann. § 34-408A; Minn. Stat. §§ 201.061(3)(a), 201.121(1), 201.121(3), 201.27(3); Wis. Stat. §§ 6.55(2)(6), 6.55(5).

107. *Id.* at 4.

108. Testimony of Maine Rep. Anne Haskell, Connecticut State Joint Committee on Government Administration and Elections, Apr. 16, 2007 (citing Maine Office of the Attorney General's Investigation Division), *available at* http://www.demos.org/pubs/Election_Day_registration_CT1.pdf.

CHAPTER SIX

FELON DISENFRANCHISEMENT

JOHN C. KEENEY JR.*

I. Introduction

In 2001, the National Commission on Federal Election Reform, cochaired by former Presidents Jimmy Carter and Gerald Ford, recommended, among other election reforms, that "each state should allow for restoration of voting rights to otherwise eligible citizens who have been convicted of a felony once they have fully served their sentence, including any term of probation or parole."[1] The commission's recommendation reflected the recognition of the disproportionate impact of disenfranchisement laws on African Americans and other minorities, thereby diluting the voting strength of communities of color.[2]

II. The State Laws

Forty-eight of the 50 states provide that citizens lose their right to vote, at least temporarily, if they are convicted of a felony.[3] Thirty-three states[4] and the District of Columbia provide for automatic restoration of voting rights upon the successful completion of the sentence, and seven more states have a conditional form of automatic restoration for some categories of former felons.[5] In other states, an ex-felon can petition for restoration of voting rights.

In addition to the states that condition forms of restoration of voting rights and limit restoration to certain types of convictions,[6] four other states permit permanent disenfranchisement of some ex-felons. These states are Alabama (some), Kentucky (all), Mississippi (some), and Virginia (all).[7] Their cumbersome and discretionary

---

* J.D. Harvard Law School (cum laude); Chair of ABA Standing Committee on Election Law. The author gratefully acknowledges the able assistance of associate Emily Saylor Gebbia in finalizing this chapter.

reenfranchisement schemes are rarely effective to restore voting rights. In such states, the National Commission on Federal Election Reform noted that the combination of the permanent loss of the right to vote and the demographics of the criminal justice system produces a significant and disproportionate effect on the black community, to the extent that as much as one-sixth of the black population is permanently disenfranchised in these states.[8]

Felon disenfranchisement has likely altered past electoral outcomes and may alter outcomes in the future. Quantification of electoral impact requires projection of how many ex-felons would have voted, how they would have voted, and whether such votes would have changed electoral outcomes. A 2002 study by professors Christopher Uggen of the University of Minnesota and Jeff Manza of Northwestern University concluded that "felon disenfranchisement laws, combined with high rates of criminal punishment, may have altered the outcome of as many as seven recent U.S. Senate elections and at least one presidential election."[9] The future impact is hard to estimate as many disenfranchisement laws have changed since 2000 and therefore in those states there will be potential participation by many newly eligible voters whose sentence, including probation and parole, has been satisfied. Even in states without changes in substantive law, changes in procedure may increase participation. For example, a 2007 Florida rule change[10] that the names of persons released from incarceration and/or supervision shall be electronically transmitted from the Department of Corrections to the Office of Executive Clemency to begin the process of restoring of civil rights may reduce delays in Florida's lengthy certification process and ultimately permit more ex-felon voters in 2008 and later elections.

In states that retain felon disenfranchisement laws, changes in data on assumptions about the rate of political participation or political preference of ex-felons compared to demographically similar nonfelons would significantly affect the accuracy of future predictions of untapped electoral potential. Despite this statistical inexactitude, felon disenfranchisement laws disproportionately impact the African American population in many states and thereby dilute its political influence by artificially depressing voting-eligible population.

III. The Judicial Decisions

Despite constituting a substantial impediment to full political participation by minority communities, felon disenfranchisement laws have been repeatedly upheld by the courts. The U.S. Supreme Court held in *Richardson v. Ramirez* that the California constitutional provision adopted in 1879 providing for felon disenfranchisement does not violate the Equal Protection Clause of the 14th Amendment.[11] The Court emphasized that Section 2 of the 14th Amendment explicitly permits states to disenfranchise those convicted of "participation in rebellion or other crime" in the context of calculation of voting representation.[12] The Court held that "those who framed and adopted the 14th Amendment could not have intended to prohibit outright in § 1 of that Amendment that which was expressly exempted from the lesser sanction of reduced representation imposed by § 2 of the Amendment."[13]

Similarly, challenges under the Eighth Amendment have been uniformly rejected on the grounds that felon disenfranchisement laws are regulatory, rather than penal, in nature, and therefore the Eighth Amendment ban on cruel and unusual punishment is not applicable.[14]

At common law, the practice of denying the vote to individuals convicted of felonies was universal. The practice dates back to ancient Athens and the penalty of "infamy" with consequent loss of the right to vote. A similar penalty was imposed in the Roman Republic for those convicted of crimes involving moral turpitude. The infamy practice of the ancient world evolved into penal statutes throughout Europe. Similar laws disenfranchising felons were adopted in the American colonies and in the early American Republic as well. Judge Friendly in *Green v. Board of Elections* noted that "eleven state constitutions adopted between 1776 and 1821 prohibited or authorized the legislature to prohibit exercise of the franchise by convicted felons. Moreover, twenty-nine states had such provisions when the Fourteenth Amendment was adopted" in 1868.[15]

The ancient lineage of such laws makes it difficult to argue that their enactment was racially motivated, despite the current racial impact. The notable exception from the Supreme Court is the decision in *Hunter v. Underwood.*[16] Distinguishing *Richardson, Hunter* holds that the constitutionality of non-racially motivated disenfranchisement laws does not protect state actions motivated by unconstitutional racial intent.[17] There, the Court struck down that part of the amended Alabama Constitution of 1901, which disenfranchised those convicted of misdemeanor crimes of moral turpitude[18] because the Court found that the 1901 expansion of disenfranchisement from felony conviction (in the 1875 constitution) to misdemeanors of moral turpitude (at the 1901 Alabama constitutional convention) "was motivated by a desire to discriminate against Blacks on account of race and the section continues to this day to have that effect."[19]

Because the misdemeanor portion of its constitution was found unconstitutional in 1985, Alabama later repealed the entirety of Article VIII of its Constitution of 1901 (including the misdemeanor portion) and replaced it with a new section disenfranchising persons convicted of felonies involving moral turpitude. In 2006 a circuit court judge in Alabama found this new section to be unconstitutionally vague and enjoined state election officials from refusing to register individuals previously convicted of felonies who were otherwise qualified to vote "[u]nless and until the Alabama Legislature passes, and the Governor signs into law, legislation specifically identifying which felonies involve moral turpitude."[20] The Supreme Court of Alabama reversed the ban, however, emphasizing that an authoritative construction of the statute by an opinion of the attorney general had specified the offenses and eliminated the vagueness.[21] This mooted plaintiffs' concern that state election officials would not register any individual with a felony conviction.

Similar challenges to arbitrary administration of disenfranchisement law may be legally cognizable. In *Thiess v. State Administrative Board of Election Law,* the district court relied on *Richardson* to reject plaintiffs' claim that the felon disenfranchisement law violated the 14th Amendment, but noted that plaintiffs' assertion that the state had administered the election laws in an arbitrary and uneven way was "by no means facially frivolous."[22] In *Williams v. Taylor,* the Fifth Circuit held: "A state may make a completely arbitrary distinction between groups of felons so as to work a denial of equal protection with respect to the right to vote when it administers a statute, fair on its face, with an unequal hand."[23] The court remanded to the district court for a determination of whether the state election board's noncompliance with statutory procedures unconstitutionally resulted in a pattern of selective enforcement.[24]

Felon disenfranchisement laws have also been challenged under Section 2 of the Voting Rights Act, alleging both vote denial and vote dilution.[25] Both are subject to the same totality of the circumstance test and the *Gingles* factors.[26] These lawsuits have been uniformly unsuccessful, some on the grounds that the Voting Rights Act is not applicable and some on the merits.[27] The Supreme Court has declined to grant certiorari to resolve the conflicting grounds on which appeals courts have upheld the dismissals.[28]

The starting point of any legal analysis is the language of the statute, which in this case is very broad. The plain language of amended Section 2 of the Voting Rights Act prohibits any voting practice or procedure that "results in the denial or abridgement of the right of any citizen of the United States to vote on account of race or color."[29] Nevertheless, application of the broad statutory language of Section 2 of the amended Voting Rights Act to felon disenfranchisement was first rejected in Tennessee in *Wesley v. Collins.*[30] The district court, applying the totality of the circumstances test, reasoned that the Tennessee disenfranchisement statute does not bear the "taint of historically-rooted racial discrimination" and "the disproportionate impact does not 'result' from a state qualification to voting based on race."[31]

In *Baker v. Pataki* an evenly divided Second Circuit affirmed by a vote of five to five the district court dismissal of a Voting Rights Act challenge to New York's felon disenfranchisement law.[32] The Second Circuit in 2006 revisited this issue in its en banc decision in *Hayden v. Pataki.*[33]

In *Hayden,* the en banc Second Circuit split eight to five in holding that Congress did not intend or understand the Voting Rights Act to encompass felon disenfranchisement statutes.[34] Thus, it reasoned that the Voting Rights Act's broad prohibition against any voting qualifications or prerequisites that resulted in a denial or abridgement of the right to vote on account of race or color did not apply to either vote denial or vote dilution claims arising out of felon disenfranchisement statutes.[35] The majority emphasized that application of the Voting Rights Act to traditional state regulation of felon disenfranchisement statutes would alter the constitutional balance between the states and the federal government, and that Congress had to make a clearer statement that it intended the Voting Rights Act to alter that federal balance.[36] The dissenting judges emphasized the act's broad use of the word "any" voting qualification or prerequisite; found no need to resort to legislative history to construe an unequivocal statutory command of "any";[37] and emphasized that the entire Voting Rights Act was an alteration of the federal-state balance in determining the qualifications of voters.[38] Because the majority had concluded that the Voting Rights Act did not apply, the court did not comment on the constitutionality of felon disenfranchisement laws under the 14th or 15th Amendments.

In *Farrakhan v. Washington* the Ninth Circuit addressed a Voting Rights Act challenge to the Washington state constitution, which provides that "all persons convicted of an infamous crime. . . . are excluded from the elective franchise."[39] The court noted as a threshold matter that felon disenfranchisement is a voting qualification and, as such, Section 2 of the Voting Rights Act is clear that any voting qualification that denies citizens the right to vote in a discriminatory manner violates the Voting Rights Act.[40] The court of appeals expressed no opinion on the merits of the Voting Rights Act claim and remanded to the district court for application of the totality of the circumstances test required by Section 2 of the Voting Rights Act.[41]

On remand in the *Farrakhan* case, the district court applied the nine-factor test of *Thornburg v. Gingles* and concluded that the totality of the circumstances did not support a Voting Rights Act violation.[42] The court found particularly probative the state of Washington's lack of history of racial bias in its decision to enact the felon disenfranchisement provisions.[43]

The en banc 11th Circuit in *Johnson v. Governor of Florida* rejected a challenge to Florida's felon disenfranchisement statute.[44] The majority noted that Florida's reenactment of the felon disenfranchisement provision in its 1968 constitution demonstrated that Florida would and did enact this provision without an impermissible motive within the meaning of *Hunter*.[45] The majority further held that neither the plain text nor the legislative history of the 1982 amendment to the Voting Rights Act declared a congressional intent to extend that act to felon disenfranchisement statutes.[46] The court noted that "we should not assume that Congress intended to produce a statute contrary to the plain text of the Fourteenth Amendment without a clear statement."[47] In addition, the majority noted that to apply Section 2 of the Voting Rights Act to felon disenfranchisement would raise grave constitutional concerns by allowing Congress, by federal statute, to prohibit a practice that the 14th Amendment specifically permitted.[48]

IV. The Constitutional Issues

In addition to Section 2 of the 14th Amendment that on its face specifically permits felon disenfranchisement "for participation in rebellion or other crime," the Qualifications Clause grants to state governments the responsibility for determining eligibility to vote.[49] Thus, there is doubt whether Congress could constitutionally ban felon disenfranchisement laws. In any event, as the Second and 11th Circuits noted, despite the Voting Rights Act's all-inclusive use of the word "any" to precede voting qualifications or prerequisites, there is little in the legislative history of the Voting Rights Act to indicate that Congress intended to apply that act to felon disenfranchisement.[50] This silence is constitutionally significant. In *City of Boerne v. Flores* the Supreme Court held that Congress may exercise its enforcement powers under the 14th and 15th Amendments only with a congruent and proportional remedy to a pattern of constitutional violations.[51] The Court urged that Congress establish a substantial legislative record of unconstitutional behavior to justify congressional enforcement under these amendments.[52] Here, Congress made no findings about felon disenfranchisement when enacting the Voting Rights Act, as amended in 1982 or thereafter. Accordingly, there is limited evidence of congressional intent at the time the Voting Rights Act was enacted.

Can Congress ban felon disenfranchisement laws in the future? Section 5 of the 14th Amendment grants Congress the authority "to enforce, by appropriate legislation," the substantive guarantees contained in Section 1 of that Amendment. This congressional power to enact "appropriate" enforcement legislation is quite broad. It is well recognized that Congress may remedy and deter state violations of constitutional rights by "prohibiting a somewhat broader swath of conduct, including that which is not itself forbidden by the Amendment's text."[53]

As the Supreme Court recognized in *Tennessee v. Lane,* "Congress' Section 5 power is not, however, unlimited."[54] Section 5 legislation must be an "appropriate remedy for constitutional violations, not 'an attempt to substantially redefine the States' legal obligations.'"[55] Of course, the constitutional line between the permitted remedial legislation and the prohibited substantial redefinition is not always apparent. Moreover, congressional power targeted at racial discrimination in voting has been given much greater judicial deference than congressional action with respect to voting that did not involve racial discrimination. Thus, in *Oregon v. Mitchell,* the Supreme Court upheld, under Section 2 of the 15th Amendment, the Voting Rights Act Amendments of 1970, which barred literacy tests and other classic tools of racial discrimination, but held to be beyond the constitutional power of Section 5 of the 14th Amendment the congressional provision that lowered the voting age from 21 to 18 in state elections.[56] The constitutional analysis is further complicated because Congress has broader powers to regulate federal (but not state and local) elections under the election clause of Article 1, Section 4 of the U.S. Constitution. *Oregon v. Mitchell* thus upheld Congress's power to lower the voting age in federal but not in state elections.

Thus, as a constitutional matter, to the extent that state disenfranchisement statutes and constitutional provisions have roots in early Greek, Roman, medieval, and colonial precedents, and are independent of racial discrimination, there are significant constitutional questions whether a future congressional ban on felon disenfranchisement would be considered remedial legislation under the 14th and 15th Amendments as opposed to the creation of a new constitutional right, which would be beyond congressional power to enact by mere statute.

V. Other Federal Statutes

Whenever a defendant is convicted of a felony in federal court, the National Voter Registration Act of 1993 requires the applicable United States Attorney's office to send a written notice to the chief state election official in the state where the defendant resides.[57] The notice must identify the defendant, the court, the offense, and the sentence. On request of a state official with responsibility for determining the effect that a conviction may have on an offender's qualification to vote, the United States attorney must supply additional available information. If the conviction is overturned, the election official must be sent additional written notice of that fact by the United States Attorney.

Similar in historical roots to felon disenfranchisement statutes is the federal statutory ban on federal jury service by ex-felons. 28 U.S.C. § 1864(b)(5) bars, from a federal jury, anyone who "has a charge pending against him for the commission of, or has been convicted in a state or federal court of record of, a crime punishable by imprisonment for more than one year and his civil rights have not been restored." This current federal statute dates back to 1948. It incorporates state statutes for restoration of civil rights; there is no federal statute for restoration of civil rights. In many cases the ban on jury service and felon disenfranchisement are directly related as voter registration lists are used to select jurors.[58]

Like the felon disenfranchisement statutes, courts have consistently upheld the federal ban on ex-felon federal jury service, despite the potential for a disproportionate impact on African Americans. In *United States v. Arce,* the Fifth Circuit determined that the statute excluding felons from jury service did not unconstitutionally discriminate against convicted felons.[59] After stating that the statute is subject to rational basis review, the court upheld the statute, reasoning that the ban serves the government's legitimate interest in protecting the integrity of juries and that banning felons is rationally related to that purpose.[60]

The Eighth Circuit in *United States v. Greene* found no equal protection violation even though African Americans are disproportionately excluded from jury service.[61] In that case the Eighth Circuit explained that a facially neutral statute is subject to rational basis review absent a showing of purposeful discrimination.[62] Applying such review, the Eighth Circuit affirmed the asserted government interest in jury probity.[63]

VI. *The International Trend*

Only 13 countries in the world permit permanent disenfranchisement.[64] Most countries among the developed nations ban post-incarceration disenfranchisement, although a few permit disenfranchisement for a certain period of time after a person is released from prison.[65] A number of countries, including Chile, the Czech Republic, Denmark, France, Germany, Guyana, Israel, Japan, New Zealand, Peru, Poland, Romania, Sweden, and Zimbabwe allow even incarcerated individuals to vote.[66]

There is a growing trend in the international community to strike down laws that deprive voting rights based on a criminal conviction. In the past five years, Canada, South Africa, the European Court of Human Rights (ECHR), and Australia each struck down such practices.[67]

In *Sauve v. Canada,* the Canadian Supreme Court struck down a provision of the Canada Elections Act that disenfranchised prisoners serving sentences of two years or more.[68] Sauve argued that the provision violated his right to equal protection under the Canadian Charter of Rights and Freedoms because it discriminated among prisoners on the basis of their sentence lengths. The court agreed, finding that the government failed to provide a purpose that justified a limitation on the right to vote.

Similarly, in *National Institute for Crime Prevention,* the South African Constitutional Court struck down a law that disenfranchised all prisoners who were serving sentences without the option of a fine because the government had failed to prove what purpose the disenfranchisement was intended to serve.[69] The court was unpersuaded that disenfranchisement was justified for the asserted government interest in not appearing "soft on crime" and ruled that the state may not "disenfranchise prisoners in order to enhance its image" nor "deprive convicted persons of valuable rights that they retain in order to correct a public misconception as to its true attitude to crime and criminals."[70]

Also, in *Hirst v. United Kingdom,* the Grand Chamber of the ECHR—a panel composed of judges representing 17 European Union nations—struck down a provision of the United Kingdom's Representation of the People Act of 1983, which disenfranchised all incarcerated prisoners.[71] Hirst claimed that this blanket voting ban was inconsistent with Article 3 of Protocol No. 1 of the European Convention on Human Rights, which ensures "the free expression of the opinion of the people in the choice of the legislature." The Grand Chamber agreed and ruled that the United Kingdom's blanket ban was not proportional to its proffered purposes of: (1) preventing crime and punishing offenders and (2) enhancing civil responsibility and respect for the law.

In *Roach v. Electoral Commissioner*, the Australian High Court held 4–2 that the Commonwealth Electoral Act provisions that bar all prisoners from voting in federal elections are unconstitutional because the laws breach sections of the constitution that provide that parliament should be "directly chosen by the people," and unlawfully breach constitutional freedoms of political participation and political communication.[72]

Currently pending is a 2007 petition with the Inter-American Commission on Human Rights challenging voter disenfranchisement in various states of the United States as violating alleged treaty obligations in the Organization of American States' *Declaration of the Rights and Duties of Man*,[73] including the declaration's principle of universal, equal, and nondiscriminatory suffrage.

VII. Conclusion

The United States remains one of the few countries to disenfranchise former felons and, due to the demographic makeup of the country's ex-felon population, such disenfranchisement disproportionately reduces the political participation of minority communities.

On a going-forward basis, the National Commission on Federal Election Reform put the fundamental policy choice most eloquently:

> We believe the question of whether felons should lose the right to vote is one that requires a moral judgment by the citizens of each state. In this realm, we have no special advantage of experience or wisdom that entitles us to instruct them. We can say, however, that we are equally modest about our ability to judge the individual circumstances of all the citizens convicted of felonies.
>
> Therefore, since the judicial process attempts to tailor the punishment to the individual crime, we think a strong case can be made in favor of restoration of voting rights when an individual has completed the full sentence the process chose to impose, including any period of probation or parole. In those states that disagree with our recommendation and choose to disfranchise felons for life, we recommend that they at least include some provision that will grant some scope for reconsidering this edict in particular cases, just as the sovereign reserves some power of clemency even for those convicted of the most serious crimes.[74]

Notes

1. Nat'l Comm'n on Fed. Election Reform, Final Report 45 (Aug. 2001), *available at* http://www.reformelections.org/ncfer.asp#finalreport.

2. The American Bar Association made a similar recommendation. In August 2003 the ABA House of Delegates approved standards on collateral sanctions that prohibit the "deprivation of the right to vote, except during actual confinement." American Bar Association, Criminal Justice Section, Standards for Criminal Justice 19-2.6(a). In its commentary, the ABA states that its premise for this standard is that "convicted persons should not lose the legal rights and privileges of citizenship." American Bar Association, Standards for Criminal Justice: Collateral Sanctions and Discretionary Disqualifications of Convicted Persons 38 (3d ed. 2004).

3. Two states, Maine and Vermont, allow prisoners to vote.

4. These states are Alaska, Arkansas, California, Colorado, Georgia, Hawaii, Idaho, Illinois, Indiana, Iowa (by July 4, 2005 Executive Order No. 42), Kansas, Louisiana, Maryland, Massachusetts, Michigan, Minnesota, Montana, New Hampshire, New Jersey, New Mexico, New York, North Carolina, North Dakota, Ohio, Oklahoma, Oregon, Rhode Island, South Carolina, South Dakota, Texas, Utah, West Virginia, and Wisconsin. Many of these automatic restoration states, however, require a reregistration in order to vote in future elections.

5. Arizona and Nevada provide automatic restoration of voting rights but only after a first conviction and not a subsequent felony conviction. Connecticut, prior to automatic reinstatement of voting rights, requires proof by the ex-felon that his sentence has been completely discharged. Delaware, Nebraska, and Wyoming impose a waiting period. The rules of the Florida Office of Executive Clemency provide for a form of automatic restoration of civil rights, including voting rights, to some classes of released felons, although action by the Clemency Office is required (Rule 9); restoration without a hearing for other categories of former felons (Rule 10); and discretionary relief upon application under Rule 6 for those not eligible under Rules 9 and 10. Missouri provides automatic restoration except for felony convictions involving voting in an election. Washington provides automatic restoration for convictions in Washington courts after 1984, but not for convictions in other states or for pre-1984 convictions.

6. *See id.*.

7. Ala. Const. art. VIII, § 177(b); Ky. Const. § 145; Ky. Rev. Stat. Ann. § 196.045(1)(e), (2)(c) (2006); Miss. Const. art. 12 §§ 241, 253; Miss. Code Ann. §§ 23-15-11, -19 (2006); Va. Const. art. 2, § 1; Va. Code Ann. §§ 24.2-427(B)(i), 53.1-231.2 (2006).

8. Nat'l Comm'n on Fed. Election Reform, Final Report 44–45 (Aug. 2001), *available at* http://www.reformelections.org/ncfer.asp#finalreport.

9. Christopher Uggen & Jeff Manza, *Democratic Contraction? The Political Consequences of Felon Disenfranchisement in the United States,* 67 Am. Soc. Rev. 777, 794 (2002).

10. Fla. Rule 5(e) note 1 of Rules of the Office of Executive Clemency (Apr. 5, 2007).

11. Richardson v. Ramirez, 418 U.S. 24 (1974).

12. *Id.* at 42–43.

13. *Id.* at 43. Applying *Richardson,* the Third Circuit upheld the district court's dismissal of a complaint that Pennsylvania's felon disenfranchisement law impermissibly distinguished in violation of the Equal Protection Clause between incarcerated felons, who

were denied the vote, and unincarcerated felons who were allowed to vote. Owens v. Barnes, 711 F.2d 25, 26 (3d Cir. 1983). It held that, under *Richardson*, the right of convicted felons to vote is not fundamental and that the state had a rational basis for disenfranchising incarcerated felons while allowing unincarcerated felons to vote. *Id.* at 27–28. *See also* Shepherd v. Trevino, 575 F.2d 1110 (5th Cir.), *cert. denied*, 439 U.S. 1129 (1979).

14. *See, e.g.*, Green v. Bd. of Elections, 380 F.2d 445 (2d Cir. 1967). For a comprehensive discussion of Eighth Amendment challenges to felon disenfranchisement laws, *see* Pamela S. Karlan, *Convictions and Doubts: Retribution, Representation, and the Debate over Felon Disenfranchisement*, 26 STAN. L. REV. 1147 (2004).

15. *Green*, 380 F.2d at 450.

16. Hunter v. Underwood, 471 U.S. 222 (1985).

17. *Id.* at 233. The unconstitutional "discriminatory taint" associated with a disenfranchisement statute has been held, however, to be removed by subsequent amendment or reenactment, which does not have a discriminatory purpose. *See* Johnson v. Governor of Florida, 405 F.3d 1214, 1224 (11th Cir.) (en banc), *cert. denied sub nom.* Johnson v. Bush, 126 S. Ct. 650 (2005); Cotton v. Fordice, 157 F.3d 388 (5th Cir. 1998).

18. *Hunter*, 471 U.S. at 232–33. In McLaughlin v. City of Canton, 947 F. Supp. 954, 975 (S.D. Miss. 1995), plaintiff alleged that Mississippi's statute that disenfranchised persons convicted of certain misdemeanors violated the Equal Protection Clause. The court applied strict scrutiny, rather than the rational-basis review of *Richardson*, reasoning that the California law upheld in *Richardson* and the sanction given to disenfranchisement in Section 2 of the 14th Amendment applied only to felonies. *Id.* at 974–75. The court struck down the misdemeanor part of the old Mississippi statute because the state failed to provide compelling justification for disenfranchising misdemeanants. *Id.* at 976.

19. *Hunter*, 471 U.S. at 233; *see also* Allen v. Ellisor, 664 F.2d 391 (4th Cir. 1981), *vacated* 454 U.S. 807 (1981). In *Allen* the plaintiff alleged that the state legislature designated the felon disenfranchisement statute's disqualifying offenses specifically to disenfranchise African Americans. *Id.* at 392. The Fourth Circuit, while holding that the statute was not facially unconstitutional, remanded to the district court for a determination of whether the statute was adopted with the intent to discriminate. *Id.* at 399. The state amended the felon disenfranchisement statute to remove the reference to specific crimes, rendering the case moot. *See* 454 U.S. 807; S.C. CODE ANN. § 7-5-120.

20. Gooden v. Worley, No. CV-2005-5778-RSV (Cir. Ct. Ala. Aug. 23, 2006), *rev'd sub. nom.* Chapman v. Gooden, No. 1051712, 2007 WL 1576103 (Ala. June 1, 2007).

21. *Id.* at 11–12.

22. Thiess v. State Admin. Bd. Election Law, 387 F. Supp. 1038, 1043 (D. Md. 1974).

23. Williams v. Taylor, 677 F.2d 510, 516 (5th Cir. 1982).

24. *Id.* at 516–17.

25. *See, e.g.*, Wesley v. Collins, 605 F. Supp. 802 (M.D. Tenn. 1985), *aff'd*, 791 F.2d 1255 (6th Cir. 1986); Johnson v. Governor of Florida, 405 F.3d 1214 (11th Cir. 2005) (en banc), *cert. denied sub nom.* Johnson v. Bush, 126 S. Ct. 650 (2005); Hayden v. Pataki, 449 F.3d 305 (2d Cir. 2006) (en banc); Farrakhan v. Washington, 338 F.3d 1009 (9th Cir. 2003), *cert. denied sub nom.* Farrakhan v. Locke, 543 U.S. 984 (2004), *on remand*, 2006 WL 1889273 (E.D. Wash. Jul. 7, 2006) (granting summary judgment for defendants).

26. *See* Thornburg v. Gingles, 478 U.S. 30 (1986). Section 2 of the Voting Rights Act is violated "where the 'totality of the circumstances' reveal that . . . 'members [of a protected class] have less opportunity than other members of the electorate to participate in the political process and to elect representatives of their choice,'" regardless of evidence of discriminatory intent. *Id.* at 43. The Supreme Court recited a number of factors relevant to a "totality of the circumstances" analysis based on a Senate Report accompanying the 1982 amendments to the Act. *Id.* These factors include:

> [T]he history of voting-related discrimination in the State or political subdivision; the extent to which voting in the elections of the State or political subdivision is racially polarized; the extent to which the State or political subdivision has used voting practices or procedures that tend to enhance the opportunity for discrimination against the minority group . . . ; the extent to which minority group members bear the effects of past discrimination in areas such as education, employment, and health, which hinder their ability to participate effectively in the political process; the use of overt or subtle racial appeals in political campaigns; and the extent to which members of the minority group have been elected to public office in the jurisdiction.

Id. at 44–45.

27. The Sixth and Ninth Circuits have held that the Voting Rights Act is applicable to felon disenfranchisement laws, but have dismissed the cases on the merits. *Wesley*, 791 F.2d 1255; *Farrakhan*, 338 F.3d 1009. The Second and 11th Circuits, in closely divided en banc opinions, have held that that Voting Rights Act is inapplicable. *Hayden*, 449 F.3d 305; *Johnson*, 405 F.3d 1214.

28. *Bush*, 126 S. Ct. 650; *Farrakhan*, 543 U.S. 984; Muntaqim v. Coombe, 543 U.S. 984 (2004).

29. 42 U.S.C. § 1983(a).

30. Wesley v. Collins, 605 F. Supp. 802 (M.D. Tenn. 1985), *aff'd*, 791 F.2d 1255 (6th Cir. 1986).

31. *Id.* at 813.

32. Baker v. Pataki, 85 F.3d 919 (2d Cir. 1996) (en banc).

33. Hayden v. Pataki, 449 F.3d 305 (2d Cir. 2006). Another case, Muntaqim v. Coombe, 449 F.3d 371 (2d Cir. 2006) that had been consolidated with *Hayden* for oral argument before the en banc court was dismissed for lack of standing.

34. *Hayden*, 449 F.3d at 322–23.

35. *Id.*

36. *Id.* at 326.

37. *Id.* at 346.

38. *Id.* at 357.

39. *Farrakhan*, 338 F.3d 1009.

40. *Id.* at 1016.

41. *Id.* at 1020.

42. *Farrakhan*, 2006 WL 1889273, at *7–*9 (E.D. Wash. July 7, 2006).

43. *Id.* at *8.

44. Johnson v. Governor of Fla., 405 F.3d 1214 (11th Cir. 2005) (en banc), *cert. denied sub. nom.* Johnson v. Bush, 126 S. Ct. 650 (2005).

45. *Id.* at 1224.

46. *Id.* at 1234.

47. *Id.*

48. *Id.*

49. U.S. CONST. art. 1, §2, cl. 1.

50. *Hayden,* 449 F.3d 305; *Johnson,* 405 F.3d 1214.

51. City of Boerne v. Flores, 521 U.S. 507, 519 (1997).

52. *Id.* at 530–31.

53. Nev. Dept. of Human Resources v. Hibbs, 538 U.S. 721, 727 (2003).

54. Tennessee v. Lane, 124 S. Ct. 1978, 1986 (2004).

55. *Hibbs,* 538 U.S. at 728 (quoting Kimel v. Fla. Bd. of Regents, 528 U.S. 62, 88 (2000)).

56. Oregon v. Mitchell, 400 U.S. 112 (1970).

57. 42 U.S.C. § 1973gg-6(g).

58. *See* United States v. Lewis, 10 F.3d 1086 (4th Cir. 1993) (approving the use of voter registration lists as a means of random jury selection even if minorities are underrepresented on those lists due to a "history of discrimination"); *see also* United States v. Johnson, 973 F. Supp. 1111, 1113 (D. Neb. 1997) ("This court has long used voter registration lists as the means of forming its jury pool, and this practice is specifically contemplated by [The Jury Selection Act,] 28 U.S.C. § 1863.").

59. United States v. Arce, 997 F.2d 1123 (5th Cir. 1993). *Accord* United States v. Greene, 995 F.2d 793 (8th Cir. 1993); United States v. Foxworth, 599 F.2d 1 (1st Cir. 1979).

60. *Arce,* 997 F.2d at 1127.

61. *Greene,* 995 F.2d at 796.

62. *Id.*

63. *Id.* Section 1864(b)(5) has been held not to violate the Sixth Amendment's fair cross-section requirement. To make a prima facie case for a constitutional violation under this amendment, a defendant must show: (1) the group excluded is a distinctive part of the community; (2) the group's representation in the jury pool is not fair and reasonable in relation to the number of these groups in the community; and (3) the underrepresentation is the result of a systematic exclusion from jury selection. Duren v. Missouri, 439 U.S. 357 (1979). The court in United States v. Best upheld the constitutionality of the statute on Sixth Amendment grounds, asserting that barring convicted felons is not a constitutional violation even if a disproportionate number of African Americans were disenfranchised. 214 F. Supp. 2d 897 (N.D. Ind. 2002). The court quoted the Seventh Circuit, which had earlier held that "if blacks are underrepresented on the jury list because of legitimate juror qualifications, such as age, then the . . . jury selection system does not unconstitutionally exclude blacks." *Id.* at 903 (quoting Davis v. Warden, Joliet Corr. Inst. at Stateville, 867 F.2d 1003, 1015 (7th Cir. 1989)).

64. *See* Petition to the Inter-American Commission on Human Rights for a Thematic Hearing on Felony Disenfranchisement Practices in the United States and the Americas

16–17, *available at* http://www.sentencingproject.org/Admin%5CDocuments%5Cnews% 5Cfd_PETITION%20TO%20IACHR_final_formatted.pdf [hereinafter Petition to the Inter-American Comm'n]. For example, in Seychelles, the government permanently disenfranchises all individuals who are sentenced to prison. *Id.* at 7. Jordan permanently disenfranchises anyone sentenced to one year or more in prison. Law of Election to the House of Deputies, Law No. 22 for the Year 1986. Tonga permanently disenfranchises individuals sentenced to two years or more in prison. CONST. TONGA art. 23. In the Dominican Republic, permanent disenfranchisement is reserved for crimes against the state. CONST. DOMINICAN Rep. art. 14.

65. Petition to the Inter-American Comm'n at 12. Chilean courts are permitted to disenfranchise individuals convicted of committing crimes against the state for a ten-year time period. CONST. CHILE art. 8. In the Philippines, persons sentenced to a prison term of one year or more are barred from voting for a period of five years. Petition to the Inter-American Comm'n at 14.

66. *See, e.g.*, Bundeswahlgesetz [Election Code] § 12, ¶ 4, third sentence. Some countries limit those incarcerated individuals who may vote based on the length of their sentence or the category of crime for which convicted. For example, New Zealand suspends the right to vote of prisoners serving sentences of (1) imprisonment for life, (2) preventative detention, or (3) imprisonment for three years or more. Electoral Act 1993, § 80(1). Guyana disenfranchises persons incarcerated for electoral offenses, GUYANA CONST. art. 159, § 4; Chile disenfranchises those incarcerated for committing crimes against the state, CONST. CHILE art. 8.

67. Sauve v. Canada (Chief Electoral Officer) [2002] 3 S.C.R. 519 (Can.); Hirst v. United Kingdom (No. 2), 38 Eur. H.R. Rep. 40 (Eur. Ct. H.R. 2004); Nat'l Inst. for Crime Prevention and the Reintegration of Offenders (NICRO), Erasmus & Schwagerl v. Minister of Home Affairs, CCT 3/04 (S. Afr., 2004).

68. *Sauve,* [2002] 3 S.C.R. 519.

69. *Nat'l Inst. for Crime Prevention,* CCT 3/04.

70. *Id.*

71. *Hirst,* 38 Eur. H.R. Rep. 40.

72. *Roach v. Electoral Comm'r* [2007] HCA 43; 81 ALJR 1830; 2007 WL 2774526 (30 Aug. 2007).

73. Petition to the Inter-American Comm'n, *supra* note 63.

74. NAT'L COMM'N ON FED. ELECTION REFORM, FINAL REPORT 45 (Aug. 2001), *available at* http://www.reformelections.org/ncfer.asp#finalreport.

CHAPTER SEVEN

SECTION 5 AND THE VOTING RIGHTS ACT
REAUTHORIZATION AND
AMENDMENTS ACT OF 2006

ABIGAIL THERNSTROM*

I. Introduction: The Rush to the VRARA

Most politicians cannot risk raising questions about civil rights protections already in place. And thus, with scarcely any debate, in the summer of 2006 Congress passed the Fannie Lou Hamer, Rosa Parks, and Coretta Scott King Voting Rights Act Reauthorization and Amendments Act (VRARA), which amended and extended Section 5 of the Voting Rights Act (VRA), giving it a new expiration date of 2031.[1] In the House of Representatives the vote on July 13 was 390 to 33, with many of the small band of opponents objecting primarily to a bilingual ballot requirement, arguably the least important of the issues on the table. A week later, the vote in the Senate was 98–0.

The president quickly signed the bill into law on July 27—not even waiting for the occasion of the 41st anniversary of the 1965 Voting Rights Act just ten days later. A signing ceremony on, say, the Edmund Pettis Bridge would have been symbolically arresting, but the president chose haste over political splash. Altogether it was a rush job. Section 5 and other temporary provisions of the Voting Rights Act were not due to expire until 12 months later.

Almost no debate, little dissent, and a president painfully eager for some good press: what a sad tale of censored and self-censored questions about an enormously complicated issue. The 1965 statute was passed in the context of massive black disenfranchisement. Four decades later, America is racially unrecognizable. A revolution in the status of blacks and the state of race relations has occurred.[2] African American voters are important political players with the power to make or break Democratic candidates. Was Section 5, the most draconian of the temporary

---

* Senior fellow at the Manhattan Institute for Policy Research; Vice-chair of the U.S. Commission on Civil Rights.

provisions, still essential in 2006 and well beyond? The question surely demanded serious consideration.

II. The Original Logic of the Preclearance Provision

America had changed by 2006 and so had the Voting Rights Act. In order to explore the legitimacy of the latest extension and amendment of Section 5, it is important to go back to the original structure and logic of the preclearance provision. It was only the shocking circumstances of egregious 15th Amendment violations that initially justified the unprecedented federal intrusion on traditional state prerogatives. In 1965, the act's constitutionality depended both on the emergency of southern blacks still kept from the polls and on a flawless design that perfectly targeted for preclearance only those states that deserved to be in federal receivership with respect to their election procedures. The obvious question, then, is whether a much-altered setting—and indeed, an amended design—continues to support such an extraordinary provision.

In the original statute, every provision was designed to attack the clear moral wrong of deliberate disenfranchisement in the Jim Crow South. It had both permanent and temporary sections. Section 2, the act's permanent opening provision, restated in stronger language the promise of the 15th Amendment, while Section 3 gave federal courts permanent authority to appoint "examiners" (registrars) or observers where necessary to guarantee 14th and 15th Amendments voting rights. Those federal officers could be sent to any jurisdiction in the nation.

The temporary provisions of the act—essential to making the statute the effective instrument for racial change that it was—constituted emergency action. Section 4 contained a statistical trigger designed to identify the states and counties targeted for federal intervention. No southern state was singled out by name. Instead, jurisdictions that met two criteria—the use of a literacy test and total voter turnout (black and white) below 50 percent in the 1964 presidential election—were "covered."

Literacy tests were constitutional, the Supreme Court had held in 1959, but the framers of the act knew the South was using fraudulent tests to stop blacks from registering. Thus, those who drafted the legislation took the well-established relationship between literacy tests and low voter political participation in the South, and used the carefully selected 50 percent turnout figure as circumstantial evidence indicating the use of intentionally disenfranchising tests. They chose the 50 percent cutoff by working backwards—knowing which states were determined to maintain white political supremacy and then looking at political participation figures. That point is extremely important because subsequent amendments would "update" the trigger using turnout figures for later presidential elections, which bore no relation to a known history of deliberate disenfranchisement. Thus the list of covered jurisdictions came to include many that were arbitrarily targeted.

From the inferred presence of egregious and *intentional* 15th Amendment violations in the states that had a literacy test and low voter turnout, important consequences followed. Literacy tests in the covered jurisdictions were suspended and, without needing judicial approval (mandated by Section 3) but at the discretion of the Attorney General, federal "examiners" and observers could be sent to monitor elections. In addition, Section 5 stopped those covered states and counties identified by the statistical trigger in Section 4 from instituting any new voting procedure in the absence of prior federal "preclearance."[3] Only changes that were shown to be nondiscriminatory could be approved.

The point of Section 5 was thus to reinforce the suspension of literacy tests. Section 4 (the statistical trigger) identified jurisdictions that required emergency intervention. Preclearance made sure the effect of that ban stuck. It was a prophylactic measure—a means of guarding against renewed disenfranchisement, renewed efforts to stop blacks from registering and voting. As such, it was unique in American law. As voting rights scholar Richard L. Hasen has noted, "Never before (or since) has a state or local jurisdiction needed permission from the federal government to put its own laws into effect."[4] It "stands alone in American history in its alteration of authority between the federal government and the states. . . ." University of Pennsylvania law professor Nathan Persily has written.[5] Moreover, although not made explicit, it was crafted to hit only one region of the country—another "never before." And in asking permission to alter an electoral rule or practice, covered states carried the burden of proving their innocence.

Attorney General Katzenbach briefly explained the need for such a harsh and targeted provision prior to the passage of the act. "Our experience in the areas that would be covered by this bill," he said, "has been such as to indicate frequently on the part of state legislatures a desire in a sense to outguess the courts . . . or even to outguess the Congress . . ."[6] Banishing southern literacy tests might not suffice; new disenfranchising devices could be created.

But for changes in voting procedure to be rejected, Katzenbach noted, they would have to have the effect of denying the rights guaranteed by the 15th Amendment.[7] And numerous witnesses at the hearings reassured their audience that those rights, which the entire purpose of the act was designed to secure, were expected to be narrowly defined. Thus Roy Wilkins, executive director of the NAACP, spoke of the need to protect the citizen "from the beginning of the registration process until his vote has been cast and counted."[8]

That narrow definition of disenfranchisement could not survive long. Already in 1964, in *Reynolds v. Sims*, the Supreme Court had concluded that "[t]he right to suffrage can be denied by a debasement or dilution of the weight of a citizen's vote just as effectively as by wholly prohibiting the free exercise of the franchise."[9] Inevitably, the one-person, one-vote decisions, with their redefinition of disenfranchisement to include dilution, had an impact on the Court's interpretation of Section 5 of the Voting Rights Act as well.

In addition, both a surge in southern black registration and a change in civil rights sensibilities shifted attention from access to results. By roughly 1970, in employment, contracting, and education the commitment to pure antidiscrimination law had been replaced by a new emphasis on racially just outcomes. With respect to voting, the mere freedom to register and cast a ballot had come to be seen as securing formal, but not substantive, equality. Civil rights advocates wanted policies that promised to put blacks in legislative office. Thus Section 5 became a means of guarding against efforts to diminish the political strength of the new black vote in racially suspect states and counties, as well as a device to stop new, inventive efforts to keep blacks from the polls.

As a consequence, at-large voting, annexations, redistricting, and other changes that had the potential to dilute black ballots became subject to federal preclearance. (Annexations that increase the proportion of whites in a city may diminish the power of the minority vote.) But the notion of protecting African American citizens from southern racism—the notion at the core of the 1965 statute—was not lost as long as Section 5 applied only to the states that were identified by the original trigger for coverage embedded in Section 4.

III. Changing the Trigger, Losing the Logic

A. THE 1970 AND 1975 AMENDMENTS

The statistical trigger was amended, however, in 1970 and again in 1975. And, as a consequence, the clean lines and logical structure of the original act were lost. In 1965 the preclearance provision was scheduled to sunset in five years; at the time, such intrusive federal power, were it to last any longer, seemed constitutionally questionable. And yet once the legitimacy of the act was firmly established,[10] amendments that extended and strengthened the emergency provisions were passed with relative ease.

Thus, in 1970 both Sections 4 and 5 (the two being inseparable) were renewed for another five years; literacy tests were banned nationwide for that same period; and coverage was expanded to include states and counties that employed such tests and in which voter turnout in 1968 was less than 50 percent. [11]

The change in the trigger—the use of the 1968 turnout figures—extended the geographical reach of federal authority, giving the act a more national cast. Jurisdictions covered in 1965 (on the basis of voter participation in 1964) would remain covered—even if turnout had subsequently risen to above 50 percent. But they would now be joined by three boroughs in New York City that had a literacy test but no history of black disenfranchisement and by other scattered counties.

Turnout in those New York boroughs (but not the city's other two) had dropped a few percentage points in the low-turnout 1968 presidential election, and thus the trigger identified them as racially suspect and subject to preclearance.

In 1975 Section 5 was again both renewed and amended. The renewal was for seven years in order to ensure federal oversight over redistricting in the covered jurisdictions after the 1980 census. The trigger was updated to rest on turnout figures in the 1972 presidential election as well, and the national ban on literacy tests was made permanent. In addition, the definition of a literacy test was expanded to include English-only election materials, which were equated with fraudulent southern tests that barred blacks from the polls. The formula for Section 5 coverage became low voter participation and the use of ballots (or other voting material) provided only in English where more than 5 percent of the voting-age citizenry were members of a single "language minority" group. As a result, Texas, Arizona, and Alaska in their entirety and counties in South Dakota, Michigan, Florida, and California were added to the list of jurisdictions subject to Section 5.

And yet, surely if English-only ballots were "disenfranchising," bilingual election materials were a sufficient remedy. Moreover, while the southern commitment to keeping blacks from the polls had made Section 5 necessary in 1965, the absence of bilingual election materials in the Southwest, Alaska, and elsewhere did not suggest equivalent racism. Finally, while the 1965 statute had mentioned no group explicitly (although the disenfranchisement of blacks was the obvious concern) in 1975 four groups were specifically named: Asian Americans, Alaskan Natives, American Indians, and persons of Spanish heritage. The list was never explained; at the congressional hearings there was almost no discussion of discrimination involving any group other than Mexican Americans.

B. THE 1982 EXTENSION

In 1982 Congress voted a straight 25-year extension of Section 5, leaving unchanged the reliance on the 1972 turnout figures to determine coverage. Remarkably, those political participation data, now more than 30 years out of date, are still today the basis upon which preclearance coverage is determined, although some of the states and counties covered had no history of disenfranchisement and many of those in the South now have high rates of black political participation. Section 5 coverage has thus become increasingly arbitrary over the decades.

With the 1982 extension, the expiration date became 2007. It was that pending expiration, of course, that prompted congressional action a year early, as described at the outset of this article. The emergency that made Section 5 so essential in 1965 is long over, and yet the emergency powers bestowed by the act have been greatly expanded and are now assured a life of 66 years unless Congress revisits the 2006 statute.

C. THE CHANGING FOCUS OF SECTION 5: FROM DISENFRANCHISEMENT TO INCREASED PROTECTION

As already indicated, as early as 1970 ensuring basic disenfranchisement ceased to be the focus of Section 5. Newly instituted at-large voting, annexations, and revised districting maps that fragmented minority voting strength—changes in the electoral setting that left minority voters with less than their "full" electoral power—became the central concern of civil rights advocates. The desire to extend preclearance to all new districting plans and annexations in Texas was the chief motivation behind the 1975 amendments. The point of the 1975 amendments—unlike that of the 1965 act—was not access to the polls for citizens disenfranchised in clear violation of the 15th Amendment, but increased protection for minority candidates through the advantageous drawing of single-member districts. In 1965 Section 5 was a means of reinforcing the suspension of the literacy tests; in 1975 the definition of literacy tests was expanded to secure in Texas and elsewhere the benefit of protection against vote dilution that preclearance brought.

But protection against vote "dilution" required a definition of an undiluted vote. And, as Justice O'Connor acknowledged in 1986, "any theory of vote dilution must necessarily rely to some extent on a measure of minority voting strength that makes some reference to the proportion between the minority group and the electorate at large."[12] That point was forthrightly recognized in the preclearance decisions involving annexations, which are viewed as "voting changes" since they have the potential to alter the balance of power between racial and ethnic groups in a city. An annexation will not be precleared unless the municipality elects its governing legislative body from single-member districts drawn to provide roughly proportional racial representation.[13]

IV. Redistricting Cases

A. *BEER:* TESTING FOR RETROGRESSION

Redistricting cases are quite different from annexation decisions. In *Beer v. United States* (1976),[14] the Supreme Court held that Section 5 barred changes that would result in a "retrogression in the position of racial minorities with respect to their effective exercise of the electoral franchise."[15] The decision squared with the prophylactic purpose of the provision, and relegated to actors remote from the scene—the D.C. court and Department of Justice—a limited, and thus manageable, task: preventing backsliding.

Section 5 by 1976 was no longer confined to the South with its terrible history of black disenfranchisement; it was no longer a response to the emergency of continuing and pervasive 15th Amendment violations; the logic of the both elements of the trigger (low voter turnout and the use of traditional literacy test) was gone;

but, at least with respect to the preclearance of districting plans, *Beer* retained the core idea of making sure that a new method of election did not leave blacks with fewer legislative seats and thus less political power than they had previously possessed. Both the U.S. Department of Justice and the D.C. court disliked *Beer* and its retrogression test from the outset. The decision allowed jurisdictions to maintain the status quo, even when that meant sticking with two majority-minority districts where, in fact, four could be drawn. Or zero, when at least one could be drawn. In its *Brief for the United States,* the attorney general had argued that alternative New Orleans maps would contain more majority-black districts, and the submitted plan should not be precleared.[16] In subsequent years, the DOJ continued to insist on "fairly drawn" districting plans—districting plans that promoted proportional racial and ethnic officeholding—and while the Supreme Court reaffirmed the *Beer* test in a 1983 decision,[17] as of 2000, at least, four Justices remained convinced that "the Court was mistaken in *Beer.*"[18]

B. *BOSSIER I:* SEPARATING SECTIONS 2 AND 5

That sense of a "mistaken" interpretation informed DOJ enforcement of Section 5 in the 1980s and even more markedly, in the 1990s. The provision protects against changes in electoral procedure that have the "effect" or "purpose" of "denying or abridging the right to vote on account of race or color." Retrogression was the test of discriminatory effect. But it could be ignored. Objections to submitted electoral changes could rest on other grounds: a finding of suspected discriminatory purpose, for instance. Alternatively, the attorney general could conclude that the new method of election violated Section 2 of the act, which "allowed a finding that voting rights had been violated if "the totality of circumstances" showed that the "political processes . . . [were] not equally open" to blacks and Hispanics.

The two provisions—Sections 5 and 2—were miles apart. Section 5 required a before-and-after comparison. Had the proposed change in the method of voting left minority voters worse off, relative to what they had been before? Section 2, on the other hand, demanded a complicated assessment of the electoral environment—the setting in which voting took place. Have minority voters had, in some absolute sense, an equal electoral "opportunity"? Nevertheless, in 1987 Justice Department guidelines for administrating Section 5 were issued, incorporating Section 2 standards into Section 5 so that a suspected violation of the Section 2 "results" test was also read as a finding of discriminatory "effect," prohibited by Section 5.[19] The decision to allow preclearance objections to rest on the unprecedented ground that they violated Section 2 of the act was a change not sanctioned by either the actual language of Section 5 or the congressional record preceding the revision of Section 2.[20]

The incorporation of Section 2 standards into the preclearance provision came to an end in 1997, when in *Reno v. Bossier Parish* (*Bossier I*)[21] the Supreme Court put a stop to the pretense that Section 5 had been implicitly rewritten in 1982. Sections 5 and 2 "combat different evils" and thus "impose very different duties upon the States," Justice O'Connor concluded. Were we to hold otherwise, she went on, "compliance with § 5 [would become] contingent upon compliance with § 2." The standards for Section 2 would replace those of Section 5.[22]

That is, "retrogression, by definition, requires a comparison of a jurisdiction's new voting plan with its existing plan . . . [while] the very concept of vote dilution implies—indeed, necessitates—the existence of an 'undiluted' practice against which the fact of dilution may be measured." Any other reading would "shift the focus of § 5 from nonretrogression to vote dilution, and . . . change the § 5 benchmark from a jurisdiction's existing plan to a hypothetical, undiluted plan."[23] Of course, the hypothetical could only be a plan ensuring minority officeholding in proportion to the black population—a point Justice Breyer's dissent explicitly acknowledged.[24]

C. *BOSSIER II:* DEFINING "DISCRIMINATORY PURPOSE"

Three years later, in *Bossier Parish II,*[25] for the first time the Supreme Court addressed the definition of discriminatory purpose in Section 5. Could the Justice Department refuse to preclear a submitted districting plan on the ground that the jurisdiction's failure to draw a "better" map—i.e., one that provided a maximum number of majority-minority districts—might suggest discriminatory purpose? It is important to recall that, under Section 5, suspicion is enough to sink a plan; the burden of proof is on the state or county to prove an absence of discrimination.

Under Section 5, only districting plans that are intentionally retrogressive violate the ban on purposeful discrimination, Justice Scalia wrote for the Court. Appellants, he said, would recast Section 5's phrase "'does not have the purpose and will not have the effect of x' to read 'does not have the purpose of y and will not have the effect of x.'"[26] They "refuse to accept the limited meaning that we have said preclearance has in the vote-dilution context." A precleared plan, whether the question is discriminatory purpose or effect, is only "a determination that the voting change is no more dilutive than what it replaces, and therefore cannot be stopped in advance under the extraordinary burden-shifting procedure of § 5, but must be attacked through the normal means of a § 2 action."[27]

The civil rights community regarded *Bossier Parish II* as a devastating blow to the enforcement of Section 5. The Court, in its view, had "fundamentally redefined—and weakened—the purpose requirement."[28] The civil rights community could live with *Bossier Parish I;* very few preclearance objections rested on a violation of Section 2, undoubtedly due in great part to the relatively difficult evidentiary demands made by the provision.[29] By contrast, a quarter of all objections in the 1980s were based on suspected discriminatory intent, and that figure rose to 43 percent in the 1990s.[30] High on the list of priorities for the civil rights community in 2006 was thus overturning *Bossier Parish II*—a point to which I will return below.

D. *ASHCROFT*: DEFINING "REPRESENTATION"

Bossier I and *II* brought an abrupt end to the enormous interpretive liberty that the Justice Department and the D.C. district court had enjoyed in interpreting Section 5 for the better part of two decades. But three years later, in *Georgia v. Ashcroft*,[31] the Supreme Court sanctioned a different sort of definitional license, which received, however, a somewhat mixed reception from the established civil rights bar.[32]

Ashcroft involved districting for the Georgia Senate. The state had gone to the D.C. court seeking a declaratory judgment that its districts did not violate Section 5.[33] A three-judge panel had refused preclearance, even though 10 out of 11 black state senators had supported the submitted map, along with 33 out of 34 black state representatives.[34] The Supreme Court vacated the judgment, and remanded the case for further consideration consistent with a fresh analysis of the retrogression standard.[35]

The plan had lowered the percentage of black voters in some districts (although not below 50 percent), but increased the number of districts certain to elect white Democrats. The Court explained the logic: "The goal of the Democratic leadership—black and white—was to maintain the number of majority-minority districts and also increase the number of Democratic Senate seats."[36] More Democratic seats would mean more black representation. "No party contests that a substantial majority of black voters in Georgia vote Democratic."[37] Excessive concentrations of black voters benefited Republicans.[38] Congressman John Lewis (as well as the black leadership in the state) had signed on to the plan, since, as Lewis put it, he believed it was "in the best interest of African American voters . . . to have a continued Democratic-controlled legislature in Georgia."[39]

Not for the first time, Justice O'Connor had become concerned that a maximum number of safe black districts did not necessarily maximize black representation, and that indeed minority "representation" was not so easy to define.[40] The Court had never "determined the meaning of 'effective exercise of the electoral franchise,'" O'Connor acknowledged.[41] Who counts as a "representative"? The Court's answer: White Democrats elected in "coalition" or "influence" districts could be considered "representative" of minority voters.[42] "Coalition" districts were those under 50 percent black in which black voters could nevertheless elect their candidates of choice by forming reliable coalitions with members of other racial and ethnic groups.[43] An "influence" district was one in which minority voters "may not be able to elect a candidate of choice but can play a substantial, if not decisive, role in the electoral process," thereby ensuring attention to their interests.[44] There were other factors to be weighed, such as the leadership positions held by white incumbents who had been supported by black voters.

"The power to influence the electoral process is not limited to winning elections," O'Connor continued.[45] Section 5 gives states drawing legislative districts the flexibility to choose substantive over descriptive representation—the freedom to place more importance on the likely sensitivity of elected officials to minority interests than on their racial identity. The provision thus allows districting plans designed to increase the number of white Democrats although the cost might be seats previously totally safe for black incumbents.[46] It was a risk, however, that the black majority leader of the Democratic-controlled senate and the black chairman of the redistricting subcommittee had been willing to take.[47] About a third of the Democratic legislators were black, as was the state attorney general who defended the plan in court. The logic behind the support of these powerful black politicians was clear. They were worried that Georgia was tipping Republican, as indeed it began to do with the election in 2002 of the first Republican governor since 1868, followed in 2004 with the victory of both GOP candidates for the U.S. Senate. A greater dispersion of black voters could help elect more white Democrats, they believed.[48]

"*Georgia v. Ashcroft* may be a dubious piece of jurisprudence," Robert Bauer, a Democratic Party operative, wrote on a blog site devoted to commentary on regulating the political process.[49] "But there is something there worth taking seriously, which is respect for politics—for 'horse-trading' and the like by those elected to do precisely that and to answer for it." [50] Bauer made an important point. *Ashcroft* had flaws, but it was a blow for political sense. The Court had recognized that the normal districting process involves a complicated weighing of numerous political objectives.[51]

The Court in *Ashcroft* had said (in effect), let legislators be legislators. And let black legislators make the deals they see as politically beneficial to their constituents. If they agree to a plan that protects white Democrats, they are politicians, not "Uncle Toms." In 1965 politics as usual in a state like Georgia could not be trusted, but the entire black establishment had been a partner in the post-2000 redistricting process.

There was a fundamental problem with the Court's message, however: It was at odds with the core of the Voting Rights Act, the whole point of which had been to deny covered jurisdictions the privilege of running their own political shop. Distrust of the South was the foundation on which the temporary, emergency provisions in the 1965 act had been built. And that distrust still ran very deep among civil rights advocates.

There was another difficulty. If a federal law guaranteeing minority voters "the ability to elect the candidates of their choice" was still essential in 2003, *Ashcroft* was no guide. It provided no coherent legal standards to govern an inevitably limited administrative preclearance process. It tried to solve one definitional problem (the unsettled meaning of the "effective exercise of the electoral franchise") only to create others. When was an "influence" district influential?[52] When did a white incumbent hold committee or other legislative power invaluable to black constituents? With *Ashcroft,* Justice Potter Stewart's famous definition of pornography applied equally to the question of minority representation: Judges and DOJ attorneys were expected to know it when they saw it.[53]

V. The Redistricting Cases and the 2006 Amendments

The amendments to Section 5 in 2006 were driven by the reaction of the civil rights community to the decisions in *Bossier II* and *Ashcroft.* As early as the 1970s, preclearance had begun to emerge as an instrument to redistribute political power among racial and ethnic groups in order to ensure racially fair representation—"fairness" being defined as proportional racial and ethnic officeholding to the degree that race-conscious districting maps could provide it. But that rewriting process greatly accelerated in the 1980s and 1990s. In the latter decade, particularly, the Justice Department rested Section 5 objections mainly on a freewheeling definition of discriminatory purpose (with violations of Section 2 as an alternative). Thus, a failure to create the maximum number of majority-minority districts when redrawing a legislative map after a decennial census was treated as evidence of suspicious intent.[54]

The Supreme Court's two *Bossier* decisions reinstated retrogression as Section 5's definition of discriminatory effect. Once again, the question became whether the proposed new map left minority voters with less political power than they previously had. Other maps might provide more safe majority-minority districts, but an entitlement to a more racially "just" plan was a matter for federal courts to sort out in Section 2 or 14th Amendment cases. Ensuring racial equity in some absolute sense was not the purpose of Section 5, and such decisions were, in any case, beyond the limited capacity of DOJ attorneys tasked with administrative preclearance. Inevitably, their knowledge of the submitted jurisdiction was crude and the 60-day time constraint imposed by the statute put the resolution of complicated questions involving the balance of power between white and minority voters under one districting plan versus another beyond their reach.

Neither suspected discriminatory purpose (very broadly defined) nor Section 2 could be used as the basis of Section 5 objections after 2000. But in 2003 *Ashcroft* gave the Justice Department a new framework within which to assess a fair distribution of minority and white political power. DOJ attorneys could weigh the varying effectiveness of coalition, influence, or safe majority-minority districts, as well as the legislative power of a white incumbent in preserving minority representation in a revised plan. Whatever its virtues, however, *Ashcroft* blurred the distinction between retrogression and racial equity anew. It asked the Justice Department to weigh extremely complex matters having to do with nature of representation—matters normally and properly decided by state legislators engaged in redistricting—with the burden of proving nondiscrimination still on the submitting jurisdiction. Only the emergency of 15th Amendment disenfranchisement had justified substituting the judgment of federal attorneys for that of state political actors. *Ashcroft* revived the question of the constitutional legitimacy of preclearance.

The 2006 amendments to Section 5 overturned *Ashcroft,* but the rejection of that decision did not answer critics who questioned whether a statute intended to enfranchise southern blacks kept from the polls more than four decades ago was still on solid constitutional ground. The emergency of black disenfranchisement that legitimized unprecedented federal power over state and local electoral affairs in 1965 had been declared likely to last at least another quarter century.

"Significant progress" had been made, the VRARA acknowledged. "However, vestiges of discrimination continue to exist . . . [that] prevent minority voters from fully participating in the electoral process." Protecting the right to "full" participation—to casting "meaningful votes"—was the stated purpose of the act.[55]

"Despite the progress made by minorities under the Voting Rights Act of 1965," the statutory language continued, "the evidence before Congress reveals that 40 years has not been a sufficient amount of time to eliminate the vestiges of discrimination following nearly 100 years of disregard for the dictates of the 15th amendment. . . ." Election practices such as "annexation, at-large voting, and the use of multimember districts" have been "enacted to dilute minority voting strength."[56] Interestingly, no mention is made in the statutory list of single-member districting plans that crack or pack minority voters, even though districting maps that fail to maximize minority officeholding have been a chief complaint in civil rights circles. Presumably, those who drafted the statute recognized the danger of an implicit endorsement of proportional racial and ethnic representation.

One might assume, on the basis of the statutory language as well as the House report, that these were still problems serious enough to justify a 25-year extension of extraordinary protection against deliberate 15th Amendment violations. Deliberate disenfranchisement was, of course, the sole rationale for the extraordinarily intrusive federal power built into the act. In fact, between 1995 and 2004, there were a total of only 46 objections to districting changes and 31 to "methods of election" (a category that includes at-large voting and multimember districts). Even those numbers are inflated, since many of the objections were based on suspicion of discriminatory purpose, with purpose given the broad definition that the Court struck down in *Bossier II* in 2000. And, before *Bossier I* in 1997, some were based on findings of Section 2 violations.

If these numbers suggest that the obstacles to political participation that justified Section 5 in 1965 are still with us, at what point would the evidence suggest the era of disenfranchisement is over? And how did Congress arrive at its pessimistic conclusion that preclearance would still be needed for the first third of the 21st century?

In the decades since 1964, Hispanics have been increasingly assimilated into mainstream American society[57] and there has been a revolution in the status of blacks and the state of race relations. Congressman John Lewis recognized the new reality in Georgia in his deposition in *Ashcroft*. "There has been a transformation. It's a different state, it's a different political climate, it's a different political environment. It's altogether a different world we live in, really," he said. And he went on: "We've come a great distance . . . [I]t's not just in Georgia, but in the American South, I think people are preparing to lay down the burden of race."[58]

The pessimism that Congress embraced in passing the 2006 statute—in sharp contrast both to the hard data on racial progress and to Congressman Lewis's celebration of that change—arguably carries a heavy cost. The denial of racial change potentially locks the Justice Department and the D.C. District Court into too narrow a definition of minority representation. When the white South feared black voices, it was legitimate to assume that only black voices could represent black interests. By now, such an assumption is not only woefully out of date, it may skew the whole districting process in ways that do not serve minority voters well, as the Supreme Court suggested in *Ashcroft*. "[T]he maximization of majority-minority districts in Georgia 'artificially push[ed] the percentage of black voters within some majority black districts as high as possible,'" the Court noted. Wasting black votes was the consequence.

A. AN EVEN MURKIER PROVISION

The 25-year extension of Section 5 in the face of transformative racial change, particularly in the South, thus raises legitimate questions about the constitutionality of the emergency provisions—questions that have not be seriously contemplated for four decades. Was there still a "congruence and proportionality between the injury to be prevented or remedied and the means adopted to that end"?[59] Numerous witnesses at the 2006 congressional hearings expressed doubts about the constitutionality of the proposed extension for 25 years—a number for which there was no particular justification. The group included a number of distinguished law professors specializing in voting rights. As Daniel Tokaji, professor of law at the Ohio State University's Moritz College of Law, pointed out in May 2006: "Among the most striking aspects of the discussions of VRA renewal . . . [was] the significant divide that appear[ed] to exist between the civil rights and scholarly communities over Section 5 of the VRA."[60]

Overturning *Bossier II* and *Ashcroft* has also made a murky provision even more difficult to understand and enforce. The language intended to assuage the anger over *Bossier II* explicitly separated "purpose" and "effect" in Section 5—giving each term a distinct meaning. Election-related changes deny or abridge the right to vote if they have either the purpose or effect of "diminishing the ability of any citizens of the United States on account of race or color . . . to elect their preferred candidates of choice." And while "effect" still refers to retrogressive impact, "purpose" is defined as "any discriminatory purpose."

Was the Justice Department now free to return to its pre-*Bossier II* use of suspected discriminatory purpose to object to every districting plan that seemed racially unfair by the measure of safe minority seats in rough proportion to the population? A series of 14th Amendment Supreme Court decisions[61] had put a stop to the most egregious forms of racial gerrymandering in the service of maximizing black and Hispanic officeholding, but those rulings stopped far short of declaring race-driven districting (of a slightly more subtle sort) unconstitutional.[62] With the passage of the VRARA, what sort of renewed pressure could the Justice Department bring on jurisdictions to "improve" on their submitted districting maps?

The statutory language and the accompanying congressional reports are both opaque. *Beer* was still controlling, both the House and Senate Judiciary Committee Reports on the VRARA stated plainly.[63] The House report described *Ashcroft* as having allowed "the minority community's own choice of preferred candidates to be trumped by political deals struck by State legislators purporting to give 'influence' to the minority community while removing that community's ability to elect candidates."[64] The notion of an "influence" district was too "nebulous," it stated;[65] such districts might even "effectively shut minority voters out of the political process . . . [and turn them] 'into second class voters who can influence elections of white candidates, but who cannot elect their preferred candidates, including candidates of their own race.'"[66]

Permitting trade-offs between influence and guaranteed officeholding was thus "inconsistent with the original and current purpose of Section 5."[67] The point of the provision is "to ensure . . . that gains made by minority voters over the course of decades are not eroded."[68] In other words, its purpose was to prevent backsliding, as *Beer* had held 30 years earlier. Nevertheless, unless "preferred candidates" were by definition members of the minority group (as *Beer* had assumed), the criteria by which to judge backsliding were unclear. It was even possible to interpret the new language as "*Ashcroft*-lite." Legislators could not substitute influence districts for sure-to-elect districts, but sure to elect whom? Did white candidates—which, in practice, would mean white Democrats—ever count?

The Senate Judiciary Committee Report was a bit different. "Ability to elect" districts were defined as those in which minority voters were a naturally occurring majority, while there was no such restriction mentioned in the House Report. The aim of the amendment to the Section 5 effects test, the committee said, was to "prevent the substitution of coalition or influence districts for naturally occurring majority-minority districts."[69] The "language does not protect any district with a representative who gets elected with some minority votes." Rather, it protects only compact majority-minority districts in which minority citizens are "selecting their 'preferred candidate of choice' with their own voting power."[70]

The legislation also aimed to close the door on a danger implicit in the Court's decision in *Georgia v. Ashcroft:* "increased substitution of partisan interests for the ability of minorities to elect their preferred candidates of choice."[71] Minority voters were almost all Democrats. But the legislation was not "intended to preserve or ensure the successful election of candidates of any political party—even if that party's candidates generally are supported by members of minority groups."[72] The influence districts that the *Ashcroft* Court had viewed as important to count in assessing retrogression, "if seen as a replacement for opportunities for minority voters to elect representatives of their choice, would simply become a rationale for creating Democratic Party gerrymanders."[73]

The actual statutory language left much unclear. And the different House and Senate reports (a difference that greatly irritated members of the House Judiciary Committee)[74] provided very little additional guidance. Both committees agreed on a return to *Beer,* but for most of the last 30 years, the Justice Department was resting objections on grounds other than retrogression as defined in 1976. Thus, there has been, in fact, very little experience with actually enforcing *Beer*—putting aside the point that annexation cases are judged by an entirely different standard.

VI. Section 5 Today

A. A BLANK CHECK

In important respects, the 2006 amendments of Section 5 appear to have handed the Justice Department (and the D.C. court) a blank check. The circumstances under which voting section attorneys in the civil rights division will now label electoral changes as arguably tainted by discriminatory purpose have yet to be seen. Suspicion, it cannot be emphasized too strongly, is all that is required to justify an objection. As for the meaning of discriminatory effect, all bets are off. The Democrats and Republicans on the Senate Judiciary Committee could not even agree on the definition of key terms in the amendments they voted on.

They did agree that the *Beer* standards had been revived. But, aside from the sparse administrative and judicial record of decisions that actually enforced retrogression as it was understood in 1976, there is another problem: in civil rights time, the *Beer* ruling is now ancient history. That was the point the *Ashcroft* Court understood, and that Congress rejected.

Ashcroft was an effort to fix the act to respond to dramatically altered racial conditions. The VRARA was in part an attempt to fix problems that *Ashcroft* had created. I have described the decision as a mixed bag. It lacked coherent legal standards (when were blacks in the minority nevertheless truly "influential"?), and it could not be squared with the deep distrust of the South that was so integral to the 1965 act. Indeed, Section 5 was in tatters after the decision. It substituted substantial subjectivity in judging preclearance submissions for the relatively straightforward notion of assessing the level of minority officeholding before and after a new districting map was drawn.[75]

The *Beer* Court understood that only a before-and-after comparison was appropriate to a swift and crude administrative process. And it assumed that the Justice Department (or the D.C. court) in assessing submissions for preclearance would count the number of minorities in office and the likely number after the proposed change in the method of voting. That assumption made sense as long as descriptive representation was a good gauge of the level of minority political power—as long as it was safe to say that in the South only blacks in office gave voice to black voter concerns. But that assumption was outdated by 2003 when *Ashcroft* was decided.

B. A BROKEN TRIGGER

The VRA was emergency legislation. The whole act had been built on the knowledge that in one region of the country 15th Amendment violations were rampant—indeed woven into the fabric of the political system. Preclearance had a clear purpose: stopping southern racists from finding a way around federal constraints on their racism. The legitimacy of Section 5 depended entirely on its application only to racially suspect localities, which could be rightly expected to prove their innocence before acquiring approval for voting changes.

But today, the allegations of discrimination against minority voters in 2000 and 2004 involved counties in Florida, Ohio, and elsewhere not covered by preclearance. Controlling for differences in socioeconomic and citizenship status, the South is no longer a distinctive region with respect to levels of minority and white electoral participation, as noted earlier. The trigger no longer works; racial change has obliterated the difference between states (and other jurisdictions) that are covered by Section 5 and those that are not, and thus the story contained in *Ashcroft* is one of Georgia blacks as major political players in drawing the districting map that reduced black concentration in some districts in exchange for increasing the likelihood the Democrats could hold on to the state senate. Only one black senator voted against the plan.[76]

Congress had overturned *Ashcroft,* but continuing racial change will surely force the civil rights community to deal once again with the questions that decision attempted to answer in refashioning Section 5 as a provision appropriate to the 21st century. The 2006 VRARA guarantees a "full" and "effective" vote to blacks and Hispanics. But, as *Ashcroft* had pointed out, a "full" vote, in today's context, may mean an ability to form coalitions with whites or to influence election outcomes in order to maximize Democratic officeholding. How long can voting rights advocates dismiss that idea—embraced by all but one black legislator in the Georgia senate?

VII. Conclusion: Section 5 Tomorrow

At some point, other questions that *Ashcroft* tried to answer will surely reach the Supreme Court once again. What is the measure of minority representation? How much protection from white competition do black and Hispanic candidates still need? Who counts as a candidate of choice for minority voters? Are minority voters sometimes better served when the legislative process worked as it did in Georgia with black legislators maximizing Democratic seats rather than maximizing safe black seats? The answers Congress gave in the summer of 2006—when both parties refused to acknowledge what a relic from the past Section 5 now is—may not seem so appealing down the road.

The "application of overly abstract moral or legal ideals of equality to political processes, or the institutional entrenchment of specific and static understandings of political equality at particular moments in time, can interfere with the complex, dynamic processes through which material power is organized effectively in democratic politics," Richard Pildes has written.[77] Section 5 is a perfect example of the point. In the early years, it was essential to securing black representation in the one-party, racially exclusionary South. It was not designed to adapt to the changing politics of that region, however. The Supreme Court could attempt to "modernize" the provision (*Ashcroft*), but it was a period piece, unsuited to a much more complex time in which black legislators and voters had real power in a competitive two-party context. And today, the interpretation given Section 5 in the VRARA is a brake on black participation in the politics of negotiation and trade-offs that normally characterize redistricting—a process that might entail the cost of fewer safe minority seats with the benefit of more representatives responsive to the preferences of black and Hispanic voters.

The sooner Congress or the Supreme Court revisits the preclearance provision, the better. All voters need protection from impediments to a truly democratic process, but yesterday's problems are not today's. Fresh thinking for a different time is in order.

Notes

1. Pub. L. No. 109-246, 120 Stat. 577 (codified as amended at 42 U.S.C. §§ 1973–1973bb-1 (2006).

2. For an extended examination of the changing status of blacks and changing racial attitudes, see generally STEPHAN THERNSTROM & ABIGAIL THERNSTROM, AMERICA IN BLACK AND WHITE: ONE NATION, INDIVISIBLE (1997). The data are now over a decade old, racial progress has continued apace in the years since the book was published.

3. Originally, Section 5 applied to Alabama, Georgia, Louisiana, Mississippi, South Carolina, Virginia, and most counties in North Carolina. These were the only jurisdictions identified by the Section 4 statistical trigger: low registration or turnout in the 1964 presidential election combined with the use of a literacy test. The turnout figures were the only ones of consequence, since registration could be higher than 50 percent, but if the turnout was under that figure, the trigger kicked in.

4. Richard L. Hasen, *Congressional Power to Renew Preclearance Provisions, in* THE FUTURE OF THE VOTING RIGHTS ACT 81 (David L. Epstein et al. eds., 2006).

5. *The Promise and Pitfalls of the New Voting Rights Act,* 117 YALE LAW JOURNAL, 174, 177 (November, 2007).

6. Hearings before Subcommittee No. 5 of the Committee on the Judiciary, U.S. House of Representatives, 89th Congress, 1st session on H.R. 6400 and other proposals to enforce the Fifteenth Amendment to the Constitution of the United States (1965) 60.

7. *Id.*

8. *Id* at 379.

9. Reynolds v. Sims, 377 U.S. 533, 555 (1964).

10. South Carolina v. Katzenbach, 383 U.S. 301 (1966).

11. The jurisdictions newly covered as a consequence of the 1970 amendments were four districts in Alaska, eight counties in Arizona, two counties in California, three counties in Connecticut, one county in Idaho, ten towns in New Hampshire, three counties in New York, 18 towns in Maine, nine towns in Massachusetts, and one county in Wyoming.

12. Thornburg v. Gingles, 478 U.S. 30, 84 (1986). *Thornburg* was a Section 2 case, but the point applies equally well to the Section 5 context.

13. *See* City of Petersburg, Va. v. United States, 354 F. Supp. 1021 (D.D.C., 1972); City of Richmond, Va. v. United States, 376 F. Supp 1344 (D.D.C. 1975), *rev'd,* 422 U.S. 358 (1975).

14. Beer v. United States, 425 U.S. 1310 (1976).

15. *Id.* at 141.

16. MAURICE T. CUNNINGHAM, MAXIMIZATION, WHATEVER THE COST: RACE, REDISTRICTING, AND THE DEPARTMENT OF JUSTICE 70 (2001).

17. City of Lockhart, Tex. v. United States, 559 F. Supp. 581 (1981), *rev'd,* 460 U.S. 125 (1983). *Lockhart* overturned a district court ruling that made clear the lower court's persistent commitment to subverting the high Court's test.

18. See, for instance, the dissents of Justices Stevens, Breyer, Souter, and Ginsburg in Reno v. Bossier Parish Sch. Bd. (*Bossier II*), 528 U.S. 320, 342 (2000) in which all four concur that "the Court was mistaken in *Beer* when it restricted the effect prong of § 5 to retrogression."

19. Department of Justice, 28 C.F.R. Part 51 Procedures for the Administration of Section 5 of the Voting Rights Act of 1965. The revision of procedures was sent out for comment on May 6, 1985, and adopted on January 6, 1987. When Section 2 was amended in 1982, it was assumed that only courts would adjudicate questions arising under the provision, but the Justice Department expanded the retrogression (backsliding) test to include an assessment of absolute electoral opportunity—as measured by criteria that allowed a great deal of subjectivity—for purposes of administrative preclearance. *See Remarks of John R. Dunne,* 14 CARDOZO L. REV. 1127, 1128 (1993) ("Under its regulations, the Civil Rights Division may also interpose an objection if it finds that the submitted plan 'clearly violates' section 2 of the Voting Rights Act."). The 1987 guidelines had been sent out for public comment in 1985. But that document stirred considerable controversy, and at the end of August 1986, at an American Political Science Association panel on the Voting Rights Act (which I chaired), William Bradford Reynolds, then the U.S. Assistant Attorney General for civil rights, suddenly announced he had changed his mind. In assessing electoral changes in the Section 5 jurisdictions, the civil rights division would stick to the purpose and effect questions writ-

ten into the provision itself; those who wished to challenge a method of voting on Section 2 grounds could litigate the matter in a local federal district court. Reynolds's about-face instantly triggered a well-organized campaign by civil rights activists, congressional hearings, and a House subcommittee on constitutional and civil rights report. And in the 1987 guidelines Reynolds flip-flopped again. Section 2 was back in the preclearance picture. On the well-organized campaign, see CUNNINGHAM, *supra* note 16, at 26–27.

20. As the Court said in the first of the two decisions that will be discussed below, in rewriting Section 2, Congress made no mention of a consequent revision of Section 5. There was, it is true, a footnote in the 1982 Senate report, which was engineered by civil rights advocacy groups who knew that the vote on the act was imminent and that only proponents would notice it. But in 1982, Congress not only amended Section 2; it renewed Section 5. It did so, the Court noted, "without changing its applicable standard. We doubt that Congress," it went on, "would depart from the settled interpretation of § 5 and impose a demonstrably greater burden on the jurisdictions covered by § 5 . . . by dropping a footnote in a Senate Report instead of amending the statute itself." Reno v. Bossier Parish Sch. Bd. (*Bossier I*), 520 U.S. 471, 484 (1997).

21. *Bossier I,* 520 U.S. 471.

22. *Id.* at 477. The decision was followed by an amendment (in 1998) of the Justice Department regulations governing the enforcement of Section 5. The change eliminated the reference to a "clear violation" of Section 2 as a basis to deny preclearance. 28 C.F.R. 51.54 (2001).

23. *Bossier I,* 520 U.S. at 479–480.

24. *Id.* at 494. Justice Breyer dissenting.

25. *Bossier II,* 528 U.S. 320.

26. *Id.* at 329.

27. *Id.* at 335.

28. Peyton McCrary, Christopher Seaman & Richard Valelly, *The Law of Preclearance: Enforcing Section 5, in* THE FUTURE OF THE VOTING RIGHTS ACT 21 (David L. Epstein et al. eds., 2006).

29. Only 1 percent of objections were based on violations of Section 2 in the 1980s, with the figure rising to 2 percent in the 1990s. *Id.* at 26, table 2.2.

30. *Id* at 26.

31. Georgia v. Ashcroft, 195 F. Supp. 2d 25, 31 (D.D.C. 2002), 539 U.S. 461 (2003).

32. The ACLU's Laughlin McDonald viewed *Ashcroft* as dangerous, in that it might "allow states to turn black and other minority voters into second-class voters, who can 'influence' the election of white candidates, but cannot elect candidates of their choice, or if they so choose, of their own race." Laughlin McDonald, *Why the Renewed Voting Rights Act Will Pass Constitutional Muster—Despite Predictions That the Roberts Court May Strike It Down,* FINDLAW, June 09, 2006, http://writ.news.findlaw.com/commentary/20060609_mcdonald .html. On the other hand, Rep. John Lewis, in a deposition submitted to the D.C. court, had strongly backed the plan, advocating that the court grant preclearance. Transcript of Record at 15–16, 18. ("Direct Testimony of John Lewis") *Georgia v. Ashscroft,* 195 F. Supp. 2d of 25 (D.D.C. 2002) In addition, a number of legal scholars who were strongly identified with the plaintiffs' bar saw *Ashcroft* as a welcome recognition of a changed South—a recognition that

would actually aid the fulfillment of black political aspirations. *See* Samuel Issacharoff, *Is Section 5 a Victim of Its Own Success?*, 104 COLUM. L. REV. 1710 (2004).

33. *Ashcroft,* 195 F. Supp. 2d at 31.

34. *Ashcroft,* 539 U.S. at 471.

35. *Id.* at 491.

36. *Id.* at 469.

37. *Id.*

38. *See id.* at 469 (Sen. Brown's statement regarding the design of the Senate plan); *id.* at 470 ("[W]e [African Americans] have a better chance to participate in the political process under the Democratic majority than we would have under a Republican majority," Charles Walker, the Senate majority leader, had testified.).

39. *Ashcroft,* 195 F. Supp. 2d at 92.

40. *Ashcroft,* 539 U.S. at 480. Justice O'Connor had earlier raised the point in the Section 2 context. For instance, concurring in Thornburg v. Gingles, 478 U.S. 30, 87–88 (citations omitted), she noted that "the phrase 'vote dilution,' in the legal sense, simply refers to the impermissible discriminatory effect that a multimember or other districting plan has when it operates 'to cancel out or minimize the voting strength of racial groups.' This definition, however, conceals some very formidable difficulties. Is the 'voting strength' of a racial group to be assessed solely with reference to its prospects for electoral success, or should courts look at other avenues of political influence open to the racial group?"

41. *Id.* at 479, 480 (citing *Beer,* 425 U.S. at 141).

42. *See id.* at 483 ("The State may choose, consistent with § 5, that it is better to risk having fewer minority representatives in order to achieve greater overall representation of a minority group by increasing the number of representatives sympathetic to the interests of minority voters.").

43. *Id.* at 481.

44. *Id.* at 482.

45. *Id.* at 482 (quoting *Thornburg,* 478 U.S. at 99 (O'Connor, J., concurring)).

46. *Id.* at 482.

47. In actuality, it turned out to be no risk at all. In the two districts with black incumbents in which the black population had been reduced, those incumbents won overwhelmingly under the revised plan. The incumbent in a third district in which the black proportion had also been lowered had been white. This history of electoral success in the districts at issue in the litigation is summarized in Richard Pildes, Response to Written Questions from Senator John Cornyn, Supplement to Original Testimony, *The Continuing Need for Section 5 Preclearance: Hearing Before the S. Judiciary Comm.,* 109th Cong. (May 16, 2006).

48. The Senate Black Caucus "wanted to maintain" the existing majority-minority districts and at the same time "not waste" black votes, the Director of Georgia's Legislative Redistricting Office testified. *Ashcroft,* 539 U.S. at 469. Black votes were "wasted" when a majority-black district contained more black voters than black candidates needed to prevail.

49. Posting of Robert F. Bauer on More Soft Money Hard Law Blog, *Thinking About the Politics of Georgia v. Ashcroft and its Critics,* http://moresoftmoneyhardlaw.com/updates/voting_rights_act_redistricting_issues.html?AID=742 (June 6, 2006). Bauer was counsel to the Democratic Senate Campaign Committee and the Democratic House Campaign Committee.

50. *Id.*

51. *Ashcroft,* 539 U.S. at 485–87.

52. In dissent, Justice Souter wrote: "Whatever one looks to, however, how does one put a value on influence that falls short of decisive influence through coalition? Nondecisive influence is worth less than majority-minority control, but how much less? Would two influence districts offset the loss of one majority-minority district? Would it take three? Or four? The Court gives no guidance for measuring influence that falls short of the voting strength of a coalition member, let alone a majority of minority voters. Nor do I see how the Court could possibly give any such guidance. The Court's 'influence' is simply not functional in the political and judicial world." *Id.* at 495 (Souter, J., dissenting). Although I agree with him on this point, Justice Souter in this dissent is arguing for a return to the status quo ante in interpreting the preclearance provision, a proposal that I cannot sign on to, for reasons that should be apparent.

53. In a famous concurrence Justice Potter Stewart quipped that while hard-core pornography is hard to define, "I know it when I see it." Jacobellis v. Ohio, 378 U.S. 184, 197 (1964) (Stewart, J., concurring).

54. See Cunningham, *supra* note 16, *passim,* for an excellent discussion of the freewheeling use of suspected discriminatory intent to object to districting plans that provided for less than a maximum number of possible majority-minority districts.

55. Pub. L. No. 109-246, § 2(b)(1)(2).

56. *Id.* at § 2(b)(7) and (b)(4).

57. *See* Dowell Myers, Immigrants and Boomers: Forging a New Social Contract for the Future of America (2007), ch. 6; Jeff Grogger & Stephen Trejo, Falling Behind or Moving Up? The Intergenerational Progress of California's Mexican American Population (2002); Linda Chavez, *The Great Assimilation Machine,* Wall St. J., June 5, 2007, A23.

58. Direct Testimony of John Lewis, quoted in Miller, *supra* note 32, at 15–16, 18. Rep. Lewis, it should be noted, however, did support the 2006 VRARA.

59. That was the standard the Court had set in judging the constitutionality of federal statutes in City of Boerne v. Flores, 521 US 507, 520 (1997).

60. Posting of Daniel Tokaji to Election Law Blog, http://electionlawblog.org/archives/005582.html (May 11, 2006, 8:42 AM). Harvard Law Professor Helen Gerken made the same point: "[V]irtually all the mainstream civil rights groups seem to have endorsed the deal, whereas there aren't many academics offering full-throated support for the bill in its current form." Election Law Blog, *id.,* 12:59 PM. Scholars and the organized civil rights community were normally a more or less united group, but spokespersons for the latter were both more alarmed by *Ashcroft* and more convinced of the importance of overturning the decisions than voting rights experts on law faculties. Thus Prof. Richard Hasen, Loyola Law School, was concerned that "there is not much of a record of recent state-driven discrimination that Congress could point to supporting renewal." *Congressional Power to Renew the Preclearance Provisions of the Voting Rights Act After* Tennessee v. Lane, 66 Ohio St. L.J. 177 (2005). Hasen goes on to conclude: "Under the existing and muddled Supreme Court precedents, it is far from clear whether Congress will be able to make the case to satisfy the Supreme Court that the 'uncommon' preclearance rationale is 'congruent and proportional' to prove intentional racial discrimination in voting by covered jurisdictions today. For this

reason, supporters of the renewed law would do themselves a service to explore alternative bases for Congressional power, including congressional power under the Guarantee Clause." *Id.* at 206–207. In calling the preclearance rational "uncommon," he was simply referring to the unique Section 5 demand that jurisdictions prove their innocence—the burden of proof thus being on the defendant—justified by the unique historical circumstances when the statute was passed in 1965. Other scholars, in their own voice and with their own priorities and suggestions, shared Hasen's concern. See posts organized under "Guest Law Professor Bloggers on Voting Rights Act Renewal" Election Law Blog, http://electionlawblog.org.

61. See, e.g., Shaw v. Reno, 509 U.S. 630 (1993); Miller v. Johnson, 515 U.S. 900 (1995).

62. As *Miller* explained, racial considerations have to be shown to be the predominant motivation behind particular districting lines in order for a court to find a 14th Amendment violation. But "[r]edistricting legislatures will . . . almost always be aware of racial demographics." *Miller*, 515 U.S. at 916. Such awareness does not pose a constitutional problem.

63. Comm. on the Judiciary, Report on the Fannie Lou Hamer, Rosa Parks, and Coretta Scott King Voting Rights Act Reauthorization and Amendments Act (VRARA), H.R. Doc. No. 109-478 (2006) [hereinafter House Report], at 69, 71 ("This change is intended to restore Section 5 and the effect prong to the standard of analysis . . . articulated by the Supreme Court in *Beer v. United States* . . ."). Comm. on the Judiciary, Report on the Fannie Lou Hamer, Rosa Parks, and Coretta Scott King Voting Rights Act Reauthorization and Amendments Act (VRARA), S. Doc. No. 109-295 (2006) [hereinafter Senate Report], at 19 (The VRARA "re-adopts—and clarifies further—the *Beer* standard.").

64. House Report, *supra* note 61, at 69.

65. *Id.* at 68, n. 183.

66. *Id.* at 69.

67. *Id.*

68. *Id.*

69. "By focusing solely on the protection of naturally occurring legislative districts with a majority of minority voters, the reauthorization bill ensures that minority voters will not be forced to trade away solidly majority-minority districts for ambiguous concepts like 'influence' or 'coalitional.'" Senate Report, *supra* note 61, at 20–21.

70. *Id.* at 21. The point is further spelled out: "By limiting non-retrogression requirements to districts in which [minority citizens] are able with their own vote power to elect 'preferred' candidates of choice—not just a candidate of choice settled for when forced to compromise with other groups—the bill limits section 5 to protecting those naturally occurring, compact majority-minority districts with which section 5 was originally concerned."

71. *Id.* at 20.

72. *Id.* at 21.

73. Testimony of Theodore S. Arrington, Chair, Dept. of Political Science, University of North Carolina, *The Continuing Need for Section 5 Pre-Clearance: Hearing Before the S. Committee on the Judiciary*, 109th Cong. (May 16, 2006), *quoted in* Senate Report, *supra* note 61, at 20.

74. That irritation was expressed unequivocally in the additional views attached to the Senate Report by Senators Leahy, Biden, Feinstein, Feingold, Kennedy, Kohl, Schumer, and Durban.

75. That subjectivity was on full display in a Justice Department staff memo written a few months after the 2003 decision, although kept under wraps for two years, and then leaked to the *Washington Post* in early December 2005. The memorandum was published as a supplement to Dan Eggen, *Justice Staff Saw Texas Districting as Illegal: Voting Rights Finding on Map Pushed by DeLay Was Overruled*, WASH. POST, Dec. 2, 2005 at A01, *available at* http://www.washingtonpost.com/wp-dyn/content/article/2005/12/01AR2005120101927.html.

76. *Ashcroft*, 539 U.S. at 472.

77. Richard H. Pildes, *Forward: The Constitutionalization of Democratic Politics*, 18 HARV. L. REV. 28, 84 (2004).

Editor's Note: Section 5 was one of the most hotly contested provisions when Congress enacted the Voting Rights Act 1965 and reauthorized it in 1982 and 2006. The widely divergent views expressed in the VRA's legislative history and later judicial decisions about the need, efficacy, and constitutionality of Section 5 are represented in Chapters 7 and 8, each setting forth contrasting perspectives of two eminently qualified experts.

CHAPTER EIGHT

REPORTS OF MY DEMISE HAVE BEEN OVERSTATED: ASSESSING THE CONSTITUTIONALITY OF THE RECENTLY RENEWED SECTION 5 PRECLEARANCE PROVISION OF THE VOTING RIGHTS ACT

KRISTEN CLARKE*

I. Introduction

In July 2006, Congress voted to reauthorize and extend the Section 5 preclearance provision of the Voting Rights Act,[1] which has long been hailed as the nation's most effective civil rights law. The various guarantees and prohibitions contained within the act have, together, helped make tangible the goal of real political equality while providing both minority voters and minority-preferred candidates with meaningful access to the political process. However, it is Section 5, the key provision of the act and the focus of this chapter, that provides an extraordinary remedial measure to prevent and deter discrimination in places that have long-standing and particularly egregious histories of voting discrimination. Specifically, Section 5 requires pre-approval of new voting changes in order to prevent certain jurisdictions from implementing laws that intentionally discriminate against or worsen the position of minority voters. Section 5 has helped make considerable improvements in the integrity of the political process in many parts of the country that have had a checkered past with respect to full minority-voter participation.

Despite the significant role that Section 5 has played, some commentators have argued that the Supreme Court's recent line of federalism cases raises concerns

* Co-Director of the Political Participation Project of the NAACP Legal Defense and Educational Fund.

about whether or not the Section 5 preclearance provision of the Voting Rights Act is vulnerable to a constitutional challenge. Indeed, the first constitutional challenge to the recently reauthorized Section 5 provision was mounted by a small Texas-based utility district only days after the bill was signed into law.[2] In that case, *Northwest Austin Municipal Utility District Number One v. Gonzales (NAMUD v. Gonzales)*, the plaintiff utility district seeks to "bail out" under Section 4(a) of the act in order to terminate its status as a covered jurisdiction and end its preclearance obligations pursuant to Section 5. The utility district has argued that if the court deems it ineligible to bail out, then Section 5 should be struck down as unconstitutional because, in its view, there was insufficient evidence in the congressional record to support the continuing need for and reauthorization of Section 5. The utility district has also argued that Section 5 should be deemed unconstitutional because Section 5 fails to satisfy the congruence and proportionality test articulated by the Supreme Court in *City of Boerne v. Flores*.[3] *See* infra Section IV. At the time of press, the three-judge panel had heard oral argument and a final decision had not yet been rendered on plaintiff's claims.

In this chapter, I consider recent rulings addressing the Supreme Court's posture on federalism and separation of powers concerns and suggest that the Voting Rights Act's preclearance requirement is likely to withstand scrutiny under this framework. However, I take that analysis a step further by assessing the weight of evidence proffered both for and against renewal of Section 5 during the 2006 congressional hearings conducted in the House and Senate. Describing what that evidence reveals, the House Judiciary Committee reported that

> [V]oting changes devised by covered jurisdictions resemble those techniques and methods used in 1965, 1970, 1975, and 1982 including: enacting discriminatory redistricting plans; switching offices from elected to appointed positions; relocating polling places; enacting discriminatory annexations and deannexations; setting numbered posts; and changing elections from single member districts to at large voting and implementing majority vote requirements. The Committee received testimony indicating that these changes were intentionally developed to keep minority voters and candidates from succeeding in the political process.[4]

In stark contrast to the arguments presented by the utility district in *NAMUD v. Gonzales*, I argue that the legislative history underlying Congress' 2006 reauthorization of Section 5 bolsters the strength of this extraordinary statutory provision. In doing so, it reduces the likelihood that the provision would be struck down under any *Boerne*-type constitutional challenge which may require an overruling of prior precedents such as *South Carolina v. Katzenbach* and *City of Rome v. United States*, both of which upheld previous reenactments of Section 5 as consistent with Congress's 15th Amendment authority.[5]

II. The Preemptive Role of the Section 5 Preclearance Provision

Section 5, one of the critical provisions of the Voting Rights Act, is unique because it deals with voting discrimination in a preemptive manner and responds to the inability of a more tedious case-by-case approach to effectively redress these problems on a broad scale. In essence, Section 5 places a temporary hold on election practices or procedures in certain "covered jurisdictions" and requires that any voting change be submitted for federal preclearance before it can be implemented. Covered voting changes range from relocation of a polling place to the adoption of a new redistricting plan. Jurisdictions can obtain preclearance by filing a Section 5 declaratory judgment action in the U.S. District Court for the District of Columbia, or administratively by submitting the voting change to the U.S. Department of Justice.[6] In either the judicial or the administrative context, the jurisdiction bears the burden of proof and must establish that the proposed voting change neither has the purpose and nor has the effect of denying or abridging the right to vote on account of race or color or [language-minority group].[7] Until the voting change is precleared, the change is deemed legally unenforceable.[8]

Although a voting change may be precleared, that determination does not mean that the change necessarily complies with various other provisions of the Voting Rights Act or Constitution. The Section 5 review process is very limited in scope, and preclearance of a change does not shield the change from a future challenge that may be mounted on other grounds. For example, a redistricting plan that has been precleared may still be challenged by private parties or by the Attorney General as violating Section 2 of the Voting Rights Act or any other applicable provision of state or federal law. Section 5 is unique and distinct from the act's Section 2 vote dilution provision, which represents another key feature of the act. Whereas Section 5 looks solely and exclusively at whether a proposed change worsens the status quo position of minority voters vis-a-vis the status quo, Section 2 more broadly looks to see whether the status quo is one that provides minority voters a meaningful level of access. In other words, Section 5 bars jurisdictions from further impairing minority voting strength while Section 2 allows plaintiffs to challenge practices or procedures that dilute minority voting strength.[9]

III. Testing the Arguments of Opponents

A. BURDENS ASSOCIATED WITH SECTION 5 COMPLIANCE

Section 5 opponents, including the plaintiff utility district in *NAMUD v. Gonzales*, argue that the statute exacts exceedingly high costs and burdens on covered jurisdictions. During a September 17, 2007, oral argument before a three-judge panel of the D.C. District Court, counsel for the utility district argued that Section 5 is a "scarlet letter" placed on those jurisdictions forced to comply with its mandate. These claims bear a striking resemblance to the federalism claims mounted by state-rights activists following the act's initial passage in 1965. In particular, opponents from both eras claim that Section 5 intrudes on local and state sovereignty; discourages jurisdictions from freely pursuing voting changes; imposes administrative burdens with respect to the preparation and submission of changes to the Justice Department; and prevents jurisdictions from putting newly enacted voting changes into immediate force and effect. These claims are either inaccurate or irrelevant to the constitutional inquiry, but have rhetorically helped fuel the arguments presented by a small cadre of voting rights opponents. These claims also ignore inherent features of Section 5 that act to limit its reach and scope and respect constitutional constraints. These features, including the geographical limits placed on its scope, termination dates, bailout, and bail-in mechanisms, together help "ensure Congress' means are proportionate to ends legitimate under § 5 [of the 14th Amendment]."[10]

B. REVISING THE COVERAGE FORMULA

Although there are a number of grounds on which opponents mount challenges to the constitutionality of Section 5, the coverage formula underlying Section 5 is subject to the most frequent attack and critique. The coverage formula is used to identify those jurisdictions that are subject to the act's preclearance requirements. The legislative record reveals that many VRA opponents generally called for revisions to or updating of the "coverage formula" codified in Section 4 of the act. Opponents argued that the formula was outdated and should, therefore, be revised to reflect voter registration or turnout rates during more recent presidential election periods under the presumption that such revisions would capture areas that have been the sites of recent voting rights litigation but have not previously been covered under the act. Here, opponents often distort the coverage formula by focusing solely on the formula's reliance on data that dates back to presidential elections in the 1960s and 1970s.[11] However, in actuality, the formula also considers whether the jurisdiction employed a voting test or device that, in concert with low voter registration or turnout rates from designated election periods, operate as proxies for identifying jurisdictions with a long history of discrimination.

Congress entertained a series of amendments during the 2006 reauthorization that would have altered the coverage formula but, after careful deliberation and debate, chose to reject these proposals. For example, the late Rep. Charles Norwood of Georgia introduced an amendment (Amendment 1183) that would have altered the coverage formula to rely on a "rolling test based off of the last three presidential elections," in place of the 1964, 1968, and 1972 presidential elections.[12] In outlining the basis for his amendment, Norwood claimed that Georgia has been "put in the penalty box of Section 5" and noted that black voter registration and turnout rates had seen improvement in Georgia. In staunch opposition to the amendment, Rep. F. James Sensenbrenner, then-Chairman of the House Judiciary Committee, observed that Norwood's reconstruction of the coverage formula would have weakened Section 5 and eliminated the provision's ability to deal with long-standing problems of voting discrimination.[13] Sensenbrenner noted that the amendment ignored "the past history of discrimination and discriminatory voting practices" and highlighted the fact that the act's coverage formula had been upheld by the Supreme Court on three occasions.[14] In addition, Rep. Norwood's amendment would have terminated the covered status of a number of states despite evidence that voting discrimination continued in these areas. After weighing arguments both for and against revision of the coverage formula, Congress chose to preserve it in its current form.

Moreover, opponents overlook the fact that Congress retains sweeping power and authority under the enforcement sections of the 14th and 15th Amendments to pass "firm [legislation] to rid the country of racial discrimination in voting."[15] Thus, it was within Congress's broad discretion under the Reconstruction Amendments to use its enforcement authority to retain the coverage formula which, in its well-considered judgment, effectively targets areas critical to the goal of eliminating real and documented problems of ongoing voting discrimination.[16] Certainly, Congress needs to illustrate some degree of reasonableness in the exercise of this discretion. However, the record of ongoing discrimination and the successful track record underlying Section 5 enforcement stands as evidence of the effectiveness of the coverage formula in identifying those areas where the threat of potential voting discrimination is the greatest. Indeed, the Supreme Court has recognized that the Voting Rights Act, in its present form, is the exemplar of congressional enforcement power under the Reconstruction Amendments.

C. DISTORTING THE GOALS OF SECTION 5 AND ARGUMENTS OF RACIAL BALKANIZATION

Some opponents to Section 5 argue that the preclearance process promotes racial gerrymandering and an unnecessary overreliance on race. Abigail Thernstrom, a senior fellow at the conservative Manhattan Institute, and one of the most vocal opponents of Section 5, testified that "[w]hen the state treats blacks as fungible members of a racial group, they become, in Ralph Ellison's famous phrase, "invisible men," whose blackness is their only observed trait. But that view—the view that individual identity is defined by race—is precisely what the civil rights movement fought so hard against."[17] These arguments make a number of false presumptions about the kind of conduct discouraged and encouraged by Section 5 (see Chapter 7).

First, Thernstrom presumes that any and all considerations of race are what Congress sought to eliminate through the passage of the Voting Rights Act. However, the congressional records underlying the initial enactment of the act and the subsequent reauthorizations make clear that Congress sought to redress real (not imagined or fabricated) problems of racial discrimination in the political process.[18] Indeed, Congress recognized that race-conscious remedial action is sometimes necessary because high levels of racially polarized voting can interact with discriminatory districting schemes to prevent blacks, Latinos, and other minorities from having equal access to the political process. Statistical experts who have thoroughly examined voting patterns concluded that voting often remains racially polarized in the covered jurisdictions. For example, Theodore Arrington, who served as an expert in a Section 2 challenge to at-large elections in Charleston County, South Carolina, observed that he "found there the most extreme polarized voting I think I have ever seen, and I have been doing this work since 1985."[19] With respect to the covered state of Louisiana, Dr. Richard Engstrom observed that out of 90 elections that he analyzed between 1991 and 2002, 78 of them (86.7 percent) showed racial divisions in candidate preferences and "extraordinarily strong preferences of one group favoring candidates different from the other."[20] With respect to Texas in the post-2000 redistricting cycle, the Supreme Court observed that voting discrimination persists throughout Texas as made evident by "particularly severe" racially polarized voting in which the "Anglo citizen voting-age majority will often, if not always, prevent Latinos from electing the candidate of their choice."[21] Given this political reality, it was perfectly reasonable for Congress to decide that Section 5 remained necessary to address the ongoing influence that race plays in our electoral process. Because racially polarized voting is such a critical aspect of the Section 5 inquiry, in many circumstances, as it declines as a feature that infects the electoral process, Sections 5 becomes less of an obstacle for covered jurisdictions. Section 5 aims to achieve the race neutrality for which Thernstrom seems to yearn but recognizes that meaningful steps must be taken to curb both discriminatory conduct and actions taken in the context of racial polarization. Thus, Thernstrom describes her vision of utopia without setting forth steps to get there.

Second, Thernstrom and other opponents claim that Section 5 requires gerrymandering, which she describes as the maintenance of "majority-black and -Hispanic districts, drawn to ensure minority officeholding roughly in proportion to the minority population." This statement is false and distorts the goal and purpose of Section 5. Indeed, Section 5 prohibits only those voting changes that reduce or diminish minority voting strength. Moreover, Section 5 does not prohibit *any* reduction in the minority population percentage of a particular district. Instead, it only bars those reductions that would meaningfully diminish the opportunity for minority voters to elect candidates of their choice, which, as noted, occurs when racially polarized voting interacts with discriminatory districting systems to exclude minority voters from the political process. Thus, the Justice Department has routinely precleared proposed voting changes that significantly reduce the percentage of minority voters in a district unless there is evidence that minority voters will lose the equal opportunity to elect candidates of their choice in the face of that reduction. The Justice Department may also object to such a change if there is evidence showing that these particular reductions were motivated by a discriminatory purpose. For example, it is not uncommon for jurisdictions to take steps to fracture or crack politically cohesive groups of minority voters. However, the point should be underscored here that the Section 5 analysis is a very rigorous and thorough one that tests the circumstances under which minority voters maintain access while providing significant flexibility to jurisdictions with respect to the kinds of voting changes they might adopt. Section 5 simply does not require the "maximization" or "gerrymandering" that opponents claim. It does, however, proscribe minimization of minority voting strength or chipping away at the fragile status of minority voters in the covered jurisdictions.

IV. Digging Through the Congressional Record: Assessing Evidence of Ongoing Voting Discrimination

Opponents suggest that Congress has exceeded its authority in renewing Section 5 by pointing to the Supreme Court's ruling in *City of Boerne v. Flores* and its progeny, which, in the view of some commentators, places greater restrictions on congressional enforcement powers under the Reconstruction Amendments. Under *Boerne,* Congress can use its remedial authority under the Reconstruction Amendments[22] after identifying a problem deemed to be of great constitutional magnitude and scope.[23] The Religious Freedom Restoration Act at issue in *Boerne* was deemed to go beyond the constitutional scope of congressional authority because, among other reasons, the legislative record lacked any example of unconstitutional discrimination within the last 40 years.[24] While opponents take the view that *Boerne's* congruence and proportionality test changes existing law, analysis of the ruling and its progeny make clear that *Boerne* merely elaborates on existing law, reaffirms the Court's earlier rulings in *Katzenbach* and *Rome,* and, most importantly, recognizes the same distinction between substantive and remedial legislation observed by the Court in *Katzenbach.*

The congruence and proportionality test set forth in *Boerne* requires courts to engage in a three-part inquiry to first identify the constitutional right that Congress seeks to protect through the legislation in question.[25] If it is determined that the particular set of rights that Congress seeks to protect are ones subject to heightened scrutiny, then Congress is generally accorded greater flexibility in constructing a remedy.[26] The second prong of that test requires courts to assess the "gravity of the harm" that Congress seeks to prevent.[27] However, such an assessment cannot be undertaken in a vacuum and instead "'must be judged with reference to . . . historical experience.'"[28] It is this second prong of the congruence and proportionality test that is the focus of this chapter, as the evidence of discrimination and weight of the legislative record are important tools to be used by courts in determining whether the harms that Section 5 seeks to prevent are sufficiently grave to warrant the particular prophylactic response embodied in the preclearance provision. Finally, courts must also consider whether the contested statute presents an "an appropriate response" to the harm that the statute seeks to redress.[29]

From *Boerne*, we understand that for a congressional act to survive constitutional scrutiny, historical information should generally be complemented by more contemporary evidence of ongoing discrimination. Thus, the older presidential election turnout figures that are used, in part, to construct the coverage formula for purposes of determining which jurisdictions are covered under Section 5 must be supplemented by recent and contemporary evidence of continued voting discrimination in those areas.[30] Indeed, analysis of the record reveals an unbroken chain of voting discrimination in the covered jurisdictions that begins at the time of the Voting Rights Act's inception and can be traced to modern times.

After extensive debate and hearings, and with significant consideration of evidence of ongoing voting discrimination in the jurisdictions subject to the act's special requirements, Congress deemed it necessary and appropriate to secure the protections afforded by Section 5. Based on the evidence presented regarding the effectiveness of the statute between the 1982 and 2006 period, Congress opted for an extension of 25 years. Moreover, Congress developed a record showing the numerous ways that jurisdictions continue to suppress minority voting strength.[31] The record shows that voting discrimination still exists on a wide scale and confirms that Section 5 helped stop various discriminatory voting changes from being put into effect.[32] These proposed changes come in various forms including redistricting plans, at-large elections, candidate qualification requirements, annexations, and polling place relocations. These changes were adopted both in small towns and state-wide.

This section provides an overview of the various kinds and types of evidence represented in the congressional record. What this evidence illustrates, most importantly, is that Section 5 represents a "congruent and proportional" piece of legislation that responds to grave levels of ongoing voting discrimination in those areas covered under the act.

In the congressional record included important evidence regarding the number and scope of objections interposed by DOJ to various proposed voting changes attempted by covered jurisdictions. For example, the House Judiciary Committee Report included among its findings a table detailing more than 700 objections between 1982 and 2005. This high number stands against fewer than 700 objections interposed between 1965 and 1981.[33] This evidence illustrates that Section 5 continued to play an important role in the more contemporary period and functioned to stop ongoing voting discrimination. Indeed, Congress found that "attempts to discriminate persist and evolve, such that Section 5 is still needed to protect minority voters in the future."[34] Most interestingly, the record amassed by Congress during the 2006 reauthorization bears remarkable resemblance to the record underlying the 1975 reauthorization, upheld in *City of Rome,* and most certainly exceeded the breadth and scope of records underlying the congressional adoption of the Family and Medical Leave Act at issue in *Nevada Department of Human Resources v. Hibbs*[35] and Title II of the ADA at issue in *Tennessee v. Lane.*[36]

A. EVIDENCE OF INTENTIONAL DISCRIMINATION

Congress analyzed a range of evidence that illustrated the breadth and depth of ongoing voting discrimination including DOJ objections, Section 2 violations, Section 5 enforcement actions, requests for more information issued by DOJ to officials seeking administrative preclearance of a voting change, withdrawals of Section 5 submissions, Section 5 declaratory judgment actions brought in the D.C. District Court, and deployments of federal observers. Some of the strongest evidence is yielded by an examination of DOJ objections. Indeed, one such analysis of objections interposed between 1980 and 2005[37] revealed that 436 of 722 (more than 60 percent) included discriminatory intent as at least part of the grounds for the objection. This latter point makes clear that even the retrogressive effect prong of Section 5 tends to capture conduct accompanied by evidence of discriminatory purpose.

B. DOJ OBJECTIONS

1. *Evading Obligations Under Section 5.* Perhaps some of the stronger evidence regarding the effectiveness of Section 5 lies in its deterrent effect. Numerous experts provided evidence regarding this deterrent effect as evidenced by jurisdictions that withdrew proposed voting changes from the administrative preclearance process after receiving requests from the Justice Department for more information underlying the adoption of the change.[38] However, standing alongside the evidence that Section 5 deters and discourages discriminatory behavior is equally compelling evidence that many jurisdictions flagrantly disregard the requirements of Section 5. These jurisdictions seek to evade the retrogression prohibition of Section 5 by submitting the same objectionable voting change for preclearance while making very cursory or inconsequential alterations to the form of the change. In other instances, these jurisdictions will employ evasive tactics in the hopes of bypassing the requirements of the act altogether. Here, I offer a few poignant examples from the congressional record that illustrate the recalcitrance that persists among many covered jurisdictions.

The long-standing battle over Mississippi's registration system illustrates the ineffectiveness of case-by-case litigation as a tool to block discriminatory voting practices. This example also illustrates the continuing need for Section 5 given the state's resistance and intransigence surrounding its registration system. During its

1890 constitutional convention, the State of Mississippi adopted a dual registration system, which required voters to register separately for municipal and nonmunicipal elections. In 1987, in *Operation PUSH v. Allain*, the court determined that the dual-registration requirement was motivated by a discriminatory purpose.[39] Despite this ruling, Mississippi subsequently put in a place a new registration system and failed to submit the voting change to the Justice Department for a requisite preclearance determination. As permitted by the statute, private citizens filed a successful Section 5 enforcement action forcing the state to submit the change.[40] Following its administrative review of that change, the Justice Department interposed an objection after finding that the dual-registration system had a racially discriminatory purpose and effect. Subsequently, the Mississippi legislature moved to adopt a unitary registration system but these efforts were vetoed by then-Governor Kirk Fordice.[41] This prompted a group of private citizens to file another suit that eventually led to the adoption of a unitary registration system.[42]

Morehouse Parish, Louisiana, provides another example of resistance and recalcitrance among the covered jurisdictions. After a 1991 Section 5 objection to its attempt to pack African American voters in the City of Bastrop, the Morehouse Parish Police Jury made cosmetic changes and resubmitted the same plan. The DOJ interposed an objection once again, and the police jury subsequently resubmitted the same plan with mere cosmetic changes. Only after the DOJ objected a third time in 1992 did the police jury address the substantive problems with the first objection and draw district lines that did not unnecessarily pack African American voters.[43]

2. Resisting Change to the Status Quo. The congressional record also contains numerous contemporary examples of jurisdictions taking discriminatory steps to deny minority voters political access in the face of growing minority population. Often, these kinds of changes emerge at moments in which minority voters are poised to become the numerical majority in a particular jurisdiction.

The Town of Kilmichael, Mississippi, provides a very compelling and recent example of a jurisdiction unwilling to allow natural shifts in population to take their course.[44] The House Judiciary Committee Report described the actions of Kilmichael officials as ones "intentionally developed to keep minority voters and candidates from succeeding in the political process." 2000 U.S. Census data revealed that Kilmichael had become majority African American, and these changing demographics naturally inspired a number of African American candidates to run for city office. However, three weeks prior to the election, the white incumbent mayor and all five white members of the Board of Aldermen canceled the election. The Department of Justice interposed an objection to the cancellation that eventually compelled the City to reschedule and move forward with the election. Most notably, once that election was conducted, African Americans won the mayoral seat and three of the five aldermanic positions.[45]

3. *Racial Selectivity.* The discretionary judgment calls by election officials, and official actions that result from them, all represent voting changes that are subject to Section 5 preclearance.[46] Indeed, comparing and contrasting official actions taken with respect to white voters and minority voters can also reveal powerful evidence of ongoing vote discrimination. For example, in 2003, DOJ objected to a proposed annexation for the Town of North, South Carolina, after finding that officials had "been racially selective in its response to both formal and informal annexation requests" received from white and black residents. While "white petitioners have no difficulty in annexing their property to the town," DOJ found that "town officials provide little, if any, information or assistance to African-American petitioners." The evidence showed that race was "an overriding factor in how the town responds to annexation requests."[47]

4. *Discriminatory Redistrictings.* Most recently, the Supreme Court observed in *LULAC v. Perry*, a challenge to a mid-term Congressional redistricting plan, that the State of Texas eliminated minority electoral opportunity despite growing numbers of politically cohesive Latino voters. The Court observed that the redistricting plan "bears the mark of intentional discrimination that could give rise to an equal protection violation."[48] In addition, the Court noted that despite a state's legitimate efforts to address various redistricting principles during the redistricting process, states cannot use these principles to "justify the [negative] effect on minority voters."[49] Although the Court's findings were made in the context of a Section 2 challenge to the redistricting plan, the Section 5 process is similarly aimed at ferreting out those changes that place voters in a worse position and often those changes may not have been adopted with any malice or apparent discriminatory intent.

In 2002, the DOJ objected to a redistricting plan for the Florida House of Representatives that dropped the minority population to a level that would have made it "impossible for these Hispanic voters to continue" to elect candidates of their choice. After the objection, a Hispanic majority-minority district was restored in Collier County.[50] Both the Texas and Florida examples illustrate the need for Section 5's protections at the federal, state, and local levels of redistricting.

5. *Declaratory Judgments.* In addition to examining objections interposed by the Department of Justice to a series of retrogressive and discriminatory voting changes, Congress also undertook careful analysis of declaratory judgment actions brought in the District Court for the District of Columbia. Although done with relative infrequency, some jurisdictions covered by Section 5 opt to go to the D.C. District Court to obtain judicial preclearance of a proposed voting change. It is often unclear what motivates jurisdictions to pursue this method of preclearance because it is relatively more costly, time-intensive, and laborious than pursuing preclearance through the administrative process. However, many jurisdictions that seek judicial preclearance are aware of the potentially problematic aspects of their proposed voting change and may hope to obtain a more favorable outcome than they would from the Justice Department. Several of the unsuccessful declaratory judgment actions, highlighted during congressional hearings, are worth noting here.

The D.C. District Court denied judicial preclearance to a plan that sought to implement an at-large method of election for the Sumter County Council in South Carolina.[51] Interestingly, despite the denial of preclearance, the county continued to discriminate, drawing a DOJ objection to a different voting change as described below.[52] In the declaratory judgment action, the court found that the county "failed to carry their burden of proving that the legislature did not pass Act 371 in 1967 for a racially discriminatory purpose at the insistence of the white majority in Sumter County."[53] In addition, the court noted that the at-large method of election would have diminished "the value of the then increasing voting strength of the black minority" and may have also had the residual effect of "prevent[ing] formation of a black majority senate district."[54] Finally, the court observed that a single-member plan would likely have provided the opportunity for black voters to elect candidates of their choice in three of seven districts.[55] Beyond this unsuccessful declaratory judgment, Sumter County has also drawn a number of objections from the Justice Department. As recently as 2002, the Justice Department deemed objectionable a proposed redistricting plan for the county that would have otherwise diminished minority voting strength.[56] In particular, the letter observed that "in three of these four, black [districts] voters will continue to have the ability to elect candidates of their choice. Our analysis, however, shows that this is not true for the fourth district."[57]

Another noteworthy example involves Louisiana's efforts to seek judicial preclearance of its 2001 redistricting plan for the State House of Representatives. Among other potentially problematic reductions in black population percentages of majority black districts around the state, the proposed plan also eliminated a majority black district in Orleans Parish. This district clearly provided black voters the opportunity to elect candidates of their choice. However, the state sought to eliminate this district outright arguing, initially, that it was necessary in order to guarantee whites proportional representation in Orleans Parish.[58] The state chose to eliminate this district in the face of white population loss over the prior decade in the region admitting that their precise goal was to diminish black opportunity in order to increase the electoral opportunity of white voters. At one point, the state altered its legal theory in the case perhaps recognizing that its justification was without support in any of the case law describing the Section 5 standard. The D.C. District Court issued an order "condemning the Louisiana House of Representatives for a mid-course revision in its litigation theory and tactics."[59] Ultimately, the state withdrew its request for declaratory judgment and entered into an eve-of-trial settlement that restored the black opportunity district in Orleans Parish.

6. Section 5 Enforcement Actions. A number of jurisdictions seek to evade their preclearance obligations under Section 5 by simply failing to obtain preclearance for a particular voting change. When this occurs, the Attorney General or private individuals can bring a Section 5 enforcement action to stop the jurisdiction from implementing or enforcing the change until preclearance is obtained. Whether such action is brought by private individuals will depend on the circumstances leading up to the adoption change, including the amount of public notice preceding any relevant local meetings and any publicity that followed the adoption of the change. There is no shortage of evidence of Section 5 enforcement actions brought, in large part, by private individuals seeking to ensure that jurisdictions comply with the mandate of Section 5 and obtain preclearance for a contested voting change. Most recently, in *North Carolina State Board of Elections v. United States,* a three-judge district court enjoined North Carolina Board of Elections from implementing the state court's 2002 legislative redistricting plan before it was precleared by the court or the Justice Department.[60] In *United States v. State of Georgia,* a three-judge court enjoined the State of Georgia from administering or implementing, or attempting to administer or implement its redistricting plan until preclearance was obtained pursuant to Section 5.[61] Although enforcement actions are not evidence that a contested voting change is retrogressive or discriminatory in violation of Section 5, these actions do make clear that jurisdictions routinely move to implement voting changes, often large in scope, while failing to comply with the mandate of federal law.

V. Conclusion

The *Boerne* line of cases tout the VRA as an exemplary model of congressional legislation under the enforcement sections of the 14th and 15th Amendments. These cases also make it clear that Congress is at the height of its power when it acts to protect a fundamental right such as the right to vote from continuing threats of invidious racial discrimination.[62] Congress acted on that power in opting to renew the act for an additional 25 years and conveying a deep commitment to the aspirational goals of democratic equality. Most importantly, the record amassed by Congress during the reauthorization period illustrates the intensity with which Congress studied and analyzed the problem of ongoing voting discrimination. Given these factors, any court should be reluctant to upset well-considered congressional judgment.

Notes

1. 42 U.S.C. 1973.
2. Northwest Austin Municipal Utility District Number One v. Gonzales (*NAMUD*), No. 06-01384 (D.D.C. Feb. 5, 2007).
3. City of Boerne v. Flores, 521 U.S. 507, 525 (1997).

4. H.R. Rep. No. 109-478 (2006), at 36.

5. South Carolina v. Katzenbach, 383 U.S. 301, 308 (1966); City of Rome v. United States, 446 U.S. 156, 166 (1980).

6. Preclearance determinations obtained through the Justice Department are final. Indeed, the Supreme Court has held that the Attorney General's decision not to interpose an objection to a submitted change is unreviewable and cannot be contested in court. Morris v. Gressette, 432 U.S. 491 (1977).

7. 42 U.S.C. 1973c.

8. Any federal district court can enjoin any attempt to implement the change prior to the granting of a declaratory judgment of preclearance. *See* South Carolina v. United States, 589 F. Supp. 757 (D.D.C. 1984). These kinds of suits, generally called Section 5 enforcement actions, bar jurisdictions from prematurely implementing voting changes.

9. Many members of the voting rights bar generally refer to Section 2 as the sword and Section 5 as the shield in voting rights efforts. *See, e.g.,* Heather K. Way, Note, *A Shield or a Sword? Section 5 of the Voting Rights Act and the Argument for the Incorporation of Section 2,* 74 Tex. L. Rev. 1439 (1996).

10. *City of Boerne,* 521 U.S. at 533.

11. Numerous witnesses who presented testimony to Congress offered compelling justifications for keeping the coverage formula intact despite the objections raised by opponents. Testimony of Drew Days, Alfred M. Rankin Professor of Law, Yale Law School, *Understanding the Benefits and Costs of Section 5 Pre-clearance: Hearing Before the S. Committee on the Judiciary,* 109th Cong. 8, 32–33 (May 17, 2006). For example, Drew Days highlighted the "the past reliability of the formula in appropriately targeting jurisdictions for pre-clearance with a historical pattern of voting discrimination." May 17, 2006 Hearing, at 32–33. Long-time voting rights litigator Armand Derfner observed that the coverage formula functioned as a "litmus test [that] was remarkably accurate in pinpointing those places where the malignancy existed and in generally leaving alone those places where it did not." *Id.* at 73. Finally, Professor Nathaniel Persily cautioned that "abandoning a seemingly neutral [coverage] formula for ad hoc judgments about the relative threat certain jurisdictions pose necessarily opens one up to charges of political cherry-picking and threatens both the passage and survival of section 5 at the Court." *Id.* at 135.

12. James Thomas Tucker, *The Politics of Persuasian: Passage of the Voting Rights Act Reauthorization Act of 2006,* 33 Notre Dame J. of Legis. 205, 254–255 (2007).

13. *Id.; see also* H. Rep. 109-554, at 2 (2006).

14. *Id.* at H. Rep. 109-554, at 2 (2006). *Katzenbach,* 383 U.S. at 329–30 (court upheld Section 5 and observed that the coverage formula was "rational."); County Council of Sumter County, S.C. v. United States, 555 F. Supp. 694, 707 (D.D.C. 1983) (a post-1982 reauthorization challenge to the constitutionality of Section 5 based, in part, on allegation that coverage formula was outdated; Plaintiff noted that that more than 50 percent of eligible citizens in South Carolina and Sumter County were registered to vote, but the three-judge panel rejected arguments reasoning that Section 5 "had a much larger purpose than to increase voter registration in a county like Sumter to more than 50 percent" and noting that "Congress held hearings, produced extensive reports, and held lengthy debates before deciding to extend the Act.").

15. *Katzenbach*, 383 U.S. at 315; *City of Rome v. United States*, 446 U.S. 156 (1980) (upholding reenactment of Section 5).

16. *See* U.S. CONST. amend. XIV, § 5; amend. XV, § 2.

17. Testimony of Abigail Thernstrom, Senior Fellow, the Manhattan Institute, and Vice-Chair, U.S. Commission on Civil Rights, *Understanding the Benefits and Costs of Section 5 Pre-Clearance: Hearing Before the S. Comm. on the Judiciary*, 109th Cong. (May 16, 2006).

18. In particular, Congress, in 2006, concluded that "the 'exceptional conditions' cited in South Carolina v. Katzenbach continued to exist in 1970, 1975, 1982, and 1992 such that Congress appropriately found that the temporary provisions were still needed. On each occasion, Congress examined the extent to which minority citizens were able to fully participate in the electoral process and weighed the record against the continued need for the temporary provisions." During each prior reauthorization period, Congress deemed it necessary to extend the temporary provisions of the Act to ensure protection of minority voters. H.R. REP. NO. 109-478, at 8–9.

19. Testimony of Theodore S. Arrington, Chair, Dept. of Political Science, University of North Carolina, *The Continuing Need for Section 5 Pre-Clearance: Hearing Before the S. Committee on the Judiciary*, 109th Cong. 20, 27–28 (May 16, 2006).

20. Testimony of Richard Engstrom, Professor, The University of New Orleans, *Voting Rights Act: Section 5 of the Act—History, Scope, and Purpose: Hearing Before the House Subcommittee on the Constitution of the Committee on the Judiciary*, 109th Cong. 49, 50 (October 25, 2005).

21. League of United Latin American Citizens v. Perry (*LULAC*), 126 S. Ct. 2594 (2006).

22. All of the Court's *Boerne* decisions have arisen in the context of Section 5 of the 14th Amendment, but the Court has suggested the analysis is the same under Section 2 of the 15th Amendment. *See* Lopez v. Monterey, 525 U.S. 266, 282–83 (1999) (citing *City of Boerne*, 521 U.S. at 518).

23. City of Boerne, 521 U.S. at 530–32; Kimel v. Fla. Bd. of Regents, 528 U.S. 62 (2000); Bd. of Treasurers of the Univ. of Ala. v. Garrett, 531 U.S. 356 (2001).

24. City of Boerne, 521 U.S. 507. Another point raised by the *Boerne* Court is that the weakness in the congressional record was not the Religious Freedom Restoration Act's most serious shortcoming. *Id.* at 531. Similarly, the *Kimel* Court noted that the lack of a record is not determinative. 528 U.S. at 91.

25. Tennessee v. Lane, 541 U.S. 509, 522 (2004); *Garrett*, 531 U.S. at 365.

26. The Supreme Court has held that "any alleged infringement of the right of citizens to vote must be carefully and meticulously scrutinized." Reynolds v. Sims, 377 U.S. 533, 562 (1964).

27. *Lane*, 541 U.S. at 523.

28. *See Katzenbach*, 383 U.S. at 308.

29. *Lane*, 541 U.S. at 530.

30. Moreover, in *Lopez*, the only case involving a post-*Boerne* challenge to Section 5, the Supreme Court upheld the constitutionality of the Section 5 preclearance provisions in the context of the substantial "federalism costs" of preclearance. 525 U.S. at 269.

31. *See Renewing the Temporary Provisions of the Voting Rights Act: An Introduction to the Evidence: Hearing Before the Sen. Jud. Comm.*, 109th Cong. 2d Sess, S. Hrng. No. 109-555 (2006).

32. *Id.* at

33. *See* H.R. Rep. No. 109-478, at 5 (2006).

34. H.R. Rep. No. 109-478, at 21.

35. Nev. Dept. of Human Resources v. Hibbs, 538 U.S. 721 (2003).

36. *Lane,* 541 U.S. 509.

37. Peyton McCrary et al., *The End of Preclearance as We Knew It: How the Supreme Court Transformed Section 5 of the Voting Rights Act,* 11(2) Mich. J. Race & L. 275 (Spring 2006); *see also* Nov. 1, 2005, Hearing, at 96.

38. *See* Luis Ricardo Fraga & Maria Lizet Ocampo, *The Deterrent Effect of Section 5 of the Voting Rights Act: The Role of More Information Requests, in* Democracy, Participation, and Power: Perspectives on Reauthorization of the Voting Rights Act (Ana Henderson ed., 2006). Fraga and Ocampo conclude that requests for more information (MIRs) "increased the impact of the DOJ on submitted changes by 110%, i.e., doubling the number of changes that were not precleared by the DOJ." Testimony of Luis Ricardo Fraga & Maria Lizet Ocampo, "The Deterrent Effect of Section 5 of the Voting Rights Act: The Role of More Information Requests" *Voting Rights Act: Evidence of Continued Need: Hearing Before the House Subcommittee on the Constitution of the Committee on the Judiciary,* Vol. II, 109th Cong. 2537, 2553 (March 8, 2006). Long-time civil rights attorney Robert McDuff observed that Section 5 has tremendous deterrence value. McDuff testified: "I cannot tell you how many times I have talked to legislators, city council members, lawyers in the State Attorney General's Office, or lawyers for localities who have really now internalized sort of the goals of Section 5, and who, when voting changes are being made, assess the impact on all groups, all racial groups, and reach out to all groups, to try to determine if a solution can be developed that satisfies everyone's concerns in light of the very deep racial fault line that still exists in the south and in other parts of the country due to the history of discrimination." Testimony of Robert B. McDuff, Attorney, Jackson, Mississippi, *Modern Enforcement of the Voting Rights Act: Hearing Before the S. Committee on the Judiciary,* 109th Cong. 21, 26 (May 10, 2006).

39. Operation PUSH v. Allain, 674 F. Supp. 1245, 1251–1252 (N.D. Miss. 1987)

40. *See* Young v. Fordice, 520 U.S. 273 (1997).

41. For extensive history concerning the struggle around Mississippi's dual-registration system, *see* Brenda Wright, *Young v. Fordice: Challenging Dual Registration Under Section 5 of the Voting Rights Act,* 18 Miss. Cl. L. Rev. 67 (1997).

42. Young v. Fordice, No. 95-CV-197, slip op. (S.D. Miss. July 24, 1995) (No. 95-2031).

43. Letters from John. R. Dunne, Assistant Attorney General, Civil Rights Division, U.S. Department of Justice to Ray Yarbrough, President, Morehouse Paris Police Jury (Sept. 27, 1992); *see also* Debo P. Adegbile, *Voting Rights in Louisiana 1982-2006* at 27 (forthcoming S. Cal. Rev. L. Soc. Justice 2008) (article on file with author).

44. Indeed, Judge David Tatel of the D.C. Circuit questioned the claims presented by counsel on behalf of the plaintiff utility district (in *NAMUD v. Gonzales*) that Congress did not receive sufficient evidence of discrimination in the covered jurisdictions to authorize the extension of Section 5. Judge Tatel introduced examples of discriminatory voting changes

adopted in Kilmichael, Mississippi, and the Town of North, South Carolina, very early on during the Sept. 17, 2007, oral argument to test the weight of plaintiffs' claims in this case. *See* Transcript of Oral Argument Before Three-Judge Court, *NAMUD* No. 06-01384 (transcript on file with author).

45. 152 Cong. Rec. H5176–77.

46. *See* Foreman v. Dallas County, Tex., 521 U.S. 979 (1997) (holding that fact that county was exercising its "discretion" pursuant to state statute when it adjusted procedure for appointing election judges did not compel finding that county could make such change without obtaining preclearance).

47. Letter from R. Alexander Acosta, Assistant Attorney General, U.S. Department of Justice, to H. Bruce Buckheister, Mayor, Town of North, Sourth Carolina (Sept. 16, 2003) (available at http://www.usdoj.gov/crt/voting/sec_5/ltr/1_091603.html).

48. *LULAC,* 548 U.S. at 34.

49. *Id.* at 35.

50. Letter from Ralph F. Boyd, Jr., Assistant Attorney General, U.S. Department of Justice, to Honorable John M. McKay, President, Florida Senate, and Honorable Tom Feeney, Speaker, Florida House of Representatives (July 1, 2002) (available at http://www.usdoj .gov/crt/voting/sec_5/ltr/1_070102.htm).

51. *Sumter County,* 555 F. Supp. 694 (D.D.C. 1983).

52. Letter from Ralph F. Boyd, Jr., Assistant Attorney General, U.S. Department of Justice, to Charles T. Edens, County Chairperson, Sumter, South Carolina (June 27, 2002) (available at http://www.usdoj.gov/crt/voting/sec_5/ltr/1_062702.htm).

53. *Sumter County,* 555 F. Supp. at 36.

54. *Id.* at 38.

55. *Id.* at 37.

56. *See infra* note 52.

57. *Id.*

58. Louisiana House of Representatives et. al. v. Ashcroft (D.D.C. 2002).

59. Order Denying Defendants' Motion for Summary Judgment, No. 02-0062, at *1 (D.D.C. Feb. 23, 2003) (on file with author).

60. N.C. State Bd. of Elections v. U.S., 208 F. Supp.2d 14 (D.D.C. 2002).

61. United States v. Georgia, 1996 WL 480861 (N.D. Ga. 1996).

62. In *Boerne,* the Supreme Court also observed that the VRA was enacted to protect the fundamental right to vote against racial discrimination. In apparent confirmation of this point, the Supreme Court described congressional powers as at their "zenith" when enacting remedial legislation that addressed problems that lie at the convergence of race and fundamental rights. "Put in simple terms," *Boerne* and its progeny unmistakably stand for the proposition that "when Congress acts to protect a fundamental right or when it acts to protect a suspect or quasi-suspect class, its powers are generally broader than when it acts to promote equality more generally." *See also* Pamela S. Karlan, *Section 5 Squared: Congressional Power to Extend and Amend the Voting Rights Act,* 44 Hou. L. Rev. 1 (2007) (discussing *Lane, Hibbs,* and United States v. Georgia, 126 S. Ct. 877 (2006) and observing that when "Congress acts to protect a fundamental right or when it acts to protect a suspect or quasi-suspect class, its powers are generally broader than when it acts to promote equality more generally.").

CHAPTER NINE

SECTIONS TWO AND FIVE AS AMENDED BY THE VOTING RIGHTS ACT REAUTHORIZATION AND AMENDMENTS ACT OF 2006

BENJAMIN E. GRIFFITH*

DAVID D. O'DONNELL**

I. Introduction

The Voting Rights Act of 1965[1] has been called the "crown jewel" of the Civil Rights Movement. Its enactment into law came only after many bloody protests, confrontations, and highly publicized marches by African Americans. What they were seeking was nothing less than basic electoral access, full participation in the political process, equal opportunity, and fundamental justice. The VRA provided the federal government and private citizens with effective means to overcome the vestiges of racial discrimination and institutional subjugation of minority communities throughout the United States, in every phase of the electoral process, from voter registration, ballot access, and casting votes to participation in the electoral process on equal footing with other voting groups.

This chapter will focus on two key provisions of the Voting Rights Act, Section 2 and Section 5, considered the most effective weapons in the fight to "attack the blight of voting discrimination"[2] in our nation. We'll examine the relationship between these provisions, which "differ in structure, purpose and application"[3] and which have been called "two of the weapons in the Federal Government's formidable arsenal,"[4] and their interplay with the 14th Amendment. Many who have smelled the smoke of the battle in litigation under the VRA would also agree these sections have been the most potent weapons in that arsenal. We will conclude this chapter with a candid assessment of continued federal enforcement of these sections of the

---

* Chair, ABA Section of State and Local Government Law; ABA Standing Committee on Election Law; J.D., University of Mississippi School of Law, 1975; Partner, Griffith & Griffith, Cleveland, Mississippi.

** J.D. Mississippi, 1985; Partner, Clayton O'Donnell, PLLC, Oxford, Mississippi.

VRA and how aggressive adherence to the original purpose of the act may be the key to its successful application and effectiveness.

Sections 2 and 5 have long been understood "to combat different evils and, accordingly, to impose very different duties"[5] on state and local governments. Both have been extraordinarily effective in ameliorating the effects of institutional racism in every phase of the electoral process. With President George W. Bush's signing into law the Fannie Lou Hamer, Rosa Parks, and Coretta Scott King Voting Rights Act Reauthorization and Amendments Act[6] on July 27, 2006, extending a strengthened version of Section 5 for another 25 years, our nation entered a new era in the ongoing struggle to protect, preserve, and strengthen voting rights of racial and ethnic minorities.

II. Background and Overview of Section 2

Section 2 of the Voting Rights Act prohibits voting practices and procedures that discriminate on the basis of race, color, or membership in a language-minority group. It offers protection against invidious barriers to a minority group's right to freely participate in the electoral process. Thus, Section 2, as amended in 1982, expressly prohibits the use of any standard, practice, or procedure that "results in a denial or abridgement of the right of any citizen . . . to vote on account of race or color." A "denial or abridgement" is proven if the evidence shows that members of the minority group have "less opportunity than other members of the electorate to participate in the political process and to elect representatives of their choice." Section 2 then identifies the "extent to which members of a protected class have been elected to office" as the principal evidence of minority "access" or "lack of access," but then emphasizes that the section is not to be construed as establishing "a right to have members of a protected class elected in numbers equal to their proportion in the population." Thus while the cognizable right of Section 2 is "equality of opportunity" of the minority electorate, not a right of proportionate electoral success for minority candidates, the evaluation of minority candidate success at the polls as the principal measure of equal opportunity has generated a fair degree of controversy and commentary.[7]

The federal government and private citizens employed Section 2 during the decade following its enactment to remove the more readily identifiable impediments to minority access to the electoral process such as the poll tax, literacy tests, white candidate slating, and other discriminatory barriers to minority access. Over the course of time these barriers were eliminated from the electoral landscape and the courts began to turn their attention to claims of "minority vote dilution," that is, that the operation of certain redistricting plans or at-large election systems, combined with past and present social and economic conditions, caused minorities to suffer a "diminution" in their collective voting strength and thus their relative opportunity to participate in the electoral process, even though the direct barriers to participation had been removed.

A. VOTE DILUTION

The Supreme Court first considered the viability vel non of minority group vote-dilution claims in the case of *Whitcomb v. Chavis,* which involved a claim by black citizens that the use of a multimember state legislative districting scheme uncon-stitutionally diluted their voting strength.[8] Evaluating the plaintiffs' dilution claim under the original version of Section 2, which simply mirrored the 15th Amend-ment's prohibition of state electoral practices or procedures that "deny or abridge the right to vote on account of race or color," the Court applied a "results" test that did not burden a Section 2 plaintiff with proving that the state "intended" to discriminate on the basis of race.[9] The Court gave credence to the "vote dilution" theory advanced by the plaintiffs, holding the appropriate inquiry to be whether the lack of success of minority candidates, in relation to their proportionate share of the general population, was attributable to the minority electorate having less oppor-tunity than other voting groups "to participate in the political process and to elect legislators of their choice."[10] Finding that the plaintiffs failed to demonstrate an actionable "vote dilution" claim under the 14th Amendment, the *Whitcomb* Court held that absent evidence of a lack of access to the political system, the lack of proportionate representation was insufficient, in itself, to establish a constitutional violation.[11] While the Court recognized that the at-large electoral scheme caused the voting power of the minority electorate to be "cancelled out," as measured by the lack of proportionate success of minority candidates, the Court held that without proof that the minority electorate had "less opportunity" than other similar groups in the electoral scheme to participate in the electoral process, because of their sta-tus as the "minority" electorate, an actionable claim could not be stated under the Equal Protection Clause.[12] The proof showed that there were "strong differences" between the minority electorate and nearby communities in terms of housing con-ditions, income and educational levels, rate of unemployment, juvenile crime, and welfare assistance and that the minority electorate voted heavily Democratic, while the district's white majority electorate regularly voted for the Republican candidates, usually resulting in the defeat of the minority-preferred candidates.[13] Not finding any structural impediments to minority access to the political process, the Court concluded that the failure of the minority electorate to have legislative seats in num-bers equal to its proportionate share in the general population emerged "more as a function of losing elections than of built-in bias against" a minority electorate.[14]

Thus, in *Whitcomb,* the Supreme Court assessed the plaintiff's minority vote-dilution claim by scrutinizing impediments to access of the minority electorate to the political process, and ultimately determined that although there was an obvious lack of proportionate representation, the losses experienced by the minority candidates were not attributable to the candidate's status as the "minority preferred candidate" but rather were the function of race-neutral choices by the majority electorate, that is, the party affiliation of the candidates involved in a given election.

Two years later, in *White v. Regester,* the Supreme Court again confronted a minority vote-dilution challenge to a multimember districting scheme, but this time determined that the operation of the electoral scheme impermissibly "diluted" the minority electoral strength.[15] The Court reiterated the standard established in *Whitcomb,* that a minority group must prove "that its members had less opportunity than did other residents in the district to participate in the political processes and to elect legislators of their choice."[16] In *White,* the Supreme Court for the first time applied a "totality of the circumstances" test to the minority's vote-dilution claim and found that the past and present acts of discrimination against the minority electorate, conjoined with the operation of the multimember districting scheme, impermissibly diluted the minority electorate's voting strength.[17] According to the Court, the "fundamental" aspect of the plaintiff's minority vote-dilution claim consisted of proof that the minority electorate was actively and effectively excluded from the slating, nominating, and electoral processes.[18] Thus, although the Court found that the more objective attributes of the multimember electoral scheme, such as the majority vote requirement and the multimember district itself, were not "in themselves improper nor invidious," they exacerbated the effect of the truly invidious and discriminatory efforts existing at other points in the electoral process which combined to exclude or minimize minority access to the electoral process.[19]

In 1980, the Supreme Court rejected the "results" test of *White* and *Whitcomb,* substituting an "intent" test to be applied in deciding minority vote-dilution claims under Section 2 and the 14th and 15th Amendments. In *City of Mobile v. Bolden,* the Supreme Court determined that proof of an invidious purpose by the government in the adoption and maintenance of the challenged electoral scheme was essential to a minority vote-dilution claim brought under Section 2 and the Constitution.[20] The Court found that an analysis of the *Zimmer v. McKeithen* factors, which were devised to give definition to the "totality of the circumstances" test of *White v. Regester,* were "relevant," but insufficient to establish the existence of a "discriminatory purpose" behind the government's continued maintenance of the electoral scheme.[21]

Congress reacted quickly to the *Bolden* decision in 1982 by amending Section 2 to provide that electoral procedures and practices that "result in" the denial or abridgement of the minority electorate's access to the electoral processes are violative of Section 2 of the act.[22] The legislative history accompanying the 1982 amendments to Section 2 expressly states that Congress intended to "codify" the results test employed in *Whitcomb* and *White.*[23] The Senate report makes clear that by amending Section 2 Congress intended to encompass "minority vote-dilution claims" within the proscriptions of the section, while broadening the potential scope of the act by specifically rejecting the *Bolden* intent test in favor of the results test applied in *White* and *Whitcomb*.[24] According to the Senate Report, a proper application of the results test requires courts to "distinguish between situations in which racial politics play an excessive role in the electoral process, and communities in which they do not."[25] The report expands on the results test of *Whitcomb* and *White* by listing various factors that the courts should apply in assessing vote-dilution claims. Thus, in addition to assessing the relative access of the minority electorate to the political processes by examining the success rates of minority candidates for political office, the report directed courts to examine the actual voting practices of the minority and majority electorates, which the report referred to as "racial bloc voting"[26]—an inquiry not found in either *White* or *Whitcomb*. According to the report, a finding that "race" was the predominant determinant of political preference within a given electoral scheme was essential to a successful Section 2 vote-dilution claim.[27]

B. ELEMENTS OF A VOTE-DILUTION CLAIM

The *Thornburg v. Gingles* decision was the Supreme Court's first occasion to construe amended Section 2.[28] The Court essentially clarified the elements of an actionable minority vote-dilution claim under amended Section 2 by devising a three-part set of preconditions that the Court deemed to be necessary, but not in and of themselves sufficient, to establish a minority vote-dilution claim. First, the minority electorate must demonstrate that they are sufficiently numerous and geographically compact to constitute a majority-minority single member district. Second, the minority electorate must be "politically cohesive." Third, there must be a showing that the majority electorate consistently votes as a block so as to regularly result in the defeat of the minority-preferred candidate.[29] The first two *Gingles* preconditions are essentially "remedy oriented" in the sense that the minority electorate must retain the attributes of a distinct political group within the general electorate, and that they are sufficiently large to form an effective voting majority in a proposed reconfigured single member districting scheme. The third precondition, that is, "white bloc voting," was elevated by the *Gingles* Court to a central and essential role within the minority vote-dilution inquiry. Proof of the third precondition involves a two-step process of identifying the "minority-preferred candidate" and then an examination of the majority voting patterns in relation to the success or the non-success of the minority-preferred candidate.

In making this assessment and reaching the ultimate determination of whether or not there is vote dilution, the court should use the Senate Report factors, those factors identified in the legislative history of Section 2, *Johnson v. DeGrandy*.[30] Moreover, the vast majority of the circuits agree that the focus of Section 2 is not on whether minorities are able to elect other minorities to office, but whether minority voters are able to elect minority-preferred candidates to office. In that regard the trial court may give appropriate weight and consideration to whether and to what extent minority-preferred candidates who were white as well as those who were African American have been elected to office in the jurisdiction in question.[31] In making the requisite searching analysis of the present political reality of an electoral system under challenge in a Section 2 vote-dilution case, moreover, the cause of or explanation for the defeat or success of minority-preferred candidates is also relevant in the totality of circumstances inquiry.[32] Failure to establish any of the "necessary preconditions" is fatal to a plaintiff's Section 2 claim.

1. Senate Report Factors. As the Supreme Court noted in *Gingles,* the Senate Judiciary Report that accompanied the 1982 Voting Rights Act Amendments elaborated on the nature of Section 2 violations and the proof required to establish those violations, specifying certain "objective factors" and enhancing factors that typically may be relevant to a Section 2 claim.

The Senate Judiciary Committee in its report accompanying amended Section 2 identified nine factors, gleaned from *White, Whitcomb* and other preamendment vote-dilution cases, considered to be relevant in determining whether or not there has been a violation.

In elaborating on the nature of a Section 2 violation and the proof required to establish such a violation, the Senate Report specified certain "objective factors" and "enhancing factors" that typically may be relevant to a Section 2 claim. These factors were culled from *White v. Regester* and the decision of the Fifth Circuit Court of Appeals in *Zimmer v. McKeithen.*[33] These Senate Report factors necessarily call for evidence of the circumstances of the local political landscape, and include, but are not necessarily limited to, the following:

1. The extent of any history of official discrimination in the state or political subdivision that touched the right of the members of the minority group to register, to vote, or otherwise to participate in the democratic process.
2. The extent to which voting in the elections of the state or political subdivision is racially polarized.
3. The extent to which the state or political subdivision has used unusually large election districts, majority vote requirements, anti-single-shot provisions, or other voting practices or procedures that may enhance the opportunity for discrimination against the minority group.
4. If there is a candidate slating process, whether the members of the minority group have been denied access to that process.
5. The extent to which members of the minority group in the state or political subdivision bear the effects of discrimination in such areas as education, employment, and health that hinder their ability to participate effectively in the political process.

6. Whether political campaigns have been characterized by overt or subtle racial appeals.
7. The extent to which members of the minority group have been elected to public office in the jurisdiction.

Additional factors that may be probative include:

8. Whether there is a significant lack of responsiveness on the part of elected officials to the particularized needs of the members of the minority group.
9. Whether the policy underlying the state or political subdivision's use of such voting qualification, prerequisite to voting, or standard, practice or procedure is tenuous.[34]

The list of Senate Report factors is neither comprehensive nor exclusive, and "there is no requirement that any particular number of factors be proved, or that a majority point one way or another."[35]

Rather than engaging in a mechanical application of the *Gingles* preconditions and the Senate Report factors, the courts are obliged to consider all evidence reflective of the extent to which minority voters are currently able to participate in the political process and to elect candidates of their choice.

2. *Special Circumstances Doctrine.* The Special Circumstances Doctrine can be traced to language that appears in the third *Gingles* precondition of legally significant white racial bloc voting, by which plaintiffs are required to show that "the white majority votes sufficiently as a bloc to enable it—in the absence of special circumstances, such as a minority candidate running unopposed, . . . usually to defeat the minority's preferred candidate."[36] Since minority electoral success can and is often invoked as a defense to a vote-dilution claim, the doctrine of special circumstances is often invoked by plaintiffs in order to discount or nullify the probative value of evidence of minority electoral success in order to improve their ability to establish a Section 2 violation.

These fundamental principles were reaffirmed in *Growe v. Emison*.[37] Justice Scalia spoke for a unanimous Court when he described the interrelationship between the *Gingles* preconditions:

> The "geographically compact majority" and "minority political cohesion" showings are needed to establish that the minority has the potential to elect a representative of its own choice in some single-member district. . . . And, the "minority political cohesion" and "majority bloc voting" showings are needed to establish that the challenged districting thwarts a distinctive minority vote by submerging it in a larger white voting population. . . . Unless these points are established, there neither has been a wrong nor can be a remedy.[38]

On the practical side, *Gingles* also addresses the nature of evidentiary proof considered relevant to identifying "minority preferred candidates" and the nature and extent of "white bloc voting." The Court noted that the trial court "relied principally" on extreme case analysis and bivariate ecological regression statistical evidence in assessing "how" the minority and majority electorates voted in particular elections.[39] The Court observed that the statistical techniques essentially yielded "estimates" of the voting patterns of the respective electorates, including precinct-level estimates of the percentages of members of each race who voted for minority candidates over the span of dozens of electoral contests.[40] The *Gingles* Court approved the trial court's evaluation of the presented statistical data, which included a consideration of the existence and strength of any "correlation" between the race of the voter and the selection of certain candidates, whether the revealed correlation was "statistically significant," and whether the differences in minority and majority electorate voting patterns was "substantively significant."[41]

III. Racial Gerrymandering Under the 14th Amendment: Appearances Do Matter

The process of revising voting district boundaries, either as a remedy for a Section 2 vote-dilution violation or as a consequence of the need to reapportion the numerical size of voting districts consistent with the one-person, one-vote principle, will typically involve the consideration and application of "traditional race-neutral districting principles" by legislatures. These traditional criteria—district compactness, nonseparation of communities of interest, minimization of boundary changes, and incumbency protection—will generally guide redistricting decision making. There are occasions, however, where the race of voters may be included in the applied redistricting criteria (as when fashioning a Section 2 remedy) or where legislators are simply "conscious" of race during the districting process but do not use race as a criterion in any real sense. Yet the use of race as the predominant consideration renders the resulting districting scheme constitutionally suspect as a racial classification under the 14th Amendment's Equal Protection Clause. Differentiating between the use of race in redistricting in its more benign form and the use of race that results in the creation of a racial classification within the meaning of the 14th Amendment is a "delicate task."[42]

The central mandate of the Equal Protection Clause is "racial neutrality in government decisionmaking."[43] This mandate prohibits purposeful discrimination against individuals on the basis of race. In 1993, it was applied to prohibit racial gerrymandering of a congressional district in *Shaw v. Reno*.[44] The Court, speaking through Justice Sandra Day O'Connor, drew the line between (1) impermissible racial gerrymandering by which voters are deliberately segregated into districts on the basis of race without compelling justification, and (2) permissible race-conscious state decision making. As the Court put it, "we believe that reapportionment is one area in which appearances do matter."[45] In invalidating a serpentine North Carolina congressional district with boundaries drawn predominantly on the basis of race, the Court said:

> A reapportionment plan that includes in one district individuals who belong to the same race, but who are otherwise widely separated by geographical and political boundaries, and who may have little in common with one another but the color of their skin, bears an uncomfortable resemblance to political apartheid. It reinforces the perception that members of the same racial group—regardless of their age, education, economic status, or the community in which they live—think alike, share the same political interests and will prefer the same candidates at the polls. We have rejected such perceptions elsewhere as impermissible racial stereotypes. . . . By perpetuating such notions, a racial gerrymander may exacerbate the very patterns of racial bloc voting that majority-minority districting is sometimes said to counteract.[46]

Shaw v. Reno has been characterized by many in the civil rights community as a judicial backlash against majority-minority districts. It was much more than that. The Court did indeed call into question those majority-minority districts that, despite being race-neutral on their face, were drawn predominantly on the basis of race, subordinating traditional nonracial districting criteria, in a manner that could not rationally be understood as "anything other than an effort to separate voters into different districts on the basis of race."[47] Justice O'Connor emphasized that the black electorate is not monolithic. She correctly equated the North Carolina redistricting plan aimed at maximizing black voting strength to "political apartheid," and reasoned that a plan grounded on purposeful segregating of minority voters in majority-minority districts would only "reinforce the perception that members of the same racial group—regardless of their age, education, economic status, or the community in which they live—think alike, share the same political interests, and will prefer the same candidates at the polls."[48] On the contrary, African Americans are not monolithic in their views on a wide variety of such hot button issues as affirmative action. Indeed, "many are strongly in favor of affirmative action, of course, but others are ambivalent . . . , and still others are strongly opposed."[49]

In a series of decisions following *Shaw v. Reno*, the Court applied the exacting "strict scrutiny" standard of review when evaluating the constitutionality of redistricting plans challenged as racial gerrymanders, to which it declined to accord traditional judicial deference accorded the legislative decision-making process, a cornerstone of federalism. While acknowledging that the need to address a Section 2 vote-dilution violation through redistricting constitutes a "compelling governmental interest," the Court has found on only one occasion that the districting scheme under "strict scrutiny" review was "narrowly tailored" to serve the articulated "compelling governmental interest."[50] Given the rarity that a challenged redistricting scheme will survive the rigors of strict scrutiny, the central and deciding focus will usually involve the question of whether race "predominated" the redistricting effort. Although the relevant evidence may sometimes reveal direct proof of the decision maker's motivation to achieve certain racial proportions within the districting scheme at the expense of other race-neutral criteria, most often the chief evidence of the subordination of race-neutral criteria is circumstantial; that is, the extent to which the resulting districts are irregular or noncompact in shape.

In *Shaw v. Hunt*,[51] the Court held that a state's reapportionment scheme will not survive strict scrutiny if it is proven to be predominantly based on race without sufficient regard to, or in subordination of, traditional districting criteria and is not shown to be narrowly tailored to serve a compelling state interest. In *Lawyer v. Department of Justice,* the Court made it clear that it would nonetheless make every effort not to preempt the role of legislative bodies performing their task of redistricting and reapportionment and would continue to call for traditional judicial deference to that role by giving the state or local government body "the opportunity to make its own redistricting decisions so long as it is practically possible," provided the government body chooses to take that opportunity.[52]

The Court adopted a mixed motive analysis in *Bush v. Vera*,[53] applying the mixed-motive formulation of *Mount Healthy City Board of Education v. Doyle*,[54] to determining whether race has predominated over or trumped other nonracial traditional districting principles such as party affiliation.

Justice O'Connor's concurring opinion in *Bush v. Vera* was seen by many as a more accurate and comprehensive statement of the law than the majority opinion. Justice O'Connor said that compliance with Section 2's results test is a compelling state interest that can coexist in principle and practice with *Shaw v. Reno* and its progeny.[55] One of the state's goals in creating the three congressional districts in question was to produce majority-minority districts, but other goals, particularly incumbency protection, played a role in drawing the district lines; the lower court's determination that race was the predominant factor in the drawing of the districts had to be sustained. According to Justice O'Connor, "The district court had ample bases on which to conclude both that racially motivated gerrymandering had a qualitatively greater influence on the drawing of district lines than politically motivated gerrymandering, and that political gerrymandering was accomplished in large part by the use of race as a proxy."[56] Moreover, the State of Texas in its Section 5 submission explained the drawing of one of the districts in exclusively racial terms, and this was coupled with an admission contained in legislative e-mail communications with the Department of Justice "written at the end of the redistricting process that incumbency protection had been achieved by using race as a proxy."[57] Such evidence was bolstered by other objective evidence strongly suggesting the predominance of race in the district plans and demographic maps. As Justice O'Connor noted, "political considerations were subordinated to racial classifications in the drawing of many of the most extreme and bizarre district lines. . . . The fact that racial data were used in complex ways, and for multiple objectives, does not mean that race did not predominate over other considerations. The record discloses intensive and pervasive use of race both as a proxy to protect the political fortunes of adjacent incumbents, and for its own sake in maximizing the minority population of District 30 regardless of traditional districting principles. District 30's combination of a bizarre, non-compact shape and overwhelming evidence that that shape was essentially dictated by racial considerations of one form or another is exceptional. . . ."[58]

Leading scholars and litigators in the voting rights field have placed great weight on Justice O'Connor's concurring opinion in *Bush v. Vera*, distilling from her concurrence the following helpful principles for state and local government entities involved in the redistricting process.[59]

1. As long as states do not subordinate traditional criteria to race, they may intentionally create majority-minority districts without coming under strict scrutiny.
2. A state may have to create majority-minority districts where the three *Gingles* preconditions (compactness, minority cohesion, and white bloc voting) are satisfied.
3. A state's interest in avoiding Section 2 liability is compelling governmental interest.
4. A district drawn to avoid Section 2 liability is narrowly tailored so long as it does not deviate substantially, for predominantly racial reasons, from the sort of district a court would draw to remedy a Section 2 violation.
5. Districts that are bizarrely shaped and noncompact and that otherwise neglect traditional principles and deviate substantially from the sort of district a court would draw are unconstitutional, if drawn for predominantly racial reasons.

IV. Background and Purpose of Section 5, as Amended in 2006

Originally enacted in 1965, Section 5 of the VRA essentially "freezes" voting practices and procedures that were in place in certain "covered" jurisdictions at the time of Section 5's enactment. As such, Section 5 is "status quo" legislation that requires any change in voting practices and procedures to be reviewed under a "nonretrogression" standard and precleared by the Attorney General or the United States District Court for the District of Columbia before they are deemed effective. The covered jurisdiction has the burden of demonstrating that the proposed voting change does not have the purpose or effect of retrogressing the electoral position of racial minorities.

Section 5 of the Voting Rights Act of 1965, as amended, imposes substantial "federalism costs" on covered states and political subdivisions, requiring them to preclear any voting change or change in voting laws, practices, or procedures that those jurisdictions seek to administer. The 15th Amendment permits such an intrusion into state sovereignty. Preclearance under Section 5, when required, entails a certain amount of federal intrusion into state and local policymaking. It may be administratively requested through a formal submission to the Attorney General of the United States, or judicially through a declaratory judgment action, provided the action is brought in the United States District Court for the District of Columbia.

A. SECTION 5 RETROGRESSION TEST

Section 5 has much more limited purpose than Section 2. In jurisdictions covered by Section 5, the dual and significantly different requirements of nonretrogression and nondilution must be satisfied. Section 5 is designed to combat retrogression, which requires a comparison of a jurisdiction's new voting plan with its existing plan and implies that the jurisdiction's existing plan is the benchmark against which the affected voting change is measured.[60] There is no single statistical measure of whether a proposed voting change has a retrogressive purpose or effect. Although nonretrogression often means maintaining the number of effective majority-minority districts and minority "influence" districts within the proposed scheme as compared to the benchmark plan, the courts and the DOJ are directed to examine the totality of the circumstances germane to the presence vel non of an invidious purpose or retrogressive effect, including the ability of minority voters to elect candidates of their choice, the extent of the minority group's opportunity to participate in the political process, and the feasibility of creating a nonretrogressive voting plan. The Court has adhered to an analytical framework for identifying legislative purpose based on multiple factors set forth in *Village of Arlington Heights v. Metropolitan Housing Development Corp.*[61]

B. SCOPE OF SECTION 5: LIMITED TO COVERED JURISDICTIONS

Section 5 applies to specific covered jurisdictions under a statutory trigger. It provides a centralized review procedure through the United States Justice Department's Civil Rights Division and the United States District Court for the District of Columbia by which covered jurisdiction must first submit and obtain federal approval for changes in voting, electoral systems, and practices before those changes can become effective. Its purpose is much more limited than Section 2. Section 5 is distinct from Section 2, particularly for covered jurisdictions, in that compliance with Section 2 is neither necessary nor sufficient to obtain preclearance from DOJ or the D.C. District Court.

C. RELEVANCE OF SECTION 2 EVIDENCE TO PROVE RETROGRESSIVE INTENT OR DISCRIMINATORY PURPOSE UNDER SECTION 5

Discriminatory effects of dilution under Section 2 are relevant to a determination of whether a given voting change has a discriminatory purpose or effect under Section 5.[62]

The most significant interplay between Section 2 and Section 5 is seen in the redistricting process. That interplay usually takes place in a field of political litigation that imposes heavy demands on Article III judges and captures the attention of elected officials who comprise legislative bodies and other governmental entities made up of single-member districts and multimember districts.

The redistricting process is essentially about reallocating political power through (1) equalizing district population under the one-person, one-vote standard of the 14th Amendment, and (2) complying with the nonretrogression command of Section 5 for covered jurisdictions, and the nondilution standard of Section 2 for all jurisdictions.

The traditional alliance between the Justice Department's Civil Rights Division and private plaintiffs has been the subject of judicial scrutiny, most notably in *Miller v. Johnson*,[63] where the Supreme Court rejected race-based redistricting efforts grounded on a black maximization agenda and an attempt to create "safe" minority seats in several of Georgia's congressional districts.

1. *Key Section 5 Decisions.* *Allen v. State Board of Elections*:[64] The Supreme Court held that Section 5 should apply not only to changes in electoral laws but to any practices that might dilute minority voting strength.[65]

Beer v. United States:[66] The Supreme Court's holding in *Beer* set forth the nonretrogression standard in the following words:

> A legislative reapportionment that enhances the position of racial minorities with respect to their effective exercise of the electoral franchise can hardly have the "effect" of diluting or abridging the right to vote on account of race within the meaning of Section 5. We conclude . . . that such an ameliorative new legislative apportionment cannot violate Section 5 unless the new apportionment itself so discriminates on the basis of race or color as to violate the constitution.[67]

The retrogression standard's application was further broadened in *City of Lockhart v. United States*,[68] wherein the Supreme Court upheld preclearance of an electoral change that did not *improve* the position of minority voters, stating, "[a]lthough there may have been no improvement in [minority] voting strength, there has been no retrogression either." Thus, in *City of Lockhart,* since the new electoral change did not "increase the degree of discrimination against blacks," it was accordingly entitled to be precleared under Section 5 of the Voting Rights Act.[69] It was on this point that Justice Thurgood Marshall dissented in *City of Lockhart,* chastising the majority for reducing "Section 5 to a means of maintaining the status quo," insofar as it held that Section 5 could only forbid electoral changes that *increased* discrimination.[70] Justice Marshall's criticism of the majority was that such a view of the retrogression standard would permit a jurisdiction to adopt "a discriminatory electoral scheme, so long as the scheme is not more discriminatory than its predecessor," a view and approach that Justice Marshall condemned as "inconsistent with both the language and purpose" of Section 5 of the Voting Rights Act.[71]

In *Lopez v. Monterey County (Lopez I)*,[72] the Supreme Court held that where California had enacted legislation effecting changes in the method for electing county judges, Monterey County was nonetheless required to seek Section 5 preclearance before it could give effect to those changes. This is true even though the county arguably was just implementing a state law without exercising any independent discretion. Monterey County had adopted and implemented six judicial consolidation ordinances without seeking Section 5 preclearance. The Court reasoned that "Congress designed the preclearance procedure to forestall the danger that local decisions to modify voting practices will impair minority access to the electoral process and will accomplish this by giving exclusive authority to pass on the discriminatory effect or purpose of an election change to the Attorney General or the United States District Court for the District of Columbia."[73]

Following remand and a second appeal, the issue before the U.S. Supreme Court was whether Monterey County was required to pursue Section 5 preclearance for state-sponsored and legislatively authorized voting changes that it sought to administer. The Supreme Court in *Lopez II* held that a covered political subdivision seeks to administer a voting change and thus is required to seek Section 5 preclearance of a voting change (1) even where it exercises no independent discretion in giving effect to a state-mandated voting change, and (2) even where the voting change it implements is required by the superior law of a noncovered state.[74]

In holding that Section 5's preclearance requirement does not require a covered jurisdiction to exercise discretion or a policy choice, the Supreme Court noted that Congress had enacted the Voting Rights Act with its trigger phrase "seek to administer," without limiting the Section 5 preclearance requirement to discretionary actions of a covered jurisdiction.

The Supreme Court in *Lopez II* held that a covered political subdivision seeks to administer a voting change and thus is required to seek Section 5 preclearance of a voting change (1) even where it exercises no independent discretion in giving effect to a state-mandated voting change, and (2) even where the voting change it implements is required by the superior law of a noncovered state.[75]

In holding that Section 5's preclearance requirement does not require a covered jurisdiction to exercise discretion or a policy choice, the Supreme Court noted that Congress had enacted the Voting Rights Act with its trigger phrase "seek to administer," without limiting the Section 5 preclearance requirement to discretionary actions of a covered jurisdiction.[76]

On the contrary, according to the Court, Section 5 reaches nondiscretionary acts by covered jurisdictions that seek to comply with a state's superior law.[77] Moreover, to the extent that a partially covered state enacts legislation that affects covered local government entities such as cities or counties, Section 5 preclearance is required. In this regard the Supreme Court noted that it as well as the Justice Department had assumed that Section 5 preclearance was required whenever a noncovered state effects voting changes in covered counties, at least as far back as *United Jewish Organizations v. Carey.*[78] In numerous instances Section 5 cases had been decided based on the assumption that laws enacted by a partially covered state must be precleared before they can take effect in covered political subdivisions, citing *Shaw v. Reno, Johnson v. DeGrandy,* and *United States v. Onslow County.*[79]

Finally, the Supreme Court accorded deference to the Attorney General's interpretation of Section 5, noting that Section 5's preclearance requirement had consistently been applied to a covered county's nondiscretionary efforts to implement a voting change required by state law, even though the state itself was not a covered jurisdiction.[80]

In *Reno v. Bossier Parish School Board (Bossier I),* the Court held that Section 5 preclearance of a covered jurisdiction's voting standard, practice, or procedure may not be denied solely on the basis that it violates Section 2 of the Voting Rights Act.[81] The Court rejected the Attorney General's position that Section 2 of the Voting Rights Act is effectively incorporated into Section 5, but concluded nonetheless that Section 2 evidence of a redistricting plan's dilutive impact may be relevant even though it is not dispositive of a Section 5 inquiry.[82]

The relationship between Section 2 of the Voting Rights Act and Section 5 was explored in depth by the United States Supreme Court in *Bossier I.* In holding that Section 5 preclearance of a covered jurisdiction's voting standard, practice, or procedure may not be denied solely on the basis that it violates Section 2 of the Voting Rights Act, the Court rejected the Attorney General's long-held position that Section 2 is effectively incorporated into Section 5. The Court concluded nonetheless that Section 2 evidence of a redistricting plan's dilutive impact may be relevant even though it is not dispositive of a Section 5 inquiry.[83] In conducting an inquiry into a covered jurisdiction's motivation in enacting voting changes and in considering such evidence according to the majority, the analytical framework of *Arlington Heights v. Metropolitan Housing Development Corp.* should be looked to for guidance.[84]

The opening line of Justice O'Connor's majority opinion in *Bossier I* promised much: "Today we clarify the relationship between §2 and §5 of the Voting Rights

Act of 1965. . . ."[85] The Court rejected the Justice Department's position that Section 2 violations may form the basis for denying Section 5 preclearance, a position which "would inevitably make compliance with §5 contingent upon compliance with §2."[86] The Court further held that "Section 2 evidence" may be relevant to prove that a covered jurisdiction had retrogressive intent and that it enacted a redistricting plan or other electoral change with a discriminatory purpose:

> The fact that a plan has a dilutive impact . . . makes it "more probable" that the jurisdiction adopting that plan acted with an intent to retrogress than "it would be without the evidence." To be sure, the link between dilutive impact and intent to retrogress is far from direct, but "the basic standard of relevance . . . is a liberal one" and one we think is met here.[87]

In *Reno v. Bossier Parish School Board (Bossier II)*, the Court rejected the Justice Department's efforts to blur the distinction between Section 2 and Section 5 by shifting the focus of Section 5 from nonretrogression to vote dilution and by changing the Section 5 benchmark from a jurisdiction's existing plan to a hypothetical, undilutive plan.[88] The Court refused to extend Section 5 to discriminatory but nonretrogressive vote-dilution purposes, criticizing the Justice Department's reading of the Section 5 preclearance provision as one that "would also exacerbate the 'substantial' federalism costs that the preclearance procedure already exacts, . . . perhaps to the extent of raising concerns about Section 5's constitutionality."[89] The majority opinion in *Bossier II* emphasized that "proceedings to preclear apportionment schemes and proceedings to consider the constitutionality of apportionment schemes are entirely distinct. §2 and §5 are different in their structure, purpose and application, and impose different duties upon state and local government bodies."[90] With regard to the limited meaning that Section 5 preclearance has in the vote-dilution context, Justice Scalia speaking for the majority in *Bossier II* emphasized that preclearance

> does not represent approval of the voting change; it is nothing more than a determination that the voting change is no more dilutive than it what it replaces, and therefore cannot be stopped in advance under the extraordinary burden-shifting procedures of §5, but must be attacked through the normal means of a §2 action. As we have repeatedly noted, in vote-dilution cases §5 prevents nothing but backsliding, and preclearance under §5 affirms nothing but the absence of backsliding.[91]

2. *Pouring Old Poison into New Bottles.* In a lengthy opinion concurring in part and dissenting in part with the majority in *Bossier II*, Justice Souter was joined by Justices Stevens, Ginsburg, and Breyer in complaining that Congress did not intend to let state and local governments "pour old poison into new bottles."[92] Justice Souter's fundamental complaint was that the majority's constricted interpretation of Section 5 would require the Justice Department to approve a redistricting plan with a known discriminatory effect, leaving too much wiggle room for discrimination and mischief. Justice Souter warned that such a narrow statutory construction on Section 5 would force executive and judicial officers of the United States "to preclear illegal and unconstitutional voting schemes patently intended to perpetuate discrimination."[93]

Brenda Wright, managing attorney at the National Voting Rights Institute, observed that if the Supreme Court's interpretation of Section 5's purpose prong in *Bossier II* had been applied during Section 5's first 35 years,

> Congressman John Lewis of Georgia probably would not have won election to the U.S. Congress in 1986. In the early 1980's, Georgia enacted a discriminatory congressional redistricting plan that fragmented the Black population in the Atlanta area. The Georgia legislator who headed the redistricting committee openly declared his opposition to drawing so-called Negro districts, except that he did not use the word "Negro"; he used the racial epithet. Because of the clear evidence of racism behind the plan, the Justice Department objected even though the plan was not retrogressive. Georgia then withdrew the district and the result was that Congressman Lewis was able to win election. But under the Bossier Parish (II) decision, the Department of Justice would have been obliged to approve Georgia's original discriminatory plan.[94]

It was as if the Court was just warming up when it required the Justice Department to preclear proposed voting changes that had a clear discriminatory purpose. The Supreme Court's decision three years later in *Georgia v. Ashcroft*[95] marked a major departure from the *Beer* retrogression standard. Up until 2003 retrogression had been defined as a failure to preserve the ability of minority voters to elect candidates of their choice. *Beer* held that in evaluating submitted voting changes under Section 5, the retrogression standard ensured that "the ability of minority voters to participate in the political process and to elect candidates of choice is not diminished by the voting change."[96] Stated differently, the *Beer* retrogression standard had been interpreted up until 2003 to mean that covered state and local governments had to protect existing minority electoral gains and were prohibited from taking actions that would lower the percentage of minority voters in a given majority-minority district.[97]

Some commentators criticized the *Ashcroft* decision as a retreat from the goal of pursuing full participation by racial minority groups in the political process, replacing a clear standard with an unclear one that equated minority influence with election of minority-preferred candidates, inviting and shielding vote dilution. Others described the Court's majority opinion as a "perversion of retrogression," stating that

> [t]here is no way that the Court can with a straight face use totally different analyses in Section 5 (retrogression) and Section 2 (totality of the circumstances) cases,

while at the same time using a Section 2 analysis to restrict the effectiveness of Section 5. That, however, is what the Court did in *Ashcroft*.[98]

The *Ashcroft* decision was not without its supporters, however, particularly those who saw no particular harm in a decision that allowed unpacking of some majority-minority districts that did not dilute minority voters' electoral influence.[99] Professor Carol M. Swain has taken the position that *Georgia v. Ashcroft* was a sensible decision that allowed politicians greater latitude to create influence districts and to forge coalition districts by unpacking majority-minority districts and dispersing minority voters in what had been relatively safe majority districts, thereby allowing for the creation of more opportunities for minorities to form coalitions and exert influence on politicians outside their own racial and ethnic groups. Moreover, the unpacking of majority-minority districts in traditionally Democratic districts would not bar the election of qualified minority politicians with consistently proven abilities to garner white crossover votes. According to Professor Swain, *Ashcroft*

> was a good decision that would have benefited minority voters by making it easier for them to elect a slate of politicians who shared their policy views. *Ashcroft* gave legislators an opportunity to craft districts that enhanced the electoral prospects of Democrats rather than focusing on the reelection prospects of minority incumbents and it empowered minority voters by acknowledging the changes that had taken place in race relations across the South and particularly in Georgia.[100]

3. Impact of VRARA of 2006. In the hearings preceding passage of the VRARA, the House Subcommittee on the Constitution, House Judiciary Committee, found that it was necessary to extend Section 5, one of the temporary provisions of the VRA set to expire in 2007, but it was also necessary to "fix" provisions of Section 5 to clear up erroneous statutory interpretations by the U.S. Supreme Court in *Ashcroft* and *Bossier II*.[101]

Bossier II generated much criticism from the civil rights community and from past and present Justice Department attorneys. Its impact on the VRA's strength was addressed during the congressional hearings on the renewal of Section 5, the primary concern being that it weakened Section 5's ability to prevent covered jurisdictions from enacting discriminatory voting practices. One proponent remarked "I think that *Bossier(II)* is indeed like a cancer, eating away at the Voting Rights Act."[102]

Bossier II was also attacked as a misconstruction of the plain meaning of the discriminatory purpose test, draining the "purpose" test of any practical meaning in the preclearance process. Proponents told the House Subcommittee that the plain meaning of the word 'purpose' encompassed "any and all discriminatory purposes, not merely a purpose to cause retrogression," but that if Section 5's purpose prong only covered a "retrogressive" purpose, then a jurisdiction whose elected body never had minority representation "could continue to adopt new redistricting plans, intentionally designed to freeze out minority voting strength, and Section 5 would provide no protection."[103]

Before it was amended by the VRARA, Section 5's purpose test would only apply if by chance a covered "jurisdiction were to intend to cause a retrogression in minorities' electoral opportunity, but somehow messes up and adopts a change that, in fact, is not retrogressive. This is highly unlikely to occur, and in fact, in the nearly 5 years since *Bossier Parish (II)* was decided, the Justice Department has reviewed approximately 76,000 voting changes and no such incompetent retrogressor has appeared."[104]

The VRARA modified Section 5 to restore the pre-*Bossier II* discriminatory purpose standard. The new subsection (c) to Section 5 added reads as follows: "The term 'purpose' in subsections (a) and (b) of this section shall include any discriminatory purpose."[105]

According to a representative of the NAACP Legal Defense and Educational Fund, Inc., "this modification would allow the DOJ, or the reviewing three-judge panel, to interpose objections or deny declaratory judgments in situations where sufficient evidence of discriminatory intent exists such that the submitting jurisdiction cannot meet its Section 5 burden."[106]

The modification to Section 5 also accomplished another important goal. *Bossier II* was founded on the Court's interpretation of statutory language. In a similar manner, the Court in *Bossier I* had used Congress's failure to clarify Section 5's statutory language to justify its decision that the effects prong was limited to "retrogressive" effects. The legislative history now makes it clear that the VRARA's modification to Section 5 was intended to avoid any implication that Congress ratified *Bossier II* by aligning the purpose prong with constitutional standards.[107]

While this amendment was seen by proponents at an important fix to Section 5, the *Beer* retrogression doctrine was not removed, and a realistic tactical decision had to be made over what battles were winnable in light of the 2006 composition of Congress, particularly with Section 5 set to expire in 2007. Proponents were "stuck" with the *Beer* analysis "and the convoluted DOJ regulations incorporating the *Beer* analysis," prompting some to complain "[i]t is sad, however, that Congress did not go further and eliminate the *Beer* analysis so that the DOJ, the District court and community activists could use Section 5 instead of resorting to more costly Section 2 litigation."[108]

The VRARA's modification to Section 5 also corrected what proponents saw as "the unwarranted shift in statutory interpretation" as a result of the *Ashcroft* decision by restoring the ability to elect standard.[109]

The VRARA added new subsections (b) and (d) to Section 5 that provided:

(b) Any voting qualification or prerequisite to voting, or standard, or practice, or procedure with respect to voting that has the purpose of or will have the effect of diminishing the ability of any citizens of the United States on account of race or color, or in contravention of the guarantees section forth in section 1973b(f)(2), to elect their preferred candidates of choice denies or abridges the right to vote within the meaning of subsection (a) of this section.

(d) The purpose of subsection (b) of this section is to protect the ability of such citizens to elect their preferred candidates of choice.[110]

This amendment to Section 5 was designed to eliminate the "totality of the circumstances" test and the justification (or "excuse") for removing dilution of minority voter strength from the Section 5 analysis and require the Justice Department to interpose objections to vote-dilutive plans submitted under Section 5.[111]

V. VRARA After the 2010 Census: A Peek into the Future

LULAC v. Perry was the first voting rights opinion issued by the Roberts Court, in the absence of Justice Sandra Day O'Connor and with the votes of a new Chief Justice and Justice Alito.[112] Six highly fractured opinions in *LULAC v. Perry* reflected the widely divergent views of the nine Justices. These opinions also provided us with a window of opportunity to evaluate how the Voting Rights Act and its 2006 reauthorization, the VRARA, will fare during the next decade.

This case focused on Republican-led Texas Legislature's mid-decade congressional redistricting plan that, inter alia, dismantled a congressional district that was previously represented by an Hispanic. The action of the state legislature was alleged to have deprived Hispanics of the ability to elect the candidate of their choice. Specifically, the challenged redistricting plan replaced a judicially created plan crafted just a few years before with one that shifted over 8 million Texans into new districts. Many of the districts in their new form were less compact, communities of interest were fragmented, and the redistricting plan was motivated by a predominantly partisan purpose. Moreover, a majority African American district was cracked without offsetting the loss in black voters' ability to elect preferred candidates elsewhere.[113]

In a 132-page decision consisting of six separate opinions, reminiscent of *Bakke* decades earlier, one can identify four key holdings of the case:

1. The Texas state legislature's decision to override a valid, court-drawn redistricting plan mid-decade was not an unconstitutional political gerrymander.
2. Sufficient evidence showed minority cohesion and majority bloc voting among Latino voters in the redrawn Congressional District 23.
3. A newly drawn congressional district in which Latinos were barely a majority did not offset the loss of a potential Latino opportunity district as result of redistricting.

4. The totality of the circumstances showed the redistricting plan for District 23 constituted vote dilution in violation of Section 2 of the Voting Rights Act.

Was politics driving the redistricting process in *LULAC v. Perry?* Following its 2003 plurality decision in *Vieth v. Jubeliere,* and the evident inability to muster a majority that would hold that partisan gerrymandering challenges were nonjusticiable political questions, the Supreme Court was understandably without a principled basis to determine how to measure impermissible partisan effect in *LULAC v. Perry.* The Court's reaction in 2006 to cries of political gerrymandering was the judicial equivalent of a yawn. One example suffices. During oral argument, when counsel for one of the appellants complained that the only reason the redistricting plan as issue was passed "was to help one political party gain more seats in the Congress at the expense of the other," Justice Scalia replied: "Wow. That's a surprise."[114]

Chief Justice Roberts, writing in a separate opinion, echoed concern over the consequences of VRA-driven race-based districting and how such a process has supplanted if not become the equivalent to minority electoral opportunity. Of such racial sorting, the Chief Justice objected to giving the courts any further role in "rejiggering the district lines under §2":

> I do not believe it is our role to make judgments about which mixes of minority voters should count for purposes of forming a majority in an electoral district, in the face of factual findings that the district is an effective majority-minority district. It's a sordid business, this divvying us up by race.[115]

Notwithstanding the fractured opinions in *LULAC v. Perry,* the collective positions of the nine Justices do provide insight into how the Roberts Supreme Court, following the decennial census scheduled for April 2010, will interpret and apply key concepts and elements of the Voting Rights Act, as amended and extended. These are some of the key areas to watch:

1. *Geographical Compactness.* The *Gingles* preconditions provide a roadmap that aids in the evaluation of the potential effectiveness of majority-minority districts. The focus is on whether the minority community is numerous and sufficiently geographically compact, with internal consistency and cohesion in its voting choices, to enable it as the majority of the population to elect minority-preferred candidates, even in the presence of legally significant white racial bloc voting. The Section 2 compactness inquiry should take into account traditional districting principles such as maintaining communities of interest and traditional boundaries; the compactness inquiry under Section 2 embraces different considerations from the compactness inquiry in the equal protection context, the latter referring to the compactness of the contested district rather than the compactness of the minority population, with evaluation of the contours and relative smoothness of district lines to determine whether race was the predominant factor in drawing those lines, a district is rendered noncompact for Section 2 purposes if it combines two communities of interest that are separated by enormous geographical distance and contain populations with disparate needs and interests, with differences in socioeconomic status, education, employment, health and other characteristics. "A district that reaches out to grab small and isolated minority communities is not reasonably compact, and a district that combines two far-flung segments of a racial group with disparate interests does not provide the opportunity that §2 requires or that the first *Gingles* precondition of geographical compactness contemplates."[116] "The mathematical possibility of a racial bloc does not make a district compact."[117] Justices Souter and Ginsburg would hold that the *Gingles* precondition of compactness is satisfied by showing that minority voters in a reconstituted or putative district constitute a majority of those voting in the primary of the dominant party, defined as the party tending to win in the general election.

2. *Minority Electoral Opportunity.* Ensuring minority groups an equal opportunity to participate in the political process and to elect representatives of their choice is critical to advancing the ultimate purposes of Section 2; Justices Scalia, Thomas, and Alito and Chief Justice Roberts rejected the claim in *LULAC v. Perry* that the state intended to minimize Latino voting power. They would sanction as constitutional the state legislature's political gerrymandering by removing voters from a district because they voted for Democrats and against the Republican incumbent, even if it so happened that the most loyal Democrats were black Democrats and the state was conscious of that fact. They would also uphold the state legislature's political and nonracial objective, finding no prohibited racial classification if district lines merely correlated with race because they were drawn on the basis of political affiliation, which corresponds with race.

3. *Minority Influence Districts.* It is possible to state a Section 2 claim for a racial group that makes up less than 50 percent of the population, provided it can be shown that voters in that group constitute a sufficiently large minority to elect their candidate of choice with the assistance of crossover votes; the mere fact that African Americans have influence in a district does not suffice to state a Section 2 claim; the opportunity to elect representatives of their choice requires more than the ability of minority voters to influence the outcome between some candidates, none of whom is their candidate of choice; the presence of influence districts where minority voters may not be able to elect a candidate of choice but can play a substantial role in the electoral process relevant to a Section 5 analysis and a relevant consideration under Section 5 of the Voting Rights Act, but the failure to create an influence district does not run afoul of Section 2; Justices Souter and Ginsburg would hold that a Section

2 vote-dilution claim can prevail without the possibility of a district percentage of minority voters above 50 percent, that replacing a majority-minority district with a coalition district with minority voters making up fewer than half constitutes impermissible retrogression under Section 5, that protection of the minority voting population in a coalition district should be protected much as a majority-minority bloc would be.

4. *Candidates of Choice.* The fact that African Americans voted for an Anglo Democrat candidate in primary and general elections could signify he is their candidate of choice; without a contested primary, such a fact, assuming the presence of racial bloc voting, could also be interpreted to show that Anglos and Latinos would vote in the Democratic primary in greater numbers if an African American candidate of choice were to run, especially in an open primary system; the fact that African American voters preferred an Anglo Democrat to Republicans who opposed him does not make him their candidate of choice; the ability of African American voters to aid in an Anglo Democrat's election in a district does not make that district an African American opportunity district for purposes of Section 2, and Section 2 does not protect that kind of influence.

5. *Communities of Interest.* The recognition of nonracial communities of interest reflects the principle that a State may not assume from a group of voters' race that they think alike, share the same political interests, and will prefer the same candidates at the polls; legitimate yet differing communities of interest should not be disregarded in the interest of race; "[t]he practical consequence of drawing a district to cover two distant, disparate communities is that one or both groups will be unable to achieve their political goals." In some cases members of a racial group in different areas that are in close proximity, such as rural and urban communities, can share similar interests and form a compact district, but cannot be made a remedy for a Section 2 violation elsewhere "if the only common index is race and the result will be to cause internal friction."

6. *Proportionality.* Proportionality, whether the number of districts in which the minority group forms an effective majority is roughly proportional to its share of the population in the relevant area, is a relevant factor in the totality of circumstances; when a vote-dilution claim is framed in statewide terms, as where racially polarized voting and possible submergence of minority votes throughout a state, proportionality should be looked at and decided on a statewide basis; proportionality is always relevant evidence in determining vote dilution, but never itself dispositive; placing undue emphasis on proportionality risks defeating the goals underlying the Voting Rights Act; the role of proportionality is not to displace an intensely local appraisal of a challenged district or to allow a state to trade off the rights of some against the rights of others; proportionality provides some evidence of whether the political processes leading to nomination or election in the state or political subdivision are not equally open to participation. There is no magic parameter for determining proportionality, and "rough proportionality" must allow for some deviations; Chief Justice Roberts and Justice Alito would adhere to the standard announced in *DeGrandy* that a finding of proportionality can defeat Section 2 liability even if a clear Gingles violation has been made out.

VI. Practice Pointers for Legislative Personnel Involved in the Redistricting Process

Cromartie v. Hunt provides a good list of potential topics to discuss with legislators about to embark on the redistricting process once the Census 2000 results come in.

1. Public or private statements, speeches, e-mail communications, etc. are fair game in the evidence-gathering process. Recall the "smoking gun e-mails" from the *Cromartie* trial.[118]

2. Be careful and circumspect in bringing key players into the legislative decision-making process. Each of those key players may be a potential witness on the issue of motive and purpose.

3. As early in the redistricting process as possible, identify and articulate clearly the relevant and applicable traditional districting criteria, and then apply those criteria consistently throughout the process.

4. Understand and adhere to clear legal guidelines for implementing the race-predominant standard, bearing in mind that a deviation from a consistent race-neutral methodology or an overemphasis on race to the point that race-consciousness may be characterized as race-predominance and may lead to a successful constitutional challenge, strict scrutiny analysis, and invalidation of racially gerrymandered districts.

5. Consideration should be given to the rigorous *Daubert* standard when legislators are trying to decide whether and to what extent experts should be retained and utilized during the legislative decision-making process. Indeed, there are experts upon experts in the field of statistical analysis, demographics, evaluation of exogenous and endogenous electoral evidence, racial bloc voting analysis, race-predominance analysis, and many other discrete evidentiary subcategories. It is not premature for a legislative body or committee to make a preliminary assessment of a redistricting expert's reasoning, methodology, and credibility during that legislative process. An early *Daubert* assessment of experts whose reports, findings, and conclusions may be central to any viable redistricting plan may indeed provide valuable evidentiary support at a trial years later.

Lawyer v. Department of Justice teaches us, moreover, that a legislative body seeking to engage in race-conscious districting can navigate through the process without running afoul of the constitutional prohibition against predominantly race-based districting. It can do this by developing the requisite legislative history sufficient to satisfy the "strong showing" of necessity required for race-based remedial action, followed by a bona fide declaratory judgment action through which the legislative body can seek to establish a great likelihood of a Section 2 violation in the absence of affirmative governmental race-conscious districting.

In this process, a number of practical evidentiary considerations that may come into play during the legislative redistricting process. That process should be conducted with a constant awareness of the fact that the entire legislative history will likely be the focus of pretrial discovery in the event a subsequent racial gerrymandering challenge or an action under Section 2 or Section 5 of the Voting Rights Act is mounted. Relevant legislative evidence may include the following:

Any narrative statements, exhibits, or evidentiary materials submitted to the Section 5 Unit of the Civil Rights Division of the Justice Department, for covered jurisdictions, over the period of at least the preceding decade.

Correspondence, e-mail, faxes, and communications of any kind, nature, and description to and from the state legislature and its representatives, on the one hand, and the Attorney General of the United States and the Voting Section attorneys, on the other, during that same relevant time period, including informal telephone memoranda and summaries of contacts.

Clear, consistent, and unambiguous reference to traditional race-neutral criteria and standards such as compactness, contiguity, incumbency protection, partisan political interests, respect for political subdivision boundaries, and preservation of nonracial communities of interest in the redistricting process.

Relevant newspaper articles, television interviews, and other forms of recorded media coverage, whether on the national, state, or local level, that identify or describe the principal goals and objectives of the redistricting process, the balanced use of race along with other nonracial factors in making boundary line changes, and other public expressions of legislative purpose bearing on the issue of whether and to what extent race predominated or was merely one of many factors in the drawing of boundaries of a given district.

Notes

1. 42 U.S.C. § 1973.
2. S. Rep. No. 97-417, at 4 (1982), *reprinted in* 1982 U.S.C.C.A.N. 177.
3. Holder v. Hall, 512 U.S. 874, 883 (1994) (plurality opinion). *See generally* United States v. Blaine County, Montana, 363 F.3d 897, 906–07 (8th Cir. 2004) (In a landmark decision upholding the constitutionality of Section 2, the 8th Circuit declined to hold that

Congress was required "to find evidence of unconstitutional voting discrimination by each of the fifty states in order to apply section 2 nationwide. Finally, even if nationwide evidence were a prerequisite to national utilization of section 2, Congress had before it sufficient evidence of discrimination in jurisdictions not covered by section 5 to warrant nationwide application. . . . Thus, we conclude that Congress did not exceed its Fourteenth and Fifteenth Amendment enforcement powers by applying section 2 nationwide." The 8th Circuit also provided a helpful comparison and contrast of Section 5 and Section 2 in their scope, burden of proof, remedial purpose, evidentiary predicate, and the federalism costs exacted from state and local jurisdictions: "Unlike section 5 of the VRA, section 2 does not engage in such a pervasive prohibition of constitutional state conduct. The two sections of the VRA are dramatically different in scope. Section 5 is an extraordinary measure, which requires covered jurisdictions to submit every change in their voting procedures to the Department of Justice for preclearance. Section 5 thus places the burden of proof on the state or locality, not on the party challenging the voting procedure. . . . Because section 5 imposes such a significant burden on state and local governments, Congress had reason to limit its application to jurisdictions with a recent history of pervasive voting discrimination. Section 2 is a far more modest remedy. The burden of proof is on the plaintiff, not the state or locality. This burden is significant; Congress heard testimony that section 2 cases are some of the most difficult to litigate because plaintiffs must usually present the testimony of a wide variety of witnesses—political scientists, historians, local politicians, lay witnesses—and sift through records going back more than a century. In contrast to section 5, section 2's results test makes no assumptions about a history of discrimination. Plaintiffs must not only prove compactness, cohesion, and white bloc voting, but also satisfy the totality-of-the-circumstances test." *Id.* at 905–06) (citations omitted).

4. South Carolina v. Katzenbach, 382 U.S. 301, 308 (1966).
5. Reno v. Bossier Parish School Board (*Bossier I*), 520 U.S. 471 (1997).
6. Pub. L. No. 109-246 (2006).
7. *See* Thornburg v. Gingles, 478 U.S. 30, 50-51 (1986) (O'Connor, J., concurring).
8. Whitcomb v. Chavis, 403 U.S. 124 (1971).
9. *Id.* at 149.
10. *Id.*
11. *Id.* at 149-50.
12. *Id.* at 153.
13. *Id.* at 150.
14. *Id.* at 154.
15. White v. Regester, 412 U.S. 755 (1973).
16. *Id.* at 769–70.
17. *Id.* at 767–68.
18. *Id.*
19. *Id.* at 767.
20. City of Mobile v. Bolden, 446 U.S. at 55 (1980).
21. *Id.* at 74 (citing Zimmer v. McKeithen, 485 F.2d 1297 (5th Cir. 1973) (en banc)).
22. *See* Senate Report No. 417, 97th Cong. 2nd Sess. (1982).
23. *See* Senate Report No. 417 at 2, 20-23, 32-33, *reprinted in* 1982 U.S.C.C.A.N. at 197–201, 210–11.

24. *Id.*

25. *Id.* at 33, *reprinted at* 211.

26. *Id.*

27. *Id.* at 148, *reprinted at* 321.

28. Thornburg v. Gingles, 478 U.S. 30 (1986).

29. *Id.* at 51.

30. Johnson v. DeGrandy, 512 U.S. 997 (1994).

31. Lewis v. Alamance County, 99 F.3d 600, 610–11 (4th Cir. 1996).

32. *Id.* at 615 n.12.

33. Zimmer, 485 F.2d 1297.

34. S. Rep. No. 97-417, at 33, *reprinted in* 1982 U.S.C.C.A.N. at 211.

35. *Gingles,* 478 U.S. at 45 (quoting S. Rep. No. 97-417, at 29, *reprinted in* 1982 U.S.C.C.A.N. 177, 207).

36. *Id.* at 51.

37. Growe v. Emison, 507 U.S. 25 (1993).

38. *Id.* at 40.

39. *Id.* at 52–53.

40. *Id.*

41. *Id.* at 52–54.

42. Miller v. Johnson, 515 U.S. 900, 905 (1995).

43. *Id.*

44. Shaw v. Reno, 509 U.S. 630 (1993).

45. *Id.* at 647.

46. *Id.* at 647–48.

47. *Id.* at 646–48.

48. *Id.* at 647.

49. Puckett v. City of Louisville, 991 F.2d 796 (6th Cir. 1993) (citing Thomas Sowell, *Affirmative Action: A Worldwide Disaster,* 88(6) Commentary (Dec. 1989), and Shelby Steele, The Content of Our Character: A New Vision of Race In America (1990)).

50. Lawyer v. Department of Justice, 521 U.S. 567 (1997).

51. Shaw v. Hunt, 517 U.S. 899 (1996).

52. Lawyer v. Dept. of Justice, 521 U.S. 567 (1997).

53. Bush v. Vera, 517 U.S. 952 (1996).

54. Mount Healthy City Bd. of Educ. v. Doyle, 429 U.S. 274 (1977).

55. *Vera,* 517 U.S. at 977.

56. *Id.* at 969.

57. *Id.*

58. *Id.* at 972.

59. Mark Packman, That's Some Catch, That Catch-22: Strategies and Considerations for State and Local Government (ABA Census 2000, 2000).

60. *See* Reno v. Bossier Parish School Board (*Bossier II*), 528 U.S. 320, 334 (2000); Bone Shirt v. Hazeltine, 461 F.3d 1011, 1022 (8th Cir. 2006).

61. Arlington Heights v. Metro. Housing Redev. Corp., 429 U.S. 252, 267 (1977).

62. *Bossier I,* 520 U.S. at 486.

63. Miller v. Johnson, 515 U.S. 900 (1995).

64. Allen v. State Bd. of Elections, 393 U.S. 544 (1969).

65. *Id.* at 565–66.

66. Beer v. United States, 425 U.S. 130 (1976).

67. *Id.* at 141.

68. City of Lockhart v. United States, 460 U.S. 125 (1983).

69. *Id.* at 136.

70. *Id.* at 137.

71. *Id.*

72. Lopez v. Monterey County (*Lopez I*), 519 U.S. 9 (1996).

73. *Id.* at 23.

74. Lopez v. Monterey County (*Lopez II*), 525 U.S. 266 (1999).

75. *Id.* In Mississippi Democratic Party v. Barbour, 491 F. Supp. 2d 641, 659 (N.D. Miss. 2007), the district court, upon invalidating the state primary statute and directing the state legislature to enact certain changes in the primary system, noted that "federal courts do not need preclearance from the Justice Department to determine the constitutionality of an election procedure" (citing Connor v. Johnson, 402 U.S. 690, 692 (1971) (holding that a district court's interim remedial decree is not within the reach of Section 5)). Slip op. at 26.

76. *Id.* at 279.

77. *Id.*

78. *Id.* (citing United Jewish Organizations v. Carey, 430 U.S. 144 (1977)).

79. *Id.* at 280–81 (citing Shaw v. Reno, 509 U.S. 630; Johnson v. DeGrandy, 512 U.S. 977 (1994); and United States v. Onslow County, 683 F. Supp. 1021 (1988)).

80. *Id.* at 281–82.

81. *Bossier I,* 520 U.S. at 483–84.

82. *Id.* at 487–88.

83. *Id.*

84. Circumstantial evidence of discriminatory intent underlying a challenged electoral practice may be found by the convergence of different racial impact, the historical background of the practice revealing a series of official actions taken for invidious purposes, the specific sequence of events leading up to the challenged decision, procedural or substantive departures from normal decision-making, and statements from the legislative or administrative history that reflect on the purpose of the decision. *Arlington Heights,* 429 U.S. at 267.

85. *Bossier I,* 520 U.S. at 474.

86. *Id.* at 477.

87. *Id.* at 487.

88. *Bossier II,* 528 U.S. 320.

89. *Id.* at 336.

90. *Id.*

91. *Id.* at 335 (citing *Bossier I,* 520 U.S. at 478; *Miller,* 515 U.S. at 926; and *Beer,* 425 U.S. at 141).

92. *Id.* at 366.

93. *Id.* at 372.

94. Testimony of Brenda Wright, *Voting Rights Act: Section 5—Preclearance Standards: Hearing Before the Subcommittee on the Constitution of the House Committee on the Judiciary,* 109th Cong. 25–26 (2006), *cited in* David H. Harris, Jr. & Trish Hardy, *A Good Fix But Not the Cure—Fannie Lou Hamer, Rosa Parks, and Coretta Scott King Voting Rights Act Reauthorization and Amendments Act of 2006,* 29 N.C. Cent. L. J. 224, 239 (2007).

95. Georgia v. Ashcroft, 539 U.S. 461 (2003).

96. Harris & Hardy, *supra* note 94, at 239.

97. Pub. L. No. 109–246, 120 Stat. 577 (2006), § 2(b)(6).

98. *Id.* at 241.

99. Carol M. Swain, *Focus on the Voting Rights Act: Reauthorization of the Voting Rights Act: How Politics and Symbolism Failed America,* 5 Geo. J.L. & Pub. Pol'y 29 (2007).

100. *Id.* at 34–35.

101. Harris & Hardy, *supra* note 94, at 239.

102. *Id.* at 238, 246 n.116 (Statement of Rep. Robert C. Scott (D. Va.) before House Subcommittee on the Constitution during Preclearance Standards Hearing).

103. *Id.* at 246 n.119–120 (Statement of Mark A. Posner, Adjunct Professor, American University, Washington College of Law, and Brenda Wright, Managing Attorney, National Voting Rights Institute, before House Subcommittee on the Constitution during Preclearance Standards Hearing).

104. *Id.* at 230, 246–47 n.121 (Statement of Mark A. Posner, *supra* n.104).

105. *Id.* at 246 n.166.

106. *Id.* at 246 n.167.

107. *Id.* at 246 nn.168–170.

108. *Id.* at 246–47.

109. *Id.* at 247 n.171.

110. Public L. No. 109–246, 120 Stat. 577 (2006).

111. *Id.* at 247 n.172.

112. League of United Latin American Citizens (LULAC) v. Perry, 126 S. Ct. 2594 (2006).

113. *Id.* at 2643.

114. 2006 U.S. Trans. Lexis 20, p. 12.

115. *LULAC,* 126 S. Ct. at 2663.

116. *Id.* at 2618.

117. *Id.* at 2619.

118. Easley v. Comartie, 532 U.S. at 254.

CHAPTER TEN

THE ROLE OF DEMOGRAPHIC AND STATISTICAL EXPERTS IN ELECTION LAW LITIGATION

BENJAMIN E. GRIFFITH*
DAVID D. O'DONNELL**

I. Introduction

This chapter addresses the role of experts in election law litigation, particularly experts in the fields of demographics and statistical analysis in vote-dilution litigation under Section 2 of the Voting Rights Act.[1] Specific problems are encountered by experts and counsel employing these analytical methods in complex litigation, often entailing a global analysis of the electoral history of a jurisdiction for the past three to four decades. Timely prepared, structurally complete, and methodologically solid analysis are essential ingredients that must be blended in correct proportions in order for an expert to express relevant and reliable opinions on the discrete issues that surface in such litigation. Experts must be constantly aware of the gatekeeping role and the heavy burden that is placed on Article III judges in evaluating expert testimony under the admissibility standards set forth in Federal Rule of Evidence 702 and *Daubert,* just as federal district court judges must maintain a constant vigil over the fundamental relevance and reliability of proffered expert testimony.[2]

II. Expert Testimony and the Gatekeeper Role of Judges

Expert qualifications are not taken as gospel just because an expert tenders a 20-page curriculum vitae, nor is the *Daubert* threshold crossed in a leisurely manner.[3]

* Chair, ABA Section of State and Local Government Law; ABA Standing Committee on Election Law; J.D. University of Mississippi School of Law, 1975; Partner, Griffith & Griffith, Cleveland, Mississippi.
** J.D. Mississippi, 1985; Partner, Clayton O'Donnell, PLLC, Oxford, Mississippi.

Expert testimony in this kind of litigation is plainly the centerpiece of the plaintiff's case in chief on liability, just as it is often the bulwark of the defense.[4]

Experts may be a dime a dozen in the view of some cynics, but the unvarnished reality is that the very best, most often relied on, and consistently accepted experts in election litigation do not even amount to a dozen in number. These experts fall into two categories. Demographers generally speak to the "compactness" of minority populations and the related issues of minority population fragmentation and "packing" within voting schemes. Statisticians speak to voter behavior, which is estimated by the use of various statistical methods. The issues they are called on to elucidate for the court include voting patterns, racial polarization, racial bloc voting, present effects of past discrimination, the role of socioeconomic disparities in contributing to minority electoral participation rates, the significance of minority electoral success, interpretation of voter registration data, identification of position bias and its effect on such phenomena as windfall votes and "bounce," the statistical significance of electoral data in bivariate ecological regression analysis and homogenous analysis, and identification of the most helpful endogenous and exogenous elections. Just this brief catalogue of typical issues might explain why federal judges place voting-rights litigation on the high end of difficulty in terms of the demands on judicial resources. That is a burden to shoulder not simply with regard to assessing "admissibility" but also in according proper weight to often opposing expert views expressed through difficult jargon.

III. The Expanding Role of Experts

There is a legitimate, substantial, and increasingly important role for experts in election litigation and particularly vote-dilution litigation under Section 2. Since 1982, when amended Section 2 was enacted and first applied by the Supreme Court several years later in *Thornburg v. Gingles,* private plaintiffs and the United States have developed an increasingly effective cadre of experts in this litigation. This access to very effective and well-seasoned experts has been nothing short of phenomenal and has been aided by the revolving door between the Civil Rights Division of the United States Department of Justice and such organizations as the ACLU and Lawyers Committee for Civil Rights Under the Law, both sources of some of the very best attorneys with extensive experience representing Section 2 plaintiffs. The availability of such experts is often an issue for the defense bar during the early phases of a case. Indeed, defense counsel in this type of litigation may at times face a sharp learning curve as well as a time crunch in securing a qualified, competent, experienced experts. Once a vote-dilution complaint is filed in federal court, the clock starts ticking for the defendant to obtain the best available expert, which in turn will depend on the extent to which one or more of the *Gingles*[5] preconditions or Senate Report factors are sharply in dispute. It may also depend on whether the plaintiff, either private or the United States, has already hired that expert.

The expert ultimately retained must have the time, resources, experience, and sheer energy to undertake the requisite massive review of electoral data, demographic data, reams of statistical analyses, and unique anecdotal information. Jurisdiction-specific electoral information will often be obtainable through digging. This means a lot of digging, factual investigation, sifting of official records and files generated before we knew what a megabyte was, and interviews with scores of candidates, potential candidates, and other lay witnesses. From the defense perspective, the jurisdiction retaining the expert must be prepared to devote the necessary resources and man-power to support this effort, while remaining ever cognizant of the possibility of assessment of attorney fees and expert witness fees incurred by the prevailing party if liability is ultimately determined.

This chapter concludes that the opportunities and utility of retaining experts in the field of election litigation are expanding and can be expected to continue expanding as we enter the next decade following the 2010 decennial census.[6] The willingness and capability of federal courts to carry out their *Daubert*-based gate-keeper role must keep up with that expansion.[7]

IV. Expert Testimony in Section 2 Vote-Dilution Litigation

Proof of a Section 2 vote-dilution claim will invariably require the use of demo-graphic and statistical experts qualified to testify as to voting district compactness, the description and prediction of majority and minority group voting behavior, and, perhaps, the degree to which such behavior is motivated by racial animus. In *Thornburg v. Gingles,* the Supreme Court delineated the elements of an actionable minority vote-dilution claim under amended Section 2 of the Voting Rights Act. In *Gingles,* the Court devised a three-part set of "preconditions" which were deemed necessary yet insufficient to establish an actionable minority vote-dilution claim.[8] As to the preconditions, first, a plaintiff must establish that the minority electorate within a given electoral scheme are sufficiently numerous and geographically com-pact to constitute a majority-minority single member district. Second, the minority electorate must be "politically cohesive." Third, the proof must also show that the majority electorate consistently votes as a bloc so as to regularly result in the defeat of the minority-preferred candidates. It has been observed that the third precon-dition, that is, "white bloc voting," occupies a central and essential role within the minority vote-dilution inquiry. Proof of the third *Gingles* element requires the identification of the "minority-preferred candidate" and then an evaluation of the majority voting patterns in relation to the electoral success of the minority-preferred candidate.

Although the degree of the minority electorate's political cohesion and the degree of the majority electorate's bloc voting, as well as the identification of the minority's preferred candidate, may be proved through anecdotal evidence depending on the circumstances of a particular case, generally the satisfaction of these criteria is through statistical evidence offered by expert witnesses. In *Gingles*, for example, the plaintiffs proffered expert testimony describing "how," not "why," the minority majority electorates voted in particular elections through the use of extreme case analysis and bivariate ecological regression statistical evidence.[9] Noting that these statistical techniques essentially yielded "estimates" of voting patterns and voter behavior, as well as estimates of the percentages of the minority and majority electorates who actually voted for minority candidates in discreet electoral contests, the *Gingles* Court approved the trial court's careful evaluation of the statistical data, which included the evaluation of the strength of the "correlation" between the race of the voter and the election of certain candidates as well as whether the correlation was "statistically significant."[10]

Yet a plurality of the Justices in *Gingles* did observe that the nature of the bivariate ecological regression analysis fell short in resolving the ultimate question in a vote-dilution claim, that is, whether racial animus in the majority electorate best explains the consistent defeat of minority-preferred candidates. Subsequent lower court decisions have held that proof of the three *Gingles*, to prove "racial bloc voting," creates a rebuttable presumption that the minority-preferred candidate's defeat at the polls was the result of racial animus. Under this approach, proof of the likely causes of majority voting behavior through anecdotal and multivariate regression analysis evidence would be relevant to the ultimate issue under the totality of the circumstances analysis.

Since *Gingles*, the lower courts reviewing statistical data in vote-dilution cases have had a checkered history in terms of evaluating or even commenting on the "statistical significance" of the presented data as well as the strength of the correlations between the racial makeup of the voting age populations of each electoral district and the number of votes cast for each candidate. The concept of "statistical significance" is essential to the ultimate validity of the data because it involves a consideration of the probability that the data revealed was produced by random events as opposed to a true correlation between the variables measured by the presented regression analyses. It is also essential in establishing the relevance of the data in a *Daubert* sense.

V. Unique Justification for Applying Daubert in Election Litigation

Cromartie v. Hunt[11] provides one of the strongest justifications for applying a rigorous *Daubert* standard to the process of selecting experts who may participate and provide guidance in the legislative decision-making process for redistricting and reapportionment even prior to the threat of litigation. Indeed, there are experts upon experts in the field of statistical analysis, demographics, evaluation of exogenous and endogenous electoral evidence, racial bloc voting analysis, race-predominance analysis, and many other discrete evidentiary subcategories. Jurisdictions do not just face the prospect of litigation over legislative choices that must be made any time redistricting is required, as for example as a consequence of annexation or reapportionment. They must now consider whether to maintain or expand the number and racial density of majority-minority districts in light of the Voting Rights Act Reauthorization and Amendments Act's[12] legislative overruling of *Georgia v. Ashcroft*[13] and *Bossier II.*[14]

Given the new statutory regime that became effective in July 2006, especially for jurisdictions covered by Section 5 in its reauthorized and strengthened form, it would not be premature for a legislative body or committee to (1) select an appropriate expert, (2) engage the expert to assist in developing and formulating relevant criteria and standards that will guide a future redistricting process, and (3) undertake a preliminary assessment of a redistricting expert's reasoning, methodology, and credibility during that legislative process, *well before* the post-2010 redistricting process officially gets underway. An early *Daubert* assessment of an expert whose reports, findings, and conclusions may be central to any viable redistricting plan may provide valuable evidentiary support at a trial years later in the event of a racial gerrymandering challenge or other 14th Amendment claim.[15] Experts and seasoned voting rights litigation counsel played a central role in the legislative jockeying that ultimately led to the 2006 Supreme Court plurality's decision in *LULAC v. Perry.*[16]

VI. Daubert/Kumho Tire

The admissibility of expert evidence in federal court is governed by the standards set forth in *Daubert* and *Kumho Tire,* which are now incorporated into Federal Rule of Evidence 702. Essentially, all expert testimony, including scientific evidence, must be "relevant to the task at hand" and must rest on a "reliable foundation."[17] Rule 702 provides that expert testimony is admissible where: (1) the testimony is based on sufficient facts or data, (2) the testimony is the product of reliable principles and methods, and (3) the witness has applied the principles and methods reliably to the facts of the case. Thus, reliability asks whether the expert's reasoning or methodology is scientifically valid, and relevance asks whether that reasoning or methodology is properly applied to the particular facts at issue. In *Daubert,* the Supreme Court directed trial courts to carefully evaluate the foundation of expert testimony and suggested the use of the following nonexhaustive list of factors in assessing "reliability": (1) whether the theory or technique the expert employs is generally accepted, (2) whether the theory has been subjected to peer review and publication, (3) whether the theory can and has been tested, (4) whether the known or potential rate of error is acceptable, and (5) whether there are standards controlling the technique's operation.[18] In the end, the complexity and volume of the statistical data generated in the typical Section 2 case as well as the conclusions and opinions drawn by the proffered experts present a formidable gatekeeping challenge to federal judges charged with applying the *Daubert/Kumho Tire* and Rule 702 standard of admissibility, especially as concerns the obligation to assess the case specific relevance of the expert's methodology and conclusions.

VII. Outcome-Determinative Nature of Daubert Hearings

Litigators play for keeps in a Federal Rule of Evidence 104(a)[19] *Daubert* hearing. The plaintiff or defendant in election litigation understands the pivotal role of expert testimony in such litigation, and is also keenly aware that "nothing in either *Daubert* or the Federal Rules of Evidence requires a district court to admit opinion evidence which is connected to existing data only by the ipse dixit of the expert. A court may conclude that there is simply too great an analytical gap between the data and the opinion proffered," or it may conclude that the level of peer review to which the expert's proffered testimony has been subjected is inadequate, or it may find that the expert's proposed expert opinion lacks discernible methodology.

VIII. Demographic Expert Qualifications to Draw Redistricting Maps

In *Bone Shirt v. Hazeltine,* the Eighth Circuit upheld the trial court's admission of expert testimony in a vote-dilution case that employed bivariate ecological repression analysis and homogeneous precinct analysis over a *Daubert* challenge.[20] Finding that the statistical methods used by the plaintiffs' expert "have long been accepted by the Supreme Court," the court affirmed the trial court's *Daubert* finding that the statistical methods were "reliable" in determining the second and third *Gingles* preconditions.[21]

The district court also ultimately held that a state legislative redistricting plan under review violated Section 2 of the Voting Rights Act of 1965 because the plan diluted Indian voting strength by minimizing the number of districts in which they could select a candidate of their choice. Demographic experts utilize population data principally from U.S. Census data in determining the size and location of specific racial and ethnic groups within a given jurisdiction and evaluate communities of interest, geographic, natural land, and man-made boundaries in devising electoral districting schemes. In admitting the expert testimony of the plaintiffs' demographic expert, William Cooper, the district court found that the expert's use of single-race Indian data, while less comprehensive, did not discredit his redistricting maps or his findings, and even though he had not taught at a college or written

for a journal and was not a sociologist, political scientist, economist, or econome-
trician, "he is nonetheless credible and qualified as an expert to draw redistricting
maps. Neither his testimony nor his report require expertise in these social sciences
for purposes of providing reliable testimony about alternative redistricting plans for
South Dakota. He need not be an expert in anthropology, Sioux culture and history,
or South Dakota history to reliably report on redistricting options in South Dakota.
He can reliably base his analysis and conclusions on his experience in South Dakota
and his knowledge of redistricting."[22]

IX. Experts on Position Bias in Election Litigation

Some attribute to Mark Twain the old adage "figures don't lie, but liars sure can
figure." Others attribute it to an unnamed politician who beat his opponent despite
last-minute exit polls that said otherwise. When it comes to statistical evidence,
demographic evidence, or other evidence purporting to explain why voters vote the
way they do, woe be to the expert who arms himself with statistics, anecdotal data,
or election-related studies he never bothered to verify, understand, or tie to the specific facts of the case.

Koppell v. New York State Board of Elections[23] provides an example of expert
exclusion in this context. Plaintiffs (two state voters and an unsuccessful candidate
for New York Attorney General) challenged the constitutionality of a state election
law provision that determined the position of candidates on the ballot by lottery,
arguing that the statute violated their the First and 14th Amendment rights due to
the existence of "position bias." Position bias is a theory that a certain number of
"windfall votes" will be cast for whichever candidate has his or her name listed first
on the ballot solely by virtue of being listed in that first ballot slot.

Each party proffered expert reports and testimony regarding the existence vel non
of position bias, plaintiffs through Dr. Bain and defendants through Drs. Chapin
and Darcy. Each party moved to strike the opposition's expert on the ground that
each failed to pass muster under Daubert threshold requirements of relevance and
reliability. Plaintiffs also challenged the Chapin and Darcy reports based on defendants' failure to comply with Federal Rule of Civil Procedure 26(a)(2)(B). Following a Daubert hearing, the district court denied defendants' motion to strike Dr.
Bain's report, denied plaintiffs' motion to strike Dr. Darcy's report and testimony,
and granted plaintiffs' motion to strike Dr. Chapin's report and testimony.[24]

X. Voting-Age Population Estimates Based
on Voter Registration Data

The 11th Circuit upheld the admissibility of expert testimony with respect to population calculations based on voter registration data in Johnson v. DeSoto County

Board of Commissioners.[25] *Desoto County* focused on the use of voter-registration data as the basis for measuring voting age population (VAP), and expert opinion testimony as to voting age population proved to be outcome-determinative. The litigation was commenced as a vote-dilution action under Section 2 in which the county proffered an expert who relied on voter registration figures to opine on the county's population increase following the 1990 census.

Affirming the district court's ruling that black citizens of the county had failed to prove vote dilution in their Section 2 challenge to the current at-large method of electing the county school board and county commission, the 11th Circuit rejected the plaintiffs' claim that the district court had erroneously considered noncensus evidence based on voter registration figures. According to the plaintiffs, registration data was inherently unreliable as a measure of voting age population and could not be used to contradict census figures. The court reasoned that there is no per se rule against the use of voter registration data in voting rights cases, and that voter registration evidence had been accepted by the Supreme Court as credible and reliable.[26]

Relying on *Daubert,* the 11th Circuit also noted that it had recognized the competence of such data and that "[l]ike most evidence presented by expert testimony, we think its admissibility has to be determined on a case-by-case basis by the district court" and that in voting rights cases, "statistical evidence derived from a sampling method, using reliable statistical techniques, is admissible on the question of determining the relevant population."[27] The 11th Circuit saw no reason why evidence of calculations of the county's population derived from voter registration information should be subject to a different analysis, noting that "[t]he Supreme Court has never precluded the use of voter registration data. And, neither have we."[28] The 11th Circuit concluded that the district court focused on population as the correct criteria, and that use of evidence derived from voter registration data to show population was not impermissible, stating:

> Whether evidence derived from voter registration figures is sufficiently reliable to be admitted and considered is a determination in the discretion of the district court. . . . If the evidence is admissible, that voter registration data might not be as reliable as some other measures of population goes to the weight of the evidence, but does not preclude use of the figures by the district court.[29]

In this case, both sides presented the district judge with expert testimony on the reliability of the defendants' evidence. The defendants' expert testified about the county registration data's reliability and emphasized the lack of obstacles to registration. According to this expert, the registration data would not underrepresent the black population in 1998 because the passage of the Motor Voter law would have increased registration rates since 1991. The 11th Circuit concluded that it was not an abuse of discretion for the district court to receive and consider evidence on the demographic changes in the county, reasoning that "[t]he kinds of evidence introduced in this case are not unfit for the purpose of challenging the continuing accuracy of census data."[30]

XI. Expert Testimony on Voting Machine Downtime

Expert testimony relevant to calculating voting machine downtime was at issue in *Montgomery County v. Microvote Corp.*[31] The county sought to recover monetary damages in a suit against the seller of malfunctioning electronic voting machines and its surety, where the county had purchased the voting machines. At trial, the county presented evidence of damages through expert testimony about downtime. The defendants proffered the videotape deposition testimony of an expert, Naegele, who was admittedly qualified to testify that the voting machines met Federal Election Commission standards. The expert relied in part on a "reverse guesstimate" of the machines' downtime set forth in a document prepared by the defendant seller's sales director.

The expert did not know what this downtime document was, who created it, or how it was created, nor did he measure actual election use data. The trial court's exclusion of this expert evidence was upheld by the Third Circuit, which concluded that the data underlying the expert's opinion was not based on sound data and was unreliable, stating:

> While the District Court did not question Naegele's qualifications as an expert to offer such testimony, the testimony of a witness, who is well qualified by experience, still may be barred if it is not based on sound data. . . . The trial judge, after viewing the videotape deposition, held that the videotape was inadmissible because it was unreliable, noting that "I'm a little concerned about some of the things that were shown to him he didn't seem to know where they were from or what the source of them were. That, I find disturbing." In his deposition, Naegele indicates that he relied on a document prepared by Microvote's National Sales Director, Gary Greenhalgh, in which Greenhalgh, who was not present during the April 1996 elections, made a "reverse" "guesstimate" about the amount of time that the machines were down. Greenhalgh did not base his determination on primary data. Naegele admitted that he did not know what the document was, who created it, or how it was created. Naegele also relied on other documents, some of which apparently were derived from the Greenhalgh document. Again, Naegele could not identify the source or basis of some of these documents, and Naegele admitted that he did not measure actual election use data to determine how long the machines were down. While Naegele testified that he relied on audit trail tapes, these were a sampling of tapes that were selected by an attorney for Carson. . . . Naegele was not subjected to cross-examination at his deposition because plaintiff's attorney was not present. Under these circumstances, we conclude that the District Court did not abuse its

discretion in excluding Naegele's testimony because the court reasonably concluded that the data underlying Naegele's opinion was so unreliable that no reasonable expert could base an opinion on it.[32]

XII. Lay Testimony of Election Officials in Challenge to Voter ID Requirement

Lay testimony in election litigation should be properly admissible so long as it does not have the earmarks of expert testimony. The dividing line between the two can be a fine one, but it exists and will be enforced in the proper case. For example, in *ACLU v. Santillanes,* the district court had before it cross-motions of plaintiffs and defendants for summary judgment as to the constitutionality of an amendment to the City of Albuquerque's charter that required voters to display photo identification cards in order to vote in all future municipal elections.[33] Holding that the charter amendment violated the Equal Protection Clause, the district court found that the lay testimony of election officials was properly considered in determining whether the parties met their respective summary judgment burdens. On one hand, an undesignated expert should not be permitted to masquerade as a lay witness, giving testimony based on specialized knowledge or cloaked in technical methodology that goes far beyond personal knowledge and experience of a lay witness. On the other hand, as in this case, courts routinely admit sworn testimony that is based on a lay witness's personal experience regarding methods of operation or "tools of the trade" used by the population he or she is charged with monitoring. The district court held that

> the sworn testimony of experienced election officials based on their own personal knowledge regarding the observed behaviors of an identifiable group or class of people they are charged with monitoring (e.g., New Mexico voters or election judges). Similarly, it does not violate the Rules of Evidence to consider such sworn testimony when it is based on the personal knowledge of witnesses in other professions who have an abundance of experience observing the behavior of a particular segment of the population (e.g., homeless individuals or Native Americans who reside in Albuquerque), so long as the witness's testimony is limited to describing personal observations and is not "cloaked under any scientific or technical methodology" containing the "indicia of an expert opinion."[34]

XIII. Evidentiary Hearing Under Daubert

The district court in *Santillanes* began its analysis with an exposition of the evidentiary hearing that should be held pursuant to Rule 104(a) in determining the admissibility of expert testimony, and outlined that two-step inquiry in which a trial judge must engage to determine "whether the reasoning or methodology underlying the [expert's] testimony is . . . valid and . . . whether that reasoning or methodology properly can be applied to the facts in issue."[35] The purpose of an evidentiary hearing held pursuant to *Daubert* is to determine whether the proffered "expert testimony 'both rests on a reliable foundation and is relevant to the task at hand.'"[36] The admissibility of evidence must be established by a preponderance of the evidence,[37] and the burden of demonstrating that the testimony is competent, relevant, and reliable rests with the proponent of the testimony.

XIV. Pertinence of Daubert *Factors in Assessing Reliability*

Whether the *Daubert* factors are pertinent to assessing reliability in a particular case depends on the nature of the issue, the particular expertise of the expert, and the subject of the expert's testimony. For this reason a trial judge is obliged to consider the specific factors identified in *Daubert* where they are reasonable measures of the reliability of expert testimony. The district court in *Koppell* embraced its role as gate-keeper, recognizing that it is required ultimately to "make certain that an expert, whether basing testimony on professional studies or personal experience, employs in the courtroom the same level of intellectual rigor that characterizes the practice of an expert in the relevant field."[38] This means that the trial court is required not only to determine if the testimony is reliable, but it must also

> determine whether an expert's testimony is "relevant to the task at hand," namely, whether the expert's reasoning or methodology can be properly applied to the facts before the court. In order to determine whether the expert's testimony will "assist the trier of fact to understand the evidence or to determine a fact in issue," the testimony must not only be reliable but must be relevant in that it "fits" the facts of the case.[39]

Turning to an application of these basic *Daubert* principles to the reports at issue, the district court in *Koppell* rejected the defendants' argument that Dr. Bain's testimony and expert report failed to meet the *Daubert* standards for reliability and relevance, concluding that the Bain report and testimony met the *Daubert* threshold.[40]

XV. Daubert *Threshold of Relevance and Reliability*

An expert in voting rights litigation should be allowed to give expert testimony so long as it is based on and the product of reliable principles and methods, it is based on sufficient facts and data, and the expert has applied reliable principles and methods in a reliable manner to the facts of the case. The absence of peer review should not be dispositive of admissibility of expert testimony under *Daubert*. Exclusion of an expert's testimony solely because it would not be published in a peer review article is a misreading of *Daubert,* as a leading treatise on the Federal Rules of Evidence makes clear:

> [P]eer review is not an absolute requirement for admissibility after Daubert. For one thing, the expert's research may be too particularized to be publishable. . . . Also, the expert's research may concern a historical event that is no longer of much interest to the publication world.[41]

Conversely, when the methodology used by an expert is subject to extensive peer review, the expert's testimony is much more likely to cross the *Daubert* threshold. In *Koppell,* the plaintiffs' expert, Dr. Bain, had coauthored a 1957 monograph, "Ballot Position and Voter's Choice," in which he studied the effects of position bias in two other states. His work was subsequently cited in over 45 scholarly articles. This expert had also given expert testimony on position bias in two state cases in California. His analysis of position bias in *Koppell* was based primarily on a study that he conducted of the 1998 Democratic primary elections in New York City. He studied 79 electoral contests, including the primary for Attorney General, noting that in New York City the candidates rotated equally among all positions on a ballot on an election precinct by election precinct basis.

The plaintiffs' expert undertook to study the elections within New York City because the rotation of the candidates made it possible in theory to isolate the effects of any position bias. In conducting the study for the instant case, the expert relied on a methodology that was substantially similar to the methodology he had described in his 1957 monograph. Scrutinizing Barnes' methodology, the district court observed:

> Bain measures position bias, or effect, in two ways. First, he compares each candidate's percentage of the total vote in the ballots on which he or she appeared in first place with the candidate's percentage of the vote in all of the election district's other ballots. Any excess percentage when in first place is considered evidence of position effect. He found a position effect with a reasonable statistical significance in 65 of the contests, with an average excess percentage of 8.5 percent. The second method measures the overall "bounce" candidates receive from being in the first position. "Bounce" is the term Bain uses to describe the average percentage increase that all the candidates in a given race get from being in the first position on the ballot. As noted above, Bain's methodology has been subject to extensive peer review, and there is a great deal of literature supporting and attacking, as well as citing, Bain's monograph and his methodology. Accordingly, the Bain report meets the *Daubert* threshold for reliability.[42]

The district court emphasized that once Dr. Bain's expert report passed the *Daubert* threshold, defense objections and concerns would be relevant to the weight to be given by the trier of fact rather than to the admissibility of the expert's testimony. The court further concluded that the report met the *Daubert* threshold of relevance, noting that "[w]hile defendants have offered evidence that tends to make the Bain report less probative, they have not offered evidence that would bar its admissibility. Dr. Bain's study of the 1998 primaries was designed to determine the precise magnitude of position effect in those elections and will assist the trier of fact in determining whether there is a position effect and whether this effect rises to the level of a constitutional injury."[43]

XVI. *Failure to Pass* Daubert *Threshold*

With respect to the plaintiffs' motion to strike the expert report of the defendants' expert, Dr. Chapin, the district court in *Koppell,* upon reading the report and hearing the testimony presented, granted the motion on two separate grounds: First, the report failed to pass the *Daubert* threshold of relevance and reliability, and second, defendants had failed to set forth in a written report an adequate disclosure of the bases of Dr. Chapin's opinions, in violation of Rule 26(a)(2)(B).[44] According to the court, this expert argued that position bias did not determine the outcomes of relevant statewide primary elections from 1974 through 1998. In his report, the expert opined about the reasons for the turnout in each electoral race, discussing such factors as the salient issues in each primary election, qualities of each candidate and the relative financial advantage of each, and the popularity of each candidate among various demographic groups. In excluding the Chapin report, the district court reasoned:

> The report is apparently based upon Chapin's political experience and historical education and uses what he terms the "methodology of history." He relied on campaign literature, newspapers, conversations with certain undisclosed individuals, and his "own memories." The explanations in each instance are largely anecdotal and do not cite particular facts, pieces of literature, or articles.[45] Chapin testified that in connection with this litigation he simply studied The New York Times and The New York Daily News for the nine months prior to each primary, and looked for "every political story in every day of those two newspapers." Defendants never provided plaintiffs with the particular stories upon which Dr. Chapin relied within each nine month period. Moreover, the report does not purport to rely upon any form of quantitative analysis.[46]

XVII. Daubert *Threshold for Reliability*

Focusing on the underlying methodology supporting the theory of position bias, the district court in *Koppell* found that the Chapin report failed to meet *Daubert*'s threshold for reliability, noting that it

> does not rely upon any discernible methodology. Rather, the report is essentially a compendium of Dr. Chapin's opinions about the elections. The report barely discusses

the existence of position effect in any given election and is not methodologically sound enough to provide reliable evidence. Moreover, this methodology has not been published, tested or subject to peer review. In addition, according to his own testimony, Dr. Chapin's opinions and judgments are in many cases those he validates based on the opinions of others. When describing the basis for his judgment regarding one particular election, Dr. Chapin testified that he knew that his own judgment was correct because "everybody who was involved, including myself, felt the same way, that is to say, they all agreed."[47]

Notwithstanding the extensive political experience of this proffered expert, the district court was not impressed with the expert's lack of specific expertise in field of position bias, stating that "[t]o the extent that the report is merely relying on consensus or the opinions of others, Chapin lacks any particular expertise. Moreover, while Dr. Chapin has significant political experience, he has not asserted expertise in the area of position bias."[48]

The last straw for the district court in its evaluation of this expert was the lack of testing or peer review. The court granted the plaintiffs' motion to strike the Chapin report "because the techniques upon which Dr. Chapin relies have neither been tested nor subject to peer review, and because the analysis he provides is largely anecdotal and does not rely upon any particular type of expertise that would assist the trier of fact in rendering the ultimate determination in this action."[49]

XVIII. Failure to Provide Basis of Opinions Under Rule 26(a)(2)(B)

Rule 26(a)(2)(B) required defendants to disclose in sufficient detail the bases for their expert's opinions, but the only materials the *Koppell* defendants provided the plaintiffs as apparently forming the bases of Dr. Chapin's opinions consisted of 117 campaign finance reports, 50 pieces of campaign literature, 26 newspaper articles, and a list of date ranges for the *New York Times,* the *New York Daily News,* the *New York Post,* and *New York Newsday* covering a nine-month period. The district court concluded that "[a] list of dates, covering nine month periods, renders this disclosure meaningless and leaves plaintiffs and the Court without a clear understanding of the data upon which Dr. Darcy relied, as well as the specific bases for his opinions."[50] Since defendants failed to provide sufficiently detailed information regarding the bases of their expert's opinion, the court excluded the Chapin report.[51]

XIX. Abdication of Gatekeeper Role as Harmless Error

While *Daubert* places a heavy burden on district judges to serve as evidentiary gatekeepers, there are instances when a court's abdication of it gatekeeping role under

Daubert may be declared harmless error.[52] One such instance occurred in *United States v. Blaine County, Montana*.[53] There the Ninth Circuit upheld the district court's determination that Blaine County, Montana's at-large voting system for electing members to the county commission violated Section 2, preventing American Indians from participating equally in the county's political process. The county on appeal challenged the district court's improper admission of testimony of the United States's expert witnesses, but the Ninth Circuit concluded that while the district court's evidentiary rulings were erroneous in a limited respect, the error was harmless.

In order to show racially cohesive voting by Native American Indians in the county, the United States proffered the expert testimony of Dr. Theodore Arrington, who testified over the county's objection that in all 14 countywide elections he examined, Native American Indian voters exceeded 67 percent cohesion. The district court found a Section 2 violation and ruled for the United States, enjoining the county from holding elections under its at-large electoral system.

The Ninth Circuit upheld the admissibility of the challenged expert testimony, rejecting the county's argument that the district court did not rule on its objections to experts' testimony. The Ninth Circuit found that the district court did evaluate the reliability of Dr. Arrington's testimony. The court also rejected the county's argument that Dr. Arrington's testimony was unreliable because he relied on race-identified registration lists, but the county's own expert testified that such reliance is customary and appropriate, and Dr. Arrington's and the county expert's bivariate ecological regression analysis and homogenous precinct analysis yielded similar results. The court found no abuse of discretion in admitting Arrington's testimony and considered any error in not making the required reliability determination to be harmless.[54]

Blaine County upheld the use of race-identified registration lists as acceptable data collection methods to examine racial voting patterns. The county objected at trial to the expert testimony of the United States' experts, Drs. Arrington, Hoxie, and McCool. Acknowledging that the district court was required to make a reliability determination to fulfill its gatekeeping function under *Daubert*/Rule 702, the Ninth Circuit found that the district court had made the required reliability determination with respect to Dr. Arrington's testimony and report. It found that race-identified registration lists used by Dr. Arrington were methods of data collection consistently accepted in Section 2 vote-dilution litigation. The Ninth Circuit also held that it was not an abuse of discretion for the district court to admit Dr. Arrington's testimony.[55]

The Ninth Circuit also commented on several commonly used and accepted methods for evaluating voting patterns: bivariate ecological regression analysis (BERA) and homogenous precinct analysis. Results obtained through the use of these methodologies in assessing racial voting patterns, racial polarization, and legally significant racial bloc voting were similar to the results obtained by Dr. Arrington's use of race-identified registration lists. The Ninth Circuit rejected the county's challenge to Dr. Arrington's use of race-identified registration lists, noting that both Dr. Arrington and the county's expert, Dr. Ron Weber, had testified that race-identified registration lists were

> commonly used and acceptable tools for examining racial voting patterns. Indeed, race-identified registration lists are arguably superior to the alternatives, such as the use of census data, because they make no assumptions about registration rates in particular communities. Moreover, the notion that Dr. Arrington's analysis was methodologically flawed is belied by the fact that Dr. Arrington's and Dr. Weber's bivariate ecological regression analysis and homogenous precinct analysis yielded similar results. Finally, Dr. Arrington actually went beyond procedures used in previous section 2 cases and divided his coders into separate groups. Thus, there was no abuse of discretion in admitting Dr. Arrington's testimony and exhibits.[56]

The Ninth Circuit also addressed the trial court's apparent failure to perform its gatekeeper role when it neither determined methodological flaws in the plaintiff's expert testimony nor evaluated the reliability of that expert testimony. Its reasoning was based on the harmless error rule. Concluding that the tainted testimony was not essential to its ultimate finding of vote dilution, the Ninth Circuit held:

> We agree that the district court failed to determine the reliability of portions of Dr. Hoxie's testimony and the entirety of Dr. McCool's expert testimony, despite objections by Blaine County. The district court's decision is not reversible, however, if its failure to make the required reliability determination was harmless. . . . Because we agree that the district court failed to expressly determine the reliability of Dr. Hoxie and Dr. McCool's testimony, we do not address the County's alternative argument that their testimony should not have been admitted because it was methodologically flawed.

> We conclude that the district court's error was harmless because the tainted testimony was not essential to the district court's ultimate finding of vote dilution. . . . In any event, the first Senate factor is not critical. As *Gingles* explained, "the most important Senate Report factors bearing on § 2 challenges to multimember districts are the 'extent to which minority group members have been elected to public office in the jurisdiction' and the 'extent to which voting in the elections of the state or political subdivision is racially polarized.'" In fact, *Gingles* expressly stated that other factors, such as the first Senate factor, "are supportive of, but not essential to, a minority voter's claim." *Id.* Therefore, even if we exclude the tainted testimony, and even if we assume that testimony was critical to the district court's analysis of the first Senate factor, we would not disturb the district court's ultimate finding of vote dilution.[57]

XX. Expert Evidence and Federal Case Management

Core disclosure and expert designation requirements, expanded use of expert depositions, and selective use of Rule 104(a) hearings have combined to make *Daubert* challenges an integral part of every federal litigator's arsenal. In election litigation in which heavy reliance is placed on relevant and reliable expert testimony, *Daubert*-related concerns can reverberate through virtually every stage of the litigation, from the initial Rule 16 scheduling conference, the Rule 26(a)(2)(B) expert written report, and Rule 56 Motions for Summary Judgment to trial, posttrial motions, and appeal. *Daubert* and its progeny have significantly broadened the discretion of trial judges to exclude what could often be exposed as litigation-driven speculation driven by the ipse dixit of forensic charlatans.

XXI. Conclusion

Since 1993, this new evidentiary regime has turned federal judges into "gatekeepers" who use an analytical framework closely aligned to the wording, intent, and purpose of the Federal Rules of Evidence. In keeping with the expanded role of experts and the letter and spirit of those rules, counsel retaining an expert in election litigation should be particularly careful to heed *Daubert's* core principle that a federal judge as gatekeeper will require more than a sterling resume before a professed expert will be permitted to give expert opinion testimony.[58]

Notes

1. Voting Rights Act of 1965, 42 U.S.C. § 1973.

2. The Federal Rules of Evidence applicable to expert testimony must be considered in context. When a district court undertakes a *Daubert* analysis, it must be mindful of the other applicable evidentiary rules such as Rule 703 and 403, discussed *infra* at note 52. Rule 703 is not satisfied when an expert predicates his or her own opinion upon unfounded data or analysis. The fact that the expert relied upon the report of another expert will not relieve a plaintiff from its burden of proving the underlying assumptions contained in the report. The 2000 amendment to Rule 702 "synthesizes the Supreme Court cases and lays out three requirements that all expert testimony must meet. The clarification and synthesis will be of great assistance to the bench and bar." 3 S. SALTZBURG, M. MARTIN & D. CAPRA, FEDERAL RULES OF EVIDENCE MANUAL § 702.02[10], at 702–49 (2002). Rule 702's focus is on the manner in which the expert has acquired his or her expertise, whether through formal training, education, experience, lectures, or reading, while the focus of Rule 703 is on the types of facts particular to the litigation that provide the basis for the expert's opinion. S. GOODE & O. WELLBORN, COURTROOM HANDBOOK ON FEDERAL EVIDENCE 370 (2005). Rule 703 normally relieves the proponent of expert testimony from having to lay an elaborate foundation with regard to

the expert's basis as a prerequisite to admissibility. 29 C. Wright & V. Gold, Federal Practice and Procedure § 6262, at 186 (1997). Some courts suggest that the line dividing the scope of Rules 702 and 703 is drawn by the distinction between methodology and data: Rule 702 requires that the expert's methodology is scientifically valid while Rule 703 requires that the expert's data is reasonably reliable. This scope problem is of consequence only if the "assist" standard established by Rule 702 and the "reasonably relied on" standard of Rule 703 are truly different. But if these standards are different, the consequences could be dramatic. Professor Imwinkelreid described where to draw the line between Rules 702 and 703 in the following manner: "The fundamental dispute is whether the expression [in Rule 703] 'the fact or data in the particular case' is limited to case-specific information or whether the expression also embraces research data." E. Imwinkelreid, *Developing a Coherent Theory of the Structure of Federal Rule of Evidence 703*, 47 Mercer L. Rev. 447, 451 (1996). *Cf. Raynor v. Merrell Pharms.*, 104 F. 3d 1371, 1374 (D.C. Cir. 1997) (concluding that *Daubert* "leaves obscure" the relationship between Rules 702 and 703). The *Daubert* trilogy teaches that the factors that determine the reliability of evidence depend on the type of evidence offered, and in making this determination the trial judge can consider the validity of the methodology, whether the technique has been subjected to peer review, and whether the expert properly applied his or her methodology. Daubert v. Merrill Dow Pharms., 509 U.S. 579, 592–93 (1993). Under Rule 703, if the data underlying "the expert's opinion are so unreliable that no reasonable expert could base an opinion on them, the opinion resting on that data must be excluded." *Id.*

3. The *Daubert* factors are a nonexhaustive list of factors or inquiries considered by the court as gatekeeper when it is determining the reliability of proffered expert testimony. They do not constitute a definitive checklist, but must be tailored to the facts of the particular case. With this caveat against generalization, the courts have recognized that when a theory or technique is scrutinized in order to determine its reliability, the gatekeeper may inquire into the following:

1. Testability: Is the expert's technique or theory one that can be or has been tested or challenged in an objective sense, or is it instead simply a subjective, conclusory approach that cannot reasonably be tested for reliability?
2. Peer review and publication: Has the technique or theory been subject to peer review and publication?
3. Error rate: What is the known or potential rate of error of the technique or theory when applied?
4. Standards: Do standards and controls exist and are they maintained?
5. General acceptance: Has the technique or theory been generally accepted in the scientific community?

See Advisory Committee Note to Rule 702 (2000 Amendment), Fed. Civ. Jud. Proc. & Rules 428 (2005 ed.).

4. The typical vehicle for presenting a *Daubert* challenge is a Rule 56 Motion for Summary Judgment coupled with a Motion in Limine and Request for a Rule 104(a) Hearing, especially in those cases where exclusion of expert evidence may remove an essential element of the opposing party's prima facie case. Motions in limine under 104(a) have gained tremendous importance during the past decade in implementing the trial judge's gatekeeping role under the *Daubert* trilogy. A hearing on a motion in limine raising a *Daubert* chal-

lenge ideally should be scheduled well in advance of trial, so that its disposition will provide a maximum degree of assistance to the parties in trial preparation and, perhaps, a maximum incentive to explore settlement. REFERENCE MANUAL ON SCIENTIFIC EVIDENCE 53-54 (2d ed. Fed. Jud. Ctr. 2000).

5. Thornburg v. Gingles, 478 U.S. 30 (1986).

6. A. B. Lustre, *Post-Daubert Standards for Admissibility of Scientific and Other Expert Evidence in State Courts,* 90 A.L.R. 5th 454 (2005).

7. *See generally Frye/Daubert:* A State Reference Guide (D.R.I. Defense Library Series, 2005–07 CD); D. Bernstein & J. Jackson, *The Daubert Trilogy in the States,* 44 JURIMETRICS J. 351 (Spring 2004).

8. Gingles, 478 U.S. at 49–50.

9. *Id.* at 52–53.

10. *Id.* at 52–54.

11. Cromartie v. Hunt, 532 U.S. at 234 (2001).

12. Fannie Lou Hamer, Rosa Parks, and Coretta Scott King Voting Rights Act Reauthorization and Amendments Act of 2006, Pub. L. No. 109-246 (2006).

13. Georgia v. Ashcroft, 539 U.S. 461 (2003).

14. Reno v. Bossier Parish Sch. Bd. (*Bossier II*), 528 U.S. 320 (2000).

15. *United States v. Noxobee County, Miss.* 494 F. Supp. 2d 440 (N.D. Miss. 2007) (upholding claim of white voters who alleged intentional discrimination on the part of African-American election officials in violation of Section 2 of the Voting Rights Act of 1965, as amended).

16. League of United Latin American Citizens (LULAC) v. Perry, 126 S. Ct. 2594 (2006).

17. *Daubert,* 509 U.S. at 597 (The Federal Rules of Evidence "assign to the trial judge the task of ensuring that an expert's testimony both rests on a reliable foundation and is relevant to the task at hand"); *see also* Kumho Tire Co. v. Carmichael, 526 U.S. 137, 141 (1999).

18. Daubert v. Merrell Dow Pharmaceuticals, Inc., 509 U.S. 579, 593–94 (1993).

19. Rule 104(a) governs preliminary questions of admissibility of evidence: "[T]he trial judge must determine *at the outset, pursuant to Rule 104(a)*" whether a proffered expert will testify to scientific knowledge that will assist the trier of fact to understand or determine a factual issue. *Daubert,* 509 U.S. at 591 (emphasis added). *See generally* D. Patterson, *The Rule 104(a) Motion as a Necessary and Useful Tool,* FOR THE DEFENSE 24, 25 (Jan. 2005).

20. Bone Shirt v. Hazeltine, 336 F. Supp. 2d 976 (D.S.D. 2004), *aff'd,* 461 F.3d 1011 (8th Cir. 2006).

21. *Bone Shirt,* 461 F.3d at 1020.

22. *Bone Shirt,* 336 F. Supp. 2d at 989–90.

23. Koppell v. N.Y. State Bd. of Elections, 97 F. Supp. 2d 477 (S.D.N.Y. 2000).

24. *Id.* at 481.

25. Johnson v. DeSoto County Bd. of Comm'rs, 204 F.3d 1335 (11th Cir. 2000).

26. *Id.* at 1342.

27. *Id.* (citing Negron v. City of Miami Beach, Fla., 113 F.3d 1563, 1570 (11th Cir. 1997).

28. *Id.* at n.11 (citing Rollins v. Fort Bend Indep. Sch. Dist., 89 F.3d 1205, 1219 (5th Cir.1996) (noting that Supreme Court has not "held that voter registration is irrelevant: it is simply not the sole criterion")).

29. *Id.* at 1342.

30. *Id.*

31. Montgomery County v. Microvote Corp., 320 F.3d 440 (3rd Cir. 2003).

32. *Id.* at 448–49 (internal citations omitted).

33. ACLU v. Santillanes, 506 F. Supp. 2d 598 (D.N.M. 2007).

34. *Id.* at 625 (internal citations omitted). Santillanes illustrates the different admissibility standards applicable to lay and expert opinion testimony that are explicitly dealt with under Federal Rules of Evidence 701 and 702. Rule 701, the lay opinion rule as amended in 2000, does not distinguish between lay witnesses and expert witnesses, but rather between lay opinion and expert opinion. Under the 2000 amendment to Rule 701, opinions based on experience that amounts to "specialized knowledge" can be admitted only under Rule 702. Rule 701 as amended in 2000 provides: If the witness is not testifying as an expert, the witness's testimony in the form of opinions or inferences is limited to those opinions or inferences that are (a) rationally based on the perception of the witness, (b) helpful to a clear understanding of the witness's testimony or the determination of a fact in issue, and (c) not based on scientific, technical, or other specialized knowledge within the scope of Rule 702.

35. Koppell, 97 F. Supp. 2d at 479.

36. *Id.* at 479 (citing Zuchowicz v. United States, 140 F.3d 381, 386 (2d Cir. 1998) (quoting *Daubert,* 509 U.S. at 597)).

37. *Id.* (citing *Daubert,* 509 U.S. at 592 n.10).

38. *Koppell,* 97 F. Supp. 2d at 479.

39. *Daubert,* 509 U.S. at 480 (quoting Fed. R. Evid. 702).

40. *Koppell,* 97 F. Supp. 2d at 482.

41. 3 S. SALTZBURG, M. MARTIN AND D. CAPRA, FEDERAL RULES OF EVIDENCE MANUAL §702.02[14], at 702–60 (8th ed. 2002).

42. *Koppell,* 97 F. Supp. 2d at 480.

43. *Id.* at 480.

44. Under the 2000 Amendments, Rule 26 provides that a testifying expert must submit a signed written report prior to trial, containing

1. a complete statement of all opinions to be expressed and the basis and reasons therefore,
2. the data or other information considered by the witness in forming the opinions,
3. any exhibits to be used as support for or a summary of the opinions,
4. the qualifications of the expert and all publications authored by the expert in the past ten years,
5. the expert's compensation for his review and testimony, and
6. a list of all other cases in which the expert has testified at trial or at deposition in the past four years.

FED. R. CIV. P. 26(a)(2)(B) (2003).

45. This lack of "fit" between the expert's proposed testimony and the specific facts of the case was but one of a number of "red flags" that suggest unreliability. While not dispositive of admissibility, the presence of several of these red flags may persuade a gatekeeper to lean against admission of expert testimony:

    1. improper extrapolation

    2. reliance on anecdotal evidence

    3. reliance on temporal proximity

    4. insufficient connection between the expert's opinion and the facts of the case

    5. ruling out other possible causes

    6. insufficient foundation for the expert's opinion

    7. subjectivity.

3 S. Saltzburg, M. Martin & D. Capra, Federal Rules of Evidence Manual § 702.02[7] (8th ed., 2002). When an expert ventures into election litigation for the first time, the expert is not in a garden variety tort suit and must bring more than impressive credentials to cross the *Daubert* threshold of reliability. *Cf.* Advisory Committee Note to Rule 702 (2000 Amendment), *supra* note 3 ("The trial court's gatekeeping function requires more than simply taking the expert's word for it.").

46. *Koppell,* 97 F. Supp. 2d at 482.

47. *Id.* at 481.

48. *Id.*

49. *Id.* at 481–482.

50. *Id.* at 482.

51. *Id.*

52. A similar discretionary balancing takes place when a trial court is called on to determine the admissibility of expert testimony under Rule 403. Rules 702 and 403 "often make it difficult to tell when a court's decision rests on one provision or the other." 29 C. Wright and V. Gold, Federal Practice and Procedure § 6263, at 194 (1997). Rule 702 has been described as a particularized but more demanding version of the relevance rules; moreover, Rule 702 "demands more than what is required by the relevance rules" such as Rule 403. *Id.* at 194–95. "Thus, Rule 702 provides more power than Rule 403 to exclude evidence where its dangers are balanced against benefits." *Id.* at 196. Relevance issues concerning expert testimony usually should be resolved under Rule 702.

53. United States v. Blaine County, Mont., 363 F.3d 897 (9th Cir. 2004).

54. *Id.* at 915 n. 27.

55. *Id.*

56. *Id.*

57. *Id.* at 914–16 (quoting *Gingles,* 478 U.S. at 51 n.15 (internal citations omitted)).

58. In preparing for a *Daubert* challenge, one suggested approach is to consider some or possibly all of the following areas of inquiry:

    1. Is the expert qualified in the specific field of expertise involved? Confirm a "fit" between the expert's opinion and the field involved.

    2. Is there generally accepted body of learning, study, and experience in that field?

    3. Is the expert's testimony grounded in that body of learning, study, and experience?

4. Can the expert explain how his or her conclusion is so grounded?
5. Explain the principles of the specific field.
6. Explain the expert's methodology and steps involved in that methodology to be taken to solve the particular issue or problem.
7. Has the principle, theory, or technique been objectively tested, or can it be?
8. Has the principle, theory, or technique been subjected to peer review or publication?
9. Does the principle, theory, technique, or method have a low potential rate of error?
10. Has the principle, theory, technique, or method been generally accepted by the relevant industry as proper to be used in matters of this sort?
11. Has the principle, theory, technique, or method been used outside the litigation in which the expert's opinion or conclusion is being offered?
12. For the expert's field of expertise, can the expert show that an appropriate specific method, theory, or technique was used, tested, and subjected to peer review and publication; identify the known or potential rate of error with respect to the technique; and show that standards controlling the technique's operations are reasonable?
13. If relying solely or primarily on experience, can the expert explain and show how that experience leads to the conclusion reached, why that experience is a sufficient basis for the opinion, and how that experience is reliably applied to the facts?
14. Have all the data, items, and materials involved in the case have been inspected or reviewed?
15. If an on-site investigation or experience is appropriate, has the expert interviewed appropriate persons and inspected the appropriate site?
16. Has the expert read the appropriate learned treatises, articles, or materials in the field of expertise?
17. Can the expert identify the studies in the field relied upon, including published studies, and are those studies reliable?
18. Can the expert explain why the methodology, rates of error, and results of these studies are reasonably relied on by experts in the field?
19. If relying on experience as the basis for his or her opinion, can the expert explain what that experience consists of and how that experience leads to the opinion and conclusion reached?
20. Can the expert show and explain that the rate of error in his or her method, technique, or conclusion is low?
21. Can the expert show how he or she applied knowledge and experience in evaluating and handling the data, articles, and technical literature and making an analysis?
22. If causation is the subject of the testimony, has the expert ruled out other plausible alternative causes of the event, injury, or condition in question?
23. Is there a logical connection and no analytical gap between the data and the expert's opinion or conclusion, and can the expert explain how that data has

been bridged to the opinion or conclusion by sound inductive or deductive reasoning?

24. Was the expert's opinion or conclusion reached outside the arena of litigation?

CHAPTER ELEVEN

GOVERNMENT-ISSUED PHOTO IDENTIFICATION AND PROOF OF CITIZENSHIP REQUIREMENTS FOR VOTERS

JON M. GREENBAUM*

JONAH H GOLDMAN**

I. Introduction

For the past six years, legislators, election administrators, advocates, and academics have struggled with what type of identification voters should show before they vote or before they register. Most of the discussion has centered on the wisdom of requiring voters to show government-issued photo identification before they vote and requiring voters to show proof of citizenship before they register. The antecedents of the debate are in the chaos surrounding the 2000 election. By the 2004 presidential election, many states had some voter identification requirements and the Congress passed the first national voter identification provision through the Help America Vote Act.[1] State requirements were relatively inclusive by either allowing voters to show an expansive array of photo or nonphoto identification or allowing voters without identification to sign an affidavit attesting to their identity.[2] HAVA requires identification for first-time voter registrants who registered by mail. There were no states that required voter registrants or voters to provide documents providing their citizenship.[3]

Since the 2004 election the drum has continued to beat to convince Congress and the states to enact laws requiring government-issued photo identification and documentary proof of citizenship for voter registration.[4] Proponents of restrictive identification provisions say they are necessary to prevent voter fraud and provide voters with confidence that they are voting in fraud-free elections.[5] Conversely,

---

* Director, Voting Rights Project, Lawyers' Committee for Civil Rights Under Law.

** Director, National Campaign for Fair Elections, Lawyers' Committee for Civil Rights Under Law.

there is significant opposition to these laws because of the dearth of evidence of the existence of voter impersonation and noncitizen voting, the type of fraud prevented by these laws.[6] Additionally, these laws will result in the disenfranchisement of some eligible voters.[7] Opponents argue that these laws are pursued because of the potential political impact that they have.[8] This suspicion is compounded by where politicians come down on this issue; in nearly every case, Republicans have sponsored these provisions while Democrats have opposed.[9] Photo identification requirements have been enacted in Georgia, Indiana, Missouri, and Albuquerque, New Mexico, and documentary proof of citizenship requirements now exist in Arizona; Congress and several states have considered similar measures and declined to adopt them. Each photo identification requirement or proof of citizenship law has been challenged in court, primarily on grounds that these laws constitute a poll tax, that they violate the fundamental right to vote under the Equal Protection Clause of the 14th Amendment, and that they violate state constitutional provisions.[10] In September 2007, the Supreme Court granted a writ of certiorari in the challenge to the Indiana law. The Court's expected decision in spring 2008 will certainly influence what happens going forward.

This article will recount the state of the law regarding voter identification as of 2004, discuss the arguments that proponents and opponents of the government-issued photo identification and proof of citizenship laws have made, survey the studies and data on the subject, recap the federal legislative developments, and analyze the legal challenges to the government-issued photo identification and proof of citizenship laws that have been passed.

II. State of the Law as of 2004

Prior to the 2004 election, many states had adopted some form of required identification for voters, but no state required photo identification without providing a voter without the requisite identification a regular ballot after signing an affidavit attesting to his or her identity.[11] With a few exceptions, these laws were not challenged in court.[12] In addition, no state required voter registrants to provide proof of citizenship. The Department of Justice's administration of Section 5 of the Voting Rights Act, the identification requirements for mail-in registrants under the Help America Vote Act, and existing federal and state criminal provisions for voter fraud provided the framework for identification requirements.

A. DEPARTMENT OF JUSTICE ENFORCEMENT OF SECTION 5 OF THE VOTING RIGHTS ACT

Under Section 5 of the Voting Rights Act,[13] jurisdictions with a history of voting discrimination[14] must demonstrate to the Department of Justice or the District Court of the District of Columbia that any change they intend to make related to voting does not have the purpose or effect of discriminating against minority voters.[15] If the jurisdiction cannot meet the legal standard, it cannot implement the proposed voting change.[16]

In 1994, Louisiana passed implementing legislation for the National Voter Registration Act of 1993 that included a provision that "first-time voters who register by mail in order to identify themselves at the polls present a current driver's license or other picture identification card."[17] Louisiana submitted this "proposed" law to the Department of Justice for preclearance. Under the proposed law, voters subject to this law who did not show photo identification would not have their vote counted. The existing law required identification but not photo identification.[18] The Department of Justice blocked implementation of the photo identification law. According to DOJ's analysis, because African Americans were four to five times as likely as whites not to have photo identification, the law would have a discriminatory effect on minority voters.[19]

B. THE HELP AMERICA VOTE ACT

As the country recovered from the 2000 election debacle that threw the presidential outcome into the hands of the Supreme Court, Congress deliberated its response. The result was the 2002 passage of the Help America Vote Act, the most sweeping federal legislative foray into the mechanics of elections in history.[20]

The law touches nearly every aspect of election administration, including establishing, for the first time, a federal identification requirement. The result of a compromise, Section 303(b) of HAVA requires first-time voters who register by mail to provide identification before they cast a ballot.

The identification requirement is actually exceedingly narrow; it only applies to *first-time* voters who *register by mail*. Moreover, if the personal identifying information submitted on a mail in registration form is later verified against a state database, that voter need not show identification at the polls.[21]

Conversely, the list of acceptable identification is very broad. According to HAVA, a voter can produce current and valid photo identification or a copy of a current utility bill, bank statement, government check, paycheck, or other government document that shows the name and address of the voter. A first-time voter who registers by mail and votes absentee may provide a copy of any of the aforementioned forms of identification.[22] HAVA, however, creates a floor, not a ceiling, allowing states to impose stricter identification requirements.[23]

C. CRIMINAL VOTING FRAUD STATUTES

Before the recent wave of activity to impose voter identification and proof of citizenship requirements on the electoral process, the problems of voter fraud were addressed, at least at a federal level, by federal proscriptions on voter fraud. There are a number of federal statutes that address various kinds of election-related fraud, many of which are felonies carrying multiple-year penalties.[24]

Broadly, 18 U.S.C. §241,[25] which makes conspiracies to intimidate or threaten another person in the exercise of a constitutional right or a federally guaranteed right illegal and punishes them with up to ten years' imprisonment, has been used to combat a broad range of election misconduct.[26]

Specifically, the Voting Rights Act has been amended to prevent certain types of election misconduct.[27] Although it primarily covers federal elections,[28] the prohibitions in the Voting Rights Act cover many of the actions that form the rhetorical basis of the fight over voter identification. In addition to preventing one from providing false information about key registration information, it also criminalizes vote-buying schemes and conspiracies to vote illegally.[29] These prohibitions carry with them punishments of up to five years' imprisonment. Another section of the Voting Rights Act makes it illegal to vote more than once.[30] Courts have found that this provision includes punishing voting in the name of deceased, ineligible, or absentee voters and also carries with it a penalty of up to five years in prison.[31]

In addition, states typically have a set of statutes criminalizing various forms of voter fraud. For example, in Georgia any person who commits the following offenses can be charged with a felony and punished by prison terms (ranging from one- to ten-year maximums) and fines (ranging from $10,000 to $100,000 maximums): (1) registers as an elector while knowing that he or she is not eligible to vote, registers under a name different than his or her own, or knowingly gives false information when registering as an elector;[32] (2) willfully inserts a fictitious name, false figure, false statement, or other fraudulent entry on a voter registration card, electors list, voter's certificate, affidavit, oath, or other election document;[33] (3) willfully prepares or presents "to any poll officer a fraudulent voter's certificate not signed by the elector whose certificate it purports to be";[34] (4) votes when knowing that he or she is not a qualified elector;[35] or votes more than once in the same election.[36]

III. Arguments Made by Proponents and Opponents on the Need for More Restrictive Identification and Proof of Citizenship Requirements

Since 2004, state legislatures across the country have debated, and sometimes passed, identification and proof of citizenship requirements that are more restrictive than the pre-2004 laws. Congress has also grappled with these issues as well.[37] The most restrictive provisions require voters to show only current and valid government-issued photo identification that has certain required information such as a date of birth and an expiration date, and imposes the further requirement that voters prove their citizenship status before their registrations can be accepted.

While the details of the various provisions contemplated by the Congress and state legislatures vary, the arguments for and against the provisions remains consistent. The discussion over whether to impose government-issued photo identification requirements for voting or proof of citizenship requirements for voter registration boils down to a debate of whether these requirements protect or undercut the integrity of the elections. Proponents believe that the requirements protect the integrity of elections by reducing voter fraud whereas opponents believe that these provisions undercut the integrity of elections because they needlessly take elderly, poor, and minority voters out of the electoral process.

A. ARGUMENTS MADE BY PROPONENTS

Proponents of imposing government-issued voter identification and proof of citizenship requirements argue that they are needed to inspire confidence in the electoral process. As the National Commission on Federal Election Reform chaired by former President Jimmy Carter and former Secretary of State James Baker opined in its recommendation that states impose restrictive identification and proof of citizenship requirements: "There is no evidence of extensive fraud in U.S. elections or of multiple voting, but both occur, and it could affect the outcome of a close election."[38]

Proponents argue that elections without strict identification requirements are left open to widespread voter fraud.[39] Specifically, since the national political discussion has increasingly focused on immigration, advocates for proof of citizenship for registration and voter identification at the polls have attempted to link the issues by suggesting that the current dominant system of voter identification (the signature match) is insufficient in keeping noncitizens, and more particularly undocumented immigrants, away from the polls.[40] While the dominant arguments for voter identification and proof of citizenship are, for the most part, framed generally (i.e., preventing fraud or preventing voter fraud) occasionally proponents argue more specifically, and accurately, that voter identification will prevent ineligible voters at the polls from impersonating valid registrants.

Moreover, proponents suggest that the disenfranchising impact of requiring identification to vote cannot possibly be significant because of the ubiquity of identification in other parts of American life. Renting a movie, buying tobacco and alcohol, and boarding a plane, among other daily activities, require identification. Proponents argue our electoral system should have similar safeguards.

While proponents largely have focused on this general, "common sense" argument, there are a few specific examples they have raised,[41] including the following:

1. *Sanchez-Dornan.* In 1996 Loretta Sanchez challenged Rep. Bob Dornan, the incumbent in California's 49th congressional district. As polls closed, the race remained tight as it had throughout the day. When the ballots were counted, Sanchez came out on top by fewer than 1,000 votes. Later, accusations began flowing that Hermandad Mexicana Nacional, a liberal nonprofit, had registered a significant number of noncitizens who voted in the election. Rep. Dornan immediately challenged the outcome as the result of ineligible noncitizens going to the polls and voting.[42]

Rep. Sanchez was seated, but the House Oversight Committee investigated to determine if her victory resulted from illegal voting. The committee ended up with a majority report, which found that nearly 700 noncitizens had cast a ballot in the election.[43] A minority report further investigated that number and found that most of those alleged to have voted illegally had no intention to defraud the system, but instead were on a path to citizenship and believed that they were eligible voters.[44] After 13 months, the full House or Representatives voted to drop the challenge because Sanchez's margin of victory was greater than the majority report's finding of illegal voting.[45]

2. Ritzy the Dog, Superman, and Inflated Voter Registration Rolls. In his persistent advocacy for stricter identification requirements, Sen. Christopher "Kit" Bond (R-MO) frequently trots out (sometimes literally) the case of Ritzy Mekler. It appears that in 2000 Ritzy was on the St. Louis voter rolls. Ritzy is a springer spaniel. According to Bond, Ritzy and her four-legged counterparts make frequent appearances on the nation's voter rolls together with Superman, Mickey Mouse, and more than a fair share of Michael Jordans.[46] According to Sen. Bond, the 2000 St. Louis voting rolls had 247,135 voters registered out of a population of 258,532 eligible voters (more than 95 percent).[47] Proponents of imposing strict voter identification provisions point to the Ritzy example and similar stories across the country as a basis for imposing strict identification requirements on voters.[48]

B. ARGUMENTS MADE BY OPPONENTS

Opponents contend that that there is virtually no evidence that the voter fraud prevented by identification and proof of citizenship requirements exist, whereas there is evidence that imposing restrictive voter identification requirements will disenfranchise eligible voters, disproportionately from traditionally disenfranchised groups (such as poor, minority, young, and elderly voters).[49] Practically, vote fraud that is effective in influencing the outcome of elections requires the ability to manipulate a significant number of ballots, which is why successful schemes to manipulate election outcomes involve a few people manufacturing a significant number of votes in a short period of time.[50] According to opponents of voter identification and proof of citizenship, the constitutional protection of the right to vote trumps hypothetical concerns over voter fraud. Opponents point out that there are few examples of noncitizens voting, noting the severe penalties if one gets caught—including deportation, loss of benefits, heavy fines, and prison time.[51] Opponents argue a similar cost-benefit analysis to contradict allegations of rampant multiple voting and voter impersonation: The cost is high both in penalties and because of the sophistication and secrecy necessary to put together a successful fraud campaign; and the benefit is low, because individual voters are limited in the number of fraudulent votes they can deliver. Moreover, fraudulent voter registrants rarely show up to cast a ballot.[52]

Poll workers will be unlikely to let vote without question someone who signs a poll book as "Mickey Mouse."[53] Instead, opponents argue, manipulation of elections is perpetrated in a more institutional fashion, through decisions made by election officials[54] and other, more sophisticated tactics.

Another source of opposition to voter identification and proof of citizenship requirements is the fear that these provisions will be implemented in a discriminatory way. In part because the nation's poll workers lack sufficient training and oversight, these provisions are frequently enforced selectively against minority voters.[55]

Specifically, opponents of voter identification and proof of citizenship requirements point to a few key election irregularities that, at first blush, appear to indicate significant fraud, but on further examination grow out of a less nefarious foundation.

1. New Jersey 2005. In September 2005, less than two months before the New Jersey gubernatorial election, the state's Republican Party chairman asked state officials to investigate what he said was "evidence of people voting twice in the same election, dead people registered to vote, tens of thousands registered more than once in New Jersey and hundreds of thousands registered in New Jersey and in other states."[56]

According to a consultant hired by the New Jersey GOP, over 10,000 voters were suspected of multiple voting—some accused of voting twice in New Jersey and some accused of voting once in New Jersey and once in another state. According to the accusations, nearly 5,000 deceased New Jersians cast ballots in the previous election.

The Brennan Center for Justice investigated the allegations and found that, most likely, the cause of the irregularities was not as insidious as the allegations suggested. Instead, the group found that the overwhelming majority of the allegations were more likely explained as different people with the same names, mistakes in data entry, and poor matching protocols that the New Jersey GOP applied to the voter registration rolls and the death lists. According to the Brennan Center, it is likely that only eight voters voted twice.[57]

2. Wisconsin 2004. Amidst widespread allegations of voting fraud in the Milwaukee area during the 2004 presidential election, the Milwaukee Police Department, Milwaukee County District Attorney's Office, Federal Bureau of Investigation, and the United States Attorneys Office formed a task force to investigate what voting irregularities occurred during that election and how widespread they were.[58] The task force found some evidence of double voting, voting in names of people who probably did not vote or voting in possibly fake names; however, the list of suspected fraudulent voters was rather small[59] and the confidence that even this small number actually represented criminal activity was on shaky ground.[60] The report also found that registration drives turned in 65 registrations of voters who did not exist, although the report found no evidence that these voters actually voted and, instead, came to the conclusion suggested above, that voter registration workers were trying to defraud the registration drives they were working for in order to collect more money. The report also found that widespread administrative failures likely led to the irregularities that, at first blush, seemed to suggest voter fraud. These irregularities included data entry errors that put multiple voters at the same address and poll workers not administering poll checks and same-day registration effectively.[61]

3. Washington Gubernatorial Election. The 2004 gubernatorial election in Washington State ended with the closest margin in a statewide competition in American history.[62] After the recounts provided for under Washington State election code, the Democratic candidate, Christine Gregoire, led her Republican challenger, Dino Rossi, by 129 votes. Litigation ensued, with each side claiming that irregularities and voter fraud gave its opponent more votes than he or she deserved.[63] While the majority of the debate centered on the number of ineligible voters with felony convictions that cast ballots in the election, there were allegations that double voting and voting by dead voters had contributed to the exceedingly close vote totals. After exhaustive litigation, however, the judge found that out of the millions of votes cast in the election, 19 votes were tabulated in the name of deceased voters and six voters had voted twice.[64] Moreover, further investigation showed that at least some of the deceased voters had died after casting an absentee ballot, and some ballots were cast by loved ones with no malicious intention, but to honor the deceased voters' choice in the election.[65]

4. Department of Justice Efforts. Since the beginning of the George W. Bush administration, the Justice Department began bringing cases alleging that voter registration fraud was corrupting the electoral process and pledging to make enforcement of fraud prevention statutes more of a priority.[66] During that time, despite increasing resources and shifting the focus of election misconduct investigations and enforcement from systemic problems that will likely have an affect on the outcomes of elections to individual cases of election crimes,[67] there have been very few successful prosecutions and convictions for voter fraud.[68]

IV. Studies on the Impact of Voter Identification and Voter Fraud

Despite no conclusive study on the subject, investigations into the impact of voter identification and proof of citizenship have consistently found that about 10 percent of voting-age citizens (around 20 million people) lack a government-issued photo ID.[69] The contentious debate over the appropriate role of voter identification in the election process has produced a number of studies attempting to empirically clear up both the mystery of what impact, if any, voter identification has on disenfranchisement and what impact, if any, voter fraud has on election outcomes. While there has been no single study that has put the debate to rest, a number of studies provide helpful insight.[70]

A. EAC VOTER FRAUD AND VOTER INTIMIDATION STUDY

In 2006, the Election Assistance Commission (EAC), which was set up by HAVA, commissioned two reports pursuant to Section 241 of HAVA; one combined research and reporting on voter fraud and voter intimidation and the second report was designed to research the impact of voter identification on turnout and make recommendations for best practices relating to identification.[71]

The EAC Fraud and Intimidation Report surveyed the available research, interviewed leading experts on voting issues, compiled an exhaustive review of available press reports on the subjects, and consulted a bipartisan working group of experts on issues related to voter fraud and voter intimidation.[72] While the report submitted to the EAC called for more research to answer the questions presented with finality, there were some common themes that emerged from the preliminary research. First, although the authors found evidence that there was fraud in obtaining voter registrations (ineligible voters submitted registration forms, fictitious voters submitted registration forms, etc.) those registrations did not result in ineligible voters at the polling place. Second, the report found that absentee voting is most susceptible to voter fraud. Third, the report found that voter intimidation is still a problem throughout the country. Finally, the report found no evidence that noncitizens vote regularly.[73]

In its study of voter identification laws, the authors of the EAC report found that increased voter identification provisions may have some impact on voter turnout and that that impact falls disproportionately on minority communities. While this report also admitted to not being comprehensive, "[t]he statistical analysis suggests that stricter voter ID requirements can be associated with lower turnout. . . . Without a better understanding of the incidence of vote fraud and its relationship to voter ID, for now best practice for the states may be to limit requirements for voter identification to the minimum needed to prevent duplicate registration and ensure eligibility."[74]

B. OTHER STUDIES

Other studies found a similarly strong indication that voter identification laws have a disproportionate impact on traditionally disenfranchised voters. In Georgia, African Americans and Latinos are roughly twice as likely as whites to lack a driver's license or other state-issued photo ID.[75] Twenty-five percent of registered Georgians have no driver's license or current government-issued photo identification.[76] Researchers at the University of Wisconsin at Milwaukee found that only 22 percent of African American males in the city of Milwaukee between 18 and 24 years old had a driver's license. The same study found that whites were twice as likely to have driver's licenses as African Americans.[77] The Brennan Center for Justice at New York University Law School conducted a national survey asking respondents about their access to identification documents. Based on the results of the survey, the Brennan Center estimated that 13 million individuals do not have access to citizenship documents and that nearly 12 percent of voting-age citizens earning under $25,000 a year do not have access to a birth certificate, a passport, or naturalization papers.[78] Additionally, it was estimated that more than 20 million individuals, disproportionately from minority communities, do not have government-issued photo identification.[79]

In Indiana, the Washington Institute for the Study of Ethnicity and Race found that about 13 percent of registered Indiana voters lack an Indiana driver's license or an alternate Indiana-issued photo ID.[80] To dig deeper, households that are less likely to have an automobile, and consequently less likely to have licensed drivers, are disproportionately low income and disproportionately minority.[81]

V. Federal Legislative Efforts to Introduce More Restrictive Requirements

Advocates for stricter identification and proof of citizenship requirements began a campaign to reform laws at the federal and state level after the 2000 election, pointing to the 2000 Missouri Senate race in which Sen. John Ashcroft was narrowly defeated by Gov. Mel Carnahan, who just days before the election died in a plane crash. During that election, vast voting irregularities in the city of St. Louis caused the St. Louis Circuit Court to issue an order extending polling hours. According to advocates for identification, the irregularities, coupled with the extended hours, led to enough ineligible voters casting ballots to sway the election in favor of Carnahan.[82]

Although the veracity of the fraud claims is in serious doubt,[83] the rhetoric that came out of the chaos of that election took hold. At the federal level, the deliberations over the Help America Vote Act were characterized by differing priorities. Some involved with the deliberation advocated for making the bill a vehicle to increase requirements for identification, while others preferred to target the bill on the issues exemplified by the 2000 election debacle. In the end, the compromise discussed above in Part II was reached.

Despite its genesis in the 2000 election, the recent effort to expand the use of voter identification and proof of citizenship hit its stride in 2004 and 2005. Starting in 2004, legislatures across the country began introducing and passing restrictive voter identification requirements.[84] Strengthening the legislative efforts was the announcement in September 2005 endorsing the imposition of strict identification requirements for voting purposes by the Commission on Federal Election Reform chaired by Jimmy Carter and James Baker.[85] Despite the fact that the commission's recommendation came over a dissent by three commissioners[86] and that it was both specific and heavy with caveats requiring the other commission recommendations to be implemented before the identification recommendation,[87] advocates for restrictive voter identification requirements took the pronouncement as a clarion call reinvigorating the efforts to pass these provisions.

In addition to the state legislation, the 109th Congress also began considering strict identification and proof of citizenship requirements. Starting with the introduction of the Voter Protection Act of 2005, introduced in the Senate by Sen. Christopher "Kit" Bond of Missouri and Sen. Mitch McConnell of Kentucky, a slew of new measures were introduced that proposed strict identification requirements for all federal elections. The Voter Protection Act of 2005 would amend the HAVA identification provision to require all voters in federal elections to show "current and valid" photo identification before voting. Consequently, the amendment would remove the expansive list of identification acceptable under HAVA for first-time voters and impose the same government-issued photo identification requirement on them.[88] Finally, the bill attempted to circumvent critics' assertions that the identification requirements imposed an unconstitutional poll tax[89] by authorizing the Election Assistance Commission to permit grants to states to issue free identification. The bill did not, however, mandate that states provide free identification.[90]

In both the House of Representatives and the Senate a few bills followed the lead of the Voter Protection Act of 2005 by proposing strict voter identification laws in federal elections.[91] These bills were sponsored by Republican members of Congress and were, in large measure, a reaction to bills introduced by their Democratic counterparts that removed restrictions or addressed documented election irregularities that would have expanded the franchise by making registration easier or streamlining election administration. Most of these bills saw little, if any, action beyond their introduction.[92] Two provisions, however, made considerable progress through the legislative process.

A. SEN. MCCONNELL'S AMENDMENT TO THE COMPREHENSIVE IMMIGRATION ACT OF 2006

In May 2006, the Senate was consumed with debate over how to reform the nation's immigration laws. The issue took center stage as proponents and opponents of a bipartisan compromise battled over the ideological foundations and the specific nuances of an increasingly complicated legislative effort. Sen. McConnell, a longtime advocate of increasing voter identification restrictions, offered an amendment that would require every voter to show a "Real ID" before voting beginning in 2008.[93] Passed without any legislative debate (either in committee or on the floor) in May 2005 as an amendment to an emergency appropriation bill funding the wars in Afghanistan and Iraq and relief for the devastating tsunami in the South

Pacific, Real ID will impose on states, beginning in May 2008,[94] a new regime of issuing identification that will be used for all federal activities including boarding a plane or entering a federal government building. States must set up extensive new procedures mandating that only certain identification be used as supporting documents to issue a Real ID, requiring extensive verification and document retention requirements on supporting documentation and requiring interoperable databases so states can check information against other states' databases, among other requirements.

The amendment was offered on the floor on May 22, 2006. After debate, a motion to table the amendment was made that failed along party lines, with Democrats voting to table the motion and all but two Republicans voting against the motion; however, the next vote on the floor was a vote for cloture on the underlying Comprehensive Immigration Act of 2006 and not a vote on the amendment. The result was that the amendment was defeated on procedural grounds—because Sen. McConnell's proposed amendment did not amend any provision in the current bill, it became nongermane and could not be offered as an amendment after cloture.

B. FEDERAL ELECTION INTEGRITY ACT OF 2006

In September 2006, the Committee on House Administration, which has jurisdiction over many election-related issues, began deliberating on Rep. Henry Hyde's Federal Election Integrity Act of 2006, which would impose strict government-issued photo identification requirements before a voter casts a ballot.[95] Unlike previous bills, this bill specifically required that acceptable "government-issued photo identification" only includes identification that required the bearer to prove citizenship in order to obtain the ID.

The bill had provisions requiring states to provide free voter IDs (which could not be used for purposes other than voting) to individuals who attested that they could not afford the identification. There was no provision, however, for indigent voters to obtain underlying documentation for free. After the bill was tweaked during the committee process, it was sent to the floor, where it passed the House of Representatives on a nearly party line vote.[96] The bill did not progress through the Senate.

VI. *Case Law on Photo Identification and Proof of Citizenship Requirements in Registering and Voting*

The photo identification requirements for in-person voting that were adopted through legislation or a referendum in Georgia, Indiana, Missouri, and Albuquerque, New Mexico, in 2005 and 2006 have all been challenged legally.[97] In addition, Arizona's Proposition 200, which requires voter registrants to provide proof of citizenship, was also challenged after it was passed by voters in November 2004.

The following discussion of the cases focuses on the two primary legal theories that plaintiffs' attorneys have advanced in these cases: that a mandatory photo identification requirement or documentary proof of citizenship requirement constitutes an undue burden on the fundamental right to vote in violation of the Equal Protection Clause of the 14th Amendment and an unconstitutional poll tax under the 24th Amendment and 14th Amendments to the United States Constitution. In addition, with respect to the Arizona proof of citizenship requirement for voter registrants, there is discussion of plaintiffs' contention that it violates the National Voter Registration Act.

A. FUNDAMENTAL RIGHT TO VOTE

In the 1960s, the United States Supreme Court made clear that there is a constitutionally protected right to vote:

> Undeniably the Constitution of the United States protects the right of all qualified citizens to vote, in state as well as in federal elections. A consistent line of decisions by this Court in cases involving attempts to deny or restrict the right of suffrage has made this indelibly clear. It has been repeatedly recognized that all qualified voters have a constitutionally protected right to vote and to have their votes counted.[98]

This right to vote is contained within the Equal Protection Clause under the 14th Amendment. Over the next decade the Supreme Court found that several state laws had the effect of denying the right to vote of particular individuals, including a Texas law that denied the right to vote to members of the armed services who lived in another state before enlistment,[99] a New York law that denied the right to vote in certain school districts to individuals that did not own property or have children going to public school,[100] and a Tennessee law that required voter registrants to be residents of the state for a year and the county for three months before the election.[101] In all three cases, the Supreme Court imposed a strict scrutiny test—the law had to be necessary to achieve a compelling interest—and the defendants failed to meet their burden.[102]

The Tennessee case, *Dunn v. Blumstein,* is particularly instructive because the state's lead justification for the law was that it would "INSURE PURITY OF BALLOT BOX,"[103] the same justification made for the government-issued photo identification and proof of citizenship laws. Though the Supreme Court acknowledged that preventing voter fraud "is a legitimate and compelling goal," it also held that "it is impossible to view durational residency requirements as necessary to achieve that state interest."[104] The Supreme Court found that although durational residency requirements would prevent some people who were not residents from voting, the law was "crude" because it also excluded many legitimate residents.[105] Moreover, the court found that the durational residency requirement was not the least restrictive alternative because of several existing Tennessee laws criminalizing voter fraud, including one for registering to vote illegally, as well as a law allowing voters to be challenged at the polls for not being eligible.[106]

In *Burdick v. Takushi*,[107] the Supreme Court refined the standard for analyzing fundamental right to vote claims. It rejected the petitioner's contention that any voting regulation would be subjected to strict scrutiny. Instead it adopted a "more flexible standard":[108] the "'character and magnitude of the asserted injury'" to the right to vote is balanced against "'the precise interests put forward by the State as justifications for the burden imposed by its rule,' taking into consideration 'the extent to which those interests make it necessary to burden the plaintiff's rights.'"[109] The Supreme Court stated that when the right to vote is "subjected to 'severe' restrictions, the regulation must be 'narrowly drawn to advance a state interest of compelling importance.'"[110] In contrast, when the law imposes "'reasonable, discriminatory restrictions'" on the right to vote "'the State's regulatory interests are generally sufficient to justify' the restrictions."[111] In the case before it, the Supreme Court applied the lower level of scrutiny to a Hawaii law banning write-in ballots and found the law constitutional.[112]

The *Burdick* test has been interpreted by courts applying it to government-issued photo identification and proof of citizenship laws in various ways. Some courts have interpreted *Burdick* to require a two-level test: a law is either severe, and subject to strict scrutiny, or subject to a lower level of scrutiny that sometimes is akin to a rational basis test. Other courts characterize the test as a sliding-scale, balancing test. Perhaps even more importantly, courts have valued the right to vote in comparison to the state's regulatory interests very differently. Where a court values the right to vote such that it requires the state to justify a photo identification or proof of citizenship statute because it is likely to prevent some people from voting, the law is likely to fail because the evidence of voter impersonation and noncitizen voting is minimal. On the other hand, where a court views the state as having a great deal of latitude to introduce facially neutral, "antivoter fraud" legislation regardless of the proof of need, the law will usually be upheld.

B. POLL TAX

In 1964, the 24th Amendment to the United States constitution was ratified. Section 1 of the Amendment states:

> The right to citizens of the United States to vote in any primary or other election for President or Vice President, for electors for President or Vice President, or for Senator or Representative in Congress, shall not be denied by the United States or any State by reason of failure to pay any poll tax or any other tax.[113]

The next year the Supreme Court decided the seminal case under the 24th Amendment, *Harman v. Forssenius*.[114] In *Harman*, the state of Virginia had a $1.50 annual poll tax that a voter needed to pay at least six months before a state or federal election in order to vote.[115] In anticipation of the passage of the 24th Amendment, Virginia amended its laws in 1963 to allow voters in federal elections to submit a notarized or witnessed certificate of residency at least six months before the election.[116]

The Supreme Court held that the Virginia law violated the 24th Amendment. It stated that "a state may not impose a penalty upon those who exercise a right guaranteed by the Constitution."[117] It further found that "the Twenty-fourth Amendment does not merely insure that the franchise shall not be 'denied' by reason of failure to pay the poll tax; it expressly guarantees that the right to vote shall not be 'denied or abridged' for that reason."[118] The Court also stated that the 24th Amendment was like the 15th Amendment in that it "'nullifies sophisticated as well as simple-minded modes' of impairing" voting rights and that "'[i]t hits onerous procedural requirements which effectively handicap exercise of the franchise' by those claiming the constitutional immunity."[119] The Court found that the Virginia law "unquestionably erects a real obstacle to voting in federal elections for those who assert their constitutional exemption from the poll tax."[120] The Court found that when a law was found to be a poll tax, as in Virginia, it violated the 24th Amendment regardless of justification:

> The requirement imposed upon those who reject the poll tax method of qualifying would not be saved even if it could be said that it is no more onerous, or even somewhat less onerous, than the poll tax. For federal elections, the poll tax is abolished absolutely as a prerequisite to voting, and no equivalent or milder substitute may be imposed. Any material requirement imposed upon the federal voter solely because of his refusal to waive the constitutional immunity subverts the effectiveness of the Twenty-fourth Amendment and must fall under its ban.[121]

Accordingly, the court struck down the Virginia law for federal elections.

The next year the Supreme Court held that the Virginia's $1.50 annual poll tax for state elections violated the Equal Protection Clause in *Harper v. Virginia Board of Elections*.[122] The Court "conclude[d] that a State violates the Equal Protection Clause of the Fourteenth Amendment whenever it makes the affluence of the voter or payment of any fee an electoral standard. Voter qualifications have no relation to wealth nor to paying or not paying this or any other tax."[123] The state contended the argument that because the state could exact fees for other license, a tax on voting was constitutional as long as the tax was the same for everybody.[124] In response, the Court stated that the state's authority was limited to fixing qualifications and "wealth or fee paying has, in our view, no relation to voting qualifications; the right to vote is too precious, too fundamental to be so burdened or conditioned."[125]

In the cases discussed below, the central issue regarding the poll tax has been whether certain fees and costs that voters without the required documentation have to expend in order to obtain the documentation constitute a poll tax. The first level is fees for obtaining the required identification itself; the second level is the fees associated with obtaining documentation that is necessary to obtain the identification (for example, an individual may have to pay for a birth certificate that is needed to obtain a driver's license or nonoperator license). The third level is the practical costs, such as transportation and time, expended in order to obtain the identification. No consensus has emerged, but courts are the most likely to find that the first level of costs constitutes a poll tax and the least likely to find that the third level of costs constitutes a poll tax.

C. DISCUSSION OF CHALLENGED LEGISLATION AND REFERENDA

1. Georgia. Prior to 2005, Georgia had an identification requirement for voters that required voters to show one of 17 types of identification, or if they did not have the identification, to complete an affidavit attesting to their identity.[126] In 2005, the Georgia General Assembly dramatically changed the law in Act 53. Act 53 required voters to provide one of six types of photo identification and no longer allowed for the affidavit option if voters did not have identification.[127] At the same time, Act 53 expanded the availability of absentee voting to all eligible voters.[128]

The passage of Act 53 was controversial. Members of Georgia's black legislative delegation staged a walkout.[129] Secretary of State Cathy Cox vehemently opposed the voter identification provision for two reasons: (1) it was unnecessary because Georgia had not experienced any problems with in-person voter fraud and (2) the law would disenfranchise many eligible voters.[130] The General Assembly voted almost entirely along partisan lines.[131]

Because Georgia's history of discrimination resulted in special coverage, before the state could implement the law it needed to seek preclearance approval from the Department of Justice pursuant to Section 5 of the Voting Rights Act.[132] Under the then-existing standard, Georgia had to show that the change in the identification provision was not adopted with the purpose or did not have the effect of worsening the position of African American voters.[133] The Department of Justice granted preclearance—though later it was revealed that the career staff working on the Section 5 submission had recommended that DOJ deny preclearance approval.[134]

A broad-based coalition filed suit in federal court and sought preliminary relief.[135] The coalition proceeded primarily on two grounds: (1) the identification provision was a poll tax because it required individuals who did not have an accepted identification to pay for identification ($20 for five years and $35 for ten years) unless they claimed indigency in an affidavit; and (2) the identification provision unduly burdened the fundamental right to vote under the 14th Amendment.

The district court granted the plaintiffs' motion for preliminary injunction on both the poll tax and fundamental right to vote grounds.[136] Regarding the poll tax, the court found that "the fee waiver affidavit runs afoul of the *Twenty-Fourth Amendment*" because a voter without identification "must pay the $20 fee or sign the fee waiver affidavit, which may require the voter to swear or affirm to facts that simply are not true in order to avoid the $20 fee."[137]

With respect to the fundamental right to vote claim, the district court found that the photo ID requirement imposed a severe burden:

> Given the fragile nature of the right to vote, and the restrictions discussed above, the Court finds that the Photo ID requirement imposes "severe" restrictions on the right to vote. In particular, the photo ID requirement makes the exercise of the fundamental right to vote extremely difficult for voters currently without acceptable forms of photo ID for whom obtaining a photo ID would be a hardship. Unfortunately, the Photo ID requirement is most likely to prevent Georgia's elderly, poor, and African-American voters from voting. For those citizens, the character of their injury—the loss of the right to vote—is undeniably demoralizing and extreme, as those citizens are likely to have no other realistic or effective means of protecting their rights.[138]

The court went on to find that Georgia did not meet its burden of satisfying strict scrutiny. Moreover, the court did not find that Georgia's justification met the lower level of scrutiny because there were no demonstrated instances of in-person voter fraud, whereas no identification was required for absentee voters, though there had been documented instances of absentee voter fraud.[139]

The Georgia legislature passed a new photo identification law in 2006 that the Department of Justice precleared. The law and its implementing regulations contained three significant changes: (1) it created a new form of photo identification that voters without a driver's license or nonoperator identification could obtain, a Georgia voter registration card, (2) it required each county to provide at least one site in the county that would issue the cards for free; and (3) it set forth the requirements for obtaining the card.[140] In lieu of a photo identification, the voter's registration application, among other things, could suffice as sufficient identification to obtain a card under the implementing regulations.[141] The plaintiffs amended their complaint to reflect the change in the law and filed a motion for preliminary injunction seeking to enjoin the law for the July 18, 2006, primary and the run-off elections. The plaintiffs again relied predominantly on poll tax and fundamental right to vote claims. At the hearing, the secretary of state testified that an analysis done for her office showed that a higher percentage of African American and elderly registered voters did not have a driver's license or nonoperator identification.[142] The plaintiffs submitted a number of declarations of registered voters who swore that the 2006 ID law would negatively affect their ability to vote.[143]

The district court ruled in the defendant's favor on the poll tax claim, holding that the availability of the free voter identification card in the 2006 law cured the deficiency in the 2005 law even if some voters would incur costs of obtaining identification, such as a birth certificate, to comply with the 2005 law.[144] The court found in plaintiff's favor on the fundamental right to vote claim as it applied to the July 18, 2006, election. The court held that the 2006 law imposed a severe burden on the fundamental right to vote for much the same reasons as the 2005 law. It found that the availability of the free voter identification cards did not alleviate the burden because of the practical difficulty the affected voters would have in getting the identification in time for the July 18, 2006, election.[145] The court also found that the state failed to show that requiring the identification was necessary to prevent voter fraud because the requirement did not address the type of electoral fraud that had existed in Georgia and because of the existence of less restrictive alternatives.[146] The district court later preliminarily enjoined implementation of the law for a September 2006 election.

Meanwhile, a concurrent challenge to the 2006 law was filed in state court on the grounds that it violated the state constitution. The state court first granted a temporary restraining order enjoining the law[147] and later permanently enjoined the 2006 law.[148] The state trial court found that the Georgia constitution "guarantees the right to vote to all residents of Georgia who are (1) citizens of the United States, (2) at least 18 years of age, (3) who meet the minimum residency requirements prescribed by the General Assembly, and (4) who have registered to vote."[149] The court found that because the 2006 law denied the right to vote to some voters who met the four qualifications, it violated the Georgia constitution.[150] The state appealed to the Georgia Supreme Court. On June 11, 2007, the Georgia Supreme Court reversed the trial court on the ground that the sole remaining plaintiff lacked standing.[151] The court did not reach the merits of the Georgia constitutional claim.

After the Georgia Supreme Court decision, the federal challenge to the 2006 law proceeded to trial in August 2007. Although the federal district court had preliminarily enjoined the disputed law on the fundamental right to vote, it found in defendants' favor at trial.[152] The court first found that all of the plaintiffs lacked standing.[153] Nevertheless, the court went onto to address the merits and found that the 2006 law did not violate the fundamental right to vote.[154] The court found that the named plaintiffs did not have standing because they testified that they would be able to go to the registrar's office and obtain identification from the registrar if necessary.[155] The court then rejected the organizational standing arguments of the NAACP (the other organizational plaintiffs dismissed themselves). The court found that the Georgia NAACP president's testimony that his predecessor told him there were several members of the NAACP who did not have identification was inadequate to establish standing on behalf of the NAACP members.[156] It also rejected the argument that the NAACP had standing in its own right because it would have to reallocate resources to educate its members about the photo ID requirement. The court stated that a decision to reallocate resources is an injury of the NAACP's own making and would not be sufficient to confer standing. In doing so, the court stated that NAACP's reliance for its standing "in its own right" theory on the United States Supreme Court's decision in *Havens Realty Corp. v. Coleman*[157] and a subsequent 11th Circuit decision was misplaced because those cases involved Fair Housing Act claims and were not applicable to other claims.[158] The standard adopted by the district court for standing makes it difficult in practice to find a plaintiff who could establish standing because the person would have to be able to travel to federal court to testify but also have to credibly testify that he or she would not be able to travel to a county voter registration in order to obtain an identification.[159]

With respect to the merits, the court stated that it was applying the "*Burdick,* sliding-scale test."[160] The court found that plaintiffs failed to produce admissible evidence showing a severe burden. It found that because the individuals that testified on behalf of plaintiffs stated that they could obtain the free identification at the voter registrar's office or could vote absentee, the burden on these voters was not severe. On a macro level, the plaintiffs relied on analyses comparing the list of the registered voters to a list of individuals that had a Georgia driver's license or nonoperator identification. Georgia's match of these lists as of June 2007 found that almost 200,000 registered voters did not have a Georgia driver's license or nonoperator identification. Plaintiffs' analysis using 2006 data showed that minority voters were about twice as likely as white voters to not have a Georgia driver's license or nonoperator identification and that elderly voters were about twice as likely to not have a Georgia driver's license or nonoperator identification as the nonelderly.[161] The court discounted these analyses on the grounds that they were not reliable (though both sides had used them), that they did not show how these voters did not have access to transportation in order to receive an identification from the voter registrar, and that there was no demonstration of how many of these voters lacked the other forms of acceptable identification.[162] Accordingly, the court found that the burden of the law was not severe and so did not apply strict scrutiny.[163]

The court instead applied a rational basis analysis.[164] The court found that under rational basis analysis, the state need not demonstrate that there had been previous instances of in-person voter fraud and that the Georgia legislature had wide latitude to determine that requiring photo identification was an appropriate measure to combat voter fraud.[165]

In upholding the 2006 law at trial, the court distinguished its decisions to preliminarily enjoin the 2005 law and 2006 law. It stated that the 2006 law was different in that it did allow voters to get a free voter identification issued by the voter registrar in their county of the Department of Drivers Services, and that its earlier preliminary injunctions of the 2006 law were predicated on concerns that not enough had been done to educate voters about the identification law.[166]

On October 2, 2007, plaintiffs filed a notice of appeal of the district court's decision.[167]

2. Indiana. In 2005, Indiana passed a law that requires voters who vote in person to provide a photo identification issued by the United States or the State of Indiana that contains the voter's name and is either unexpired or had not expired at the time of the most recent general election.[168] Voters who do not have acceptable identification when they vote are permitted to cast a provisional ballot, which is counted if within the second Monday after the election, the voter appears at the county clerk or county election board and provides acceptable identification or signs an affidavit attesting to his or her identity and to his or her indigency or religious objection to being photographed.[169] Absentee voters who vote by mail do not have to provide identification—a voter must meet one of ten qualifications to vote absentee.[170]

Two sets of plaintiffs brought federal challenges to Indiana's voter identification law, and the plaintiffs and defendants both filed for summary judgment.[171] The district court granted the defendants' motion for summary judgment. With respect to plaintiffs' fundamental right to vote claim, the court found that strict scrutiny was not warranted because, according to the court, the plaintiffs "failed to submit: (1) evidence of any individuals who will be unable to vote or who will be forced to undertake appreciable burdens to vote; and (2) any statistics or aggregate data indicating particular groups who will be unable to vote or will be forced to undertake appreciable burdens in order to vote."[172] The plaintiffs had submitted an expert report that estimated that as many as 989,000 registered voters did not have a photo identification issued by the Bureau of Motor Vehicles, but the court did not consider the report in its determinations because the court found the report "utterly incredible and unreliable."[173]

The court then went on to find that the Indiana photo voter identification law was reasonably justified. The court stated that "in examining an election regulation aimed at combating fraud, courts are well-advised to pay additional deference to the legislative judgment because 'the striking of the balance between discouraging fraud and other abuses and encouraging turnout is quintessentially a legislative judgment with which we judges should not legislatively interfere unless strongly convinced that the legislative judgment is grossly awry."[174] In applying this "grossly awry" standard, the court did not find it significant that the defendants had conceded that they were "not aware of any incidents or persons attempting to vote, or voting, at a polling place with fraudulent or otherwise false identification,'"[175] because, according to the court, "the state is not required to produce such documentation prior to enactment of the law."[176]

The court also found that the law was not a poll tax because Indiana residents who do not wish to drive can receive a free photo identification card from the Bureau of Motor Vehicles.[177] The court rejected the plaintiffs' argument that the costs associated with obtaining the BMV identification, such as the cost of obtaining a birth certificate, could constitute a poll tax.[178]

The plaintiffs appealed the district court's decision to the Seventh Circuit, where it was affirmed by a 2–1 vote.[179] Both opinions focused on the fundamental right to vote claim. Judge Posner, writing for the majority, stated that "a strict standard would be especially inappropriate in a case such as this, in which the right to vote is on both sides of the ledger."[180] In Judge Posner's view, not only does a voter identification statute deny the right to vote of voters who do not have identification but it protects the right to vote because "voting fraud impairs the right to vote of legitimate voters by diluting their vote."[181] Judge Posner stated that the record of the legitimate voters who are disenfranchised by the statute is "slight" and that "a vote in a political election rarely has any *instrumental* value, since elections for political office at the state or federal level are never decided by just one vote."[182] Though he acknowledged that there was no record of voter impersonation in Indiana, he hypothesized that "the absence of prosecutions is explained by the endemic under-enforcement of minor criminal laws (minor as they appear to the public and prosecutors, at all events) and by the extreme difficulty of apprehending the voting impersonator."[183] He concluded that "the details of the elections must be left to the states."[184]

Judge Evans dissented. He stated that the Indiana voter identification should be subjected to strict scrutiny, or what he called "strict scrutiny light," and struck down "as an undue burden on the fundamental right to vote."[185] He stated that "the real problem is that this law will make it significantly more difficult for some eligible voters" to vote and that "this group is mostly comprised of people who are poor, elderly, minorities, disabled, or some combination thereof."[186] He compared this to the scant evidence of voter impersonation at the polls—"where is the justification for this law? Is it wise to use a sledgehammer to hit either a real or imaginary fly on a glass coffee table? I think not."[187]

The appellants petitioned to have the entire Seventh Circuit hear the case en banc. The Seventh Circuit denied the petition.[188] Judge Wood dissented along with three other judges.[189] The dissent stated that "when there is a serious risk that an election law has been passed with the intent of imposing an additional significant burden on the right to vote of a specific group of voters, the court must apply strict scrutiny."[190] The dissent also indicated that complete deprivations of the right to vote, like a photo identification requirement, are "severe" injuries to the voters affected and require strict scrutiny review, as compared to "minor obstacles," such as a 28-day registration deadline, which do not.[191] The dissent stated that remand was appropriate because the state's justification for the law—that it would prevent fraud at the polling place—was a disputed question of fact precluding summary judgment because "if the burden on voting is great and the benefit for the asserted state interest is small as an empirical matter, the law cannot stand."[192]

The appellants petitioned the United States Supreme Court for a writ of certiorari and certiorari was granted on September 25, 2007.[193] The Supreme Court is likely to hear argument during the 2007–08 term.

3. Arizona. Prior to the 2004 election, an individual living in Arizona could register to vote if the individual filled out a registration form, provided the identifying information in the form, and signed a statement attesting, among other things, that the individual was a citizen over the age of 18, and acknowledging that executing a false registration was a class 6 felony.[194] When arriving at the polls, the voter was required to announce his or her name and sign the signature roster.[195]

In the November 2004 election, Arizona voters passed Proposition 200, the Arizona Taxpayer and Protection Act. The proposition included findings that "illegal immigration is causing hardship to the state and that illegal immigration is encouraged by public agencies within this state that provide public benefits without verifying immigration status."[196] In addition to some changes in Arizona welfare law, Proposition 200 created new registration and voting requirements. Arizona law now requires that new applicants for voter registration show proof of citizenship,[197] and that voters who vote on Election Day provide one form of photo identification that contains the voter's name and address or two pieces of nonphoto identification that contain the voter's name and address.[198] Arizona is the only state that requires an identification that contains the voter's address.[199] The Arizona secretary of state issued procedures for proof of identification at the polls that set forth, among other things, what types of identification were acceptable,[200] the process for voters who did not have identification,[201] and special procedures for Native American voters.[202] In contrast, there is no identification requirement for voters who vote by early voting; instead, election officials check the signature on the affidavit contained within the early ballot envelope with the signature on the voter's registration form.[203] All Arizona voters are eligible to vote early either by mail or at on-site locations determined by the county recorder.[204]

In 2006, three cases filed by different groups of plaintiffs, the Gonzalez plaintiffs, the Inter-Tribal Council of Arizona (ITCA) plaintiffs, and the Navajo Nation plaintiffs, filed complaints in United States District Court seeking to enjoin implementation of the Arizona proof of citizenship requirements for voter registration and/or the identification requirements for Election Day voters under a variety of theories. The cases were consolidated.[205]

The Gonzalez plaintiffs, joined by the ITCA plaintiffs, sought a temporary restraining order prohibiting Arizona county recorders from requiring applicants who completed the Federal Mail-In Form to provide proof of citizenship. The plaintiffs relied on (1) the language of the National Voter Registration Act (NVRA), which mandated the Federal Mail-In Form; (2) the legislative history of the NVRA; and (3) a letter from the Election Assistance Commission (EAC), the agency responsible for developing the Federal Mail-In Form, to Arizona's secretary of state, stating that Arizona's decision not to accept the Federal Mail-In Form absent documentation of citizenship violated the NVRA.[206] The language of the NVRA specifies that states "shall accept and use the mail voter registration application proscribed by the

U.S. Election Assistance Commission pursuant to section 9(a)(2) for the registration of voters in elections for federal office."[207] The legislative history on this issue was particularly clear: The NVRA bill originally passed by the Senate had a provision stating that nothing in the NVRA prevented states from asking for documentation of citizenship, whereas the bill passed originally by the House did not have such a provision. In the Senate/House conference to resolve differences, the provision was taken out. The conference report stated that proof of citizenship requirements for the Federal Mail-In Form were "not necessary or consistent with the purpose of [the NVRA]."[208] The EAC relied on both foregoing authorities in the letter.[209] Nonetheless, the district court denied the motion. It found that no review of the legislative history and the agency interpretation was needed because "[p]laintiffs have not shown that the requirements of Proposition 200 conflict with the plain language of the NVRA."[210]

The ITCA and Gonzalez plaintiffs then sought a preliminary injunction on two other claims—the Equal Protection fundamental right to vote claim and the poll tax claim (the plaintiffs also included the NVRA in the motion)—and the court held an evidentiary hearing on these claims in August 2006.[211] The evidence included (1) the defendants' acknowledgement that more than 20,000 registration forms had been rejected at the time of the hearing because the applicants did not provide proof of citizenship,[212] (2) documentation of the costs required to obtain the required proof of citizenship or identification for individuals that did not have the required documents,[213] and (3) the nonexistent evidence of voter impersonation and sparse evidence of noncitizen registration and voting in Arizona.[214] The district court denied plaintiffs' motion on September 11, 2006, but did not issue its findings until October 11, 2006. The district court concluded that "'plaintiffs have shown a possibility of success of success on the merits' of some of their arguments but the Court 'cannot say at this stage of the litigation they have shown a strong likelihood.'"[215]

After the district court issued its decision denying the motion but before it issued its findings, the ITCA and Gonzalez plaintiffs appealed the decision, and moved the Ninth Circuit to stay implementation of the polling place identification requirements of Proposition 200 until it could decide the merits of plaintiffs' motion, which would have effectively enjoined Proposition 200 for the November 2006 election. The Ninth Circuit granted plaintiffs' motion.[216] The defendants appealed to the United States Supreme Court to vacate the stay and the Supreme Court did so in a per curiam opinion.[217] The Supreme Court stated that it was not expressing any opinion on the merits of the motion or the case. It vacated the stay because of "the imminence of the election," "the inadequate time to resolve the factual disputes," and the Ninth Circuit's lack of explanation as to how the district court erred.[218] The Supreme Court also recognized the underlying competing interests. It stated that "[c]onfidence in the integrity of the electoral process is essential to the functioning of our participatory democracy," while also stating that "the possibility that qualified voters might be turned away from the polls would caution any district judge to give careful consideration to the plaintiffs' challenges."[219] In a concurring opinion, Justice Stevens stated that "[a]t least two important factual issues remain largely resolved: the scope of the disenfranchisement that the novel identification requirements will produce, and the prevalence and character of the fraudulent practices that allegedly justify those requirements."[220]

The merits of the ITCA and Gonzalez plaintiffs' motion for preliminary injunction as to the proof of citizenship requirement were subsequently heard by the Ninth Circuit.[221] The Ninth Circuit concluded that

> the district court did not abuse its discretion in denying injunctive relief with respect to [the proof of citizenship] requirement, because the limited record before us does not establish that the balance of hardships and likelihood of success on the merits of plaintiffs' claims justify an injunction at this stage of the proceedings. The litigation remains pending at the district court. There, final resolution of the scope of the appropriate permanent relief can be determined on the basis of a fully developed record, and well before the next general election in 2008.[222]

Upon remand, Arizona moved for summary judgment on some of the plaintiffs' claims including the NVRA and poll tax claims. The court granted the defendants' motion. Relying on the Ninth Circuit opinion, the court disposed of the NVRA claim in one paragraph. It found that the "language of the NVRA 'does not prohibit documentation requirements.'"[223] Again relying on the Ninth Circuit opinion, the district court disposed of the poll tax claim in a paragraph. It stated that the Proposition 200 is not a poll tax because "'voters do not have to choose between paying a poll tax and providing proof of citizenship when they register to vote. They only have to provide proof of citizenship.'"[224] The undue burden claim was not part of the summary judgment motion and discovery in the case continues.

4. Missouri. In 2002, after allegations of voter fraud in Missouri in the November 2000 election and the passage of HAVA, the Missouri state legislature passed an identification statute that required voters to show one of several different types of photo or nonphoto identification.[225] Missouri Secretary of State Matt Blunt, who was elected governor in November 2004, "described Missouri's elections in 2002 and 2004 to then-Governor Bob Holden as 'two of the cleanest and most problem free elections in recent history.'"[226] Nonetheless, the Missouri state legislature enacted a new statute in 2006 that would become permanent on November 1, 2008. The statute required in-person voters to present unexpired photo identification issued by Missouri or the federal government that contains the voter's name as listed in the voter registration records.[227] The law contained exceptions for individuals born before 1941, individuals with disabilities, or people who, on religious grounds, objected to a picture being taken of them.[228] In addition, Missouri allowed

individuals who provided proper documentation to obtain a nondriver photo identification free of charge.[229] For elections before November 1, 2008, a "transitional"
law would be in place that would allow voters without the required identification
to cast a provisional ballot if they signed an affidavit attesting to their identity and
presented one of a number of permitted forms of identification.[230] The provisional
ballot would be counted if the signature of the affidavit matched the signature on
file with the election authority.[231]

A group of Missouri voters filed an action challenging the constitutionality
of the Missouri law under the Missouri and United States constitutions. The trial
court found that the identification law violated the Missouri constitution.[232] The
court found that

> [t]he photo ID burden placed on the voter may seem minor or inconsequential
> to the mainstream of our society for whom automobiles, driver licenses, and even
> passports are a natural part of everyday life. However, for the elderly, the poor, the
> under-educated, or otherwise disadvantaged, the burden can be great if not insur-
> mountable, and it is those very people outside the mainstream of society who are
> the least equipped to bear the costs or navigate the many bureaucracies necessary to
> obtain the required documentation.[233]

By a 6–1 vote, the Missouri Supreme Court held, in a per curiam opinion, that the
Missouri statute violates Missouri's equal protection clause and "Missouri's constitutional guarantee of the right of its qualified, registered citizens to vote."[234] The
Missouri Supreme Court found that the right to vote under the Missouri Constitution is more expansive than under the United States Constitution because the right
to vote is explicitly mentioned,[235] though the analysis it applied was akin to the
Burdick analysis. The Missouri Supreme Court found that the photo identification
law was a "substantial burden" on the right to vote, and thus was subject to strict
scrutiny.[236] The court based its determination on the number of registered voters
who did not have Missouri driver's licenses or photo identification as calculated
from analyses by the Office of the Secretary of State (240,000) and the Department
of Revenue (169,415) and the monetary costs associated with obtaining the identification needed to obtain a driver's license or nonoperator identification as well
as the practical costs involved in getting the identification.[237] The court stated that
under federal law, all fees that impose financial burdens are impermissible as a poll
tax, and the same would be true under Missouri law.[238] The court then found that
the statute failed to survive strict scrutiny. It held that photo identification was not
necessary because the earlier 2002 requirements had been sufficient to prevent the
limited amount of voter impersonation fraud that existed prior to 2002.[239]

Justice Limbaugh dissented on the grounds that the court did not need to decide
whether the permanent law was constitutional because it would not go into effect
until November 1, 2008, and that the transitional law was constitutional.[240]

5. Albuquerque, New Mexico. In 2005, New Mexico passed a law requiring voters to show one of numerous photo and nonphoto identifications in order to vote in person for state and federal elections.[241] There was no similar requirement enacted for municipal elections. Through an October 4, 2005, voter referendum, the City of Albuquerque enacted a requirement that in-person voters must show a photo identification that contains their name.[242] Voters without photo identification are allowed to cast a provisional ballot if they sign an affidavit attesting to their identity and provide their date of birth and last four numbers of their social security card, but those ballots are not counted unless the voter supplies the required photo identification to the election official or signs an affidavit stating that the voter has a religious objection to taking a photograph.[243] The charter provision also stated that photo identification cards would be issued by the City Clerk free of charge if the voter showed at least two of several types of identification or signed an affidavit attesting to his or her identity.[244]

Three organizations and three individuals challenged the Albuquerque photo identification law. On cross-motions for summary judgment, the district court found that the law violated the Equal Protection Clause.[245] The court applied the *Burdick* test, which it characterized as an "intermediate" scrutiny "sliding-scale" balancing test.[246] The court found that the law imposed a "significant burden on the right to vote"[247] because

> [p]laintiffs have shown that surprise or confusion about the photo ID requirement and the bureaucratic hurdles it imposes is likely to discourage—if not disenfranchise—a significant number of Albuquerque voters who appear at a polling place to vote on the next municipal election day, especially given the lack of clarity or definition in the text of the amendment itself, the absence of any specific plans for voter-education efforts to be undertaken by the City, and the fact that the City's photo ID requirement differs significantly from the identification requirements that voters have experienced in past elections."[248]

On the other side of the balance, the court found that *Burdick* requires a jurisdiction to identify a precise interest justifying the law, and not a generalized interest, and in this case the precise interest was in preventing voter impersonation fraud, not other types of voting fraud.[249] The court found "there is no admissible evidence in the record that such voter impersonation fraud has occurred with any frequency in past municipal elections."[250] It also found that not requiring identification for absentee voters presented a "significant opportunity for circumventing the fraud-prevention requirement" in the voter ID law, and "tends to undermine Defendant's argument that the amendment effectively targets the goal of preventing future instances of voter impersonation fraud."[251] In addition, it found that the voter identification requirements contained in HAVA and under New Mexico law for state elections were less restrictive alternatives.[252]

The defendants have appealed the trial court's ruling to the Tenth Circuit Court of Appeals.[253]

The foregoing cases demonstrate that the courts deciding whether a government-issued photo identification or proof of citizenship law violates the fundamental right to vote or constitutes a poll tax have adopted a range of approaches that affect voters' rights. This reflects both the vagueness of the *Burdick* test (i.e., when does a burden become a "severe" burden?) and the differing views that various courts have on individual constitutional rights as opposed to a state's legislative prerogatives. Where courts highly value the right to vote and demand that jurisdictions provide a showing of the need for these laws, the challenge will likely succeed because of the dearth of evidence of voter impersonation or noncitizen voting. Conversely, where courts are deferential to the decisions of legislators or voters and view voting as more of a privilege that can be regulated substantially than a right that can be impeded only with justification, challenges will likely fail. The upcoming decision and reasoning of the Supreme Court's disposition of *Crawford v. Marion County Election Board* is likely to go a long way in determining how the balance between the right to vote and state legislative prerogatives are balanced.

VII. Conclusion

The issue of whether government-issued voter identification laws and proof of citizenship laws are constitutional and appropriate has raged among advocates, Congress and state legislatures, and the courts. In each forum, there have been dramatically divergent views on the issue. The upcoming Supreme Court decision in *Crawford v. Marion County Election Board* will likely provide substantial clarification of the constitutional issue as it applies to government-issued photo identification. Regardless of the outcome of the *Crawford* case, we should expect that the debate over whether these measures are appropriate will continue in the years to come.

Notes

1. *See* Help America Vote Act, 42 U.S.C. § 15301; *compare* ELECTIONLINE.ORG, ELECTION REFORM BRIEFING: VOTER IDENTIFICATION (2002), *available at* http://www.electionline.org/Portals/1/Publications/Voter%20Identification.pdf [hereinafter ELECTION REFORM BRIEFING], *with* Election line.org, Voter ID Laws, *available at* http://www.electionline.org/Default.aspx?tabid=364.

2. *See* ELECTION REFORM BRIEFING, *supra* note 1.

3. *See id.*

4. *See supra* note 1.

5. *See, e.g.,* JOHN FUND, STEALING ELECTIONS: HOW VOTER FRAUD THREATENS OUR DEMOCRACY (2004); *Assessing the Conduct of the 2006 Mid-Term Elections: Hearing Before the U.S. Election Assistance Commission* (2006) (statement of Mark F. (Thor) Hearne II).

6. *See generally* Brief for the Lawyers' Committee for Civil Rights Under Law, Service Employees International Union, American Federation of State, County and Municipal Employees, Common Cause, Jewish Council for Public Affairs, and National Council of Jewish Women as *Amici Curiae* in Support of Petitioners, *Crawford v. Marion County Election Bd.*, et al., Nos. 07-21 and 07-25 (U.S. Nov. 13, 2007) [hereinafter Lawyers' Committee Brief].

7. *Id.*

8. *See* Crawford v. Marion County Election Bd., 472 F.3d 949, 950 (7th Cir. 2007) (Evans, J., dissenting) ("Let's not beat around the bush: The Indiana voter photo ID law is a not-too-thinly-veiled attempt to discourage election-day turnout by certain folks believed to skew Democratic."); Kristen Mack, *In Trying to Win, Has Dewhurst Lost a Friend?*, HOUSTON CHRONICLE, May 17, 2007 ("Among Republicans it is an 'article of religious faith that voter fraud is causing us to lose elections,' [Royal] Masset [former Texas Republican Party political director] said. He doesn't agree with that, but does believe that requiring photo IDs could cause enough of a dropoff in legitimate Democratic voting to add 3 percent to the Republican vote.").

9. See *infra* note 131 and accompanying text; Indiana Democratic Party v. Rokita, 458 F. Supp. 2d 775, 783 (S.D. Ind. 2006) ("This litigation is a result of a partisan legislative disagreement that has spilled out of the state house into the courts.").

10. *See infra* notes 97 to 253 and accompanying text.

11. *See* EAGLETON INSTITUTE OF POLITICS & MORITZ COLLEGE OF LAW, REPORT TO THE U.S. ELECTION ASSISTANCE COMMISSION ON BEST PRACTICES TO IMPROVE VOTER IDENTIFICATION REQUIREMENTS PURSUANT TO THE HELP AMERICA VOTE ACT OF 2002, PUBLIC LAW 107-252, at 9 & App. A (2006), *available at* http://www.eac.gov/clearinghouse/docs/eagletons-draft-voter-id-report/attachment_download/file (last visited Aug. 20, 2007) [hereinafter EAGLETON INSTITUTE REPORT].

12. *See id.* at App. B.

13. 42 U.S.C. § 1973c (2007).

14. Congress adopted a formula contained within Section 4 of the Act, 42 U.S.C. § 1973b, that was designed to capture these jurisdictions. The list of covered jurisdictions can be found at 28 C.F.R. pt.55 App. A (2007).

15. 42 U.S.C. § 1973.

16. *Id.*

17. Letter from Deval L. Patrick, Assistant Attorney General, Civil Rights Division, U.S. Department of Justice, to Sheri Marcus Morris, Assistant Attorney General, State of Louisiana (Nov. 21, 1994).

18. *Id.*

19. *Id.* at 2.

20. Help America Vote Act, 42 U.S.C. § 15301.

21. 42 U.S.C. § 15483(b)(3)(B).

22. 42 U.S.C. § 15483(b)(2).

23. 42 U.S.C. § 15484.

24. For a detailed discussion on the role of current federal statutes on election related fraud, *see generally* CRAIG C. DONSANTO & NANCY L. SIMMONS, FEDERAL PROSECUTION OF ELEC-

Tion Offenses 37–57 (7th ed. 2007), *available at* http://www.usdoj.gov/criminal/pin/docs/electbook-0507.pdf.

25. 18 U.S.C. §242 has also been applied to voting. That statute is much like §241, but has a color of law requirement.

26. *See, e.g.,* United States v. Saylor, 322 U.S. 385 (1944); United States v. Haynes, 977 F.2d 583 (6th Cir. 1992); United States v. Morando, 454 F.2d 167 (5th Cir. 1972).

27. *See* 42 U.S.C. s.1973i(c).

28. Many of the prohibitions in the Voting Rights Act have been read to consolidated federal and nonfederal election. *See* Donsanto & Simmons, *supra* note 24, at 42–44.

29. 42 U.S.C. §1973i(c).

30. *See* 42 U.S.C. §1973i(e).

31. United States v. Olinger, 759 F.2d 1293 (7th Cir. 1985); United States v. Smith, 231 F.3d 800 (11th Cir. 2000).

32. Ga. Code Ann. §21-2-561 (2007).

33. Ga. Code Ann. §21-2-562 (2007).

34. Ga. Code Ann. §21-2-566 (2007).

35. Ga. Code Ann. §21-2-571 (2007).

36. Ga. Code Ann. §21-2-572 (2007).

37. *See infra* notes 82 to 96 and accompanying text.

38. Commission on Federal Election Reform, Building Confidence in U.S. Elections; Report of the Commission on Federal Election Reform 18, (Center for Democracy and Election Management, American University, Sept. 2005).

39. *See* John Fund, Stealing Elections: How Voter Fraud Threatens Our Democracy (2004) [hereinafter Stealing Elections]; *Assessing the Conduct of the 2006 Mid-Term Elections: Hearing Before the U.S. Election Assistance Commission* (2006) (statement of Mark F. (Thor) Thorne II).

40. *See Hearing on Non-Citizen Voting Before House Admin. Comm.,* 109th Cong. (2006) (statement of Patrick Rogers).

41. *See* Stealing Elections, *supra* note 39.

42. *See* B. Drummond Ayres, Jr., *After Days of Counting, Dornan Race Too Close to Call,* N.Y. Times, Nov. 14, 1996.

43. *Dismissing the Election Contest Against Loretta Sanchez: Report of the Committee on House Oversight on H.R. 355 Together with Minority Views,* H.R. Doc. No. 105-416 (1998).

44. *Id.*

45. *Id.* at 1025.

46. *See* Robert Pear, *Bill to Overhaul System of Voting is Seen in Danger,* N.Y. Times, Sept. 7, 2002; *Assessing the Conduct of the 2006 Mid-Term Elections: Hearing Before the Election Assistance Commission* (2006) (statement of Mark F. (Thor) Hearne II).

47. 109 Cong. Rec. S8692 (daily ed. Aug. 2, 2001) (statement of Sen. Bond).

48. *See id.;* Stealing Elections, *supra* note 39, at 24–25. *But see infra* notes 49-68 and accompanying text suggesting that these registrations do not lead to ineligible voters at the polling place.

49. *See* Spencer Overton, Stealing Democracy: The New Politics of Voter Suppression 148–67 (2006); Tova Andrea Wang, Where's the Voter Fraud? (2006); Lorraine C. Minnite, Ph.D., The Politics of Voter Fraud (2007).

50. *See* Donsanto & Simmons, *supra* note 24, at 101. For a discussion of the steps necessary to commit the type of voter fraud prevented by these provisions, *see* Lawyers' Committee Brief, *supra* note 6, at 10).

51. See *supra* notes 24–36 and accompanying text for a discussion of criminal penalties for voter fraud.

52. *See* Ian Urbina, *Panel Said to Alter Finding on Voter Fraud*, N.Y. Times, Apr. 11, 2007, A01.

53. For a detailed response to allegations of voter fraud, *see* Brennan Center for Justice, The Truth About Fraud: Case Studies by Issue, www.truthaboutfraud.org/case_studies_by_issue.

54. Recent examples include the flawed purge list used by Florida in 2000 and 2004 to match ineligible voters with felony convictions to the voter registration rolls and a number of questionable directives made by Ohio Secretary of State Kenneth Blackwell in the 2004 presidential elections. *See* Andrew Gumbel, Steal this Vote: Dirty Elections and the Rotten History of Democracy in America 210–13 (2005).

55. *See* Asian American Legal Defense and Education Fund, The Asian American Vote: Report on the Multilingual Exit Poll in the 2004 Presidential Election (2005), *available at* http://www.aaldef.org/articles/2005-04-20_67_TheAsianAmeric.pdf.

56. Mitchel Maddux, *GOP Calls for Probe of State's Election Rolls*, The (Bergen County, N.J.) Record, Sept. 16, 2005.

57. *See* Brennan Center for Justice, The Truth About Fraud: New Jersey, 2004, http://www.truthaboutfraud.org/case_studies_by_state/new_jersey_2005.html.

58. *See* James Finch, Nanette Hegerty, E. Michael McCann & Steven M. Biskupic, Preliminary Findings of Joint Task Force Investigating Possible Election Fraud (May 10, 2005), *available at* http://www.wispolitics.com/1006/electionfraud.pdf.

59. *See id.* at 2. According to the report, the list of suspected fraudulent voters was around 100 out of over 250,000 votes cast.

60. *See id.*

61. *Id.*

62. Tova Andrea Wang, *Competing Values or False Choices: Coming to Consensus on the Election Reform Debate in Washington State and the Country*, 29 Seattle U.L. Rev. 353, 369 (2005).

63. Court's Oral Decision, Borders v. King County, No. 05-2-00027-3 (Wash. Super. Ct. 2005), *available at* www.seattleweekly.com/2005-06-08/news/borders-et-al-v-king-county-et-al.php?page=full.

64. *Id.*

65. *See* Gene Johnson, *Two Plead Guilty to Voting Twice in 2004 General Election*, Associated Press, June 2, 2005; Keith Ervin, *6 Accused of Casting Multiple Votes*, Seattle Times, June 22, 2005.

66. *See* United States Department of Justice, Fact Sheet: Protecting Voting Rights and Preventing Election Fraud, *available at* http://www.usdoj.gov/opa/pr/2002/November/02_at_641.htm.

67. *See* U.S. Election Assistance Comm. Election Crimes: An Initial Review and Recommendations for Future Study app. 3, at 4 (Dec. 2006).

68. Eric Lipton & Ian Urbina, *In 5-Year Effort, Scant Evidence of Voter Fraud*, N.Y. Times, Apr. 12, 2007.

69. *See* Comm'n on Fed. Election Reform, Building Confidence in U.S. Elections 73 n.22 (2005); Brennan Center for Justice, Citizens Without Proof: A Survey of Americans' Possession of Documentary Proof of Citizenship and Photo Identification (Nov. 2006), *available at* http://www.vote.caltech.edu/VoterID/CitizensWithoutProof.pdf [hereinafter Citizens Without Proof]; *Verification of Identity, in* To Assure Pride and Confidence in the Electoral Process: Task Force Reports to Accompany the Report of the National Commission on Election Reform, sec. VI (Aug. 2001), *available at* http://www.tcf.org/Publications/electionreform/full_tf_report.pdf

70. In addition, in Section VI, *infra*, there is discussion of the evidence presented in each case on these issues.

71. Controversy surrounded the development of these reports and their eventual release. For more information see Ian Urbina, *Panel Said to Alter Finding on Voter Fraud*, N.Y. Times, Apr. 11, 2007, A01.

72. As discussed *id.,* the EAC commissioned two consultants—one with a progressive background, one with a conservative background, to draft the report. The report turned in by the consultants was later changed by EAC staff. *Compare* Job Serebrov & Tova Wang, Voting Fraud and Voter Intimidation: Report to the U.S. Election Assistance Commission on Preliminary Research and Recommendations, Draft Report (not adopted by U.S. Election Assistance Commission), *available at* http://graphics8.nytimes.com/packages/pdf/national/20070411voters_draft_report.pdf, *with* U.S. Election Assistance Comm'n., Election Crimes: An Initial Review and Recommendations for Future Study (Election Assistance Commission, Dec. 2006). These changes were controversial and were the subject of a House Committee hearing. The report submitted by the consultants includes all of the research they compiled, while the final report omits major portions of that research.

73. *See id.*

74. *Presentation to the U.S. Election Assistance Commission: Summarizing a Report on Best Practices to Improve Voter Identification Requirements Pursuant to the Help America Vote Act of 2002 Public Law 107-252 Submitted on June 28, 2006, by The Eagleton Institute of Politics, Rutgers, The State University of New Jersey and The Moritz College of Law, The Ohio State University,* Thomas O'Neill and Tim Vercellotti, Testimony to EAC, Feb. 8, 2007 (like the EAC Fraud Report, the EAC did not endorse the findings of this report).

75. M. V. Hood III & Charles S. Bullock, III, Worth a Thousand Words? An Analysis of Georgia's Voter Identification Statute 15 (2007).

76. *See* Common Cause/Georgia v. Billups, 439 F. Supp. 2d 1294, 1311 (N.D. Ga. 2006).

77. JOHN PAWASARAT, THE DRIVER LICENSE STATUS OF THE VOTING AGE POPULATION IN WISCONSIN 1, 11 (June 2005), *available at* http://www.uwm.edu/Dept/ETI/barriers/DriversLicense.pdf.

78. *See* CITIZENS WITHOUT PROOF, *supra* note 69.

79. *Id.*

80. *See* Matt A. Barreto, et al., Washington Institute for the Study of Ethnicity and Race, *The Disproportionate Impact of Indiana Voter ID Requirements on the Electorate*, at Table 1.1b (Wash. Inst. for the Study of Ethnicity & Race, Working Paper, 2007), *available at* http://depts.washington.edu/uwiser/documents/Indiana_voter.pdf.

81. U.S. Census Bureau, Tenure by Vehicles Available by Age of Householder (2000), *available at* http://factfinder.census.gov/servlet/DTTable?_bm=y&-geo_id=D&-ds_name=D&-_lang=en&-mt_name=DEC_2000_SF3_U_H045(10 percent of American households have no available automobile while 24 percent of African American and 17 percent of Latino households have no automobile); IND. DEPT. OF TRANSP. MARKET RESEARCH PROJECT, 3.0 ENVIRONMENTAL JUSTICE PERSPECTIVES 3–36, *available at* http://www.in.gov/indot/files/market_section3.pdf (noting that, while over 90 percent of Indiana households have access to at least one automobile, one in four below-poverty Indiana households lack access to an automobile).

82. 109 CONG. REC. S8692 (daily ed. Aug. 2, 2001) (statement of Sen. Bond).

83. *See* Brennan Center for Justice, The *Truth About Fraud: Missouri, 2000*, http://www.truthaboutfraud.org/case_studies_by_state/missouri_2000.html.

84. See *e.g.*, MLL 168.823; H1408 (Miss. 2007); H 218 (Tex. 2006).

85. *See* COMM'N ON FEDERAL ELECTION REFORM, BUILDING CONFIDENCE IN U.S. ELECTIONS; REPORT OF THE COMMISSION ON FEDERAL ELECTION REFORM 18 (Sept. 2005).

86. *See id.* at 88.

87. *See* Jimmy Carter and James A. Baker III, Editorial, *Voting Reform Is in the Cards*, N.Y. TIMES, Sept. 23, 2005.

88. Voter Protection Act of 2005, S. 414, 109th Cong. (2005).

89. See *infra* Section VI for a discussion regarding opinions on whether government issued photo identification requirements for voters constitute a poll tax.

90. Voter Protection Act of 2005, S. 414, 109th Cong. (2005).

91. *See* Valuing Our Trust in Elections Act, H.R. 2250, 109th Cong. (2005); Verifying the Outcome of Tomorrow's Elections Act, H.R. 3910, 109th Cong. (2006).

92. Neither of these bills made it out of committee.

93. Amendment by Sen. McConnell to the Comprehensive Immigration Reform Act of 2006, S. 2611, 109th Cong. (2006).

94. The Real ID Act has an implementation date of May 2008, although regulations issued by the Department of Homeland Security in 2007 has extended the deadline. Sen. McConnell's amendment would have imposed Real ID before the implementation date by requiring it for voting starting in January 2008.

95. *See* Federal Election Integrity Act of 2006, H.R. 4844, 109th Cong. (2006).

96. The bill passed 228–196 with all but three Republicans voting for it and all but four Democrats voting against.

97. This case discussion in this article focuses on cases involving challenges to legislative enactments or voter referenda that require photo identification for in person voters or require voter registrants to provide documentary proof of citizenship. There are other cases

involving identification requirements since 2005 not covered here. For example, in Michigan, the Michigan Supreme Court issued an advisory opinion stating that Michigan's law, which requires voters to provide photo identification or sign an affidavit averring that they do not have photo identification, is facially constitutionally valid. The law had been originally enacted in 1996 and reenacted in 2005, but had not been enforced because of a 1997 Michigan Attorney General's opinion that the law violated Equal Protection Clause of the United States Constitution. *In re* Request for Advisory Opinion Regarding Constitutionality of 2005 PA 71, 2007 Mich. LEXIS 1582 (Mich. July 18, 2007). In addition, in Mississippi, the Mississippi Democratic Party filed suit arguing that Mississippi's "open" primary system, which allowed any registered voter to vote in the Democratic Primary, violated the First Amendment. The federal district court granted the Democratic Party's motion for summary judgment but ordered remedies not requested by the Democratic Party, including requiring the Mississippi State Legislature to pass legislation by spring 2007 that would include a photo identification requirement for voters in primary elections. Mississippi State Democratic Party v. Barbour, 2007 U.S. Dist. LEXIS 41908 (N.D. Miss. June 8, 2007); 2007 U.S. Dist. LEXIS 52141 (N.D. Miss. July 17, 2007). The court's decision resulted in a now-pending appeal not only from the defendants, but from the plaintiffs, as well as the Mississippi NAACP and the Mississippi Republican Executive Committee, both of which sought intervention after the court's order.

98. Reynolds v. Sims, 377 U.S. 533, 554 (1964) (citations omitted).

99. Carrington v. Rash, 380 U.S. 89 (1965).

100. Kramer v. Union Free Sch. Dist., 395 U.S. 621 (1969).

101. Dunn v. Blumstein, 405 U.S. 330 (1972).

102. *Carrington*, 380 U.S. at 96–97, *Kramer*, 395 U.S. at 627–33, *Dunn*, 405 U.S. at 342–60.

103. 405 U.S. at 345.

104. *Id.*

105. *Id.* at 351.

106. *Id.* at 353.

107. Burdick v. Takushi, 504 U.S. 428 (1992).

108. *Id.* at 434.

109. *Id.* (quoting Anderson v. Celebrezze, 460 U.S. 780, 789 (1983)).

110. *Id.* at 434 (quoting Norman v. Reed, 502 U.S. 279, 289 (1992)).

111. *Id.* at 434 (quoting *Anderson*, 460 U.S. at 789 (1983)).

112. *Id.* at 440.

113. U.S. Const. amend XXIV, § 1.

114. Harman v. Forssenius, 380 U.S. 528 (1965).

115. *Id.* at 530–31.

116. *Id.* at 531–32.

117. *Id.* at 540.

118. *Id.*

119. *Id.* at 540–41 (quoting Lane v. Wilson, 307 U.S. 268, 275 (1939)).

120. *Id.* at 541.

121. *Id.* at 542.

122. Harper v. Virginia Bd. of Elections, 383 U.S. 663 (1966).

123. *Id.* at 666.
124. *Id.* at 668.
125. *Id.* at 670.
126. GA. CODE ANN. §21-2-417(a) (2004). The acceptable forms of identification were
     1. A valid Georgia driver's license;
     2. A valid identification card issued by a branch, department, agency, or entity of the State of Georgia, any other state, or the United States authorized by law to issue personal identification;
     3. A valid United States passport;
     4. A valid employee identification card containing a photograph of the elector and issued by any branch, department, agency, or entity of the United States government, this state, or any county, municipality, board, authority, or other entity of this state;
     5. A valid employee identification card containing a photograph of the elector and issued by any employer of the elector in the ordinary course of such employer's business;
     6. A valid student identification card containing a photograph of the elector from any public or private college, university, or postgraduate technical or professional school located within the State of Georgia;
     7. A valid Georgia license to carry a pistol or revolver;
     8. A valid pilot's license issued by the Federal Aviation Administration or other authorized agency of the United States;
     9. A valid United States military identification card;
     10. A certified copy of the elector's birth certificate;
     11. A valid social security card;
     12. Certified naturalization documentation;
     13. A certified copy of court records showing adoption, name, or sex change;
     14. A current utility bill, or a legible copy thereof, showing the name and address of the elector;
     15. A bank statement, or a legible copy thereof, showing the name and address of the elector;
     16. A government check or paycheck, or a legible copy thereof, showing the name and address of the elector; or
     17. A government document, or a legible copy thereof, showing the name and address of the elector.
127. The acceptable forms of identification under the 2005 law were
     1. A Georgia driver's license that was properly issued by the appropriate state agency;
     2. A valid Georgia identification card issued by a branch, department, agency, or entity of the State of Georgia, any other state, or the United States authorized by law to issue personal identification, provided that such identification card contains a photograph of the elector;
     3. A valid United States passport;

4. A valid employee identification card containing a photograph of the elector and issued by any branch, department, agency, or entity of the United States government, this state, or any county, municipality, board, authority, or other entity of this state;

5. A valid United States military identification card, provided that such identification card contains a photograph of the elector; or

6. A valid tribal identification card containing a photograph of the elector. GA. CODE ANN. § 21-2-417(a) (2005).

128. GA. CODE ANN. § 21-2-380 (2005).

129. Tom Baxter and Jim Galloway, *View of Past Closed in Walkout*, ATLANTA J. CONST., Mar. 15, 2005, at B4.

130. Common Cause/Georgia v. Billups, 406 F. Supp. 2d 1326, 1332–33 (N.D. Ga. 2005).

131. In the Georgia House, 89 Republicans and two Democrats voted for Act 53 and 72 Democrats and three Republicans voted against it. In the Georgia Senate, 31 Republicans and one Democrat voted for Act 53 and 18 Democrats and two Republicans voted against it. *Id.* at 1331.

132. *See supra* notes 13–15 and accompanying text.

133. Prior to the decision in Reno v. Bossier Parish Sch. Bd. (*Bossier II*), 528 U.S. 320 (2000), the Department of Justice had interpreted the purpose prong of Section 5 to bar any voting change that had the purpose of discriminating against minority voters. In *Bossier II*, the Supreme Court interpreted the Section 5 purpose prong to bar only changes that would put minorities in a worse position prior to the change. When President Bush and Congress reauthorized the temporary provisions of the Voting Rights Act in July 2006, it restored the purpose prong to the pre-*Bossier* standard. Fannie Lou Hamer, Rosa Parks, and Coretta Scott King Voting Rights Act Reauthorization and Amendments Act of 2006, Pub. L. No. 109-246 §§ 2, 5, 120 Stat. 557–78, 580–81 (2006).

134. Dan Eggen, *Criticism of Voting Law Was Overruled*, WASH. POST, Nov. 17, 2005, at A1.

135. *Common Cause/Georgia*, 406 F. Supp. 2d 1326.

136. *Id.* at 1376.

137. *Id.* at 1370 (emphasis in original).

138. *Id.* at 1365–66.

139. *Id.* at 1366.

140. *Common Cause/Georgia*, 439 F. Supp. 2d at 1306–11.

141. *Id.* at 1310.

142. *Id.* at 1311.

143. *Id.* at 1312–13.

144. *Id.* at 1354–55.

145. *Id.* at 1349–50.

146. *Id.* at 1350–51.

147. Lake v. Perdue, No. 2006CV119027 (Fulton Co. Sup. Ct. Ga., July 7, 2006).

148. Lake v. Perdue, No. 2006CV119027 (Fulton Co. Sup. Ct. Ga., Sept. 19, 2006).

149. *Id.* at 13.

150. *Id.* at 14.

151. Lake v. Perdue, 2007 Ga. Lexis 433, at *5–6 (Ga. June 11, 2007).

152. Common Cause/Georgia v. Billups, 2007 U.S. Dist. LEXIS 68950 (N.D. Ga. Sept. 6, 2007).

153. *Id.* at *111.

154. *Id.* at *134.

155. *Id.* at *107.

156. *See id.* at *105.

157. Havens Realty Corp. v. Coleman, 455 U.S. 363 (1982).

158. *Common Cause/Georgia,* 2007 U.S. Dist. LEXIS 68950, at *106–08.

159. Indeed, the district court rejected the admissibility of affidavits of individuals who stated that they did not have identification. *Id.* at *43.

160. *Id.* at *119.

161. *Id.* at *74–75; *see also* note 74 and accompanying text. Dr. Hood was an expert hired by plaintiffs whose expert testimony regarding the racial and age analysis of a 2006 match performed by him was rejected by the court on *Daubert* grounds. A race and age analysis of the 2007 match done by Georgia, however, shows the same disparate impact on minority and elderly voters. The race and age analyzes are possible because this information is contained on Georgia's voter registration form.

162. *Common Cause/Georgia,* 2007 U.S. Dist. LEXIS 68950, at *121–22.

163. *Id.* at *129–130.

164. *Id.* at *132.

165. *Id.* at 131–34.

166. *Id.* at 125–27.

167. Notice of Appeal, Young v. Billups, No. 05-EV-201 (N.D. Ga.).

168. IND. CODE §§ 3-5-2-40.5, 3-10-1-7.2; 3-11-8-25.1 (2007).

169. IND. CODE §§ 3-11.7-5.-2.5, 3-11-8-23, 3-11-8-25.1 (2007).

170. IND. CODE §§ 3-11-10-1.2. The qualifications for voting absentee are

    1. The voter has a specific, reasonable expectation of being absent from the county on election day during the entire twelve (12) hours that the polls are open.

    2. The voter will be absent from the precinct of the voter's residence on election day because of service as:

        a. a precinct election officer under IND. CODE § 3-6-6;

        b. a watcher under IND. CODE § 3-6-8, IND. CODE § 3-6-9, or IND. CODE § 3-6-10;

        c. a challenger or pollbook holder under IND. CODE § 3-6-7; or

        d. a person employed by an election board to administer the election for which the absentee ballot is requested.

    3. The voter will be confined on election day to the voter's residence, to a health care facility, or to a hospital because of an illness or injury during the entire twelve (12) hours that the polls are open.

    4. The voter is a voter with disabilities.

5. The voter is an elderly voter.

6. The voter is prevented from voting due to the voter's care of an individual confined to a private residence because of illness or injury during the entire twelve (12) hours that the polls are open.

7. The voter is scheduled to work at the person's regular place of employment during the entire twelve (12) hours that the polls are open.

8. The voter is eligible to vote under IND. CODE §3-10-11 or IND. CODE §3-10-12.

9. The voter is prevented from voting due to observance of a religious discipline or religious holiday during the entire twelve (12) hours that the polls are open.

10. The voter is an address confidentiality program participant (as defined in IND. CODE §5-26.5-1-6).

IND. CODE §3-11-10-24.

171. Indiana Democratic Party v. Rokita, 485 F. Supp. 2d 775, 786 (S.D. Ind. 2006).

172. *Id.* at 822.

173. *Id.* at 803.

174. *Id.* at 825 (quoting Griffin v. Roupas, 385 F.3d 1128, 1133 (7th Cir. 2004)).

175. *Id.* at 792–93.

176. *Id.* at 826.

177. *Id.* at 827.

178. *Id.*

179. Crawford v. Marion County Election Bd., 472 F.3d 949 (7th Cir. 2007).

180. *Id.* at 952.

181. *Id.*

182. *Id.* at 951.

183. *Id.* at 953.

184. Id. at 954.

185. *Crawford*, 472 F.3d at 954 (Evans, J., dissenting).

186. *Id.* at 955.

187. *Id.*

188. Crawford v. Marion County Election Bd., 484 F.3d 436 (7th Cir. 2007) (en banc).

189. *Id.* at 437 (Wood, J., dissenting).

190. *Id.*

191. *Id.* at 438.

192. *Id.* at 439.

193. Crawford v. Marion County Election Bd., 76 U.S.L.W. 3154 (U.S. Sept. 25, 2007) (*cert. granted*).

194. ARIZ. REV. STAT. §16-152 (2004).

195. ARIZ. REV. STAT. §16-579 (2004).

196. 2004 Arizona Ballot Propositions, Proposition 200, at 1.

197. Under Proposition 200, an applicant can prove citizenship by providing the number of a driver's license or nonoperating license issued after October 1, 1996, that indicates that the applicant is a citizen; a photocopy of the applicant's birth certificate; a photocopy

of a passport; the applicant's United States naturalization documents or the number of the certificate of naturalization; other documents established under the Immigration Form and Control Act of 1986, or the applicant's Bureau of Indian Affairs (BIA) card number, tribal treaty card number, or tribal enrollment number. ARIZ. REV. STAT. § 16-479 (2007). BIA and tribal treaty cards that include identification number of individual tribal members do not exist. ITCA's Plaintiffs Motion for Preliminary Injunction, at 4. Registered voters who move to Arizona from out-of-state or from another Arizona county must provide proof of citizenship; registered voters who move within an Arizona county do not. ARIZ. REV. STAT. § 16-479 (2007).

198.   ARIZ. REV. STAT. § 16-579 (2007).

199.   *See* EAGLETON INSTITUTE REPORT, *supra* note 11, at App. A.

200.   The following forms of photo identification are acceptable: (1) valid Arizona driver license; (2) valid Arizona nonoperating identification license; (3) tribal identification card or other form of tribal identification; and (4) valid United States federal, state, or local government issued identification. The following forms of nonphoto identification are acceptable: (1) utility bill of the elector dated within 90 days of the election; (2) bank or credit union statement that is dated within 90 days of the date of the election; (3) valid Arizona Vehicle Registration; (4) Indian Census Card; (5) property tax statement of the elector's residence; (6) tribal enrollment card or other form of tribal identification; (7) vehicle insurance card; (8) Recorder's Certificate; and (9) valid United States federal, state, or local government-issued identification, including a voter registration card issued by the county recorder. ARIZONA SECRETARY OF STATE, ARIZONA SECRETARY OF STATE ELECTION PROCEDURES MANUAL 113–14 (2006).

201.   Voters who did not bring identification to the polls cast conditional provisional ballots that are not counted unless the voter brings the required identification to the "county recorder's office by 5:00 PM on the fifth business day after a general election that includes an election for federal office or 5:00 PM on the third business day after any other election." *Id.* at 120.

202.   Native American voters are treated differently in one instance—voters who present one form of tribal identification that contains the name of the voter are provided with a provisional ballot that is counted if the signature in the affidavit on the provisional ballot envelope matches the signature on the voter's registration form.

203.   ARIZ. REV. STAT. § 16-548.

204.   ARIZ. REV. STAT. § 16-541.

205.   *See* Gonzalez v. Arizona, 2006 U.S. Dist. LEXIS 76638, at *5 (D. Ariz. Oct. 11, 2006).

206.   *See* Joinder in Gonzalez' Plaintiffs' Ex Parte Application for Temporary Restraining Order and Order to Show Cause, *Gonzalez v. Arizona*, No. 2006-CIV-01268 (D. Ariz. 2006).

207.   42 U.S.C. § 1973gg-7(a)(2).

208.   Joint Conference Committee Report on the National Voter Registration Act of 1993, H. Rep. No. 103-66 (1993).

209.   Letter from Thomas R. Wilkey, Executive Director, U.S. Election Assistance Commission, to Jan Brewer, Arizona Secretary of State (Mar. 6, 2006).

210.   Gonzalez v. Arizona, No. 2006-CIV-01268, slip. op. at 13 (D. Ariz. June 19, 2006).

211. The Navajo Nation plaintiffs filed a separate motion for preliminary injunction on the polling place identification requirements. The district court denied this motion.

212. ITCA Plaintiffs' Reply in Support of Motion for Preliminary Injunction, at 2, *Gonzalez v. Arizona*, No. 2006-CIV-01268 (D. Ariz. 2006). The number of rejected forms is now greater than 30,000. ITCA Plaintiffs' Response to Defendants' Motion for Partial Summary Judgment, at 4, *Gonzalez v. Arizona*, No. 2006-CIV-01268 (D. Ariz. 2007).

213. ITCA Plaintiffs' Motion for Preliminary Injunction, at 11–21, *Gonzalez v. Arizona*, No. 2006-CIV-01268 (D. Ariz. 2006).

214. *Id.* at 21–22.

215. *Gonzalez*, 2006 U.S. Dist LEXIS 76638, at *16 (quoting Southwest Voter Registration Educ. Project v. Shelley, 344 F.3d 914, 919).

216. *See* Purcell v. Gonzalez, 127 S. Ct. 5, 6–7 (2006).

217. *Id.* at 5.

218. *Id.* at 7–8.

219. *Id.* at 7.

220. *Id.* at 8 (Stevens, J., concurring).

221. Gonzalez v. Arizona, 485 F.3d 1041 (9th Cir. 2007).

222. *Id.* at 1047.

223. Gonzalez v. Arizona, No. CV 06-1268-PHX-ROS, slip op. at 2 (D. Ariz. Aug. 28, 2007) (quoting *Gonzalez*, 485 F.3d at 1050).

224. *Id.*, slip op. at 3 (quoting *Gonzalez*, 485 F.3d at 1049).

225. Under the 2002 statute, voters had to provide one of the following:

    1. Identification issued by the state of Missouri, an agency of the state, or a local election authority of the state;

    2. Identification issued by the United States government or agency thereof;

    3. Identification issued by an institution of higher education, including a university, college, vocational, and technical school, located within the state of Missouri;

    4. A copy of a current utility bill, bank statement, government check, paycheck, or other government document that contains the name and address of the voter;

    5. Driver's license or state identification card issued by another state; or

    6. Other identification approved by the secretary of state under rules promulgated pursuant to subsection 3 of this section or other identification approved by federal law. Personal knowledge of the voter by two supervising election judges, one from each major political party, shall be acceptable voter identification upon the completion of a secretary of state–approved affidavit that is signed by both supervisory election judges and the voter that attests to the personal knowledge of the voter by the two supervisory election judges. The secretary of state may provide by rule for a sample affidavit to be used for such purpose.

    Mo. Rev. Stat. § 115.427.1 (2005).

226. Weinschenk v. State of Missouri, 203 S.W.3d 201, 210 (Mo. 2006).

227. Mo. Rev. Stat. § 115.427.1 (2006).

228. Mo. Rev. Stat. § 115.427.4 (2006).

229. Mo. Rev. Stat. § 115.427.7 (2006).

230. Mo. Rev. Stat. § 115.427.13 (2006).

231. *Id.*

232. Weinschenk v. State of Missouri, No. 06AC-CC00656 (Cole Co. Cir. Ct., Sept. 14, 2006).

233. *Id.* at 9.

234. *Weinschenk,* 203 S.W.3d at 204.

235. *Id.* at 212.

236. *Id.* at 215.

237. *Id.* at 206, 212–15.

238. *Id.* at 213–14.

239. *Id.* at 217.

240. *Id.* at 222.

241. The statute setting forth the identification requirements reads as follows:

As used in the Election Code [N.M. Stat. Ann. § 1-1-1 (1978)], "required voter identification" means any of the following forms of identification as chosen by the voter:

A. a physical form of identification, which may be:
   (1) an original or copy of a current and valid photo identification with or without an address, which address is not required to match the voter's certificate of registration or a voter identification card; or
   (2) an original or copy of a utility bill, bank statement, government check, paycheck, student identification card or other government document, including identification issued by an Indian nation, tribe or pueblo, that shows the name and address of the person, the address of which is not required to match the voter's certificate of registration; or
B. a verbal or written statement by the voter of the voter's name, year of birth and unique identifier; provided, however, that the statement of the voter's name need not contain the voter's middle initial or suffix.

N.M. Stat. Ann. § 1-1-24.

242. Albuquerque, N.M., City Charter, art. XIII, § 14 (Oct. 4, 2005).

243. *Id.*

244. *Id.*

245. ACLU of New Mexico v. Santillanes, 2007 Lexis 17087, at *6–7 (D.N.M. Mar. 6, 2007).

246. *Id.* at *72–78.

247. *Id.* at *96.

248. *Id.* at *96–97 (parenthetical omitted).

249. *Id.* at *98–99.

250. *Id.* at *100.

251. *Id.* at *105.

252. *Id.* at *111–12.

253. Notice of Appeal, ACLU of New Mexico v. Santillanes, No. 05-1136 (D.N.M.).

CHAPTER TWELVE

FUNCTION FOLLOWS FORM:
VOTING TECHNOLOGY AND THE LAW

STEPHEN ANSOLABEHERE*
CHARLES STEWART III**

I. Introduction

The meltdown of election systems in Florida during the 2000 presidential election exposed the tremendous difficulties of administering elections, recording and counting votes, and assuring the outcomes of very close elections. Technologies long thought to have improved on traditional hand-counted paper ballots proved to be unreliable, forcing the courts to decide how votes ought to be counted and, ultimately, who won. Over the succeeding years, local and state governments have undertaken unprecedented efforts to modernize their election systems, especially voting machines. The Help America Vote Act (HAVA) of 2002,[1] one of the few federal forays into this subject, even provided funds to buy out older types of technologies—lever machines and punch cards. States and counties have since followed two technology paths, adopting either electronic voting machines (called direct recording electronic devices, or DREs) or optically scanned paper ballots. Both technologies, though they record voters' intentions using quite different modes, put faith in computers to tabulate votes.

As these new technologies have spread, an intense backlash against the widespread adoption of computerized voting has emerged. This reaction stems from deep-seated distrust of the management of the software used to tabulate votes and the increasing removal of vote counting from the public eye and into the domain of privately held companies. Much of the vitriol toward computerization has been directed at DREs, but optical scanners have not escaped criticism either. These new

* Elting Morrison Professor of Political Science, MIT.
** Kenan Sahin Distinguished Professor and Head of Political Science, MIT.

questions leave the administration of elections in a quandary. This is the dilemma we face today. How should the United States record and count votes?

We cannot answer that question, but it deserves our fullest attention. State and local governments will continue along the two different technology paths, choosing either optical scanners or DREs, as that is all that counties can feasibly use today. Technologists have highlighted numerous security and reliability concerns with each sort of machinery. For its part, the industry that produces voting machines has responded quickly with alterations in their equipment and even new machines, such as DREs that print out a paper copy of the ballot for the voter to inspect, that meet the criticisms of computer scientists. But these problems are not going away, and they have proven resilient to simple technological solutions because they are problems of law as much as technology.

Election reform since 2000 has proceeded under a basic assumption. Adopt the right technology and the legal questions will go away. We have been guilty of this simplification ourselves. And it misses an important subtlety that we think is lacking in the consideration of voting technology. Voting technologies and election laws go hand in hand. They constrain and define each other. Nowhere is that more apparent than in the recounting of elections, which is, after all, what much of this debate is about.

Legislators and judges ought to be to make the law clearer or more transparent where possible. Technologists and administrators ought to improve the way voting machines operate and are used. But it is futile to imagine a perfect voting technology, just as it is a myth that the law is a coherent, static whole. The law is organic, and as the meaning of the vote evolves so too must voting technology. Likewise, innovations in computing and communication technology will create new ways to vote. Society will try these technologies on for size, and when they do, the law will have to change with them.

A brief history of voting makes this lesson all too obvious. Voting, when modern democracies began in the 18th century, was a public act. One merely needed to stand up or speak up to vote. As states throughout the nation abandoned *viva voce* voting in favor of written ballots in the early 19th century, laws had to be written about how the ballots would be marked, accumulated, counted, and (possibly) recounted. Once states began printing ballots in the 1890s, not only did states have to let printing contracts, they had to pass laws that specified in minute detail how ballots would be designed and how they would be properly marked.

Prior to the current round of voting technology reform, the last time the nation's attention was pulled toward voting methods was around the turn of the 20th century, when attacks on the century-old paper-based voting methods were beginning to cast doubt on the honesty of election outcomes. Movements arose, advocating for the use of mechanical lever machines. Adopting lever machines was more complex than simply deciding to purchase a bunch of machines and set them up to use.

The laws that specified how paper ballots were to be used were largely irrelevant in specifying how mechanical voting machines would be used. Candidates were listed on card inserts, ballot choices recorded on the machines were ephemeral, and no physical evidence of the vote remained after the voter exited the booth.

Once mechanical lever machines had settled into common use in much of the country, while paper remained entrenched elsewhere, voting technologies continued to grow more sophisticated. However, because laws and specific voting technologies tend to be bundled together, voting technologies tended to evolve in ways that made the new versions look like the old, so that technological advances could be adapted without a wholesale upset of election laws. Mechanical voting machines grew in size and sophistication until some versions were made that replaced the levers and mechanical works with buttons and electronics. Paper went from being marked with an X to being marked with a hole punch or a No. 2 pencil and fed through a machine for counting. While these technological advances required changes in the law to adopt the older practices to new implementations, these changes were less fundamental than deciding to move from a permanent paper ballot to an ephemeral mechanical ballot.

It is in this sense that voting technologies and laws have existed in equilibrium and have been a cause of each other. Because a major change in one would require a major change in the other, there was a tendency for localities to take the path of least resistance when they occasionally considered changing how to vote.

Because the last widespread reconsideration of how Americans vote occurred a century ago, it was perhaps natural that policymakers and others concerned about voting reform forgot about this equilibrium. If they realized it existed, the breakdowns of the technologies that were highlighted in Florida put a premium on changing the technologies and appropriating billions of dollars to make it happen fast.

The remainder of this chapter proceeds as follows. First, to help clarify the nature of the law-technology equilibrium that had been established by 2000, we develop a two-dimensional typology of voting technology that identifies the predominant features of voting technology as being the user interface (paper or machine) and the method of managing ballots (preserve them for counting or not). This typology defines four general types of voting technologies, each of which requires a different bundle of laws in order to operate and to count votes. For reasons that will be discussed, only two of the four theoretically possible technology types were developed in the 20th century, paper interfaces that saved ballots for counting and machine interfaces that destroyed ballots at the point of counting. Thus, practically speaking, the most important decision counties had to make for most of the 20th century was which of these two "cells" to reside in.

Next, we sketch out the historical development of voting technologies in the United States prior to 2000. States and localities needed reasons for deciding which of the two practical forms of voting technology to choose and, within those generic choices, which particular implementation to buy. We argue that for most of the century these choices were based on trying to maximize three qualities—security, accuracy, and speed—while obeying a budget constraint set by appropriators (county commissioners or state legislators) for whom voting technology purchase was a low-priority item. The civil rights movement added a fourth maximand, accessibility, which was already beginning to upset established methods of voting as the 20th century was coming to a close.

Third, we discuss HAVA and the effect that this law had in upsetting the cozy relationship between voting technology and law throughout the country. The first-order effects of HAVA were spelled out in the law and have led to mostly salutary changes in election practices. The most important way in which HAVA produced ambiguous second-order effects was in leading to a backlash against DREs and a movement favoring voter-verifiable paper audit trails (VVPATs). This movement gained traction, we argue, because HAVA-mandated accessibility requirements seriously disrupted the technology-law equilibrium, leaving millions of voters facing election machines that violated century-old local notions about what a clean election looked like.

Finally, we turn our attention to the legal issues that have arisen as legislatures, election boards, and courts have attempted to apply the legal standards that had grown up around one technology bundle to different bundles of technology. In particular, the addition of VVPATs to DREs invites legislatures, boards, and courts to apply paper-based legal reasoning to systems that were designed to operate best when the ballots were destroyed upon counting. Likewise, recounting optically scanned paper ballots by simply feeding them through the counters again invites an application of the law of paperless systems to paper systems. We argue that having a variety of voting technologies that differ fundamentally in how the user interface and ballot management systems are designed requires a variety of corresponding standards for recounting ballots. It would be foolish to establish a single recount criterion for all voting systems in a naïve desire to promote equal protection. What is more important is that the criteria be clear and be consistent with the design of the technologies on which votes are cast.

II. A Framework for Understanding Voting Technologies

The Caltech/MIT Voting Technology Report *Voting: What Is, What Could Be*[2] introduced a useful distinction between the functions performed by voting machines: recording votes and managing votes (including tabulation). Voters *record* their preferences when they fill out a ballot or use a DRE. Problems of usability, such as confusing user-interface formats, incorrect language, or lack of blind accessibility, arise at this stage. Failures of punch-card voting technologies in 2000, especially the infamous "butterfly" ballot, were of this sort. Vote tabulators and election officers *manage* the ballots, including tabulation of votes, security and accounting of all ballots, and certification of official results. Failures in this system are of two sorts—nonmalicious errors in counting and malicious attacks, such as destruction of ballots, stuffing ballot boxes, and stealing votes through computer programming. Counting errors result in unreliable tabulations; malicious attacks results in vote fraud. Both may alter election counts.

The Caltech/MIT team introduced the distinction as a way to optimize voting technology. They advocate separating vote recording from vote management technologies in order to allow each to best serve the required functions. Vote recording technologies should evolve to become as universally and easily usable as possible; vote management technologies should evolve to provide a secure, verifiable, and accurate count. The "frog" voting system proposed in *Voting: What Is, What Could Be* accomplishes exactly this separation. Some technologies, such as conventional DREs, move in the opposite direction and marry the vote recording technology to the vote management system.

Setting aside what is the right model for optimizing technology, the distinction allows for a useful classification of existing voting technologies. A simple typology of systems arises. In terms of vote recording, we may distinguish systems where the voter prepares a physical record of his or her preferences (or intentions) from systems where voters record votes directly into a common-use machine, one that is used by other voters as well. This distinction maps into machines versus paper ballots today (though some ancient democracies used stones and other markers). In terms of vote management, the distinction is between systems that keep every individual's intentions separately and those that maintain just a running tally. Systems that keep individual voters' ballots or preferences allow for the inspection of those votes in the event of a recount and treat the tabulator as a potentially fallible machine. Traditional hand-counted paper ballots, punch cards, and optical scan systems have a physical record of the vote prepared by the voter and those votes retained as separate bits of information in the management and tabulation of the vote. We call these TYPE ONE technologies.

Lever machines and DREs represent the opposite technologies. Voters record their preferences directly into the machines, and the machines keep a running tally of the official vote, rather than separable ballots that may be inspected by the voter at the time of voting and afterward by election officials. We call these TYPE TWO technologies. These are the dominant methods of voting, and their classification suggests a hard connection between the method of recording votes and the method of managing them. If a county opts for paper, it commits to management of individual ballots. If it chooses electronics, it commits to management of tabulations, rather than individual votes. The link between direct recording of votes and continuous tabulation led to the notion that there were just two systems: Machine Voting and Paper Voting. See Table 1.

Table 1. Classification of Historical and Current Technologies

		Ballot management system	
		Individual Votes or Ballots	**Tabulations**
Vote Recording	Paper	TYPE ONE: —Traditional hand-counted paper ballot —Punch card ballots tallied by electronic counter —Optically scanned paper ballot tallied by electronic scanner	TYPE FOUR:
	Machine	TYPE THREE: —Internet Voting (SERVE)	TYPE TWO: —Mechanical lever machine —DRE

Internet voting breaks that link. Internet ballots can be stored and posted as separate pieces of information in the management process, but they are recorded directly into a machine. DREs with separate audit trails, such as used by Nevada in 2004, may also break the hard rule that the method of recording votes dictates the method of managing and tabulating. Any system that stores individual votes or ballots for the purpose of counting, but uses an interface that does not record directly the voters' intentions, we call a TYPE THREE technology.

Table 1 raises an interesting puzzle. Is there a system in which voters record their preferences on paper ballots (separate and permanent records of their intentions) but in which only the tabulations are relevant to the certification of the vote? Is there a TYPE FOUR technology? Viewed strictly as a matter of technology, the answer is no. But hypothetically, you could have an optical scan system that shreds ballots as they are fed into the scanner.

Election law, however, creates just such systems. Some state recount laws, either as written or interpreted by courts, provide only for machine recounts, not manual recounts of ballots, unless the margin of victory falls below a very low threshold. This is analogous to having a system that records each voters' intentions, but that treats tabulations as official and discards any information not recognized by the tabulation machine. The rationale is that reading voters' intentions after the fact often introduces a heavily subjective element in the resolution of the count. At least the machine tabulator is objective.

The criticisms of direct recording electronics point to the inability to retrieve voters' intentions for the purpose of getting closer to the true count and validating the tabulator. Lack of a separate record of voters' intentions limits the ability to audit a DRE in the event of a recount or election controversy.

Both examples point to the tension between voting technology and election law. In the case of machine recounts, the election law completely redefines the technology; indeed, it creates a whole new class of technology—one that doesn't normally exist. And in both examples there arises the profound question of what the vote is. Is it the intention of the voter, or the recording in a machine? This is a matter best settled by law, though many states have let the technology provide the answer for them.

The fundamental legal question, then, is: What is a vote? Is it is intention (however discerned)? The legal ballot? The tabulation of ballots? Cast another way, is a legal ballot simply what a tabulator records?

III. The Historical Dynamics of Voting Technology Choice

The previous section sets out a typology of voting technology design and notes that virtually all practical voting systems have (until very recently) occupied a limited range of the theoretical possibilities. What explains why the observed choices of voting technologies reside in these cells? What explains why a county would choose one cell over the other?

In understanding the evolution of voting technology choice in the United States, let us assume that elections will be highly competitive and that voters generally prefer for the winner to be the one who received the most votes in a fair fight. Like all fights, the stakes of electoral competition often produce incentives for the contestants to fight unfairly. It is not overly naïve to assume that, as a first approximation, the grand sweep of voting technology evolution has been guided by attempts to increase the fairness of elections. In addition, it is important to understand that voting technologies are paid for by appropriations made by legislators whose immediate concerns are the more prosaic worries of elected officials—filling the potholes, building the schools, policing the streets, and fighting fires. Voting machines are low on the list. Consequently, elections tend to be underfunded; technological advances in voting have lagged several steps behind broader technological advances in other areas of society.

Putting these two axioms together (clean elections along with budget constraints), voting technology has largely been in service of ending the most egregious of election abuses, such as ballot-box stuffing, ballot-box theft, and chain voting, at the lowest cost possible. Sometimes, advances in voting technology could be used to achieve the twin values of clean elections and budgets constraints. For instance, by automating the counting of votes, mechanical lever machines facilitated the consolidation of precincts. Not only did precinct consolidation cut down on the immediate costs of elections, but it also reduced the number of physical locations that needed to be monitored and protected against attack on Election Day.

All told, three general goals have helped motivate the application of new technologies, mechanical and electronic, to voting since the 19th century. These have been (1) security, (2) accuracy, and (3) speed. Security has encompassed a number of concerns, from ensuring the integrity of the ballot box against maladies like ballot box stuffing to ensuring that the courier transmitting the ballot count back to the county courthouse didn't get waylaid, or worse. The concern with accuracy started with these waylaid couriers and ranged to more benign concerns, such as a realization that machines were generally better than humans in completing repetitive tasks like counting marks on pieces of paper and summing columns of numbers. Finally, speed was a concern because the longer it takes to do a vote count, the more opportunities there are to effect mischief.

A fourth goal was added during the civil rights era: accessibility. First conceived of as an issue of racial justice, accessibility of the polls to the physically disabled and language minorities has been a major motivator behind the adoption of new technologies in voting over the past half-century.

In sum, the application of new technologies to the process of voting in the contemporary, post–civil rights era is now generally in service of achieving four goals—security, accuracy, speed, and accessibility—constrained by budgets that are set by officials who may be optimizing around another set of goals.

It was precisely concerns about security, speed, and accuracy that led to the spread of mechanical lever machines in the 50 years after their first use in Lockport, New York, in 1892.[3] These machines, which found acceptance primarily in the Northeast and South, weighed up to half a ton apiece, making them virtually impossible to steal. A series of locks protected their inner workings. Ballots no longer needed to be physically counted, which sped up the count immeasurably. If a hapless courier were waylaid while carrying the count from the precinct to the courthouse, it was trivial to produce another count within minutes. Lever machines employed mechanical systems that were similar to those used in cash registers and adding machines—devices that were coming into widespread use as financial control devices.

Of course, the mechanical machines were more expensive to purchase than ballot boxes and paper ballots—at least for a single election. However, the machines could be amortized across scores of elections. As mentioned previously, the machines also facilitated the consolidation of precincts, which both increased security and decreased costs. Nonetheless, the costs of the machines *were* hard to swallow in some places, so that by mid-century, even though mechanical lever machines were the most common way of casting ballots in the United States, they still tended to be concentrated in urban areas unless there was a statewide mandate to use them everywhere.

Within the functional framework we presented in the previous section, the mechanical lever machines met election-related goals by effectively destroying the ballot as soon as it was created. That is, it provided each voter with an identical ballot face in mechanical form, allowing the voter to "mark" the ballot by moving levers. Then, when the voter pulled the lever to throw open the privacy curtain and exit the booth, two things happened simultaneously—the votes of the voter were tabulated and the voter's ballot was destroyed. This ended the ability of voters to leave telltale indications of how they voted on paper ballots, curtailed chain voting, and made it difficult to stuff ballots into the (nonexistent) ballot box.

As late as 1980, over 40 percent of all votes cast in the United States were on mechanical lever machines, even though the corrupt practices that had prompted their initial adoption had receded into the distant past.[4] Furthermore, most of the administrative advances that had originally been associated with mechanical lever machine, such as the ability to handle large numbers of votes in precincts or to establish well-regulated controls over access to voting equipment, were also available in the newer electronic voting devices that relied on paper ballots, such as optically scanned ballots and punch cards. Still, mechanical lever machines remained popular; as they were being abandoned, a significant number of jurisdictions simply switched over to new machines that seemed to differ only in having electronic tabulators rather than mechanical ones, that is, DREs.

Twenty years later, 60 percent of counties that had used mechanical lever machines in 1980 were either still using lever machines or had adopted DREs, that is, had continued to use paperless voting systems.

Even though the history of voting technologies in the early 20th century was the story of the adoption of mechanical lever machines, much of America never abandoned paper—primarily small-town America, where mechanical machines would have been a fiscal extravagance. The rapid growth of many areas that continued to use paper ballots put the criteria of fast and accurate counts at risk immediately following World War II. This paved the way for the automation of the count through the application of punch cards to voting—first used in 1964. Even though punch card technologies are contemporaneous with the mechanical technologies that lie behind lever machines, it is testimony to the low-tech ethos of early paper-based systems that it took a century to adapt this technology to paper-based voting systems.

Optical scanning technologies were introduced to voting at roughly the same time as punch cards, even though optical recognition technology was much more recent. As with punch cards, optical scanning technology did not necessarily represent a security advance, but did assist rapidly growing areas with increasing the speed and accuracy of their counts.

In the 20 years prior to 2000, counties that started with paper-based systems generally stayed with paper. Virtually no jurisdiction that was using some form of paper to vote in 1980—punch cards, hand-counted paper, or optically scanned ballots—was using either a mechanical lever machine or DRE in 2000. The upgrade path on the paper side of the voting ledger stayed with paper as an interface, even when electronics were brought in to help with the counting. Of the 1,149 counties that used hand-counted paper ballots in 1980, 53 percent had switched to optical scanning by 2000 and 9 percent had gone over to punch cards; of the 601 counties that used punch cards in 1980, 30 percent had switched to optical scanning by 2000 while almost all the others had stayed with punch cards.[5]

In light of the controversy that DREs have elicited in recent years, it is astonishing that the widespread use of mechanical lever machines and DREs prior to 2000 spurred no widespread calls for reform.[6] This is especially astonishing when we realize that the combined share of these machines was *greater* in 1980 than in 2006.

The lack of widespread controversy over paperless voting systems is easily understandable when we realize that before 2000 the decision to change voting equipment was typically made by local officials, who were making choices within the constraints provided by local laws and customs. Counties that were using paperless systems had long experience using them, and so it was unremarkable that old paperless systems might be replaced with newer ones. Most of these counties were located in states that also allowed for paper-based systems to be used, and so it was not too remarkable when a local election official switched to the more intuitive paper system. Similarly, a county election official who moved from hand-counted paper to scanner-counted paper was not dramatically changing the interface the voters used, only using an old technology to count ballots. Because the counties that abandoned hand-counted paper ballots in favor of optical scanning were larger and faster-growing than those that stayed with the traditional method, local officials could also trumpet the advantages of using computers to count ballots in counties where the task was a growing chore.[7] Officials in these counties were not facing violence and corruption. As a consequence, they found no reason to even consider mechanical or electronic options.

This is the voting world that existed in 2000 and that probably would have continued had the election of 2000 not ended with a drawn-out and divisive recount that determined the outcome of the presidential race. Evolution would have continued in ways consistent with state and local laws and with informal practices. The decrepitude of existing mechanical lever machines was already leading to their gradual retirement, in favor of a mix of optically scanned paper ballots and newer DREs. Punch cards, which were already beginning to show signs of breakdown prior to Palm Beach County in 2000, would have been replaced with optically scanned paper.[8] The same undoubtedly would have been true of many counties that continued to hold onto traditional hand-counted paper.

IV. The Success of the Help America Vote Act

The Help America Vote Act disrupted the established upgrade paths of voting technologies, especially the paper-dominated path of hand-counted paper, punch cards, and optically scanned ballots. The disruption came through the HAVA requirement that each precinct have available a form of voting that was accessible to voters with disabilities. While this requirement did not mandate the technology for accomplishing this goal, given currently available technologies, local officials faced the practical reality that DREs were the best response to the mandate. And while the mandate certainly did not require that *all* voters use these accessible machines, local officials that already used paper-based systems recoiled at the possibility of operating two different voting systems in parallel, risking greater confusion on Election Day. Consequently, the response of many local election officials to the HAVA accessibility requirements, abetted by the promise of federal funds, was to adopt DREs as the single way of voting in many communities.

Federal funds for technology upgrades were particularly important. One of the main constraints on the adoption of new technologies is cost. It is not that voting machines are expensive. Compared with any other sort of government equipment, they are cheap. Rather, voting machines are expensive for local election offices because local election offices have meager resources to carry out their charge. In an average year, before the passage of HAVA, total election administration expenditures amounted to approximately $1 billion nationwide. This figure includes labor costs, management of registration systems, office overhead, and, of course, voting machines. Registration systems and office staff costs absorb most of the county election offices' budgets. Voting machines account for only about a fifth of total expenditures on elections. Of particular importance for ongoing debates about technology, what equipment counties use is unrelated to their total expenditures on election administration.[9] HAVA provided a huge infusion of cash to upgrade county and state election systems, especially voting equipment.

The effects of HAVA on how Americans vote are clear. In the six years from 2000 to 2006, over half of all counties in the United States changed voting technologies—25 percent more than changed throughout the entire decade of the 1990s and nearly three times the turnover rate of the 1980s. Most of the counties that chose new voting equipment between 2000 and 2006 chose DREs. In stark contrast with past patterns, the vast majority (84 percent) of these new DRE counties had previously used some form of paper. DREs did not completely take over the voting machine market. Their growth came on a very low starting point. Today, approximately half of Americans vote on optical scan ballots and half on DREs. Only 1 percent use hand-counted paper, and punch cards and lever machines are extinct.

Many critics of computerized voting and of the rapid changes since 2000 agitate for expansion of hand-counted paper or wistfully long for the days of lever machines.

But by every available metric, the upgrades of voting technology funded by HAVA and state efforts have significantly improved the performance of the electoral system.

Social science research following the 2000 election developed two metrics of the reliability of vote counting methods and technologies. First, *residual votes* measure the percent of all voters for whom no vote was recorded for a particular office. The residual vote may be due to problems with the tabulators, such as programming errors or mechanical failures. It may also be due to actions taken by the voter. Some may prepare their ballots incorrectly, such as occurs when people mark optical scan ballots in a way that the scanner cannot read; others may be confused by the formatting and accidentally skip an office, such as occurs when the ballot format presents many offices on one page or screen; still others intentionally do not vote for an office.[10] Voting technologies ought not produce residual votes through any of these means, and thus residual votes should be unassociated with what technology a county uses.

A second measure of voting technology errors are *recount discrepancies*—the differential between the official count produced by a recount and the initial count of ballots. Tabulation errors that either miss votes or that assign votes to the wrong candidates will be corrected in recounting the ballots. These discrepancies also reflect problems in handling ballots not immediately associated with the programming of the tabulators, such as occurs when the election office does not tabulate all ballots or accidentally tabulates some ballots twice. Of course, machines affect processes for handling ballots, such as the ease with which absentees are incorporated. And, some technologies, notably DREs, have minimal recount discrepancies because the technology does not completely preserve the voter's intentions, only what is recorded in the machine's memory.

These measures do not capture all problems. Both measures miss cases where people accidentally vote for the wrong candidate, as much research indicates happened with the butterfly ballot in Palm Beach, Florida.[11] Designers of voting technology have focused on ways to minimize such difficulties,[12] but from the perspective of a recount, such errors are uncorrectable. Residual votes and recount discrepancies, however, do capture the two main issues that arise with resolving the tabulations produced by the initial counting of ballots. First, does the tabulation technology lose votes? Second, how close is the initial tabulation from the "truth"—or at least the official vote that would results from a more careful count?

By both measures, newer technologies appear much more reliable than hand-counted paper, lever machines, and punch cards. We conducted comprehensive assessments of residual votes from the 1980s through the 2004 election, and that analysis reveals several important facts. First, the residual vote rate historically averages slightly over 2 percent nationwide for presidential elections and approximately 4 percent for governor and U.S. Senate elections. The difference between the presidential and lower races is mostly due to intentional nonvoting, though not entirely. Second, the size of the residual vote is strongly associated with voting technology, and optical scanning seems to be the best technology, though its edge over electronics is not overwhelming. Up to the year 2000, hand-counted paper, lever machines, and optical scanning perform best in presidential elections, followed by DREs, with punch cards showing the highest rate of residual votes. Counties that switched from an older technology to optical scanning between 1988 and 2000 consistently showed long-run reductions in residual voting rates.[13] DREs and scanners adopted between 2000 and 2004 show statistically similar improvements over the technologies.[14] Further down the ballot—for governor, U.S. Senator, and U.S. House—lever machines showed the worst performance; punch cards lagged the others as well.[15]

Recount discrepancies are much harder to study, because recounts are relatively rare and systematic state reports on recounts are elusive. New Hampshire is the exception. The large number of state legislative and town elections in that state, the administration of elections at the town level, and the relatively liberal recount provisions in election laws make recounts common; in addition, the Secretary of State's office prepares a comprehensive report of the certified vote from all recounts and town votes. New Hampshire is a good case in which to contrast hand-counted paper with optical scanning, as approximately half of the towns use one technology and the other half the other. In the battle of man versus machine in the tabulation of votes, the machine wins hands down. The discrepancy between initial counts and official certified counts in these recounted races averaged only about four-tenths of one percent in towns using optical scanning, but there was a difference of nearly two percentage points in towns using paper ballots. One town with paper ballots was particularly bad, with nearly 8 percent of ballots uncounted in the initial tabulation.[16]

Taken together, the residual vote and recount discrepancies suggest that the switch to optical scanning and direct recording electronic voting machines ought to translate into a lower residual vote rate nationwide since 2000. That is indeed the case. In 2000, the residual vote rate nationwide averaged just over 2 percent. In other words, just over 2 percent of all people who voted did not vote for president. In 2004, the residual vote rate fell nearly a full percentage point, and much of that drop appears attributable to the replacement of punch cards and lever machines with optical scan and direct recording electronic voting machines. One statistical study concluded that approximately one million votes were "recovered" in 2004 because of the nationwide change in voting technologies since 2000.[17]

V. The Backlash Against the Help America Vote Act and Direct Recording Electronic Devices

HAVA had the unintended consequence of forcing hundreds of counties and millions of voters to confront dramatically new practices and expectations about how elections should be conducted. Users of punch cards were often relieved that they were to be rid of the danger of hanging chads, but a large number of counties that abandoned computer-counted paper for DREs were giving up optical scanning, which not only was a highly accurate form of voting[18] but was also consistent with the law and voting culture of the community.

It is not surprising that anti-DRE activism arose in this context and that it was nourished in such fertile ground. The most sensational of this activism centered on the work of Bev Harris, whose *Black Box Voting*[19] provided ammunition for hundreds of citizen activists around the country. A more mainstream, and arguably more effective, line of citizen activism started with David Dill, a professor of computer science at Stanford University, gaining institutional form with the Verified Voting foundation. Coupled with a steady diet of press accounts of voting machine glitches and Democratic voters' outrage over the Republican-leaning political activities of voting machine company presidents, a large plurality of voters became skeptical about the quality of election administration in the United States and resistant to the further adoption of DREs.

Criticism of DREs has focused on questioning whether they are superior to the more traditional paper-based systems on two of the traditional criteria on which voting technologies have traditionally been judged, security and accuracy. The security concerns are sometimes expressed with the more pungent worry about voting machines being "hacked." The worry here is that votes could be stolen by a rogue programmer engaging in some behavior—writing malicious code in the standard software, infecting voting machines with viruses after the fact, manipulating the electronically stored totals, and so on—that would effectively switch votes from Candidate A to Candidate B. (It should be noted that many of these concerns were theoretically possible and physically simple to implement with mechanical lever machines.)

These security concerns differ from a set of accuracy concerns that mostly pertained to trust in the interaction between the touch screen interface and the computer unit that was interpreting touches to the screen. It is well known that touch screens are prone to "alignment errors." In the context of elections, this would manifest itself by a voter touching the part of the screen naming Candidate A, but having the sensors translate the touch as being intended for Candidate B. Leaving aside this relatively benign inherent design challenge with computer touch screens, one could imagine a hack that would simply make the voter believe that a touch to Candidate A's name had led to a vote for Candidate A, with the computer recording the vote for Candidate B instead.

The concerns over security and accuracy were on trial in the disputed election involving the 13th Congressional District of Florida in 2006. This election, which resulted in an unprecedented residual vote rate on DREs used in just one county in the district, Sarasota County, has been contested on the security and accuracy of these systems.[20] Leaving aside the highly unlikely possibility that these blank electronic ballots were intentional, the arguments of both sides of the disputed election come down to questions about the security and accuracy of the DREs. The challenge by Christine Jennings (D) asked for access to the machines and the software, to ensure that the touch screens were working properly (accuracy), that the interface between the touch screens and computer were working properly (accuracy), and that the software rendering the ballots and accumulating the votes were functioning properly (security and accuracy). One counterargument by the declared winner, Vernon Buchanan (R), implied that if the machines were at fault, it was due to poor ballot designs chosen by county officials (accuracy).

Unfortunately, at least from our perspective, the courts did not open up the machines. We are less concerned with how this particular race turned out than we are with the answer to the question. This was an ideal case to put allegations of tampering to the test. Both sides acknowledged the peculiarity of the results. Questions about the roles played by bad ballot design or defective software and hardware were fundamentally unanswerable using election returns alone. We may never know the answer, since the Florida courts have not allowed the challenger independent inspection of the internal code of the machines used on Election Day and proceedings in the House of Representatives are moving slowly. Because a problem with the code was a plausible (if unlikely, in the minds of many) cause of the missing ballots, courts and the House have missed opportunities to close off all avenues for doubt. Those doubts linger, and the Jennings-Buchanan dispute became one more example for those with a penchant for conspiracy theories.

VI. The Voter-Verifiable Paper Audit Trail (VVPAT)

How to deal with these accuracy and security concerns has been the top issue in voting technology since the passage of HAVA in 2002. Providing voters with reliable feedback that their votes were accurately recorded has been the subject of considerable research by scholars, particularly in computer science and related fields such as cryptography.[21] However, the most common class of remedies falls under the rubric of the "voter-verifiable paper audit trail" (VVPAT).

VVPAT proposals come in two general forms. The first essentially has a printer attached to the electronic voting machine. After the voter has voted, *but before the voter has ended the voting session,* the printer prints what the computer has recorded as the voter's choices. The voter is able to scrutinize the paper printout and compare it to the results displayed on the computer screen. Once the voter is satisfied, she presses the "vote" button, at which time the votes are electronically accumulated as before and the paper printout is deposited in a secure box. In this first form of the VVPAT, the electronic version of the vote is considered the official ballot. The printout serves three purposes. First, the paper trail allows voters to audit the machines as they operate on Election Day—it opens up the black box. Second, the paper can serve as a backup in the event of an overt failure of the electronics.[22] Third, the paper can serve as a check on the electronic machine in a postelection audit. Absent a catastrophic machine failure, if there is a recount of the election, it is the electronic ballots, not the paper ballots, that are retabulated.

The second form of a VVPAT is similar to the first, but the computer prints out separate, scannable paper ballots. Under some variants, the paper printouts are then scanned and tabulated. In other variants, the electronic totals are generally used to certify the election, but if there is a dispute, it is the paper that is recounted. In either case, the paper ballot that is reviewed and approved by the voter serves as the official ballot.

VVPAT, from a technology perspective, is a chameleon. It merges scan technology with DRE technology to create a system that can take the shade of any of the four types we have identified in the framework illustrated in Table 1. The first form of VVPAT can operate as either a TYPE TWO technology, as it is essentially a DRE with a visible paper backup, or as a TYPE THREE technology. The second form of VVPAT can operate entirely as TYPE ONE technology, such as an optical scanner, using the computer interface to prepare the scannable paper ballot and eliminating the problems that arise when people incorrectly fill out paper ballots. Or either version can be treated in such a way as to be a TYPE THREE technology—a paper-based voting system in which only the machine tabulation is treated as the count.

Assuming for the moment the efficacy of the VVPAT concept, the complexity of the system has generated a continued debate about what this system actually is and how successfully it accomplishes its aims.

Skeptics of the security of DREs would naturally like the printed ballots to serve as the official ballot, not as a backup or as auditing devices. A strong argument against this view focuses on the reliability of printers, both intrinsically and as currently implemented. DREs were initially championed precisely because they had almost no moving parts to break down. Printers, especially the cheap ones used in many voting machines, break down frequently, leaving a real possibility that a properly cast ballot might not be recorded. Furthermore, a practical reality of printers is that technicians need access to the paper supply during the day, to deal with jams and other malfunctions. Providing a secure, tamper-proof path from paper supply to ballot box on Election Day may be practically impossible. Some DRE supporters, notably Michael Shamos, note that while no cases of electronic manipulation of the vote have been discovered, history proves that it is easy to manipulate paper ballots on Election Day. Why tempt unscrupulous electioneers?

One technological response to this criticism is, essentially, to turn the DRE into an electronic pencil. The paper inserted into the printer is the traditional optically scanned paper ballot. The voter uses the electronic machine as a marking device— the voter makes choices on the touch screen while the ovals are marked on the card by the printer. The voter then takes the card and has it scanned, just like optically scanned ballots today. Indeed, the voter need not use the mechanical device as an interface at all—at the risk of not marking the ballot at neatly as the machine and not taking advantage of the undervote protections that are also provided by DREs.

While there are public officials on both sides of the VVPAT debate, most election officials oppose the use of VVPAT under most conditions. Leaving aside the legal status of the paper printout, introducing mechanical printers just adds one more mechanical operation that can fail on Election Day, adding to the burden of harried precinct workers and adding to the possibility that voters will make mistakes. Of the two ways of implementing VVPATs, many do acknowledge that paper printouts provide an independent method of auditing, which could help improve elections in the future.

Interest in VVPATs has led a few states and localities to undertake experiments that inform the practicality of using VVPATs as official ballots. The results have not been promising. For instance, the Election Science Institute undertook a detailed study of the May 2006 primary in Cuyahoga County (Cleveland), Ohio, that compared the VVPAT materials with electronic ballots and could not reconcile the two. The most likely reason these numbers did not match was due to breakdowns in the VVPAT system. Among other things, the recount team found that almost 10 percent of the VVPAT paper tapes "were either destroyed, blank, illegible, missing, taped together or otherwise compromised."[23] Pilot projects in three Georgia counties after the 2006 general election were more successful in reconciling the paper and electronics, but the paper was so unwieldy to use, the process so labor-intensive, and the wait so long that the use of the paper trails as an official ballot likewise seems unlikely.[24]

California's revision of its election law to accommodate the use of VVPATs in recounts highlights the ambiguous legal status of the paper trail.[25] A special election to fill a vacancy in the Orange County Board of Supervisors in February 2007 put the law to the test. In a tightly fought, multicandidate field, Trung Nguyen was initially declared the victor over Janet Nguyen (no relation) by seven votes, out of almost 46,000 cast. Janet Nguyen demanded a recount. Seventy-six percent of the ballots cast in this race were paper absentees. When they were recounted by hand, there was a net shift in 14 ballots in Janet Nguyen's favor, giving her a seven-vote advantage. The question arose about how to recount the almost 11,000 Election Day ballots cast on DREs. County Registrar Neal Kelley interpreted state law as saying that the candidate requesting the recount could determine whether the electronic recount would be done by examining the paper printouts or by retabulating the electronic computer memories. Janet Nguyen chose the latter, which resulted in no change from the original recount. Janet Nguyen was declared the winner.

Trung Nguyen challenged the decision not to examine the paper trails, arguing that California law required that they be reexamined in a recount. Orange County

Superior Court Judge Michael Brenner sided with Janet Nguyen, stating that because the functioning of the machines was never disputed, "it was perfectly reasonable" just to re-tally the electronic votes without examining the printouts.[26]

The Orange County case leads to an inexorable, if ironic, conclusion about the VVPAT. By creating a chameleon technology, the designers of the VVPAT have left the meaning of voting technology entirely up to the lawmakers, be they legislators, judges, or local election officials, who have not systematically specified the relationship between the ballot management system of voting machines and what constitutes the legal ballot. What type of technology the VVPAT is and whether it accomplishes the goals of those who advocate it depends entirely on a set of legal questions that may arise on an ad hoc basis. What is the official vote, the paper record or the electronic record? What is the right way to conduct a recount, using the paper ballots or the electronic readings? Which counting method is more accurate, hand-counts of pieces of paper or computer counts? Which record of the votes is complete, the paper ballots submitted by voters or the electronic record kept with the machines?

Not all of these questions will be resolved in a manner favorable to or intended by those who designed and advocated for the VVPAT. The reason is simple. The technology, by becoming a chameleon, places very few constraints on what counts as a vote or how it can be used. Hand-counted paper and lever machines imposed heavy constraints on the conduct of elections and the meaning of the vote in the event of a recount. That is no longer true with the VVPAT, especially the form that produces individual ballots. The irony, then, is this. The advocates of the VVPAT have sought a system that would further constrain election officials and courts and would keep private interests away from the operation of elections. They have created technologies that in fact impose fewer constraints on how elections are operated and, because of their complexity, surely increase the reliance of county election offices on vendors to program the machines. Whether that is bad or good, we leave to the reader to determine. But what it has surely done is meant that election laws and not technology will define the meaning of the vote and the procedures for determining who wins. The VVPAT, then, will increase the likelihood that recounts end up in court as judges will have to determine what counts as a vote.

Notes

1.   Help America Vote Act of 2002, Pub. L. No. 107-252 (2002), 42 U.S.C. § 15301.

2.   CALTECH/MIT VOTING TECHNOLOGY PROJECT, VOTING: WHAT IS, WHAT COULD BE (July 2001).

3.   For a history of the evolution of voting technologies in the United States, see ROY G. SALTMAN, THE HISTORY AND POLITICS OF VOTING TECHNOLOGY: IN QUEST OF INTEGRITY AND PUBLIC CONFIDENCE (2006).

4. Throughout this chapter, statistics concerning the use of voting technologies were made available through Election Data Services (EDS). Election turnout figures prior to 2000 were similarly provided by EDS. Turnout figures from 2000 onward were collected by the authors.

Two good sources of 19th-century election practices in the pre-reform era are ALEXANDER KEYSSAR, THE RIGHT TO VOTE: THE CONTESTED HISTORY OF DEMOCRACY IN THE UNITED STATES (2000) and RICHARD BENSEL, THE AMERICAN BALLOT BOX IN THE MID-NINETEENTH CENTURY (2004).

5. Only three of the 601 counties had switched to DREs in the ensuing 20 years.

6. A notable exception was the computer scientist Rebecca Mercuri, who began publishing articles related to voting in the early 1990s and defended her dissertation (*Electronic Vote Tabulation: Checks and Balances,* University of Pennsylvania) mere days before the 2000 presidential election.

7. Counties that abandoned hand-counted paper between 1980 and 2000 were, on average, three times the population of those that retained hand-counted paper and had population growth rates in the 1990s that were twice that of the standpat counties.

8. The most important case of pre-Palm Beach County failure of punch cards was in the 1996 Democratic Primary in the 10th Congressional District of Massachusetts, which experienced many of the problems that were later to surface in Florida in 2000. The Massachusetts experience had already led the Commonwealth to decertify punch cards, resulting in a significant shift toward optical scanning in anticipation of the 2000 election.

9. CALTECH/MIT VOTING TECHNOLOGY PROJECT, *supra* note 2, at 48–54.

10. A very small percentage of people say they do not vote for a given office (less than one half of one percent for president).

11. Jonathan N. Wand et al., *The Butterfly Did It: The Aberrant Vote for Buchanan in Palm Beach County, Florida,* 95(4) AM. POL. SCI. REV. 793–810.

12. One example is Benjamin Bederson's application of a "Zoomable User Interface" to electronic ballots, *available at* http://www.cs.umd.edu/%7Ebederson/voting (accessed Aug. 27, 2007). Also see Ted Selker, *Fixing the Vote,* SCI. AM., Oct. 2004, at 90–97.

13. Stephen Ansolabehere & Charles Stewart III, *Residual Votes Attributable to Technology,* 67(2) J. POL. 365–89 (2005).

14. Charles Stewart III, *Residual Vote in the 2004 Election,* 5(2) ELECTION L.J. 158–69 (2006).

15. Ansolabehere & Stewart, *supra* note 13.

16. Stephen Ansolabehere & Andrew Reeves, *Using Recounts to Measure the Accuracy of Vote Tabulations: Evidence from New Hampshire Elections 1946-2002* (Caltech/MIT Voting Technology Project Working Paper # 11, 2004), *available at* http://www.vote.caltech.edu/media/documents/wps/vtp_wp11.pdf (accessed Aug. 27, 2007).

17. Stewart, *supra* note 14.

18. *See* CALTECH/MIT VOTING TECHNOLOGY PROJECT, RESIDUAL VOTES ATTRIBUTABLE TO TECHNOLOGY: AN ASSESSMENT OF THE RELIABILITY OF EXISTING VOTING EQUIPMENT, version 2 (Mar. 30, 2001).

19. BEV HARRIS, BLACK BOX VOTING: BALLOT TAMPERING IN THE 21ST CENTURY (2004).

20. In the interest of full disclosure, one of the authors of this piece (Stewart) served as an expert witness, supporting the efforts of candidate Jenkins to gain access to the electronic voting software and hardware used in Sarasota County.

21. *See, e.g.,* David Chaum, *Secret-Ballot Receipts: True Voter-Verifiable Elections,* 2(1) IEEE Security & Privacy 38–47 (Jan.–Feb. 2004); Ronald L. Rivest, *The ThreeBallot [sic] Voting System* (mimeo, Computer Science and Artificial Intelligence Laboratory, Massachusetts Institute of Technology, Oct. 1, 2006), *available at* http://people.csail.mit.edu/rivest/Rivest-The ThreeBallotVotingSystem.pdf (accessed Aug. 27, 2007).

22. This adds a lever of redundancy, since most DREs now also preserve individual ballot images electronically.

23. Election Science Institute, DRE Analysis for May 2006 Primary, Cuyahoga County, Ohio (Aug. 2006), *available at* http://bocc.cuyahogacounty.us/GSC/pdf/esi_cuyahoga_final .pdf (accessed Aug. 27, 2007).

24. Georgia Office of Secretary of State, Elections Division, Voter Verified Paper Audit Trail: Pilot Project Report (Apr. 2007), *available at* http://sos.georgia.gov/elections/VVPATreport.pdf (accessed Aug. 27, 2007).

25. The following newspaper stories provide a summary account of this case: Christian Berthelsen, *Trung Nguyen on Top by 7 Votes,* L.A. Times, Feb. 8, 2007, B1; Mike Anton, *An O.C. Supervisor—Maybe,* L.A. Times, Feb. 27, 2007, B1; Mike Anton, *O.C.'s 7-Vote Election Gap Becomes a 7-Lawyer Case,* L.A. Times, Mar. 22, 2007, B10; Mike Anton, *Recount Tightens,* L.A. Times, Mar. 24, 2007, B4; Mike Anton, *Ruling Gives Janet Nguyen a Seat as O.C. Supervisor,* L.A. Times, Mar. 27, 2007, B3.

26. Mike Anton, *Ruling Gives Janet Nguyen a Seat as O.C. Supervisor,* L.A. Times, Mar. 27, 2007, B3.

CHAPTER THIRTEEN

THE GROWTH OF EARLY AND NONPRECINCT PLACE BALLOTING: WHEN, WHY, AND PROSPECTS FOR THE FUTURE

PAUL GRONKE*
EVA GALANES-ROSENBAUM**

I. Introduction

Early or convenience voting—understood in this chapter to be laws, rules, and procedures whereby citizens can cast a ballot at a place and time other than at the precinct on Election Day—has grown steadily and inexorably in the United States over the past quarter century, and is increasingly being adopted worldwide.[1] It is a popular target for election reformers, who often identify higher voter turnout as an important goal and early voting as a tool for reaching that goal.

In this chapter, we provide a road map to the changing terrain of voting in the United States, focusing on the emergence of a new roadside attraction—early voting in its many guises and forms. First, we describe the early voting policy regime, detailing the legal requirements and administrative procedures associated with each balloting method. Second, we briefly review how rapidly early voting laws have been adopted, and how many Americans are taking advantage of these laws. Finally, to give the readers some sense of the how, where, and why of early voting, we review the main arguments made by proponents and opponents of early voting, and examine in detail how early voting reforms were implemented in Florida leading up to the 2004 campaign. While not intended to be statistically representative of the nation, Florida provides a number of important illustrations of the administrative challenges that face elections officials, candidates, and voters under an early voting regime.

* Professor of Political Science, Reed College; Director, Early Voting Information Center, Reed College.
** Associate Director, Early Voting Information Center, Reed College.

II. A Typology of Early Voting Laws and Procedures

What is "early voting"? Typically, the phrase is understood to mean any mode of balloting by which voters can cast a ballot prior to Election Day, either at a local elections office, at a satellite location, at a voting center, or perhaps in the comfort of their own home. It is important to distinguish between the mode of balloting (absentee by paper; early in person by machine, etc.) and the time that the ballot was cast. Unfortunately, in most election jurisdictions, it is virtually impossible to make this distinction. An "early" absentee ballot may be cast as early as 40 days before the election in Iowa, Wyoming, and Maine; while in many jurisdictions (e.g., California), the absentee ballot could actually have been hand-delivered to the elections office on Election Day. Some states provide for as many as 45 days of early in-person voting, while others allocate just a week. It is important for the reader to keep in mind, then, that what we refer to as "early voting" captures a diverse set of voters, including those who may have made their choice in mid-September as well as a small number who cast their "early" ballots on Election Day, and are thus not voting "early" at all.[2]

The legal requirements for voting before Election Day vary between states, mainly between "no excuse" systems and those requiring voters to prove a "special" status (physical disability, absence on Election Day, medical condition or hospitalization, etc.). One of the major shifts that has occurred over the last few decades, particularly in the last ten years, has been the movement from "excuse required" laws to "no excuse" systems, which automatically expands the early voting system immensely.[3]

The following sections provide a guide to the various types of early voting systems and the legal requirements and administrative procedures associated with each. Table 1 provides an overview to this section.

A. ABSENTEE VOTING[4]

The first method by which citizens could vote before Election Day was the absentee ballot. Introduced during the Civil War, absentee voting expanded along two parallel tracks for most of its history: military and civilian. The method was first used to allow soldiers in the Civil War, who were often posted far from home, to cast ballots in their home states. Concerns about security and privacy of votes, familiar in debates about absentee voting even today, were introduced along with this voting method in the 1860s, and once the war ended, state laws allowing for absentee voting expired or were repealed. During World War I, soldiers were again posted far from home (this time overseas), and states responded by adopting absentee laws, most of which expired after 1918. By World War II, states were accustomed

Table 1: Early Voting Systems

Early Voting System	AKA	Mechanics	Where Used
Traditional Absentee		Voters have to apply for an absentee ballot, but a limited number of reasons are allowed, such as being physically unable to make it to a polling station, being in the military (domestic or overseas), living abroad, or being away at college.	Everywhere
No-Excuse Absentee	"Vote-by-mail," "Absentee voting by mail"	Voters have to apply for an absentee ballot, but no excuse is required. Voters receive the ballot as early as 45 days before the election and must return by the date of the election. In some localities, only a ballot postmarked on or before the election counts as valid. A few states allow for permanent absentee status, whereas in most states, a voter must apply for an absentee ballot at each election.	Many states and localities
Vote-by-Mail	"Postal voting"	Voters receive a ballot in the mail approximately two weeks before the election. Ballots can be returned via mail or dropped off at satellite locations or at the county elections office.	Oregon, United Kingdom (local elections), New Zealand
In-Person Early Voting	"In person absentee balloting"	Voters have the option of casting a vote early at a satellite location or at the county elections office. In most localities, the voter simply shows up; no prior notification is required. In most jurisdictions, the same voting machinery is used for early in-person and election day balloting.	Rapidly expanding list; Texas for the longest, Georgia, Tennessee, Iowa. Many states have this reform after the 2000 election

Possible sources of confusion: In an increasing number of localities, absentee balloting can be done in person (and is often referred to as early voting) or via mail (sometimes referred to as "vote by mail"). Many localities do not distinguish between the two when reporting absentee ballot figures. In Sweden, "postal voting" is used to describe in-person voting at the post office.

to legislating absentee voting for soldiers, and responded to the declaration of war appropriately.[5] Although it didn't make the difference, the soldier absentee vote was extremely important in the 1944 presidential election.[6]

It wasn't until the Korean War that states passed absentee legislation for soldiers that did not expire at the termination of a specific conflict. Following closely behind, the 1955 Federal Voting Assistance Act expanded absentee voting from a state-by-state question to a matter of federal importance, first for uniformed personnel overseas, then for their families, and finally for civilians overseas (see below).[7]

Thirty years passed, during which voting reform focused on other sectors of the electorate; finally, in 1986 the Uniformed and Overseas Citizens Voting Act[8] (popularly referred to as UOCAVA) relaxed registration requirements and created a voting assistance program within the Department of Defense to aid overseas voters. Although absentee voting has continued to expand for the civilian population since 1986, the systems developed under UOCAVA for military voters have remained largely unchanged since the act's passage two decades ago, with the exception of some experimentation with Internet voting.

Running parallel to absentee developments for military voters was a series of expansions for civilian voters. The introduction of the "Australian ballot" in the late 19th century ensured voters (civilian and military alike) the protections we think of as common sense now: privacy while casting a ballot; uniform ballots containing all the names of eligible candidates and printed by election officials in the jurisdiction (not by party officials, as they often were previously). These regulations presented problems for civilian absentee balloting: If voters are supposed to be protected from coercion and fraud, how are these protections ensured when ballots are cast outside of the polling place? While these questions were answered to the extent that absentee voting laws were passed, it is important to note that the same concerns are *still present* in debates over early voting reform, nearly 100 years later.

Between the World Wars, many states introduced legislation allowing civilian voters with very specific reasons for not voting on Election Day to cast ballots early. They often attempted to create Australian-ballot-like protections by requiring voters to have witnesses, and restricted absentee voters in other ways—for example, to railroad workers only, or to others including business travelers, the bedridden, and the hospitalized. Where these laws conflicted with the provisions of the Australian ballot or other protections, the new laws were challenged and struck down. Throughout the following decades, states expanded their absentee laws to include similar rosters of qualifying excuses; 1955's Federal Voting Assistance Act added citizens living overseas, and the 1970 Voting Rights Act Amendments firmly established ideals of short residency requirements and absentee provisions for voters who had moved close to the time of an election, reflecting a trend in state election law reform in the 1960s.

When the 26th Amendment was passed the next year, extending the right to vote to citizens 18 years or older, absentee voting suddenly became much more relevant. Now that most college students were eligible to vote, millions of students who were attending college away from home had to be accommodated. Most states and local jurisdictions developed administrative procedures and regulations to deal with this new demand. Similarly, the 1975 Overseas Citizens Voting Rights Act[9] gave citizens without legal addresses in the United States the right to vote from their residences abroad, again placing new administrative requirements on local jurisdictions to deal with absentee voters.

The present era of "nonprecinct voting reform" was inaugurated in 1978, when California became the first state to require no excuse from a voter wishing to cast an absentee ballot. By the early 1980s, Oregon and Washington had adopted similar legislation, commonly called no-excuse or liberalized absentee voting (as opposed to traditional absentee laws, which require a demonstrable reason or proof of status for voting early). As citizens farther and farther from home acquired the right to vote, many of the absentee requirements initially present in state laws—such as the witnessing of ballots by an official—had to be abandoned; by 1992, "only eight states required a notary public" to sign off on an absentee ballot.[10]

The preceding brief history of nonprecinct voting hints at the often vast differences in how such voting methods are actually administered—that is, how voters cast the ballot via one of these systems. Even the labels used to identify each method change meaning, depending on the state or local jurisdiction. More importantly, jurisdictions have different rules governing how registered voters go about casting a nonprecinct ballot. For example, in some states with no-excuse absentee laws, voters may choose to cast an absentee ballot in person (Maine is one such state), while most states accept them only by mail. In Washington State, a ballot need only be postmarked by Election Day; all other states require that ballots arrive by the day of the election.

Legally speaking, there are variations in such things as the number of early voting sites required to be established (per precinct or county), the required provisions for disabled voters, the ways in which ballots are processed (daily or on Election Day), and so on. Some states with voting machines conduct their early in-person polling on the same machines as their Election Day polling, whereas others use paper ballots.

B. VOTE-BY-MAIL

Vote-by-mail (VBM) is, in many practical respects, no different from absentee balloting, with one crucial difference: Voters have no choice in their mode of balloting. All voters, except a few with disabilities that necessitate an alternative balloting mode, must receive their ballot by mail.[11] Voters need not cast their ballots "by mail," however—they can be hand-delivered to the county office or dropped off at other official collection centers (in Oregon, for example, library branches are alternative drop-off points).

While Oregon is thought to be the pioneer in voting by mail, in fact California local elections were the first to go fully vote-by-mail, and two (rural) counties in the state are designated "VBM counties." Oregon became the first state to run all of its elections this way in 2000, after several test elections and use of VBM for local, county, and special elections. Washington State legalized the method as a limited option for nonpartisan special elections. After significant success and public demand, odd-year nonpartisan primary elections were added (1993), then a two-year trial period allowed any election to be conducted by mail (1994 and 1995). At the time of writing, 37 of Washington's 39 counties now run all elections by mail, with 70 percent to 83 percent of voters in the remaining two counties voting absentee (de facto VBM).[12] It is a peculiarity of VBM that only two West Coast states use it, with some other western states (California, Idaho, Arizona) seriously considering it.

Absentee voting is sometimes referred to as vote-by-mail in some jurisdictions, as most absentee votes are cast via the postal system. In most cases, the two methods are identical in administrative procedure, except that absentee voting is optional (and thus requires the voter to request an absentee ballot). Thus, in Oregon and soon in Washington, VBM is the *only* election system present, while absentee balloting coexists with other systems of balloting. While use of VBM is limited in the United States, a few other countries have implemented similar systems, usually called "postal voting," usually for local elections. Canada, Australia, and New Zealand are three examples, with some pilot tests of "all postal voting" elections in the United Kingdom.[13]

C. EARLY IN-PERSON VOTING[14]

The third major convenience method is early in-person voting. In this system, voters may cast ballots during an early voting period, some days or even weeks before Election Day. Many states offer early voting stations only at elections offices; others offer them at libraries, city halls, and other municipal buildings. Still others, of which Texas is the most famous, allow voters to vote at convenience stores. Larimer County, Colorado, has pioneered the use of "voting centers," super-sized balloting locations that are placed along major commute highways and act as "super-precincts."[15] A few states offer absentee voting with the option to cast such ballots in person, rendering these options de facto early in-person voting.

Other than being able to cast a ballot early and the necessity of going to a less convenient polling place, the mechanics of most in-person early voting system are identical to precinct place voting. This may be why this has been one of the most popular nonprecinct place voting reforms. Election administrators already know what to do—the machines, the procedures, and the ballots are all the same.

III. Trends in Nonprecinct Voting

The last three decades, beginning with California's introduction of no-excuse absentee voting in 1978, can be characterized as the "Era of Nonprecinct Voting." The clearest trend during this period is growth along two axes: adoption and turnout. Growth in both dimensions was slow in the 1980s, increased in the 1990s, and exploded in the current decade. As states adopted reforms that gave voters more choices in when and how they cast their ballots, voters turned to these new methods in greater numbers. Additional states, in turn, adopted these methods, and more citizens voted this way.

As with many topics in election administration and election reform, the 2000 election is a marker point in the development of early voting. After 2000, early voting laws really took off. By the 2006 election, the consequence of all these changes was clear: The era of early voting is here to stay. Election Day has become a quaint anachronism. Election Day has turned into a multiweek marathon of campaign contacts, absentee ballot delivery, and voter mobilization.

A. THE EVOLVING LEGAL REGIME

The early voting era began in 1978, when California—a source of many legal experiments and innovations—extended absentee voting to all eligible voters in 1978. The sister West Coast states of Oregon and Washington quickly followed suit. In 1987, Texas passed a law enabling voters to cast in-person early ballots. During the 1990s, 12 more states followed the West Coast lead by allowing no-excuse absentee voting. Meanwhile, "permanent" absentee voting was introduced in Washington, creating a set of de facto by-mail voters. Texas was joined by eight other in-person early voting states,[16] with all but two (Nevada and Tennessee) offering this in addition to no-excuse absentee voting. Finally, first by administrative mandate in 1996, then by voter referendum in 1998, Oregon became the first state to conduct all elections fully by mail.

As shown in Table 2, the slow and steady growth in early voting options kicked into high gear after 2000. The 2000 presidential contest and associated legal wrangling cast a bright light on election administration in the United States. What was revealed was not very pretty. Doubts were cast about the ability of many states to track registered voters, provide secure and private methods of voting, accurately count ballots, or design proper ballots at all. This was followed in 2002 by the Help America Vote Act (HAVA), which aimed at eliminating many of the problems revealed in the 2000 election.[17] While HAVA was not intended to encourage early voting, many state legislatures responded to the new political environment by passing nonprecinct voting laws. Theoretically, these laws gave voters more convenient options for casting ballots and more control over their voting process, and thus should increase turnout. In addition, early voting gave election officials more time

Table 2: The Development of the Early Voting Legal Regime

	Traditional Absentee Voting	No Excuse Absentee	No Excuse Absentee and Permanent Absentee Status
1980s	47 states as of January 1980	CA, OR, WA	(none)
1990s	45 states as of January 1990	AK, CA, IA, ND, VT, WA, WY	WA
2000–2006	27 states as of January 2000	AK, CA, IN, IA, ME, MD, MT, NE, ND, NJ, VT	AZ, CA, CO, ME, MT, UT, WA

Notes: Figures collected by the authors. Numbers do not add up to 50 per decade because states reformed their election laws and may have a value in two cells. As noted in the text, the definition of "in-person early voting" varies across states.

to work out the problems with new voting machines and put less pressure on polling places, thus helping to improve election administration overall.

Regardless of the reason, early voting exploded after 2000. By 2006, only 15 states, mostly clustered in the northeast, retain traditional absentee voting.[18] The most common electoral regime today is a combination of no-excuse absentee balloting and early in-person voting, a regime used by 19 states at the time of this writing.

B. THE GROWTH IN EARLY VOTING

Not surprisingly, as early voting became more widely available, voters responded accordingly. Reliable figures are difficult to come by, because many states still did not discriminate between nonprecinct place and precinct place voters until the 2000 election (and some still do not). Linking election return files and voter history files can be challenging. Exit polls and preelection surveys also failed to ask respondents about their early voting behavior until well into this decade, even though solid estimates are that 14 percent of the electorate voted prior to Election Day in 2000.[19]

The quality of data reporting has improved dramatically over the past few election cycles, and should continue to increase in quality as states move to statewide voter registration and reporting systems. The best available estimates of the rates of early voting, drawing on data from mass sample surveys and from the Election Assistance Commission's Election Day survey, are that 14 percent of voters cast their ballots prior to election day in 2000, 20 percent did in 2004, and 25 percent, or more than 25 million voters, cast nonprecinct place ballots in 2006.[20]

These nationwide figures disguise substantial variation across the states, as we would expect given the varied legal regimes. Figure 1 shows the differing levels of early voting across the states. What is evident from this figure is that early voting

	In Person Early Voting	No Excuse Absentee and In Person Early Voting	Voting by Mail
1980s	TX	(none)	
1990s	NV, TN, TX	AZ, CO, HI, ID, NM, OK	OR*
2000–2006	LA, NM, NC, TN, TX	AK, AZ, AR, CO, FL, GA, HI, ID, IA, NE, NM, NC, OH, OK, SD, UT, VT, WI, WY	OR

Notes: * Oregon voters approved a November 1998 initiative adopting voting by mail for all elections. The state experimented with voting by mail in a special Senate election in 1995 and 1996, and special elections in 1993, 1995, and 1997.

is most common in the western and southwestern states, perhaps correlated with those states in which voters face both long drives to county offices and possibly long commutes in some of these cities.[21] There are a few marked exceptions, however. Citizens of Iowa and Tennessee have long shown a tendency to vote early, even though this balloting method is not particularly common in the Midwest and South. Finally note the example of Illinois, which significantly relaxed its early voting laws in 2005, allowing in-person early voting. In most states, 10 percent to 20 percent of the citizenry adopts early voting when it is first made available (e.g., Florida and Georgia in 2004), yet in Illinois, less than 6 percent of ballots were cast early in person.[22]

In summary, citizens usually respond quite favorably to early voting reforms. On average, 10 percent to 20 percent of the ballots end up being cast early once these reforms are adopted, and the figures can climb rapidly. In some cases, such as Washington State, there seems to be no upper limit on the numbers of early voters, while in others, such as Tennessee or Texas, early voting seems to top out at 40 percent of the electorate. It is not known at present why these differences exist—this remains a topic for future research.

IV. The Politics of Early Voting Reform

Thus far, we have discussed the typology of early voting laws, where these laws have been passed, and how citizens are responding to these legal changes. But why are these laws adopted in some jurisdictions and not in others? Is there any pattern to the political and legal conditions that seem to underlie early voting reform? In the

Figure 1: Nonprecinct Place Voting Rates in 2004

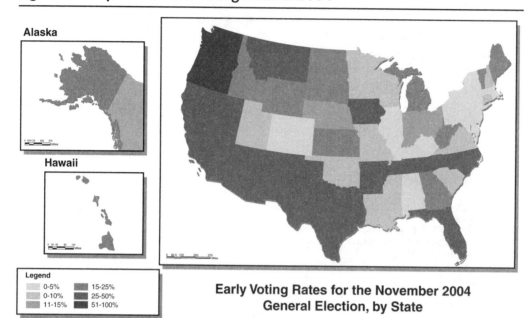

Alaska

Hawaii

Legend
0-5% 15-25%
0-10% 25-50%
11-15% 51-100%

**Early Voting Rates for the November 2004
General Election, by State**

final section of this chapter, we review the political arguments used to advocate for early voting reforms and examine the Florida experience with early voting, extended to "in person" voting (and widely publicized) in 2004. Florida is not representative of early voting states, but was chosen to illustrate how and why these laws are adopted. Florida illustrates a few salient point. First, early voting reforms are usually adopted as part of a package of election reforms intended to make voting easier, more convenient, and ideally to increase turnout. Second, there is little evidence that one or the other political party is inclined to oppose early voting—there are examples of Republican and of Democratic states adopting this reform, and examples where Republicans or Democrats opposed the change.[23]

A. WHY ADOPT EARLY VOTING?

The arguments made for early voting can be boiled down into four kinds of convenience: convenience for turning out, convenience for learning and deciding, convenience for campaign mobilization, and convenience for election administrators.

The first reason given for adopting early voting is that it is more convenient for the voter. Because the early voting period is usually more than one week long, these systems provide busy people or people with special needs a more leisurely way to cast a ballot.[24] Gimpel[25] and Haspel and Knotts[26] both point out that the accessibility of the ballot box, especially with regard to distance from one's home or workplace, can have a significant impact on whether citizens participate in elections. Those who work for an hourly wage, have long commutes, or have heavy time restraints on a November Tuesday can use early voting to participate when they have more time—like on the weekend.[27] People with physical disabilities may have access issues and can use absentee or mail ballots to alleviate these problems, or vote early in-person (when time and crowd pressure is lower and better access may be available at libraries or elections offices). Those who are non-English speakers, or who cannot read well, can receive additional help when crowds are smaller and poll workers aren't as strained. Early voting is preferred by some elections officials and voting rights advocates for the same reason—they believe it will increase turnout.

Empirical research on the turnout impact of early voting has been inconclusive. There is no clear evidence that early voting *always* increases turnout, and at least one recent study suggests that it may actually depress turnout.[28] There is certainly no agreement on how much it might increase participation. Regardless of the empirical results, the impact on turnout is almost always cited in newspaper editorials, published speeches, and legislative debates over early voting.

Second, some argue that early voting improves the quality of democratic decision making. According to these advocates, early voting allows voters the time and leisure to reflect on their voting options.[29] While these Norman Rockwellian visions of a family sitting around the kitchen table debating their electoral choices are compelling, there is little empirical evidence to date that this actually occurs. From a scientific perspective, there is no logical reason that voting *earlier* than Election Day provides *more* time to evaluate the options on the ballot. This remains an open question for future research.

Early voting may also convenience campaign organizations. While the "normal" or familiar rhythm to campaigning, building excitement and publicity up to Election Day, must be altered, the prolonged "period of voting" enables campaigns to more specifically target supporters and may allow them to run more efficient campaigns overall. Instead of bombarding supporters with reminders for a week or more, campaigns can focus their attention on supporters who have not already cast a ballot by five days before Election Day, three days before, the day before. In addition, campaigns can hold rallies and other events centered on early voting. In 2004, in Florida, campaigns bused people to early voting sites after rallies and gave people who had already voted special admission to music events.

Some have pointed out the disadvantages to campaigns, however.[30] First, campaigns risked overcampaigning if they did not have access to specific early voting records or if they did not have sufficient supporter lists. This would make campaigns much less efficient by wasting money and volunteer hours on people who had already voted and failing to mobilize those potential voters most in need of an external prompt to make them go to the polls.[31] And while the effects of political advertising are in dispute, it is possible that a longer high-intensity campaign period characterized by negative rhetoric and negative advertising is off-putting to some voters. This may be true especially of individuals who do not identify with either major party.[32]

Finally, early voting conveniences elections officials because early voting is less costly, it reduces the administrative burden of holding elections, and it improves procedural integrity. The National Conference of State Legislatures and the National Association of Secretaries of State both issued reports after the 2000 elections, and again after the passage of the Help America Vote Act (HAVA), that urge states to consider reforms that would allow early voting.[33] The empirical evidence to date supports election officials on procedural integrity. In-person early voting, absentee balloting, and vote-by-mail *do* result in a more accurate count.[34] The verdict on cost-savings is less clear. The state of Oregon claims to have saved nearly 17 percent of the costs of holding elections by adopting VBM, while in-person early voting and liberalized absentee balloting do not clearly result in a cost saving.[35] However, improved procedural integrity and flat or slightly positive cost savings have led to widespread recommendations in favor of all varieties of early voting. Major advocacy groups such as Common Cause and the AARP have also come out publicly in favor of relaxed absentee balloting and in-person early voting.

B. THE FLORIDA EXPERIENCE[36]

In the final section of this chapter, we review in detail one state's experience with early voting: the state of Florida's decision to provide in-person early voting in 2004, as part of a package of voting reforms passed in response to the 2000 election. Florida is not representative of the nation nor is it representative of early voting states, but it is an exemplar case in many ways. Demographically, Florida has become more and more like the nation at large (it has a lower proportion of African Americans and a higher proportion of Latinos than other southern states, and the median income and level of home ownership is closer to the national than to regional figures). Politically, it is one of the nation's battleground states, generally falling into the Republican camp in presidential years, although less and less reliably. Most importantly, because of the intense media scrutiny that Florida has experienced since 2000, we are able to draw on detailed coverage of election law changes in Florida.

Early voting was implemented in Florida as one of the major responses to the 2000 election. By 2004, the state legislature defined "early voting as 'casting a ballot prior to election day at a location designated by the supervisor of elections" and "passed legislation which standardizes early voting throughout the state."[37] The passage of this legislation, designed to fix certain problems and improve voting for Floridians overall, had several problems of its own (enumerated below).[38]

1. Administrative Problems. In response to the chaos of the 2000 general election, Florida adopted legislation aimed at ridding the election system of its problems. Elections officials looked to early voting as a way to increase turnout while also alleviating much of the 2000 mess: Lines would be shorter, those who needed individual assistance could be attended to, there would be fewer disputes, and ambiguity issues with ballots and laws would be resolved or never occur at all. Beginning in 2002, county elections supervisors could choose to offer early voting, but it was not uniformly required or implemented across the state until 2004. In an editorial supporting the adoption of statewide early voting, the *Palm Beach Post* asserted that "early voting would help lessen the election-day strain on facilities and systems and would diminish the demand for absentee ballots. Elderly voters who require more time would have it. Elections officials could troubleshoot potential technical problems and fix them before the mass turnout." Citing the 2000 "election day meltdown," the article continues that "if Floridians have learned anything about voting since 2000 it's that [Florida] cannot run elections on the cheap and that the more safeguards built into the system, the better."[39]

Unfortunately, there were problems with the new voting system. Under pressure to fix the problems from 2000 as quickly as possible, especially before the next presidential election, the Florida state legislature neglected to include voter protection provisions that would have mirrored the protections in other voting laws. According to Florida law, campaign supporters cannot solicit voters within 50 feet of the entrance to a polling place on the day of "any election"; however, Secretary of State Glenda Hood "decided that the early voting sites were exempt from the 50-foot barrier because they are in local government buildings to which the public must have access."[40] Furthermore, although elections supervisors in each county are allowed to open additional early voting sites, the only sites they are *required* to have are the single sites at their elections offices. This meant that, potentially, some citizens would have considerably greater or less access to early voting than others, simply based on how populous their county was, or how easy it was for them to get to the elections office.

Technology failure and ballot ambiguity was a big issue in 2000, so Florida adopted many new, largely untried, electronic voting machines. Many critics predicted problems with the new technology, particularly because it had not been tested for high-volume elections like the 2004 presidential race. Also, as most counties had never offered the option of early voting prior to this election, it was difficult to predict the actual volume of voters who would take advantage of the new voting option. Moreover, volunteers who worked at polling places were disproportionately elderly, a group least comfortable with the use of technology. As a result many polling places had staffing problems.[41] News reports of polling places that opened late or had machine failures were widespread.[42] Campaigns and their Get Out the Early Vote efforts (discussed below) were an unknown quantity in this equation: How much and how successfully they embraced early voting would also affect turnout.

2. *Getting Out the Early Vote.* One of the most important changes that results from implementation of early voting is seen in the way the two national campaigns approached Florida. Campaigns that normally would time their efforts to peak on, or just before, Election Day must now, with early voting, allocate resources in order draw in early voters, and then sustain this energy or even increase it as Election Day nears. For Florida, this meant two weeks of high-energy campaigning instead of just a few days.

This longer campaigning period had several potential advantages as campaigns transitioned from their traditional Get Out the Vote (GOTV) tactics to Get Out the Early Vote (GOTEV). First, if the campaign was run well and a party had sufficient access to early voting records, it had the ability to better target supporters by sending pamphlets, calling, and knocking on the doors of only those supporters who hadn't voted. By encouraging people to vote early, campaigns could "bank" votes well before Election Day,[43] and focus more of their money and efforts on people who hadn't yet voted, particularly on "swing" voters. In some cases, campaigns can get a good idea of whether or not they have won an election even before Election Day, based on the numbers of supporters they know have turned out for early voting.

Second, many campaigns found that early voting provided an excellent way to focus many events. Instead of general excitement-building GOTV rallies, many parties held GOTEV rallies after which attendees were transported to early voting sites. Some received "I voted early" pins that granted them free admission to concerts. Others got to meet celebrities (like Danny DeVito and Rhea Pearlman) or famous politicians at "Come vote with me" events.

While there are no solid data available on the amount of resources devoted to GOTEV efforts in Florida, they formed an important part of both Republican and Democratic Party mobilization efforts. Their increasing popularity in Florida will only increase their importance in the future.

3. *Queuing Up to Vote Early.* Unfortunately, the optimism that accompanied the state's adoption of early voting evaporated within the first few hours of actual balloting. Reports of an elected official receiving only half of a ballot when she asked for a paper copy instead of using the touch-screen machines came in around 10 AM. Subsequent hours and days yielded reports of harassment and intimidation, very long waits, people leaving discouraged.[44] One of the most high-profile reports of early voting problems in Florida came from Palm Beach County, where "One worker wearing her identification badge around her neck was throttled by an irate person 'who tried to choke her with it.'"[45] By the time Election Day rolled around, the media circus surrounding early voting made it seem like a complete failure.

Concerns about the lack of the 50-foot nonsolicitation zone in the legislation proved prudent, as many voters reported campaign supporters harassing, intimidating, or simply annoying them. Poll workers themselves complained to elections supervisors about campaigners from both major parties, and some quit because of the stress this caused. As Kam and Keller reported, "The early voting problems reveal yet another facet lawmakers failed to consider in their sweeping election reform package passed in the wake of the 2000 fiasco—the establishment of early voting sites without the same protections given to precinct locales on Election Day."[46] In some counties, early voting was nearly shut down: Early voting required considerably more staffing than traditional precinct voting.

One oft-cited problem was the number of sites available to voters. Generally, too few machines led to long lines and extended waits. More specifically, however, there was heavy criticism from many interest groups and minority communities about the lack of early voting sites in areas where black, Latino, and low-income residents could vote. When William E. Scheu replaced John Stafford as Duval County election supervisor, he quickly added sites at four regional libraries in Jacksonville, "including one on the city's northwest side, a predominantly black area" in response to the outcry. This and other areas in urban Florida had a history of elections issues and minority groups from 2000, when "27,000 ballots were mismarked and thrown out because of misleading instructions."[47]

Even at sites with an adequate total number of machines, long waits ensued because of technological limits. In Miami-Dade County, for instance, 20 sites were open for early voting. County residents were allowed to vote at any of the 20 sites. However, because machines lacked enough memory to store all the ballot forms needed to address each of the different local issues, only half of the machines at any one site could be used for ballots appropriate for local residents. The remaining machines, which largely went unused, were dedicated to ballots other than those facing the local community. As a result local residents faced long waits while about half the machines in each polling place went unused. Moreover, the publicity given to the long waits seemed to spur people to vote early for fear of an impending Election Day disaster. As shown in Figure 2, excepting the weekend dates of October 23–24 and 30–31 as well as November 1 when only two early voting sites were open, early voting increased throughout the period.

In summary, Florida encountered many difficulties in implementing early voting reforms in 2004. Some of the problems, such as long early voting lines, were also evident in other states (e.g., Georgia). Florida election officials, along with many across the nation, anticipated neither the level of interest in voting early nor the mobilization efforts targeted at this mode of balloting. Finally, elections officials took great care to avoid the problems associated with the 2000 contest, but in their efforts to make sure all ballots were counted accurately, they may have ironically dissuaded many from voting altogether. The tension between convenience, integrity, and accuracy is one that election officials continue to contend with.

Figure 2: Early Votes in Florida, by Date

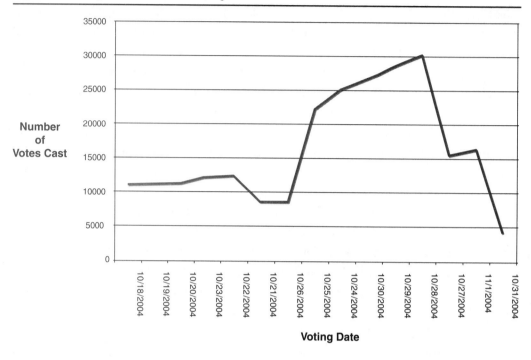

V. Conclusion

As a consequence of the controversies surrounding the 2000 election, major innovations in voter registration and election administration are well under way. Early voting, however, is a much more important change in elections administration that has been occurring for at least a decade, with little fanfare or critical examination. There are increasing calls for adopting early voting nationwide. Two pieces of legislation currently under consideration in Congress, the Ballot Integrity Act of 2007 (S. 1487) and the Voter Confidence and Increased Accessibility Act (H.R. 811, also known as the Holt Bill), would mandate no-excuse absentee balloting for all federal elections.

Early voting systems have already become or are well on their way to becoming the dominant mode by which Americans cast their ballot, and they are increasingly being adopted in other democratic nations. As a consequence of these changes, voting in America is becoming an individualized rather than a community act. Early voting may undermine the role of elections as "civic events" that bring together a community in political dialogue and participation. By individualizing voting, early voting could *dissuade* participation by newly naturalized citizens and those from traditionally disempowered communities. Finally, it is clear that voters who opt to vote early cannot draw on all the information provided by campaigns and the news media. There seems little question, then, that "[e]lection day in the United States is rapidly turning into an anachronism . . . waiting in line to cast our ballots will become the quaint notion of a bygone era."[48] Early voting and extended "election weeks" are here to stay.

This chapter provides the interested reader with a road map to this new form of balloting in the United States, focusing more on explaining the details of the process than on examining the potential consequences. Surprisingly little empirical research has examined the consequences of early voting reforms for how our elections are administered, how campaigns are being conducted, and finally, how citizens learn about elections and make their choices. Those questions remain on the agenda for future scholars, activists, and citizens.

Notes

1. Forty-six percent of the democratic nations listed in the EPIC Project database (http://aceproject.org/epic-en/vo "Voting Organizations") allow electors to cast ballots before the designated national election day. Of these nations, 34 percent allow early voting for everyone, while the remaining 66 percent limit early voting to electors who are unable, for a variety of reasons (e.g., in hospitals, living abroad, serving in the military), to cast a ballot at the local polling place.

2. Some have come to use the term "convenience" or "nonprecinct place" voting rather than "early voting" in order to differentiate between ballots cast prior to Election Day and those ballots that were not cast at the precinct (which may not have been cast prior to Election Day). In all but one state, absentee ballots must arrive at the election office prior to the day of the election (Washington State allows ballots to be postmarked on Election Day). In most states, early voting closes on the Friday or Saturday prior to Election Day. States that do not fall under Friday/Saturday deadlines are Alaska, Colorado, Hawaii, Idaho, Iowa, Maine, Minnesota, Montana, Nebraska, North Dakota, South Dakota, and Vermont (election day deadline—an odd deadline for "early" voting); and Arkansas, Indiana, Kansas, Ohio, and Wisconsin (the day before the election). Two states have early voting deadlines earlier than four days before the election: Louisiana (6 days) and Tennessee (5 days). The best illustration of the difference comes from the state of Oregon, one of the few that records the date that a ballot was processed (opened, but not counted). In recent years, between one-sixth and one-fourth of ballots were delivered to county offices on Election Day (e.g., 2004 Presidential: 16 percent; 2006 Primary: 29 percent (Oregon Secretary of State Elections Division, Ballot Return History, http://www.sos.state.or.us/elections/ballot_return_history.pdf)). However, Oregon is unusual in that it does not maintain polling places.

3. Two pieces of legislation currently under consideration in Congress, the Ballot Integrity Act of 2007 (S. 1487) and the Voter Confidence and Increased Accessibility Act (H.R. 811, also known as the Holt Bill) would mandate no-excuse absentee balloting for all federal elections.

4. See JOHN C. FORTIER, ABSENTEE AND EARLY VOTING: TRENDS, PROMISES, AND PERILS (2006) for a comprehensive review of absentee balloting. We rely heavily on Fortier's insights in this section.

5. Soldiers Vote Act (Armed Forces Absentee Voting Act), ch. 561, 56 Stat. 753 (50 U.S.C. §§ 301 et seq.) (repealed 1955) mandated absentee balloting for armed services personnel during wartime. Interestingly, the law was amended prior to the 1944 election to make such procedures recommended, not mandated. KEVIN J. COLEMAN, THE UNIFORMED AND OVERSEAS CITIZENS ABSENTEE VOTING ACT: BACKGROUND AND ISSUES (2007).

6. FORTIER, supra note 4.

7. Federal Voting Assistance Act of 1955, ch. 656, 69 Stat. 585 (42 U.S.C. §§ 1973cc et seq.).

8. 42 U.S.C. § 1973 ff.

9. Overseas Citizens Voting Rights Act of 1975, 42 U.S.C. §§ 1973dd et seq.

10. FORTIER, supra note 4, at 13.

11. In both Oregon and Washington (which at the time of this writing was nearly 100 percent voting by mail), disabled voters may cast their ballots at local jurisdictions using digital recording electronic voting machines (DREs). In Oregon, sight-impaired voters may also receive a unique Web-based ballot, which is then read and filled out using specially equipped computers. The ballot is then printed out and mailed like any other ballot. This Web-based ballot delivery system is also used in some counties for UOCAVA voters.

12. Two more counties—King and Pierce—are planning to change in 2008.

13. Matt Qvortrup, First Past the Postman: Voting by Mail in Comparative Perspective, 76 (3) POL. Q. 414–19 (2005); ELECTORAL COMM'N, DELIVERING DEMOCRACY? THE FUTURE OF POSTAL VOTING (T.U.K.E. Comm'n ed., 2004).

14. See Martha Kropf, Should the Missouri Legislature Consider Early/Advance Voting? MO. LEGIS. ACAD. (Report No. 5-2006), and Robert M. Stein, Introduction: Early Voting, 62 (1) PUB. OPINION Q. 57–69 (1998), for an extended discussion of early voting systems.

15. Information on Larimer County, Colorado's experiment with vote centers can be found at http://www.co.larimer.co.us/elections/vote_centers.cfm. The turnout impact of these centers has been studied by R.M. Stein and G. Vonnahme, Engaging the Unengaged Voter: Vote Centers and Voter Turnout 70 J. POLIT. (in press).

16. Arizona, Colorado, Hawaii, Idaho, New Mexico, Nevada, Oklahoma, and Tennessee.

17. Help America Vote Act of 2002, Pub. L. No. 107-252 (2002), 42 U.S.C. §§ 15301 et seq.

18. The most up-to-date listing of absentee and early voting laws is at Electionline.org, Pre-Election Day and Absentee Voting by Mail Rules, http://www.electionline.org/Default.aspx?tabid=474.

19. Press Release, K. Kenski, Early Voting Reaches Record Levels in 2004, National Annenberg Election Survey Show, University of Pennsylvania (2005) available at http://www.annenbergpublicpolicycenter.org/Downloads/Political_Communication/naes/2204_03_early%20voting%203_23_05_pr.pdf; Paul Gronke, Eva Galanes-Rosenbaum & Peter Miller, Early Voting and Turnout, 40(4) PS: POL. SCI. & POL. (2007).

20. Gronke, Galanes-Rosenbaum & Miller, supra note 19.

21. Paul Gronke, Early Voting Reforms and American Elections (paper presented at the annual meeting of the American Political Science Association (Chicago, Sept. 2–5, 2004)) (longer commutes are positively associated with the likelihood of casting an early ballot).

22. U.S. Election Assistance Commission, *2006 Election Day Survey* (2007) *available at* http://www.eac.gov/News/press/clearinghouse/2006-election-administration-and-voting -survey.

23. Jan Leighley, Robert M. Stein, and Christopher Owens, Early Voting and the Determinants of Vote Choice: Is Timing Everything? (paper presented at the annual meeting of the Midwest Political Science Association (Chicago, Apr. 15, 2004)) (reporting that their study shows no evidence of a partisan advantage to early voting).

24. *See, e.g.,* David B. Magleby, *Participation in Mail Ballot Elections*, 40(1) W. Pol. Q. 79–91 (1987); Priscilla L. Southwell & Justin I. Burchett, *The Effect of All-Mail Elections on Voter Turnout*, 28(1) Am. Pol. Q. 72–9 (2000); Priscilla L. Southwell & Justin Burchett, *Vote-by-Mail in the State of Oregon*, 34(2) Willamette L.R. (1998); Susan Davis, *Voting by Mail Could Improve American Democracy*, Roll Call, June 22, 2005.

25. James G. Gimpel, Joshua J. Dyck & Daron R. Shaw, *Location, Knowledge and Time Pressures in the Spatial Structure of Convenience Voting*, 25(1) Electoral Stud. 35–58 (2006).

26. Moshe Haspel & H. Gibbs Knotts, *Location, Location, Location: Precinct Placement and the Costs of Voting*, 67(2) J. Pol. (2005) at 560–573.

27. For example, the AFL-CIO, at a recent convention, considered a proposal to support the extension of Oregon's vote-by-mail election system into other states. One of the primary reasons given was that by-mail voting was more convenient for shift workers. *See* Oregon AFL-CIO, Resolution 34: Support and Expand Oregon's Vote-by-mail Elections in Other States (resolution proposed at the 2005 convention of the AFL-CIO), *available at* http://aflcio.org/aboutus/thisistheaflcio/convention/2005/resolutions.cfm.

28. James T. Smith & John Comer, Consequential Reform or Innocuous Tinkering? Another Look at Efforts to Increase Turnout in American Elections (paper presented at the annual meeting of the Midwest Political Science Association (Chicago, April 7, 2005)).

29. *See, e.g.,* Paul Gronke et al., Early Voting in Florida, 2004 (paper prepared for the annual meeting of the American Political Science Association (Washington D.C., Sept. 1, 2005)); Oregon Secretary of State's Office, http://www.sos.state.or.us.

30. Gronke, *supra* note 21.

31. Steven Rosenstone & John Mark Hansen, Mobilization, Participation, and Democracy in America (1993).

32. Stephen Ansolabehere & Shanto Iyengar, Going Negative: How Political Advertisements Shrink and Polarize the Electorate (1995).

33. Nat'l Conf. State Legislatures, Voting In America: Final Report of the NCSL Elections Reform Task Force (2001); Nat'l Assoc. Secretaries of State, New Millennium Best Practices Survey (2003); Nat'l Assoc. Secretaries of State, Election Reform: State by State Best Practices (2001); Bill Bradbury, *Vote by Mail: The Real Winner in Democracy*, Wash. Post, Jan. 1, 2005, at 23.

34. R. Michael Alvarez, Thad Hall & Betsy Sinclair, *Whose Absentee Votes Are Counted: The Variety and Use of Absentee Ballots in California*, Electoral Stud. (2008); Michael J. Hanmer & Michael W. Traugott, *The Impact of Voting by Mail on Voter Behavior*, Am. Pol. Res.

(2004); Michael W. Traugott, *Why Electoral Reform Has Failed: If You Build It, Will They Come?, in* Rethinking the Vote: The Politics and Prospects of American Election Reform 167–184 (A. Crigler, M. Just & E. McCaffery eds., 2004).

35. John Mark Hansen, Report, Miller Center for Public Affairs, University of Virginia, Charlottesville (2001). *To Assure Pride and Confidence in the Electoral Process.*

36. This section relies on P.W. Gronke, B. Bishin, D. Stevens, and E. Galanes-Rosenbaum, Early Voting in Florida, 2004 (paper presented at the annual meeting of the American Political Science Association (Washington, D.C., Sept. 1, 2005)).

37. Division of Elections, Florida Department of State, Early Voting, http://election .dos.state.fl.us/earlyvoting.shtml.

38. *Casting Your Ballot,* Fla. Today, Mar. 17, 2005. However, despite the initial bumps in the road, Florida continued early voting in 2006, even contemplating the adoption of "super-precincts" to make early voting even more convenient.

39. *Voting Early and Uniformly,* Palm Beach Post, Jan. 27, 2004, 12A.

40. Dara Kam & Larry Keller, *Early Vote Sites Report Intimidation,* Palm Beach Post, Oct. 25, 2004, 18.

41. David Paul Kuhn, *More Florida Ballot Woes On Tap?,* CBS News, July 20, 2004, *available at* http://www.cbsnews.com/stories/2004/07/20/politics/main630728.shtml.

42. In the 2002 September primary election, Rep. Carrie Meek, a ten-year congressional veteran, was turned away from the polls when election workers were unable to verify her identity when attempting to vote early.

43. Ray Suarez, "Florida Again," *Lehrer News Hour* (PBS television broadcast, Oct. 26, 2004).

44. Ray Suarez, "Voting Early," *Lehrer News Hour* (PBS television broadcast, Oct. 18, 2004); Ron Word, *New Duval Elections Supervisor Quickly Adds Early Voting Sites,* Associated Press State & Local Wire, Jacksonville, FL (Oct. 19, 2004).

45. Kam & Keller, *supra* note 40.

46. *Id.*

47. Word, *New Duval Elections Supervisor Quickly Adds Early Voting Sites, supra* note 44.

48. Gronke, *supra* note 21.

CHAPTER FOURTEEN

NUTS AND BOLTS FOR ELECTION OFFICIALS: MISSISSIPPI: A CASE STUDY

LESLIE C. SCOTT*

I. Introduction

Across the United States, local elected and appointed citizens are charged with the enormous responsibility of preparing for and conducting our elections. These individuals' responsibilities extend to elections in jurisdictions as small as a municipal ward and as large as an entire state's participation in the nationwide choice of president. The competency, skill, and character of these critical players in the process are the single most significant factors in the success of the electoral system and our nation's ability to conduct fair and free elections.

Despite this, many citizens, laypersons and attorneys alike, lack even a generalized understanding of the legal roles of local election officials and the technical requirements attendant to their responsibility to carry out their duties properly. This chapter will use Mississippi as a sample state for conducting a case study of the wide-ranging and preeminent role of local election officials in the days and weeks prior to an election, on Election Day, and in the post-election period. This nuts and bolts analysis will include by necessity the key role local election officials play in preventing voter fraud, voter suppression and intimidation, and illegal voting, as well as other abuses of the electoral process. From this analysis, it will be evident that increased attention to the work of election officials, in the form of improved selection, training, and support, is the most needed reform toward safeguarding our electoral process, the cornerstone of our democracy.

---

* Butler, Snow, O'Mara, Stevens & Cannada, PLLC.

II. General Overview

In most states in the United States, elections are conducted in a decentralized manner.[1] This means that most state election officials have little or no role in the selection, training, or governance of local election officials, nor does the state play a role in declaring the outcomes of elections conducted at the local level. Even in an election for president of the United States or a statewide election for governor, the statewide outcome is determined by a mere computation of the local elections' results. This being the case, the identification of the key players in the electoral process and examination of their legal duties and powers is critical to an understanding of election law in this country.

Because each state has a system of statutes that governs the conduct of its local election officials, with many of the types of duties set forth in common, this chapter will analyze in detail the legal requirements imposed on local and state election officials in Mississippi. From registering voters and preparing voter rolls to appointing and training poll managers, from Election Day voting and certifying election results to hearing and participating in election contests, the work of these local election officials determines just how close an election comes to being fundamentally fair and free.

III. Roles of Election Officials

Mississippi's decentralized electoral system is governed locally by political party executive committees, election commissions, and voter registrars. With the passage of the Help America Vote Act of 2002 (HAVA),[2] the role of the state's chief elections officer, the secretary of state, has increased in the area of voter roll maintenance and selection of compliant voting devices for use in all of Mississippi's 82 counties.[3] However, in no way does this heightened role in these areas supplant the ultimate authority of local officials to organize, conduct, and certify the outcomes of all of the state's elections.

A. LOCAL ELECTION COMMISSIONS

Perhaps as powerful in the area of elections in Mississippi as any other single person or group, local election commissions are responsible for overseeing the conduct of all general and special elections taking place within their jurisdictions. Under state law, there are five election commissioners in each county popularly elected by voters in county districts for four-year terms.[4] Municipal election commissioners are appointed by the governing authorities (city councils, mayor, and aldermen, for example) of their municipalities. Their numbers range from three to seven based on the municipalities' population.[5]

Each election commission elects a chair and a secretary with the chair having sole responsibility for having official election ballots printed and distributed in all general and special elections being conducted within that jurisdiction.[6] In Mississippi, and in most states, this authority is coveted since many political strategists and academics believe ballot order of candidate names affects some percentage of the votes cast.[7]

In Mississippi, local election commissioners are required to be trained 12 days per year by the staff of the state's chief elections officer.[8] In Mississippi, following the United States Congress's enactment of HAVA in 2002, with its 2006 effective date for implementation, training requirements for local officials increased substantially in order to address these election law changes and the use of newly mandated voting equipment. State law changes in 2006 increased annual training requirements for local election commissioners from six days to 12 and included the addition of eight more training days at the option of the local governing body.[9]

1. *Pre-Election Day Duties.* Local election commissions' electoral duties begin with responsibility for voter roll maintenance. Proper maintenance involves the duty to diligently secure the removal of names from the rolls of persons no longer eligible to vote in each jurisdiction according to state law. For example, the names of deceased persons, persons registering to vote in other jurisdictions, persons who no longer reside in the local jurisdiction, and persons convicted of disenfranchising crimes must be periodically removed from a county's voter rolls.[10] This ongoing responsibility is restricted in Mississippi only by the number of allowable days for which election commissioners may be paid for this work pursuant to state law.[11]

In 1997, the United States Supreme Court mandated Mississippi's compliance with the National Voter Registration Act (NVRA).[12] Following the decision, election commissions were required to follow a federally mandated procedure when removing voter names from the rolls due to a voter's change of residence. According to the NVRA,[13] and subsequent state law,[14] such voters may be removed from local voter rolls only after they are mailed a card or other written notice seeking confirmation of the change in address. This notice must be forwardable, be mailed to the voter's last known address, and contain a postage-prepaid response card to facilitate the voter's confirmation or nonconfirmation of the address change. If this notice is returned to the local election commission as nondeliverable, or if no voter response is received, or if the voter confirms a change of address outside the local jurisdiction, then the voter's name is placed on an inactive list of voters and may be removed from the rolls if he or she does not cast a ballot in the next two federal general elections following the notice's mailing. If the voter does vote in either of these two elections, he or she does so by affidavit or provisional ballot and the voter's name is automatically returned to the roll of active voters in the county.[15] These requirements have served to increase local election commission responsibilities in this area of their work, but have served the important purpose of assuring that local voter roll maintenance does not operate to improperly purge eligible voters from the rolls.

Another federal law change has operated to dramatically change the work and ease the burden of local election commissions with regard to their voter roll maintenance duties. With the adoption of HAVA in 2002, states were required to implement centralized, interactive state-wide voter registry systems for use by January 1, 2006.[16] HAVA's requirements for such systems include the ability to notify local election commissions when a voter's name is entered as a new registrant in another county in the state as well as the ability to access the state's bureau of vital statistics offices and criminal court records to provide counties with information as to voter deaths and disenfranchising convictions. These systems, if properly implemented, will greatly enhance the ability of local election commissions to carry out their voter roll maintenance responsibilities. Eventually, states' centralized voter registries may be cross-referenced against those in neighboring states to detect duplicate registrations, out-of-state deaths, and foreign convictions. Suffice it to say that HAVA's mandate in this regard, coupled with hefty federal funding to states to assist with the cost of implementing such systems, could become the single greatest legacy of HAVA. Once fully implemented and operational, the existence of centralized voter rolls will significantly affect voters' perceptions, rightly or wrongly, that voter rolls are so inflated that voter fraud is not only possible but occurring with regularity in states across the country. Voter confidence in the ability of local officials to keep up-to-date, accurate voter rolls and prevent voting by ineligible people is critical to addressing voter apathy and increasing voter participation.

Following the statutory deadlines for candidates to qualify for office, election commissions in Mississippi are also charged with the responsibility of certifying that candidates seeking local offices meet all the statutory requirements for eligibility to hold the offices they seek without contingency.[17] Mississippi law allows challenges to the qualifications of all independent and party-nominated candidates to be filed with the appropriate state or local election commission, depending on the office for which the candidate qualified.[18] These challenges are originally heard and determined by these commissions and are subject to judicial appeal.[19]

In the weeks immediately preceding an election, local election commissions in Mississippi carry out a variety of election preparation duties, all of which are essential components of successful elections. Chief among these duties is the appointment and training of poll managers.[20] Poll managers are those officials who have firsthand experience with all voters on Election Day and are responsible for overseeing Election Day voting. They open polling places, pick up and deliver ballot boxes or other supplies to the polling places, set up and turn on any electronic voting systems in place and maintain these devices' security on Election Day, meet voters and determine their eligibility to vote, and canvass and report the results of the election at that precinct after polls close.[21] If these poll managers are not carefully selected and trained, or if they fail to perform any of these duties in an ethical and responsible manner, the integrity of the election is seriously compromised.[22]

2. Post-Election Day Duties. Local election commissions' postelection duties are multiple. They must determine whether affidavit ballots should be counted[23] and must certify and deliver official, final election results from all participating precincts in the county to the secretary of state for computation and certification.[24]

The process of affidavit ballot verification is detailed and, depending on the number of such ballots, can be very time consuming. In a close race, this process is very closely scrutinized as the election commission decision on each such ballot can sway such an election's outcome. As a result, affidavit ballot decisions are frequently the subject of election contests. The local election commission's integrity, fidelity to statutory requirements, and nonpartisan discharge of this duty is essential to the safeguarding of voters' and candidates' rights to prevent illegal voting and voter fraud in accordance with statutory rules.

3. Inadequate Compensation. For all their responsibilities, in Mississippi local election commissioners' service is a part-time job compensated by payment of a per diem allowance of $84 per day in which at least five hours of work is performed carrying out either voter roll maintenance or conduct of election duties.[25] The number of per diem days per year for which Mississippi local election commissioners are entitled to be paid varies from 50 days (and an additional 15 days for each election in excess of one per year) to 240 days (and an additional 105 days for each election in excess of one per year) based on county population as determined by the most recent federal decennial census.[26]

B. LOCAL POLITICAL PARTY EXECUTIVE COMMITTEES

In Mississippi, local political party executive committees conduct party primary elections at both the municipal and county levels.[27] Executive Committee members are popularly elected at the municipal level and appointed in accordance with political party procedures, usually through party caucuses, at the county level.[28] The role of political party executive committees in primary elections is identical to that of local election commissions in general and special elections, with the exception of voter roll maintenance duties.[29] They determine all party candidate qualifications,[30] appoint and train poll workers,[31] validate affidavit ballots,[32] and certify official primary election results.[33]

C. LOCAL VOTER REGISTRARS

In Mississippi, the State Board of Election Commissioners appoints a registrar for each of the state's 82 counties, who serves a four-year term.[34] The municipal clerk of each of Mississippi's over 300 municipalities is the voter registrar for each municipality.[35] The municipal registrar, who by law also serves as a deputy county registrar to avoid dual registration requirements, is responsible for registering voters for both county and municipal elections.[36] Just as state law mandates that the municipal clerk serves as the municipal voter registrar, the State Board of Election Commissioners routinely appoints the county circuit clerk as the county voter registrar.[37] The duties of the county and municipal registrars are identical, the first and most important of which is to accept voter registration applications and place qualified applicants' names on the registration books of the proper voting precincts depending on the voters' residence.[38]

Local registrars are required by law in Mississippi to keep registration books open and keep office hours of 8:00 AM until 7:00 PM for five business days immediately prior to the 30th day before a primary or general election for voter registration purposes.[39] This time period is required to satisfy Mississippi's 30-day residency requirement for voting.[40]

In cases of physical disability, state law allows the voter registrar to visit applicants to facilitate their registration.[41] If an applicant is unable to read or write, due to disability or otherwise, Mississippi law requires the registrar to read aloud the registration application's questions and the oath and record the applicant's responses, with the execution of the oath being waived.[42]

In the fall and spring of each year, the county registrar must furnish all public schools in the county with mail-in voter registration applications to enable students who will be 18 years old before the state's next general election to register to vote in time to vote in those elections.[43]

Finally, county registrars are directed by Mississippi law to prepare and keep in their offices a complete list of persons convicted of disenfranchising crimes under the Mississippi Constitution[44] to assist local election commissions with their voter roll maintenance duties.[45] As the HAVA-mandated centralized voter registry system is implemented and interfaced with state court records of criminal convictions, the manual maintenance of such a list by the registrar should become an obsolete duty.

Practically speaking, in Mississippi and in many states, the local voter registrar is the only local election official who is a full-time, salaried public employee. For that reason, local election commissions and local party executive committees depend on the voter registrar to play a much greater role in the process of election administration than is statutorily provided. In many cases, depending on the qualifications and attention to duty of election commissioners and party executive committee members, local voter registrars either prompt the timely completion of election administration duties in their counties or carry out these duties themselves on behalf of other officials in order to ensure that elections are properly conducted.

D. STATE BOARD OF ELECTION COMMISSIONERS

By virtue of the NVRA, every state has designated a chief elections officer.[46] Under the NVRA, this officer has certain special responsibilities, including coordination of state agency-registrar duties. Carrying out these responsibilities may involve training state agency registrar representatives to conduct voter registration duties and providing advice and assistance to these agencies as needed.

Under HAVA,[47] the NVRA-designated chief elections officer in a state has duties that, if performed in accordance with HAVA requirements, serve to qualify the state for receipt of the not insignificant amount of federal funds appropriated by Congress to assist states with implementation of their HAVA-mandated election responsibilities. For example, by the time all federal appropriations authorized for this purpose under HAVA are complete Mississippi may receive as much as $34 million to assist with implementation of the centralized voter registry system and the purchase of compliant voting devices, all of which is provided to the state's chief elections officer for use in accordance with HAVA mandates.[48] The fact that these election technology decisions are allowed to be made at the state level by a statewide elected official, and not locally,[49] is a major shift of election administration responsibility from the historically complete decentralization of these functions in Mississippi and in most other states.

Otherwise, three statewide elected officials in Mississippi—the governor, the attorney general, and the secretary of state—compose the State Board of Election Commissioners,[50] which functions as a state election commission to the extent that it determines the qualifications of candidates seeking election to statewide, state district, legislative district, and judicial district offices.[51] The governor, as chair of the State Board, also determines the contents of the official sample ballot for elections involving state and state district offices, which ballot is then provided to local election commissions. Local election commission chairs ultimately decide upon and order the printing of the ballot and by law may vary the format from that submitted as a sample by the State Board, since the local official is only required to follow the sample "as nearly as practicable."[52]

IV. Nuts and Bolts

A. PRE-ELECTION DAY RESPONSIBILITIES

In Mississippi, preparations for Election Day begin with the appointment by local party executive committees in primary elections and local election commissions in general and special elections of poll managers. For each election, the commissions or committees appoint at least three and not more than 18 poll managers (based on the number of registered voters in each precinct), commonly referred to as "poll workers."[53] The poll managers in Mississippi must be registered voters of the county but not necessarily of the precincts in which they serve.[54] The commission or committee designates one poll manager at each precinct as the bailiff for that precinct.[55] Under state law, poll managers are generally charged with the responsibility of taking care that "the election is conducted fairly and agreeably to law" and judging elector qualifications.[56] The poll manager designated as the precinct's bailiff is required to enforce laws regarding the presence of persons in the polling place, campaigning in or near the polling place, and activities of party or candidate poll watchers in the polling place. In Mississippi, the bailiff has a general duty to "arrest all persons creating any disturbance at the voting place, and to enable all qualified electors who have not voted, and who desire to vote, to have unobstructed access to the polls for the purpose of voting."[57]

According to Mississippi law, in a general or special election, the poll managers "shall not all be of the same political party if suitable persons of different political parties can be found in the district."[58] Practically speaking, the election commissions in Mississippi have exercised a great deal of discretion in determining whether "suitable persons" of both political parties can be found to serve as poll managers. Depending on the philosophy of the members of a particular local election commission, political and otherwise, and the availability of capable poll managers of varying political parties, general Election Day poll managers may or may not be representative of both dominant political parties in the state.

Training of poll workers in the proper exercise of their duties is also the responsibility of local election commissions.[59] This training has become more extensive in recent years in Mississippi as older, paper-based voting systems give way to electronic voting systems called direct recording electronic (DRE) systems. This training must take place no later than five days before the election in which the poll managers will serve.[60]

In an attempt to assist with future poll worker recruitment, in 2002 Mississippi passed legislation creating the student intern poll worker program.[61] Under the legislation, local election commissions may appoint up to two students per precinct to serve during an election. The interns must be at least 16 years old by Election Day, among other requirements. While their specific duties are left to local election commissions to determine, they may not include responsibilities deemed essential poll manager functions such as deciding voter challenges, carrying out bailiff responsibilities, or tallying votes.[62] The philosophy underlying this legislation was one cognizant of the aging population of available and willing poll managers and the need for an influx of new citizens eager to take on this civic duty.

B. ELECTION DAY RESPONSIBILITIES

In Mississippi, when a voter appears at the precinct polling place to vote, the poll manager checks to see that the voter's name appears on the precinct's poll book.

If located, the voter signs the receipt book, and immediately proceeds to a voting compartment and votes.[63]

Under certain new voter identification procedures mandated by HAVA in federal elections, first-time voters who register to vote by mail must present an acceptable form of identification to the poll manager before voting.[64] The HAVA identification requirement is not imposed on military voters, disabled or elderly voters, voters who enclose one of the acceptable identification forms with their mail-in voter registration application, or voters who possess current and valid Mississippi driver's licenses or federal social security numbers and whose data match state records.[65]

In the post-HAVA era, poll workers in Mississippi are provided with poll books that are flagged to reflect those first-time voters who are required to present HAVA identification. Poll managers are charged with the responsibility of securing an acceptable form of identification or requiring the voter to vote by affidavit or provisional ballot in the absence of the required identification.[66]

In Mississippi, poll managers are also charged with determining if a voter is entitled to receive assistance in voting. State law requires that before a voter may be accompanied into the voting booth by one providing assistance, the voter must first make a request for assistance of the poll managers and the managers must be satisfied that the voter is either blind, physically disabled, or illiterate and needs help to mark a ballot before assistance is allowed. (With the increased use of disability-accessible DRE voting devices since HAVA's enactment, most of these reasons no longer serve to justify a request for assistance.) After satisfying the threshold criteria, only the voter designates the person to accompany and assist him in the act of voting. In Mississippi, the only persons ineligible to provide assistance are the voter's employer or employer's agent or an officer or agent of the voter's union.[67]

Another important Election Day poll manager responsibility in Mississippi elections is that involving challenges to voter qualifications and decisions regarding these challenges. By the proper handling of such challenges, poll managers have the opportunity to prevent both fraudulent voting and voter intimidation. By law in Mississippi, only certain individuals in the polling place may legally challenge a voter's qualifications. They are

1. Any candidate whose name is on the ballot in that precinct.
2. Any candidate representative or poll watcher of a candidate whose name is on the ballot in that precinct.
3. Any political party poll watcher in that precinct.
4. Any qualified elector (registered voter) in that precinct.
5. Any poll manager in the precinct where a challenged person is attempting to vote.[68]

In Mississippi elections, challenges to a voter's qualifications may only be made on one of the following grounds:

1. The voter is not a registered voter in that precinct.
2. The voter is not the registered voter under whose name he or she is attempting to vote.
3. The voter has already voted in the election.
4. The voter is not a resident of the precinct where he or she is registered.
5. The voter has illegally registered to vote.
6. The voter has taken his or her ballot outside the polling place.
7. The voter is disqualified by law.[69]

It is the singular responsibility of the poll managers in Mississippi to vote and to determine the validity of all challenges made to voters' qualifications in the precincts where they serve.[70] In Mississippi, there are three possible outcomes to any such challenge. First, if a majority of the precinct's poll managers determine that the challenge is frivolous or not made in good faith, they must disregard it and the voter proceeds to vote as if not challenged. Second, if the poll managers unanimously determine that it is clear, either by admission of or statement by the voter or from official documents, that the challenge is well taken, they must reject the vote and it is not counted. Finally, if poll managers cannot agree unanimously that a challenge is proper, or are not convinced it is frivolous or made in bad faith, then the ballot is marked "challenged." These ballots are separated from the other ballots or votes at the closing of the polls, counted, and reported separately. Rejected ballots are not counted at all.[71]

The conduct of affidavit voting in Mississippi is one of the greatest challenges facing poll managers, especially in light of an increase in such balloting due to HAVA identification requirements and other new procedures involved in Election Day voting. Such voting, often called "provisional" voting in other states, occurs when a voter's name does not appear on the poll books or legally required voter identification is not presented. Under Mississippi law as well as under HAVA, in the absence of one of the required forms of identification for some voters, the voter must be given the opportunity to cast an affidavit ballot. This ballot is different from a regular Election Day ballot because it requires the voter to affirm that he or she is entitled to vote in the precinct in question. In addition, affidavit ballots are not automatically counted by poll managers after polls close along with all the unchallenged ballots. Affidavit ballots are merely returned by poll managers to a central location at the close of Election Day for examination and validation, if appropriate, by local party executive committees in primary elections and local election commissions in general and special elections.[72]

In Mississippi, absentee ballots are cast either by mail or in the office of the county or municipal voter registrar, depending on the particular status of the voter and the reason for applying to vote by absentee ballot.[73] When the registrar receives these ballots and before ballot boxes are released for distribution to the precincts, the registrar places absentee ballots, along with the corresponding absentee ballot applications completed by the voters, in the appropriate precinct boxes.[74] At the close of the polls on Election Day, poll managers at each precinct begin the process of examining these ballots and deciding whether they should be counted.

When reviewing each absentee ballot, poll managers announce the name, address, and precinct of each. Then they begin their analysis of the ballot, application, and ballot envelope. The examination process consists of verifying that (1) the voter's signature on the application favorably compares with that on the ballot envelope,[75] (2) the voter's signature on the ballot envelope is across the flap of the envelope (mandatory requirement for the ballot to be counted);[76] and (3) all absentee ballots and applications that are required to be notarized are in fact properly notarized.[77] If the absentee ballots meet all statutory requirements, the poll managers count these ballots at that time and include them among their reported precinct totals.[78]

In addition to reviewing and counting eligible absentee ballots at the closing of the polls, poll managers in Mississippi open the ballot boxes (or perform an electronic function for the same purpose on DRE devices) and proceed to determine the vote counts for the precinct. This is a public process and can be observed by the general public and specifically by candidates and/or candidate representatives so long as there is no "unnecessary interference, delay or encroachment upon the good order of the duties and proceedings of the managers."[79] These totals are recorded and transmitted to the executive committee or election commission, depending on whether the election is a party primary or general or special election, by the responsible poll manager for certification of final results.[80]

C. POST-ELECTION DAY DUTIES

1. *Certification of Election Results.* In Mississippi primary elections for county, county district, and single-county legislative district offices, county party executive committees must meet one to two days after the primary and certify party nominees or the names of those facing second or run-off primary elections.[81] This information must be transmitted to the Mississippi Secretary of State within ten days of the primary election.[82] Within ten days after the first or second primaries for statewide, state district, or multicounty legislative district offices, state political party executive committee chairs must transmit to the Mississippi Secretary of State the party vote by precinct in each county.[83]

In Mississippi general and special elections, within ten days after the election the local election commissions must certify final results and declare winners in county, county district, and single-county legislative district elections. Likewise, within the same ten-day period, these commissions must transmit to the Mississippi Secretary of State certified vote totals for their counties for all statewide, state district, and multicounty legislative district elections.[84] Not later than 30 days postelection, the Mississippi Secretary of State must "sum up the whole number of votes given for each candidate" for state district and multicounty legislative district offices and declare those with the largest number of votes "duly elected."[85]

2. *Election Contests.* Except for the federal laws governing election contest procedures for candidates for federal office,[86] election contests are governed by the laws of the various states. In Mississippi, primary election contests are first heard and decided by local or state election officials, depending on the office involved in the contest.

In Mississippi primary elections, any person contesting the election of another as a party nominee for local office must file a petition within 20 calendar days after the election with either the municipal or county political party executive committee (if the contested election involves a municipal, county, or single-county legislative district office) or the state political party executive committee (if the contested election involves a statewide, state district, or multicounty legislative district office).[87] The local political party executive committee then meets at the call of its chair or any three of its members to consider or hear the contest. Notice of the contest hearing date is provided to interested parties, and by majority vote, the contest is decided and the local committee declares the primary election's true results.[88] In contests of Mississippi primary elections for state, state district, or multicounty legislative district offices, the state political party executive committee chair, on receipt of a primary election contest petition, directs the appropriate county executive committee chair to investigate the petition's allegations and report findings to the state committee. After receipt of the report, and by majority vote, the state committee decides the contest and declares the true primary results.[89]

These Mississippi administrative bodies have the legal authority to subpoena witnesses and documents to aid in their investigations and hearing of primary election contests.[90] Appeals of these contests may be filed with the local trial courts for de novo review and on appeal are judicially reviewed on the records below.[91] An exception to this rule in Mississippi is that appeals of contests heard by the State Executive Committee are reviewed de novo by the trial courts in Hinds County, the State Committee's county of residence.[92]

An interesting aspect of party primary election contests in Mississippi is that the county election commissioners of the county involved in the contest are required to attend the trial court hearing on the contest. By law, they act as "advisors or assistants in the trial and determination of the facts, and as assistants in counts, calculations and inspections, and in seeing to it that the ballots, papers, documents, books and the like are diligently secured."[93] Although Mississippi law expressly provides that the trial judge makes all final determinations as to facts and law in the case, the final contest decision is considered to be rendered by this "special tribunal" with election commissioners being allowed to submit dissents, if any.[94]

In contests of Mississippi general or special elections, petitions must be filed with trial court clerks within 20 calendar days after the election; are original judicial, rather than administrative, proceedings; and are tried to juries.[95]

V. *Case Studies:* Gnemi *and* Brown

In Mississippi, two recent court cases, one state and one federal, serve as real-life illustrations of the problems encountered by candidates and the breakdown of the electoral process when local election officials fail to carry out their responsibilities in accordance with law.

In the case of *Waters v. Gnemi,* the Mississippi Supreme Court examined a party primary election in which almost every statutory rule as to postelection ballot security was violated at every level of local election management.[96] As a result, certified results were set aside and a new election was ordered that delayed the general election and cast the electoral process in that Mississippi county in a very poor light.

Gnemi, an incumbent county district official running for reelection, was certified by the local party executive committee as the second-place finisher in the primary and placed in a second, or run-off, primary to determine the party nominee. Some two weeks later, after a recalculation of the vote, Gnemi was advised by the executive committee that his opponent had won outright and that no second primary was needed. No new party certification of this result took place. During the two-week post-election period prior to the recalculation, second primary ballots had been ordered by the executive committee and absentee ballots had been voted.[97]

Gnemi decided to avail himself of the statutory precontest remedy of examining the contents of those ballot boxes from his district's precincts.[98] When Gnemi appeared at the appointed time to conduct the examination, he was not presented with the six sealed ballot boxes from his district, which should have been delivered by poll managers on election night and preserved intact thereafter.[99] Instead, he was presented with two taped-up cardboard boxes allegedly containing the commingled ballots from his six precincts. The local circuit clerk and voter registrar, who was charged by law with securing ballot boxes until expiration of the contest period, advised Gnemi that primary election ballot box contents had been emptied and combined so she could make Election Day ballot boxes available for the upcoming second or run-off primary.[100] Also produced to Gnemi at this time were two documents signed by a county election commissioner (by law, not involved in the conduct of party primary elections) that he had reviewed ballots from the six Election Day ballot boxes and placed them in the cardboard boxes. Following his examination of the two boxes' contents, Gnemi filed a petition contesting the primary outcome. The party executive committee denied his petition and he filed a sworn petition for review with the local trial court. The lower court ruled for Gnemi and ordered a new primary election. His opponent appealed.

On appeal, the Mississippi Supreme Court affirmed the lower court decision ordering a special primary election. In its opinion, the court discussed at length the handling of ballots by local officials following the primary election. After noting that the involvement of a local election commissioner in the primary was improper, the court discussed ballot box security, pointing out several ways in which the security requirements had been breached in the case. Because such requirements are "premised on eliminating fraudulent or corrupt practices and insuring a just and trustworthy result," the court went to great lengths in its opinion to discuss these thoroughly.[101]

Ultimately, the *Gnemi* court held that the ballot boxes involved in the primary contest were never properly locked and sealed and that they were not taken into custody and safeguarded by the circuit clerk as required by law. Rather, according to the court, the boxes' contents were commingled and placed in insecure, taped, farmers-market cardboard boxes. Consequently, the court ruled that the contents of these boxes lost their evidentiary value.[102] Because of the "gross deviation and total departure form mandatory election procedure" by the local executive committee, the court ruled that the result of the primary election was "completely undermined as all indicia of reliability were compromised." Therefore, the court reasoned that the conduct of a new election was "not only an appropriate remedy, it was the only remedy."[103] Since these violations precluded Gnemi from even being able to detect fraud, the court held that allegations of fraud were not necessary to Gnemi's success in the contest.

The *Gnemi* scenario is undoubtedly election management at its worst, though no allegations or findings of purposeful misconduct were made. In the case of *United States v. Brown*,[104] however, the United States Department of Justice alleged and the court found racially motivated manipulation of the election process in a Mississippi county by the chair and members of the local party executive committee and local election commission, all in violation of Section 2 of the Voting Rights Act of 1965.

In *Brown*, the facts developed at the trial of the case revealed that the executive committee chairperson (Brown), the circuit clerk, the executive committee, and the election commission had complete control over all county electoral activity, "from voter registration, to voter roll maintenance, to voting itself, and to canvassing returns and certifying election results."[105] In this acknowledged "unconventional, if not unprecedented" use of the Voting Rights Act, these black election officials were accused of using their majority position in the county to discriminate against white citizens much the same as whites had historically discriminated against blacks there.[106]

Holding that Section 2 affords no less protection to white voters than to any other class of voters, the district court in *Brown* found numerous instances of discriminatory conduct sufficient to determine that the Voting Rights Act had been violated. In its Section 2 analysis, the court wrote that it did not have "to look far to find ample direct and circumstantial evidence of an intent to discriminate against white voters."[107] Principally, the court found that Brown, in particular, was "firmly of the view that blacks . . . should hold all elected offices [in the county] to the exclusion of whites."[108] Among the other specific findings were that Brown, as chair of the county executive commission, recruited black candidates to run for office when he knew they failed to meet candidate residency requirements; that the defendants conducted racially motivated abuses of the absentee ballot process in the county involving hiring teams of notaries to secure sworn absentee ballots from black voters and ensuring their being counted by putting in place a nearly all-black force of loyal poll managers to ignore or reject proper challenges of black voters' absentee ballots; that Brown and others hired 103 black poll managers out of a total of 110 appointed to serve in the 2003 primary election; that the defendants conducted unsolicited and otherwise improper voter assistance for black voters; that the defendants engaged in disparate enforcement of Mississippi's law against campaigning at or near polling places on the basis of race; and finally, that Brown and other defendants made illegal demands for party loyalty from voters as a prerequisite for primary voting, as reflected in an open letter published in 2003.[109] In the letter, the defendants included a list of 174 white voters who would be challenged and rejected if they attempted to vote in the primary election.

Based on these and other facts, the *Brown* court held that the defendants "administered and manipulated the political process in ways specifically intended and designed to impair and impede participation of white voters and to dilute their votes."[110] In finding a legal violation of Section 2 of the Voting Rights Act, the court concluded that "[n]o one could reasonably argue that an election official's racially motivated decision to count the votes of black voters while rejecting those of white voters is discrimination that can be countenanced under any view of Section 2. In purpose and effect, that is what has occurred in this case."[111]

In both *Gnemi* and *Brown*, powerful local election officials neglected or intentionally disregarded the legal requirements attendant to their duties. In the *Gnemi* case, it is clear that a candidate's right, along with the preeminent expectation of the public, to ascertain whether an election's certified outcome was correct was completely thwarted by the incompetent discharge of duties. In *Brown*, local minority election officials' collective zealous but misguided mentality resulted in the unfortunate and unanticipated use of a corrective weapon created years ago to preserve black minority voting rights as a remedy. In each case, the importance of the legal and ethical functioning of local election officials is clear in the prevention of voter fraud, voter intimidation, and candidate and voter qualification.

VI. Conclusion

In a state like Mississippi, HAVA has brought about much needed changes, including a renewed emphasis on training of those officials who are ultimately responsible for the conduct of elections across the state. The *Gnemi* and *Brown* cases are only the latest in a long history extending back some 50 years during which Mississippi has struggled to make meaningful the critical right to vote for all of its citizens—a right so dependent on local election officials.[112] Perhaps as a result of their struggles, most Mississippians today, including its election officials, uniquely understand the importance of the franchise and the need to zealously guard against its erosion. Better-trained, more professional election administration is central to Mississippi's and other states' continued progress toward making the ideal of free and fair elections a reality.

A Mississippi jurist eloquently expressed the view of most Mississippians, as well as citizens throughout our country, on the special role voting plays and the significance of the proper exercise of authority by election officials in our democracy when he wrote:

> The right to vote has become the brightest star in the American constitutional firmament. It has been secured and extended in five of our last twelve amendments which are the public expression of an enduring national consensus. It is free speech, but with a bite, for it is the one form of speech where others may be made to listen despite their dissent or disinterest. Each election sees a convergence in space and time when each of us by law is as equal as we were created. By sovereign decree, no one of us at such a moment has greater power or wealth or standing in the human race than the most miserable wretch who slouches toward the polls to vote and thus to affirm, anonymously and to the world, that he can feel and fear and despair and dream. . . . Election day is more than a ritual renewal of the social contract. It is at once the workhorse of the pragmatic, secular state and, because it works, the political precondition of human hope.[113]

Notes

1. ELECTIONLINE.ORG, WORKING TOGETHER? STATE AND LOCAL ELECTIONS COORDINATION 1 (Election Reform Briefing, Sept. 2002), *available at* http://www.electionline.org/Portals/1/Publications/Working%20Together.pdf.

2. Pub. L. No. 107-252 (Oct. 29, 2002).

3. Pub. L. No. 107-252, §§ 301, 303 (Oct. 29, 2002); MISS. CODE ANN. §§ 23-15-165, 23-15-211.1.

4. MISS. CODE ANN. §§ 23-15-211, 23-15-213.

5. MISS. CODE ANN. § 23-15-221.

6. MISS. CODE ANN. § 23-15-213.

7. Jon A. Krosnick, *In the Voting Booth, Bias Starts at the Top*, N.Y. Times, Nov. 4, 2006.

8. Miss. Code Ann. § 23-15-211(2), (3), (5).

9. Miss. Code Ann. § 23-15-211(5).

10. Miss. Const. 1890 § 241; Miss. Code Ann. § 23-15-153.

11. Miss. Code Ann. § 23-15-153.

12. 42 U.S.C.A. §§ 1973gg et seq. (2000); Young v. Fordice, 520 U.S. 273 (1997).

13. 42 U.S.C.A. § 1973gg-6(a)(4); 42 U.S.C.A. § 1973gg(b); 42 U.S.C.A. § 1973gg(c) (2000).

14. Miss. Code Ann. 23-15-153(1).

15. 42 U.S.C. § 1973gg(b) (2000).

16. Pub. L. No. 107-252, § 303 (Oct. 29, 2002).

17. Miss. Code Ann. §§ 23-15-359(8), 23-15-361(5).

18. Miss. Code Ann. § 23-15-963(1). *See* Powe v. Forrest County Elec. Comm'n, 163 So. 2d 656 (Miss. 1964) (holding that state and local commissions are authorized to determine candidate qualifications).

19. Miss. Code Ann. § 23-15-963(4)–(7).

20. Miss. Code Ann. §§ 23-15-231, 23-15-235, 23-15-239.

21. Miss. Code Ann. §§ 23-15-247, 23-15-251, 23-15-261.

22. *See* Clark v. Rankin County Dem. Exec. Comm., 753 So. 2d 753 (Miss. 1975) (poll managers allowed counting of ballots to begin before polls closed, causing the court to overturn the election results and order a new election to be held).

23. Miss. Code Ann. § 23-15-573.

24. Miss. Code Ann. § 23-15-603.

25. Miss. Code Ann. § 23-15-153. In 2007, the Mississippi State Legislature voted to increase the per diem amount to $84 per day from a previous amount of $70 per day.

26. Miss. Code Ann. § 23-15-153(2)(a)–(j).

27. Miss. Code Ann. §§ 23-15-171, 23-15-263.

28. Miss. Code Ann. §§ 23-15-171, 23-15-313, 23-15-1053.

29. Miss. Code Ann. § 23-15-31.

30. Miss. Code Ann. §§ 23-15-299(7), 23-15-309(4).

31. Miss. Code Ann. § 23-15-265.

32. Miss. Code Ann. § 23-15-573.

33. Miss. Code Ann. §§ 23-15-597, 23-15-599(1), (2).

34. Miss. Code Ann. §§ 23-15-223.

35. *Id.*

36. Miss. Code Ann. §§ 23-15-223, 23-15-35.

37. Miss. Code Ann. § 23-15-223.

38. Miss. Code Ann. §§ 23-15-31, 23-15-33, 23-15-35.

39. Miss. Code Ann. § 23-15-37(2).

40. Miss. Code Ann. § 23-15-11.

41. Miss. Code Ann. § 23-15-37(4).

42. Miss. Code Ann. § 23-15-39(7).

43. Miss. Code Ann. § 23-15-37(5)(a).

44. MISS. CONST. 1890 § 241.

45. MISS. CODE ANN. § 23-15-151.

46. 42 U.S.C. § 1973gg-8 (2000).

47. Pub. L. No. 107-252 (Oct. 29, 2002).

48. *See* Secretary of State of Mississippi, Mississippi's Compliance with HAVA, Frequently Asked Questions, www.sos.state.ms.us/elections/HAVA/HAVA.asp.

49. Pub. L. No. 107-252 § 303(a)(1) (Oct. 29, 2002).

50. MISS. CODE ANN. § 23-15-211(1).

51. MISS. CODE ANN. § 23-15-359(8).

52. MISS. CODE ANN. § 23-15-367(1), (3).

53. MISS. CODE ANN. §§ 23-15-231, 23-15-235.

54. MISS. CODE ANN. § 23-15-231.

55. *Id.*

56. MISS. CODE ANN. §§ 23-15-233.

57. MISS. CODE ANN. § 23-15-241.

58. MISS. CODE ANN. § 23-15-231.

59. MISS. CODE ANN. § 23-15-239(1).

60. *Id.*

61. MISS. CODE ANN. § 23-15-240.

62. MISS. CODE ANN. § 23-15-240(2).

63. MISS. CODE ANN. § 23-15-541.

64. Pub. L. No. 107-252 § 303(b)(1) (Oct. 29, 2002). Under HAVA, acceptable forms of identification, if required, include a current photo ID, a copy of a utility bill, bank statement, a government check, paycheck, or other government documentation with the voter's name and address included.

65. Pub. L. No. 107-252 § 303(b)(3) (Oct. 29, 2002).

66. Pub. L. No. 107-252, §§ 303(b), 302(a) (Oct. 29, 2002). HAVA requires that all voters required to vote affidavit ballots under HAVA be able to learn if their ballots were counted or not and, if not, why, via a free access system. (§ 302(a)(5)).

67. MISS. CODE ANN. § 23-15-549. *See* O'Neal v. Simpson, 350 So. 2d 998 (Miss. 1977) (purposes of and proper procedures for voter assistance).

68. MISS. CODE ANN. § 23-15-571(1)(a)–(e).

69. MISS. CODE ANN. § 23-15-571(3).

70. MISS. CODE ANN. § 23-15-571(2).

71. MISS. CODE ANN. § 23-25-579. *See also* Misso v. Oliver, 666 So. 2d 1366 (Miss. 1996) (poll manager duties regarding rejected and challenged ballots).

72. MISS. CODE ANN. § 23-15-573.

73. MISS. CODE ANN. § 23-15-627. For absentee ballot requirements in Mississippi, see MISS. CODE ANN. §§ 23-15-621 et seq. and 23-15-711 et seq.

74. MISS. CODE ANN. §§ 23-15-625, 23-15-637.

75. MISS. CODE ANN. § 23-15-639. *See* Pegram v. Bailey, 708 So. 2d 1307 (Miss. 1997).

76. MISS. CODE ANN. § 23-15-633.

77. MISS. CODE ANN. §§ 23-15-641, 23-15-631, 23-15-635, 23-15-719. *See* Shannon v. Henson, 499 So. 2d 758 (Miss. 1986); Fouche v. Ragland, 424 So. 2d 559 (Miss. 1982).

78. Miss. Code Ann. § 23-15-639.

79. Miss. Code Ann. § 23-15-581.

80. Miss. Code Ann. §§ 23-15-595, 23-15-601.

81. Miss. Code Ann. § 23-15-597(1).

82. Miss. Code Ann. § 23-15-599(2) (a).

83. Miss. Code Ann. § 23-15-599(1) (a).

84. Miss. Code Ann. §§ 23-15-601(1), 23-15-603.

85. Miss. Code Ann. § 23-15-605. In statewide races, Mississippi law requires that vote totals be directed by local election commissions to the "seat of government," through the secretary of state, and delivered to the Speaker of the Mississippi House of Representatives when he or she convenes the opening session of the House in January of the year immediately following the November general election.

86. Federal Contested Elections Act of 1969, 2 U.S.C.A. §§ 381 et seq. (1969); *see* Jeffrey A. Jenkins, *Partisanship and Contested Election Cases in the Senate, 1789-2002*, 19 Stud. Am. Pol. Dev. 53–74 (Spring 2005).

87. Miss. Code Ann. §§ 23-15-921, 23-15-923.

88. Miss. Code Ann. § 23-15-921.

89. Miss. Code Ann. § 23-15-923.

90. Miss. Code Ann. § 23-15-925.

91. Miss. Code Ann. §§ 23-15-927, 23-15-929, 23-15-931, 23-15-933.

92. Miss. Code Ann. § 23-15-931.

93. Miss. Code Ann. § 23-15-931.

94. *Id. See* Waters v. Gnemi, 907 So. 2d 307 (Miss. 2005), for a discussion of a party primary contest in which local election commissioners became involved in primary election management, thus compromising the role they should have played as a part of the judicial "special tribunal."

95. Miss. Code Ann. § 23-15-951. An exception to this process in Mississippi occurs in contests of general or special elections for state legislative offices. Only the state legislature hears these contests in accordance with the internal procedures of the chamber in which the contested seat is located. Miss. Const. 1890 Art. IV, § 38; Miss. Code Ann. § 23-15-955.

96. *Gnemi, 907 So. 2d 307.* In the interest of disclosure, note that the author was one of the attorneys representing Gnemi on appeal in this case.

97. *Id.* at 311, 312.

98. Miss. Code Ann. § 23-15-911 (1972). In 2003, Holmes County used an OMR (optical mark reader) voting system. Such a system operated with paper ballots that were read when scanned through an OMR. Thus, the actual marked Election Day ballots were available for Gnemi's examination.

99. Miss. Code Ann. §§ 23-15-591, 23-15-595.

100. *Gnemi, 907 So. 2d at 313.*

101. *Id.* at 329, 330. The statutes violated included Miss. Code Ann. § 23-15-591 (immediate postelection handling of boxes requiring locks and seals); Miss. Code Ann. §23-15-911(1) (maintenance of box security before and after any candidate examination of contents requiring relocking and resealing of boxes by party executive committee after

canvassing precinct results, safekeeping by circuit clerk, and relocking and resealing after candidate examination); MISS. CODE ANN. § 23-15-595 (circuit clerk responsibility to place on each box a lock and numbered metal seal similar to railroad freight car seals when in the clerk's custody).

102. *Gnemi*, 907 So. 2d at 331.

103. *Id.* at 335.

104. United States v. Brown, 494 F. Supp. 2d 440 (S.D. Miss. 2007).

105. *Id.*, citing JEFFREY JACKSON & MARY MILLER, MISSISSIPPI PRACTICE SERIES: ENCYCLOPEDIA OF MISSISSIPPI LAW § 6 (2003).

106. *Id.* at 443.

107. *Id.* at 449.

108. *Id.*

109. *See generally id.* at 452–473.

110. *Id.* at 485.

111. *Id.* at 486.

112. Hamer v. Campbell, 358 F.2d 215 (5th Cir. 1966); United States v. State of Miss., 339 F.2d 679 (5th Cir. 1964); United States v. Duke, 332 F.2d 759 (5th Cir. 1964); United States v. Dogan, 314 F.2d 767 (5th Cir. 1963); James v. Humphreys County Bd. of Election Comm'rs, 384 F. Supp. 114 (N.D. Miss. 1974); Frazier v. Callicutt, 383 F. Supp. 15 (N.D. Miss. 1974); Graham v. Waller, 343 F. Supp. 1 (S.D. Miss. 1972); United States v. State of Miss., 256 F. Supp. 344 (S.D. Miss. 1966); O'Neal v. Simpson, 350 So. 2d 998 (Miss. 1977).

113. Wilbourn v. Hobson, 608 So. 2d 1187, 1196 (Miss. 1992) (Robertson, J., concurring).

CHAPTER FIFTEEN

ELECTION CHALLENGES INVOLVING
CANDIDATES FOR FEDERAL OFFICE

TOMMIE S. CARDIN*
LESLIE C. SCOTT**

I. Introduction

Questionable practices designed to influence votes in federal elections are as old as the Republic itself. With the historic events of the 2000 U.S. presidential election, modern-day election practices affecting candidates for federal offices have once again been thrust to the forefront. The advancements of modern technology in the election arena seem to underscore the old adage that the more things change, the more they stay the same. Indeed, while technology has introduced new grounds for election contests, the traditional methods of influencing elections remain. Modern-day challenges to federal elections run the gamut from questioning practices surrounding new technology to more traditional grounds such as challenging candidate qualifications. Regardless of the changes, one factor will always remain constant: human nature. Consequently, there will always be fertile ground for legal challenges in federal elections as long as our Republic exists.[1]

II. The Sources of Challenges to Federal Elections

A. HOUSE, SENATE, PRESIDENT

The United States Constitution establishes the various elected federal offices and prescribes the qualifications for those offices. A member of the U.S. House of Representatives must be at least 25 years old, have been a U.S. citizen for seven years,

* Butler, Snow, O'Mara, Stevens & Cannada, PLLC.
** Butler, Snow, O'Mara, Stevens & Cannada, PLLC.

and be a resident of the state which he seeks to represent.[2] A member of the U.S. Senate must be at least 35 years old, have been a U.S. citizen for nine years, and be a resident of the state which he seeks to represent.[3] The term for members of the House is two years[4] and for members of the Senate six years.[5] The qualifications for president of the United States are set forth as well as the electoral method for selecting the president every four years.[6]

Significantly, while setting forth these specific qualifications for office, the Constitution affords each state the latitude of establishing the "times, places, and manner of holding elections for Senators and representatives."[7] After granting the states the power to run their own elections for federal offices, the Constitution then provides that each chamber "shall be the judge of the elections, returns and qualifications of its own members."[8] Consequently, the U.S. Constitution has established a dichotomy when it comes to the election of candidates for federal offices. That is, by delegating to each state the ability to determine the time, manner, and place for federal elections, state law necessarily governs how federal elections will occur and what methods will be used to carry out those elections. On the other hand, the Constitution affords each chamber the ultimate authority to determine the election of its members.

Respecting this dichotomy, courts have consistently held that Congress is the exclusive arbiter of the election of its members.[9] Thus, each chamber is responsible for handling election contests of its members. In this regard, contests follow the procedures established by each chamber. Dating back to 1798, the U.S. House of Representatives has had some type of statutory procedure in place providing for a method of discovery in election contests involving its members.[10] Congress enacted a new statute in 1851 to replace the 1798 procedure, and this statute remained in place until 1969.[11] With adoption of the Federal Contested Elections Act of 1969, Congress established a statutory procedure intended to modernize the process for bringing contests in the House.[12] This procedure provides that within 30 days after the duly authorized elections official certifies the results of the election, the contestant shall file written notice of contest with the Clerk of the House.[13] The process may be initiated by a member, someone outside of the House, or the House itself.[14] The notice is to state with particularity the grounds for contest and is to be served on the contestee.[15] Within 30 days of service, the contestee shall serve a written response and may assert various affirmative defenses or, if necessary, seek a more definite statement.[16] The burden of proof rests with the contestant to prove he or she is entitled to the contestee's seat, even if the contestee does not respond.[17] Thereafter either party may depose witnesses within certain prescribed time periods and seek documents from them via subpoena.[18] The parties prepare a record consisting of depositions, papers, and exhibits that is filed with the Clerk and upon which the contest shall be heard along with any briefs submitted by the parties.[19] The House may allow reimbursement of reasonable expenses incurred in the contest, including reasonable attorneys' fees, to any party in an election contest.[20] These procedures have remained in effect since 1969, with the subpoena provisions having specifically been held constitutional as recently as 1997.[21]

The House's own internal operating rules come to bear in these contests as well.[22] The election contest is handled by the Committee on House Administration.[23] After completing its examination of the election, the House Administration Committee reports to the full House by way of resolution with recommendation, and the full House then takes final action.[24] The House can take a variety of actions such as dismissing the challenge, declaring which candidate should be seated, refusing to seat anyone until an investigation is completed, calling for a new election, declaring the challenger unqualified to contest the election, and paying for the contestant's cost of prosecuting the contest.[25] The decision of the House is final and no court has jurisdiction to change that decision.[26]

From 1933 to 2005, the House considered 105 contested election cases; in most, the contestee prevailed.[27] The grounds for contests have varied with many of them being alleged fraud or other irregularities.[28] Given that the contestant must prove that the outcome of the election was affected by the alleged irregularities, most contests filed since adoption of the Federal Contested Elections Act of 1969 have been dismissed for failure of contestants to meet the requisite burden of proof.[29]

On the Senate side, not surprisingly, there is a different procedure for contests involving its members. To begin with, there is no statutory procedure set forth as there is with the House. Consequently, the Senate approaches each contest on a case-by-case basis and has greater flexibility in addressing each case.[30] In the Senate, the filing of a contest is not as limited as in the House. Rather, in addition to the losing candidate or a member, private citizens, public or private associations, or state governmental units may file a contest.[31] The contestant files a petition, which can take any form, and can be filed at any time as opposed to a certain period of time as set forth in the House.[32] Once filed, the contest is taken up by the Committee on Rules and Administration.[33] Between 1789 and 2002, there were 132 contested election cases in the Senate.[34] These contests fell into the following general categories: fraud, corruption, or bribery (28); serious irregularities not involving criminal actions such as failure to protest security of ballot boxes, voting by those not registered, failure to protest ballot secrecy, and the like (32); Civil War and Reconstruction issues (24); illegal appointment by governor (26); lack of qualifications (15); and other (7).[35] Of these cases, the contestant prevailed in 93.[36] The number of contested elections in the Senate began to drop off considerably following Reconstruction and have not been common since then.[37]

What happens if one wishes to contest a presidential election? There is no statutory procedure or any other procedure established for any legislative body to adjudicate the contest of a presidential election. Instead, each state is left to certify its results in presidential elections and any challenge thereto will likely find itself embroiled in both state and federal courts, as most vividly illustrated by the 2000 contest in the State of Florida between George W. Bush and Al Gore.[38]

One state that has become even more pivotal in the presidential race due to the partisanship divide in the country has recently taken action that will likely result in even greater confusion in the event of a challenge to a presidential race in that state. Due in part to the problems encountered in the 2004 presidential election, the Ohio legislature adopted amendments to its election code in 2006. One unique amendment was to codify that henceforth all contests of federal elections "shall be conducted in accordance with the applicable provisions of federal law."[39] The State of Ohio has thus banned its judiciary from having the authority to adjudicate any contest of a federal office.[40] This approach presents an intriguing dilemma: What to do in the event of the contest of a presidential election in Ohio? This dilemma becomes not too far-fetched when one considers that Ohio now serves as a swing state in modern presidential elections.[41] How would the contest of the presidential race in Ohio now proceed with the statutory requirements that all contests of federal elections be done according to federal law? There is no federal law for contesting a presidential election other than the principles set forth in *Bush v. Gore*, which supposedly, according to the Court, are to have limited precedential value.[42] Presumably this statute would result in the normal procedure being followed for House and Senate candidates since their procedures do exist in federal law. However, by taking this novel approach, the State of Ohio has now engrafted yet another layer of confusion onto what is already a somewhat chaotic process at best when it comes to contesting the results of a presidential election.

B. STATE LAW

Even though courts have steadfastly held that Congress holds exclusive jurisdiction over deciding the election fate of its own members, there is some authority providing that state courts can rule on issues challenging the conduct of election officials in enforcing (or failing to enforce) state election laws prior to certification of the results in federal elections.[43] Regardless of whether a contest originates in state courts or in the respective chamber of Congress, state law will always play a critical role in election challenges because the procedure for conducting federal elections is prescribed by statute in each respective state.

Finding consistency among 50 separate election codes can be quite a challenge because no two states' election procedures are identical. In the United States, there is a wide variety in how the election process is set up and controlled. Essentially, states have either a centralized or decentralized system of elections. In a centralized system, state election authorities control most aspects of statewide and local elections.[44] In a decentralized system, local jurisdictions maintain control over all elections with minimal involvement of state election officials.[45] There is a great deal of disparity among the 50 states as to the degree of involvement of state authorities in governing elections. As one study puts it, "Fifty states and 50 systems has been used to describe election administration in the United States, but a more accurate description would be 50 states—and hundreds of systems."[46]

III. Modern-Day Challenges to Federal Elections

Some 20 years ago, most complaints in election contests fell into basically three categories: (1) wrongful acts or omissions by election officials; (2) unlawful conduct by the winning candidate or supporters; and (3) candidate eligibility.[47] Given the allegations of misconduct occurring in the 2004 and 2006 federal election cycles, it is somewhat surprising that there is a dearth of federal election contests of recent vintage based on the more traditional categories of misconduct by election officials or candidates and supporters.[48] Rather, the most prominent challenges in federal races arising out of recent election cycles have been grounded in the emerging field of voting technology.

New technology is being implemented for the sake of election reform, but it is also ushering in a new set of issues ripe for election challenges. In 2002, Congress passed the Help America Vote Act[49] (HAVA) in an attempt to cure some of the evils exposed during the 2000 presidential race challenge in Florida. One aspect of HAVA was to mandate the use of disability accessible voting equipment, resulting in the implementation of direct recording electronic (DRE) or "touch-screen" voting devices in many jurisdictions. Use of these machines has begun to prompt election challenges in federal races (and others) grounded in theories uniquely related to their operation, maintenance, and functioning.

A. VOTING MACHINES

One of the hotly contested challenges in a federal election that continues to be fought currently centers around the use of DREs. In perhaps one of the most ironic turns of event in the 2006 midterm congressional elections, a challenge to a federal election emanated from implementation of cutting-edge technology in an open congressional seat created by the decision of the incumbent, Katherine Harris, to run for the U.S. Senate. Katherine Harris was the former Florida secretary of state who gained national prominence during the *Bush v. Gore* wrangling in 2000. As the chief elections officer for the State of Florida during the 2000 presidential election, Harris was a central figure in the *Bush v. Gore* contest as she ultimately certified a Bush victory in that state. In the wake of the *Bush v. Gore* controversy, the State of Florida implemented the use of touch-screen computer voting machines in the place of the punch-card machines that had produced the infamous "hanging chad" saga. When Harris decided to seek election to the U.S. Senate, Republican Vern Buchanan and Democrat Christine Jennings ran against each other in the general election in November 2006 for the 13th District seat.

Out of a total of 238,249 votes cast, Jennings lost by 369 votes.[50] However, what raised eyebrows was a significant undervote of 18,412 votes that occurred in one of the five counties comprising the congressional district.[51] An undervote occurs when voters vote in all other races on the ballot, but not the race in question. The undervote in Sarasota County, which was the only county that Jennings carried out of the five comprising the district, was significantly higher than in the other counties. Sarasota County alone, while accounting for approximately half of the total votes cast in the congressional race, experienced 86 percent of the district's undervote.[52] Florida law provided for automatic recounts given the closeness of the race; both a machine and a manual recount yielded a Buchanan win by 369 votes.[53]

Questioning the reason for the large undervote, Jennings filed suit in state court challenging the election and attempting to obtain the source code for the electronic voting machines to examine whether the equipment malfunctioned.[54] Jennings sought this source code for the voting machines in Sarasota County, where the bulk of the undervote occurred, asserting that experts needed to review that information in order to determine whether a voting machine malfunction resulted in the large undervote. The state and county defendants in the litigation refused to provide any information pertaining to the source code and related software on the grounds that such constituted proprietary trade secrets.[55] The trial court denied Jennings's request for the source code.[56] She appealed, and the Florida Court of Appeals upheld the trial court's ruling denying her access to the source code.[57] According to the appellate court, Jennings had failed to meet her burden of proof that review of a nonfinal discovery order was necessary in order to avoid irreparable harm.[58]

Jennings's state court challenge proceeded simultaneously with a notice of contest that she filed with the U.S. House of Representatives on December 20, 2006, pursuant to the Federal Contested Elections Act of 1969.[59] In her notice of contest filed with the House, Jennings asserted that the primary reason for the large undervote was the "pervasive malfunctioning of electronic voting machines."[60] Several studies have been conducted by various experts reaching different conclusions about whether machine malfunctioning resulted in the large undervote in the Jennings-Buchanan election. The State of Florida Elections Division conducted an audit of the election and found no evidence of malfunctioning of the voting machines.[61] Florida also hired outside experts to review the source code of the voting machines and this team found no evidence of machine malfunction.[62] These experts suggested that confusion over the ballot design probably was the cause of most of the problem.[63] Yet another study, however, refutes the suggestion that poor ballot design was the primary cause of the undervote problem. This independent study, conducted by Cornell University government professor Walter Mebane and Stanford University computer science professor David Dill, concluded that the excessive undervote in Sarasota County cannot be properly explained by an analysis of the ballot format and cannot be properly understood without further investigation.[64]

Charged with the task of conducting further investigation of the Jennings contest, the three-member Task Force of the Committee on House Administration rejected Jennings's request for a source code review by her own experts as flawed and partisan.[65] But the task force voted 2–1 to instruct the Government Accountability Office (GAO) to conduct an investigation and report back the results.[66] On August 3, 2007, the GAO reported to the task force that it had examined the source code for the electronic voting machines and found no malfunctions explaining the undervotes.[67] On October 2, 2007, however, the GAO released a statement to the task force calling for additional testing on the voting machines to try to obtain further assurance that the machines did not cause the undervote.[68] The GAO concluded that previous tests conducted by the State of Florida and Sarasota County failed to provide adequate assurance that the machines did not cause the undervote.[69] The GAO recommended "(1) a firmware verification test, (2) a ballot test, and (3) a calibration test be conducted to try to obtain further assurance that the [DREs] used in Sarasota County during the 2006 general election did not cause the undervote."[70] Meanwhile, the House provisionally seated Republican Vern Buchanan at the beginning of the 110th Congress in January 2007, and he has served in that capacity throughout the continuing contests.[71] And, on July 19, 2007, Jennings announced that she will run again for the 13th District seat.[72] By the time the GAO completes its testing of the voting machines and reports its findings, the election for the 13th District will likely be imminent. This saga will have lasted an entire congressional term and may not even be resolved by the 2008 election.

Besides demonstrating new grounds for contesting an election when electronic voting machines are used, the Jennings-Buchanan challenge also illustrates the dichotomy at play between state and federal law in federal election contests. Jennings chose both a state and federal avenue for pursuing her contest. Proceeding in state court, she asserted that she should be entitled to review the source code for the voting machines used in her election. Her contest in the House of Representatives asserted that the voting machines malfunctioned and that a review of the source code is necessary. Jennings is pursuing all avenues available in an effort to overturn the results of her election. Interestingly, almost two years later, she still awaits a final resolution by either forum.

The use of DREs in Florida during the 2004 elections spawned another legal challenge by a member of the U.S. House of Representatives—Democratic Rep. Robert Wexler. Rep. Wexler lodged a challenge to the manual recount procedures in counties using paperless touch-screen voting machines.[73] Under Florida law, two methods of voting are allowed: optical scan ballots or touch-screen voting machines.[74] At the time of Rep. Wexler's challenge, 15 of the 67 counties in Florida used the touch-screen voting machines and the remaining counties used optical scan ballots.[75] Florida law provided for a manual recount procedure in certain close elections and with optical scan ballots, there was a paper trail by which to verify votes, but with the touch-screen machines, since they were paperless, there was no paper trail available for the recount procedure.[76] As such, the manual recount procedure for optical scan ballots differs from the voting machines because of the existence of paper in one and not the other.

Rep. Wexler asserted that because touch-screen voting machines were not capable of providing for the type of manual recounts under Florida law due to the lack of any paper records, then the State of Florida had violated the equal protection and due process rights of voters in counties using touch-screen machines.[77] The United States District Court for the Southern District of Florida held that Florida's manual recount laws did not violate voters' equal protection or due process rights, and on appeal the United States Court of Appeals for the 11th Circuit affirmed the district court's opinion.[78] Framing the issue somewhat differently than the district court, the 11th Circuit held that the intermediate level of scrutiny under constitutional law analysis should be applied rather than the highest level of scrutiny.[79] Applying the intermediate level test, the 11th Circuit held that "Florida [had] important reasons for employing different manual recount procedures according to the type of voting system a county uses" and that these deficiencies were necessary due to the technological differences of the systems.[80] The court further held that the manual recount procedures established under Florida law were "justified by the State's important regulatory interests" and do not rise to the level of a constitutional violation.[81] Significantly, the U.S. Supreme Court refused to grant certiorari in the *Wexler* case and thus it stands as law of the land.[82]

The *Wexler* holding is important because it establishes that the lack of ability to verify electronic votes with paper evidence does not per se result in a constitutional violation. If the state can establish an important governmental interest for conducting its recount procedures for paperless machines in this manner, then the procedure will pass constitutional muster. Thus, a constitutional challenge to the methodology of a recount procedure will likely not be as effective as being able to demonstrate a malfunction of the machinery that affects the outcome of an election.

Florida is not alone in having faced election woes in federal elections post *Bush v. Gore* as a result of the use of electronic voting machines. Ohio was the swing state that determined the winner of the 2004 presidential race in electoral votes.[83] Following the election, there were numerous allegations of fraud and abuse, particularly focusing on Cuyahoga County, the most populous county in the state.[84] The results in Ohio were suspicious to many due to the inconsistency between the exit polls and the actual votes.[85]

Amazingly, amidst all of the allegations of voter fraud and abuse pertaining to the presidential race of 2004 in Ohio, nothing culminated in sustainable litigation effecting any changes in the use of touch-screen voting machines. What did come out of the allegations of abuse in Ohio was the first-ever independent audit of election results in the United States.[86] The Cuyahoga County Board of Elections commissioned this audit and it was conducted by numerous party representatives and other voter-group representatives along with the Center for Election Strategy at Cleveland State University.[87]

The "Top Tier Recommendations" of the audit included making independent audits a routine part of the election process and to "[r]econsider the feasibility and wisdom of supporting two major voting systems: optical scan and DRE touch screens."[88] As to the DRE machines, the audit questioned whether they could support the turnout in a presidential election, noted that election workers were not highly trained in operation of the machines, and, significantly, opined that DRE machines "present considerably greater hurdles to cost-effective and complete auditing than do paper optical scan ballots."[89] Finally, the audit recommended that independent technical professionals rather than election system vendors should perform a comprehensive evaluation of the election database to ensure no database corruption.[90]

As the Ohio audit points out, the reliability of DREs can be questionable and there certainly remain issues that need to be addressed to offer verification of actual votes cast. Unless these issues are addressed adequately by the jurisdictions that choose to use DRE devices, litigation is sure to follow.

A group of civic organizations and individuals in Ohio filed suit after the 2004 presidential election on an interesting peripheral issue involving voting machines. The group filed suit against Ohio Secretary of State Kenneth Blackwell and other elected officials and private contractors alleging that they developed and implemented procedures for placement of voting machines in a racially discriminatory manner that resulted in a shortage of machines in areas of highly concentrated African American population.[91] Plaintiffs sought an injunction requiring the county election boards to preserve all ballots (paper and electronic) from the 2004 presidential race so as to allow those ballots to be available for review as part of their racial discrimination challenge.[92] The court issued the injunction and directly ordered each election board to preserve the ballots.[93] The underlying racial discrimination claim involving the placement of voting machines was not addressed.

All of the allegations surrounding the 2004 elections in Ohio resulted in numerous amendments to the Ohio election code. These amendments affected a full range of issues in the election process, and seemed to be directed at curing many of the alleged evils that had occurred in the 2004 election. Apparently in response to the litigation filed pertaining to the alleged discriminatory placement of DRE devices, the amendments provided that, beginning in the year 2013, the secretary of state must establish a minimum number of DRE machines that a county must have, based on a formula, if that county chooses to use DRE machines.[94]

B. CANDIDATE QUALIFICATIONS

In spite of the prominent role taken by election contests of federal elections involving the use of electronic voting equipment, several modern-day challenges have centered on the more traditional basis of candidate qualifications. Two recent challenges in different congressional races that were grounded in the claim that the apparent winners lacked the requisite qualifications to serve in Congress illustrate the role that federal courts will take when confronted with the contest of candidate qualifications in a federal race. Unsuccessful candidate J. Patrick Lyons, who ran for the Sixth Congressional District of Tennessee in 2004, challenged the election of his opponent, incumbent Bart Gordon, on a theory that he was ineligible to serve as a member of Congress for multiple reasons.[95] Lyons contended that the U.S. Constitution requires an incumbent to resign his seat before seeking reelection.[96] Lyons claimed that Gordon was therefore ineligible to seek reelection because he had not resigned beforehand.[97] Also, Lyons argued that as an inactive member of the State Bar of Tennessee, Gordon was a "judicial officer" who could not simultaneously serve in the Congress.[98] Lyons asserted that Gordon's service as a member of the U.S. House would therefore violate the U.S. Constitution and constitute insurrection or rebellion against the United States, rendering him constitutionally barred from serving in Congress.[99]

Lyons filed a notice of contest in the House, which dismissed the contest.[100] Thereafter Lyons filed suit in federal court seeking relief. The district court dismissed Lyons's suit, holding that the House had exclusive jurisdiction over contested elections involving its members.[101] The court also noted that the decision by the House in an election contest is not judicially reviewable.[102]

Patti Cox challenged incumbent James Otis "Jim" McCrery of the Fourth Congressional District in Louisiana and she lost. Cox filed two suits following the election, one in federal court and the other in state court. Both suits were identical in the nature of the claim: Cox asserted that McCrery sold his residence in Shreveport before the election and thus was not an inhabitant of Louisiana at the time of his election and therefore did not meet the qualifications set forth in the U.S. Constitution to serve as a member of Congress.[103]

The court first addressed a motion to remand the action, which was originally filed in state court and removed to the district court. In denying the motion to remand, the court held that the issue of qualifications for membership in the U.S. Congress was a matter of interpretation and application of the Qualifications Clause of the U.S. Constitution and thus properly a federal question sufficient to invoke federal jurisdiction.[104]

Moving to the merits of Cox's claim, the court held that Congress has the exclusive authority to judge the qualifications of its own members.[105] The court recognized that Congress, in exercising this authority, had adopted the Federal Contested Elections Act of 1969, a specific statutory procedure for contestants to follow in challenging the election of any House member.[106] Holding that the House of Representatives held exclusive jurisdiction to decide the claims raised by Cox, the district court dismissed her suit without prejudice.[107]

As these two recent cases illustrate, contestants of federal elections challenging the qualifications of a candidate will encounter an exercise in futility by seeking relief in federal courts. Simply put, federal courts will not entertain election contests involving the qualifications of members of Congress. The ultimate battleground for these contests will be Congress.

IV. Reform Proposals

As new grounds emerge that form the basis for challenging federal elections, reform measures appear on the horizon. Lawmakers and various professional associations and groups continue to weigh in with possible solutions. Currently, potential reform is embodied in pending federal legislation as well as in recommended practices adopted by several advisory bodies.

A. LEGISLATION

Rep. Rush Holt (D-NJ) has reintroduced legislation in the 110th Congress to address a variety of election activities, most prominent among those being the requirement that voting machines be used that have a verifiable paper trail.[108] The Holt bill, H.B. 811, designated as the Voter Confidence and Increased Accessibility Act of 2007, is in large part a response to the prominent Jennings-Buchanan disputed race in Florida's 13th Congressional District.[109] The bill would also allow more access to source code information, which is the specific relief sought by Christine Jennings in her state court action in Florida.[110] The measure has at least 179 cosponsors in the House and, with a current Democratic majority, appears poised for adoption.[111] In the Senate, Senator Dianne Feinstein (D-Calif.) has called for an investigation by the Government Accountability Office of the voting machines used in Sarasota County during the Jennings-Buchanan election in 2006 as well as elections in 2004.[112]

B. ADVISORY GROUPS

The Help America Vote Act of 2002 established the United States Election Assistance Commission (EAC) to assist the nation's election officials with the implementing best practices designed to enhance the integrity of elections.[113] The EAC has developed, among other things, a comprehensive "Best Practices Tool Kit" designed to cover election practices for election administration officials.[114] The EAC has even received input from the National Institute of Standards and Technology, an agency that usually deals with a panoply of devices and items having nothing to do with elections, concluding that electronic voting without paper records is unacceptable.[115] In spite of this conclusion, the technical guidelines committee of the EAC refused to adopt a resolution recommending use of electronic voting only if there is independent verification of the results.[116] The EAC technical guidelines committee supported the necessity for paper verification in the future, but refused to recommend that requirement for existing machines.[117]

Election issues became such a national concern following the 2000 presidential election that a prominent study commission was established with former President Jimmy Carter and former Secretary of State James Baker serving as cochairs. The Commission on Federal Election Reform, also known as the Carter-Baker Commission, conducted a study of elections in the United States and developed a comprehensive set of recommendations that, if followed, would undoubtedly enhance confidence in elections in this country. One theme woven throughout the commission's recommendations was that of uniformity among the states. The commission recommended measures that would promote uniformity of voter registration, interoperability among states, verification and counting of provisional ballots, and voter identification.[118] The commission made several practical and specific recommendations that would address several of the issues forming the basis for election contests in federal races based on electronic voting machine malfunctioning. Regarding the issue of verifying the vote count of electronic voting machines, the commission recommended that Congress pass a law requiring that all voting machines be equipped with a voter-verifiable paper audit trail.[119] A copy of source codes should be put in escrow for future review by qualified experts if necessary.[120] Both of these recommendations would likely have prevented or certainly lessened the rancor in the Jennings-Buchanan contest in Florida.

V. Conclusion

New voting technology has resulted in election contests in federal races based on novel grounds. This trend will likely continue until either courts or legislators act to provide definitive guidance. A positive consequence of this activity has been a renewed focus and emphasis on what can be done to enhance public confidence in elections and to avoid contests. While federal elections in America will never be foolproof due to the element of human involvement, hopefully reform measures currently being debated around the county will bolster the ability of election officials to ensure fair elections at the federal level as well as other levels.

Notes

1.   American history is replete with instances of ballot fraud, voter intimidation, voter suppression, and a variety of other practices calling significant elections into question dating back to colonial days. For an excellent chronicle of the history of election fraud in America

since the early days of the Republic, *see* Tracy Campbell, Deliver the Vote: A History of Election Fraud, an American Tradition—1742-2004 (2005). This chapter will explore modern-day election challenges involving candidates for federal offices and will not address the law of recounts except to the extent that such laws may be one aspect of a particular challenge.

2. U.S. Const. art. I, § 2.

3. U.S. Const. art. I, § 3.

4. U.S. Const. art. I, § 2.

5. U.S. Const. art. I, § 3.

6. U.S. Const. art. II, § 1, amend. XII.

7. U.S. Const. art. I, § 4.

8. U.S. Const. art. I, § 5.

9. R.T. Kimbrough, Annotation, *Jurisdiction of Courts to Determine Election or Qualifications of Member of Legislative Body, and Conclusiveness of Its Decision, as Affected by Constitutional or Statutory Provision Making Legislative Body the Judge of Election and Qualification of Its Own Members*, 107 A.L.R. 205 (1937).

10. *See* Dornan v. Sanchez, 978 F. Supp. 1315, 1319 (C.D. Cal. 1997).

11. *Id.* at 1320.

12. 2 U.S.C.A. §§ 381 et seq. (2007).

13. 2 U.S.C.A. § 382 (2007).

14. *Dornan*, 978 F. Supp. at 1319.

15. 2 U.S.C.A. § 382 (2007).

16. 2 U.S.C.A. § 383 (2007).

17. 2 U.S.C.A. § 385 (2007).

18. 2 U.S.C.A. §§ 386–391 (2007).

19. 2 U.S.C.A. § 392 (2007).

20. 2 U.S.C.A. § 396 (2007).

21. *Dornan*, 978 F. Supp. at 1322.

22. *See* H.R. Doc. No. 108-241 (2005) (109th Congress House Rules Manual); H.R. Res. 6, 110th Cong. (2006) (enacted).

23. C-SPAN'S Capitol Questions, *What Is the House Procedure for Resolving Contested Elections . . .*, C-SPAN.org (May 3, 2000), www.c-span.org/questions/weekly93.asp.

24. *Id.*

25. *Id.*

26. *See* Dornan v. Sanchez, 955 F. Supp. 1210, 1212 (C.D. Cal. 1997).

27. L. Paige Whitaker, House Contested Election Cases: 1933 to 2005, at 1–44 (CRS Report for Congress, Oct. 26, 2006).

28. *Id.* at 1.

29. *Id.*

30. *See* Jeffery A. Jenkins, *Partisanship and Contested Election Cases in the Senate, 1789-2002*, 19 Stud. Am. Pol. Dev. 53-74 (Spring 2005).

31. *Id.* at 54.

32. *Id.*

33. *Id.* at 55.

34. *Id.*

35. *Id.* at 58–59.

36. *Id.* at 59.

37. As an interesting aside, Jeffery A. Jenkins has analyzed the extent to which political partisanship has influenced election contests in the Senate. He concludes that while election contests were a part of a party-building strategy for the House in the late 19th century, no such evidence exists of a similar strategy in the Senate at least as a primary means of party development. *See* Jenkins, *supra* note 30, at 66–74.

38. *See generally* Bush v. Gore, 531 U.S. 98 (2000).

39. Ohio Rev. Code Ann. § 3518.08(A) (West 2007).

40. *See generally* Edward B. Foley, *The Analysis and Mitigation of Electoral Errors: Theory, Practice, Policy,* 18 Stan. L. & Pol'y Rev. 350, 368 (2007).

41. *See* Editorial, *In Search of Accurate Vote Totals,* N.Y. Times, Sept. 5, 2006, at http://www.nytimes.com/2006/09/05opinion/05tue1.html?scp=1&sq=ln+search+of+accurate+vote+totals.

42. *See* Bush v. Gore, 531 U.S. at 109.

43. *See* Kimbrough, *supra* note 9.

44. Electionline.org., Election Reform Briefing, Working Together? State and Local Election Coordination 1 (Sept. 2002), http://www.electionline.org/Portals/1/Publications/Working%20Together.pdf.

45. *Id.* at 2.

46. *Id.* at 3.

47. *Developments in the Law, Elections, Post-Election Remedies,* 88 Harv. L. Rev. 1298, 1312–14 (1975).

48. Both the 2004 and 2006 federal elections were rife with allegations of misconduct across the country. In the 2006 Maryland Senate race between Democrat Benjamin Cardin and Republican Michael Steele, paid workers were bused in from Pennsylvania on Election Day and passed out allegedly misleading fliers in and around Baltimore. *See* Matthew Mosk and Avio Thomas-Lester, *GOP Fliers Apparently Were Part of Strategy,* Wash. Post, Nov. 13, 2006, at B1. In Mississippi, a federal district court concluded that tactics employed by an African American chair of a county Democratic executive committee discriminated against white voters during the 2004 elections. *See* United States v. Brown, 494 F. Supp. 2d 440, 449, (S.D. Miss. 2007). And, in Ohio, there were allegations that the Republican Secretary of State, Kenneth Blackwell, employed numerous tactics and made judgment calls in the 2004 presidential race resulting in the disenfranchisement of many Democratic voters. *See generally* Kennedy, *infra* note 85. Democrats also claimed intimidation tactics by Republican operatives participating in a "strike force" team sent from Texas to make intimidating calls to likely voters. *Id.* None of these instances resulted in any contest of a federal election.

49. Help America Vote Act of 2002, Pub. L. No. 107-252 (2002), 42 U.S.C. §§ 15301 et seq.

50. Walter R. Mebane Jr. & David L. Dill, *Factors Associated with the Excessive CD-13 Undervote in the 2006 General Election in Sarasota County, Florida* 2 National Science Foundation, Grant No. CNS-0524155 (Jan. 23, 2007).

51. Notice of Contest Regarding the Election for Representative in the One Hundred Tenth Congress from Florida's Thirteenth Congressional District, In the United States House of Representatives, *Christine Jennings v. Vern Buchanan,* 7 (Dec. 20, 2006).

52. *Id.* The Notice of Contest filed by Jennings in the U.S. House of Representatives outlines in statistical detail the disproportionate undervote in Sarasota County at 6–12.

53. *Id.* at 5–6; Mebane & Dill, *supra* note 50, at 2.

54. *See* Jennings v. Elections Canvassing Comm'n of Fla., 2006 WL 4404531 (Fla. Cir. Ct. 2006).

55. *See* Notice of Contest, *supra* note 51, at 26.

56. *See Jennings, supra* note 54.

57. Jennings v. Elections Canvassing Comm'n of Fla., 958 So. 2d 1083, 1084 (Fla. Dist. Ct. App. 2007).

58. *Id.*

59. *See* Notice of Contest, *supra* note 51, at 1.

60. *Id.* at 2.

61. Editorial, *Deplorable Delay in District 13*, HERALD TRIB. (Sarasota, Fla.), June 30, 2007, *available at* http://www.heraldtribune.com/article/20070622/OPINION/706220394/1030.

62. *Id.*

63. Christopher Drew, *Panel Cites Voter Error, Not Software, in Loss of Votes*, N.Y. TIMES, Feb. 24, 2007, at http://www.nytimes.com/2007/02/24/us/politics/24voting.html?ref=us.

64. *See* Mebane & Dill, *supra* note 50, at 1–2.

65. Press Release, Committee on House Administration, Task Force Denies Jennings' Proposed Review of Source Code (May 2, 2007), *available at* http://gop.cha.house.gov/mediapages/PRArticle.aspx?NewsID=1464.

66. *Id.*

67. Press Release, Committee on House Administration, GAO Looks for Answers in Florida's 13th District (Aug. 3, 2007), *available at* http://gop.cha.house.gov/mediapages/PRArticle.aspx?NewsID=1490.

68. Statement of Nabajyoti Barkakati, Senior-Level Technologist: Applied Research and Methods, before the Task Force on Florida-13, Committee on House Administration, House of Representatives, *Further Testing Could Provide Increased but Not Absolute Assurance That Voting Systems Did Not Cause Undervotes in Florida's 13th Congressional District*, 110th Cong. (Oct. 2, 2007), *available at* http://www.gao.gov/news.items/d0897t.pdf.

69. *Id.* at 3.

70. *Id.*

71. Rachel Kapochunas, *Sarasota Officials Freeze Election Data, as Jennings Battle Wages On*, N.Y. TIMES, Feb. 2, 2007, at http://www.nytimes.com/cq/2007/02/02/cq_2229 .html?pagewanted=print.

72. Jeremy Wallace, *Jennings to Run for Congress Again*, HERALD TRIB. (Sarasota, Fla.), July 20, 2007, *available at* http://www.heraldtribune.com/article/20070720/NEWS/707200305.

73. Wexler v. Anderson., 452 F.3d 1226 (11th Cir. 2006).

74. *Id.* at 1228.

75. *Id.*

76. *Id.*

77. *Id.* at 1231.

78. *Id.* at 1234.

79. The 11th Circuit framed the issue as "whether Florida's manual recount procedures, which vary by county according to voting system, accord arbitrary and disparate treatment

to Florida voters, thereby depriving voters of their constitutional rights to due process and equal protection." *Id.* at 1231.

80. *Id.* at 1233.

81. *Id.*

82. Wexler v. Anderson, 549 U.S. ___, 127 S. Ct. 934, 166 L. Ed. 2d 703 (No. 06-401) (Jan. 8, 2007).

83. *See* Editorial, *In Search of Accurate Vote Totals, supra* note 41.

84. *Id.*

85. Robert F. Kennedy, Jr., *Was the 2004 Election Stolen?*, Rollingstone.com, June 1, 2006, www.rollingstone.com/news/story/10432334/was_the_2004_election_stolen; Ron Baiman & Kathy Dopp, Nat'l Election Data Archive, The Gun is Smoking: 2004 Ohio Precinct-Level Exit Poll Data Show Virtually Irrefutable Evidence of Vote Miscount (Jan. 23, 2006), http://electionarchive.org/ucvAnalysis/OH/Ohio-Exit-Polls-2004.pdf.

86. Kathy Dopp, Nat'l Election Data Archive, First U.S. Scientific Election Audit Reveals Voting System Flaws but Questions Remain Unanswered (May 7, 2007), http://electionarchive.org/ucvAnalysis/OH/CuyahogaElectionAudit.pdf.

87. Cuyahoga County Collaborative Audit Comm. & Cleveland State Univ. Center for Election Integrity, Collaborative Public Audit of the November 2006 General Election (Apr. 18, 2007), http://urban.csuohio.edu/cei/public_monitor/cuyahoga_2006_audit_rpt.pdf.

88. *Id.* at 5-6.

89. *Id.* at 6.

90. *Id.*

91. King Lincoln Bronzeville N'hood Ass'n v. Blackwell, 448 F. Supp. 2d 876, 877 (S.D. Ohio 2006).

92. *Id.*

93. *Id.* at 880.

94. Ohio Rev. Code Ann. § 3506.22(A)(B) (West 2007).

95. Lyons v. Gordon, No. Civ. A. 05-00870RMC, 2006 WL 241230 (D.D.C. Feb. 1, 2006).

96. *Id.* at 1.

97. *Id.*

98. *Id.*

99. *Id.*

100. *Id.* In addition to filing a notice of contest in the 109th Congress, Lyons had previously filed an almost identical contest in the 108th Congress, which was dismissed as well. *See* Whitaker, *supra* note 27, at 43–44.

101. *Lyons*, 2006 WL 241230, at *3.

102. *Id.*

103. Cox v. McCrery, No. Civ. A. 06-2191, 2007 WL 97142 (W.D. La. Jan. 5, 2007).

104. *Id.* at 2.

105. *Id.*

106. *Id.* at 3.

107. *Id.*

108. Mark Wegner, *Measure Introduced to Require Paper Trail in 2008 Voting I,* Cong. Daily (Feb. 7, 2007), *available at* 2007 WLNR 2373514.

109. Kat Zambon, *Holt Bill Clears Committee as Republican Amendments Shot Down,* Electionline.org. May 10, 2007, *available at* http://electionline.org/Newsletters/tabid/87/ ctl/Detail/mid/643/xmid/251/xmtid/3/Default.aspx. One of the cosponsors of H.B. 811 is Rep. Robert Wexler (D-Fla.), who also has been an active litigant challenging Florida law pertaining to recount procedures for voting machines; *see Wexler,* 452 F.3d 1226. Also, Rep. Holt raised a parliamentary inquiry about the legality of the election of Republican Vern Buchanan to the 13th Congressional District seat in Florida at the beginning of the 110th Congress; *see* Kapochunas, *supra* note 71.

110. Jeremy Wallace, *House Committee Unlikely to Rush District 13 Voting Inquiry,* Herald Trib. (Sarasota, Fla.), Jan. 6, 2007, *available at* http://www.heraldtribune.com/apps/pbcs .dll/article?AID=/20070106/NEWS/701060410.

111. Sean Greene, *Rep. Rush Holt Reintroduces Updated Paper Trail, Audit Bill,* Election-line.org, Feb. 8, 2007, *available at* http://www.electionline.org/Newsletters/tabid/87/ctl/ Detail/mid/643/xmid/3/Default.asp.

112. Lesley Clark, *Top Senator Calls for Electronic-Voting Probe,* Bradenton Herald (Bradenton, Fla.), Feb. 15, 2007, *available at* http://www.bradenton.com/election_2006/ story/12389.html.

113. *See* U.S. Election Assistance Comm'n, Best Practices in Administration, Management and Security in Voting Systems and Provisional Voting: A Tool Kit for Election Administrators and Stakeholders: Issue One, http://www.eac.gov/election/practices/bpea/ bp-welcome?portal_status_message=changes+saved.

114. *Id.*

115. Editorial, *The Road to Reliable Elections,* N.Y. Times, Dec. 11, 2006, *available at* http:// www.nytimes.com/2006/12/11/opinion/11mon1.html?ex=1323493200&en=b903020b16fl b57b&ei=50908&partner=rssuserland&eme=rss.

116. *Id.*

117. *Id.*

118. Comm'n on Federal Election Reform, Report, Building Confidence in U.S. Elections 79–87 (Sept. 19, 2005), http://www.american.edu/ia/cfer/report/full_report.pdf.

119. *Id.* at 81.

120. *Id.* at 82.

CHAPTER SIXTEEN

BAILOUT UNDER THE VOTING RIGHTS ACT

J. GERALD HEBERT*

I. Introduction

Following years of struggle for voting rights, culminating in the violent response to marchers in Selma by law enforcement officers on the Edmund Pettis Bridge, Congress—led by the encouragement of President Lyndon Johnson—passed the Voting Rights Act (VRA).[1] Now, four decades later, the VRA is regarded as the most successful piece of civil rights legislation ever enacted. Most recently, the special provisions of the act were renewed as the Fannie Lou Hamer, Rosa Parks, and Coretta Scott King Voting Rights Act Reauthorization and Amendments Act of 2006. The VRA generally seeks to accomplish two things: providing minority ballot *access,* and ensuring once access is granted that minority votes aren't *diluted* through various election schemes.[2]

The VRA is composed of both permanent provisions and temporary, renewable provisions. Several of the temporary provisions apply only to jurisdictions "covered" as a result of a specific formula.[3] One of these provisions, controversial from the time of enactment, requires covered jurisdictions to preapprove all voting-related changes through either a declaratory judgment from the District Court for the District of Columbia or approval from the Attorney General.[4] This process, contained in Section Five of the original act, is commonly known as preclearance.[5] Congress provided a way for covered jurisdictions to exempt themselves, or "bail out,"[6] from coverage (and therefore the preclearance requirements) by obtaining a declaratory judgment from the District Court for the District of Columbia.[7] This chapter examines the history, benefits, intent, operational procedure, and effect of the bailout

---

* J.D. Suffolk University School of Law; Solo practitioner in Alexandria, Virginia; Executive Director and Director of Litigation for the Campaign Legal Center, Washington, D.C.

option. Additionally, while a relatively small number of jurisdictions have bailed out in recent years, the vast majority of covered jurisdictions have not done so. This chapter also examines why more jurisdictions have not bailed out.

II. History of Bailout and the Current Bailout Provisions

The Voting Rights Act, including the initial bailout provision, was signed into law in 1965. The initial bailout provision did not allow a political subdivision to bail out independently if covered only because it was in a state that was entirely covered.[8] Shortly after the VRA was enacted, a lawsuit challenged the act's constitutionality. In *South Carolina v. Katzenbach*, the Supreme Court upheld the VRA—including the coverage formula and bailout provisions—as appropriate exercises of congressional authority under Section 2 of the 15th Amendment.[9] Specifically addressing the bailout provision, the Court found that though a determination that a jurisdiction would be subject to the act's special provisions (through application of the coverage formula) is not reviewable by a court,[10] "[i]n the event that the formula is improperly applied, the area affected can always go into court and obtain termination of coverage under §4(b), provided of course that it has not been guilty of voting discrimination in recent years. This procedure serves as a partial substitute for direct judicial review."[11] As Justice Powell would note a decade and a half later, the bailout option helped to alleviate any cause for concern that the VRA unconstitutionally exceeded Congress's authority.[12]

The temporary provisions of the VRA were renewed in 1970, 1975, 1982, and 2006.[13] Although the 1970 and 1975 amendments did not make any substantive changes to the bailout provisions, the 1982 renewal did amend the bailout requirements. The amended requirements enabled political subdivisions in wholly covered states to bail out independently.[14] Additionally, the bailout requirements "were changed to recognize and reward good conduct rather than making jurisdictions await a fixed expiration date without consideration of their record."[15] These updated requirements, along with bailout for political subdivisions, remain in effect today.[16] Under these requirements, jurisdictions seeking bailout must show that, *in the previous ten years:*

1. No test or device has been used to determine voter eligibility with the purpose or effect of discrimination;[17]
2. No final judgments, consent decrees, settlements, or agreements have been entered against the jurisdiction as a result of racially discriminatory voting practices, and there are no pending lawsuits alleging such practices;
3. No federal examiners or observers have been sent to the jurisdiction;
4. The jurisdiction has complied with the preclearance provision, has not implemented a change without preclearance, and has repealed all preclear-

ance changes objected to by the Attorney General or District Court for the District of Columbia; and

5. There have been no objections by the Attorney General or District Court for the District of Columbia to changes submitted for preclearance, and there are no pending preclearance requests.[18]

In addition the jurisdiction must show *at the time it seeks bailout* that it has

1. Eliminated any inhibitive or dilutive voting or election procedures;
2. Made constructive efforts to eliminate intimidation or harassment of minority voters; and
3. Made constructive efforts to increase minority voter participation, such as expanding convenience of registration and voting, along with appointment of minority election officials throughout all stages of the registration and election processes.[19]

States or political subdivisions seeking bailout must also demonstrate that all governmental units that exist within the subdivision's territory meet all of the bailout qualifications.[20]

Since the 1982 amendments took effect,[21] 14 jurisdictions have bailed out.[22] All of these bailouts are jurisdictions in Virginia. Bailouts are pending for two additional jurisdictions, Amherst and Page Counties in Virginia. The jurisdictions that have bailed out thus far were not only able to establish compliance with the VRA dating back at least ten years, but also were able to show that the current electoral process was equally open to all citizens in its borders. Indeed, voting changes made by these jurisdictions over the years (and precleared by the Department of Justice (DOJ)) were at least neutral in racial effect, and many of the precleared voting changes actually improved minority voting opportunities.

Demographically, most jurisdictions that have bailed out thus far have had a relatively small percentage of minority population: eight jurisdictions had a minority population of less than 5 percent; four jurisdictions had a minority population of between 5 and 10 percent; and two jurisdictions, Middlesex County and Essex County, had a minority population percentage of 20 percent and 39 percent, respectively, at the time of bailout.

III. Process of Obtaining a Bailout

In handling bailouts for covered jurisdictions, I have divided the process of seeking a bailout into three phases. In the first phase, I gather relevant information on the jurisdiction. In the second phase, I take the gathered information and present it to the Department of Justice for independent review of bailout eligibility. If DOJ independently concludes that bailout is appropriate, it will consent to the bailout. In the final phase, assuming the jurisdiction has been found bailout-eligible by DOJ, I prepare the necessary legal papers and file them in the D.C. Court seeking entry of a declaratory judgment from a three-judge panel. The VRA also requires special publication of notice of bailout actions. Each phase is described in some detail below.

A. PHASE I: GATHERING INFORMATION

Once a jurisdiction decides to explore bailout, it should begin the process of gathering information needed to determine if the jurisdiction actually meets the bailout criteria set forth in the VRA. According to the VRA, "[t]o assist the court in determining whether to issue a declaratory judgment under this subsection, the plaintiff shall present evidence of minority participation, including evidence of the levels of minority group registration and voting, changes in such levels over time, and disparities between minority-group and non-minority-group participation."[23] For the most part, the threshold criteria for establishing a bailout are present in nearly all covered jurisdictions: the absence of a test or device as a prerequisite to vote or voting; no federal examiners have been assigned to the jurisdiction; and the absence of a court finding that the jurisdiction has denied the right to vote on account of race, color, or membership in a language-minority group, and so on. These assessments are easily made.

What is left, then, is the need to gather information that tends to show that all citizens of the jurisdiction enjoy an equal opportunity to participate effectively in the political process. Among other things, the jurisdiction should gather census data; the method of election of candidates for the jurisdiction and all elective bodies within it (e.g., at-large or from districts); the racial composition, location, and convenience of registration and polling places; and so on. Other relevant data that shed light on the level of "minority participation" include the number of minority candidates in past elections, how these candidates fared in the election, and the number of minority-group members who have worked in the voter registration office or who served as poll officials on Election Day.

In essence, the jurisdiction should gather those data relevant to the bailout criteria set forth in the statute so as to assess bailout eligibility.[24] If the jurisdiction determines that it is eligible for bailout, then the assembled data and information can be submitted to the Attorney General so that DOJ can assess independently whether the jurisdiction meets the statutory requirements for bailout.

B. PHASE II: SUBMISSION OF DATA TO AND GAINING CONSENT OF DOJ

The purpose of Phase II is to submit the data from Phase I to the Department of Justice for independent review and to secure DOJ's consent to bailout. Technically, the VRA allows jurisdictions to file for bailout with the District Court for the District of Columbia without first obtaining consent from DOJ. However, while there is no requirement to obtain consent from DOJ, the best course of action is to first seek the Attorney General's consent to bailout before petitioning the court. If a bailout lawsuit is filed before consulting with DOJ, and DOJ raises objections, the two choices available at that point for the jurisdiction are not good: either take on DOJ in contested litigation (costly and what is perhaps a losing cause), or withdraw the suit while the jurisdiction attempts to work out its differences with DOJ. For the same reason, if a jurisdiction determines that the data gathered during Phase I do not support bailout, the jurisdiction should not move forward at that time with the bailout process. Rather than risk costly litigation, the jurisdiction should instead develop a plan for bringing itself into compliance with the VRA.

The bailout provision of the VRA provides that "[n]othing in this section shall prohibit the Attorney General from consenting to an entry of judgment if based upon a showing of objective and compelling evidence by the plaintiff, and upon investigation, he is satisfied that the State or political subdivision has complied with the requirements . . . [for bailout]."[25] DOJ conducts an independent investigation to verify and establish bailout eligibility as required by law.[26] If DOJ confirms that the jurisdiction is eligible for bailout, it notifies the jurisdiction that it will consent to the bailout. If DOJ were to identify problems that preclude bailout eligibility, it presumably would bring these problems to the attention of the jurisdiction and insist on corrective action.[27]

As a part of obtaining bailout, the VRA requires a jurisdiction to publicize notice of bailout proceedings. The statute states, "[t]he State or political subdivision bringing such action shall publicize the intended commencement *and* any proposed settlement of such action in the media serving such State or political subdivision and in appropriate United States post offices."[28] Notice is required so that interested parties are aware of the bailout and can intervene if they desire.[29]

The notice requirement can be handled in two different ways. First, the jurisdiction can publish notice immediately prior to filing papers with the court in the manner required by the VRA. Presumably, this notice would come after obtaining DOJ's consent to bailout, as the statute also mandates that notice of any "proposed settlement" be publicized as well. This type of notice comes late in the bailout process and gives the minority community inadequate time to consider the full ramifications of the bailout issue. Of course, the minority community will likely have been contacted by DOJ as part of its independent review, and learning about the bailout process in such a manner may fuel suspicions in the minority community that the jurisdiction is trying to "pull a fast one," or worse.

Alternatively, the jurisdiction could first give notice of the intent to seek a bailout, and later give notice after obtaining DOJ's consent to bailout. Most of the jurisdictions that have bailed out thus far have used this second, two-step method of giving notice. When approached this way, the first notice is given early in the process—either after the jurisdiction has completed its own investigation and decided to move forward with bailout or after the jurisdiction has submitted its data to DOJ and DOJ is undertaking its own independent review.

While the VRA doesn't require it, my experience is that the best approach is to give notice early and hold a public hearing on bailout. The hearing should be advertised in the local media and post offices. Holding a public hearing not only provides the public with notice that the jurisdiction intends to seek a bailout, it also gives the jurisdiction an opportunity to explain the bailout process and its implications for minority voters. Misinformation, such as a belief that a bailout will take away minority voting rights, can easily be corrected in a question-and-answer public hearing. The hearing also gives the minority community an opportunity to give feedback to local officials, including election officials, about how they perceive the electoral process and bailout. Thus far, one thing has been clear: Minority voters are, as they should be, deeply concerned about their right to vote. These voters need assurance that a bailout will not diminish their voting rights. If this assurance is not forthcoming and fully understood, the jurisdiction should not expect minority voters to support bailout. Ways to assure minority voters of continued protection of voting rights are addressed later in this chapter.

Though most of the legal documents necessary for a bailout are given to the court in Phase III, the jurisdiction gives two documents to DOJ during Phase II—a stipulation of facts and a consent to bail out. After DOJ consents to bailout and signs these two documents, the jurisdiction gives its second notice, again following the procedures required in the VRA. This notice must be given before filing documents with the court.

C. PHASE III: OBTAINING DECLARATORY JUDGMENT

Upon notification by the Department of Justice that it will consent to the bailout, counsel for the jurisdiction should prepare all of the legal documents necessary to complete bailout in the District Court for the District of Columbia. In addition to the complaint, it will be necessary to prepare a request for three-judge court and a motion to approve the bailout judgment. The documents from the bailouts to date, available on PACER, provide good prototypes for these filings.[30]

The time necessary to complete a bailout from start to finish varies from jurisdiction to jurisdiction. Phase I can typically be completed in one to two months. Phase II takes anywhere from two months to one year. Phase III is usually completed within one to six months.

IV. Impact of Bailout

Bailout affects both the jurisdiction and the voters therein. First, because preclearance is no longer required for a bailed-out jurisdiction, the burden of proof of whether or not a voting change is discriminatory is shifted from the formerly covered jurisdiction to voters. As noted earlier, Congress passed the VRA (and preclearance provision) in response to repeated and continued threats to minority voters' rights. The Supreme Court stated, "Congress had found that case-by-case litigation was inadequate to combat widespread and persistent discrimination in voting."[31] By requiring preclearance, Congress placed the burden of proving discrimination on *jurisdictions* covered by the coverage formula rather than on *voters*. This burden shift was described by the Senate Judiciary Committee's 1982 Report on the Voting Rights Act Extension: "The effectiveness of section 5 rests in part on the fact that a submitting jurisdiction bears the burden of showing that a proposed modification is not discriminatory in purpose or effect."[32] After a bailout the jurisdiction is like all uncovered jurisdictions, putting on voters the burden of proving a voting change is discriminatory.

However, the VRA contains a fallback provision for bailed-out jurisdictions. Under this provision, if within ten years the previously covered jurisdiction is found to have executed a change that would not have received preclearance when covered, then declaratory judgment providing for bailout is vacated and the jurisdiction comes back under coverage.[33] This helps ensure that a previously covered jurisdiction remains true to the purposes of the VRA.

Regardless of bailout status, all permanent provisions of the VRA—including the Section 2 ban on discriminatory voting practices and procedures—remain intact after bailout.[34] Only the special provisions for jurisdictions under coverage are affected by bailout.

V. Why Haven't Other Jurisdictions Bailed Out?

Although there are hundreds of covered jurisdictions subject to the special provisions of the VRA and thus theoretically eligible for bailout, to date only 14 have bailed out.[35] As explained below, bailouts are cost-effective and the bailout process is not burdensome. So if the financial benefit of a bailout outweighs the costs of continued preclearance, why haven't more jurisdictions bailed out? A number of factors likely explain why relatively few jurisdictions have sought a bailout thus far. This section examines these factors and proposes possible solutions.

1. *Lack of Knowledge.* As I speak to local election officials at various conferences, I have found that many local officials are unaware of the bailout option.[36] Those who are aware of bailout lack basic knowledge of the process. The lack of knowledge about bailout can be reduced if governmental authorities (e.g., state secretaries of state, state boards of elections, local government associations, and the Department of Justice) disseminate more information to local election officials. There is no reason why, for example, the Department of Justice cannot advise covered jurisdictions of the availability of bailout. To the extent such information would produce more bailout efforts, such a move would have two salutary effects: (1) it would result in a complete review of a covered jurisdiction's electoral process (and all political subdivisions or governmental units therein), and (2) to the extent there were problems which precluded bailout, they would be identified and corrected.

2. *Cost and Administrative Burden.* Local officials may mistakenly believe that bailing out is not cost-effective or is administratively difficult. While obtaining a bailout does involve some cost, the cost is modest. Moreover, there are also costs associated with preclearance submissions continuing indefinitely. The cost of bailing out will vary depending on a number of factors, such as the size of the jurisdiction and the number of local governmental units. If local election officials are willing to gather the data for Phase I rather than having legal counsel do so, the overall cost of the bailout can be reduced. In fact, when the jurisdiction gathers the data, the legal fees for the entire process of obtaining a bailout are less than $5,000. Most covered jurisdictions can afford such costs, which when measured against continued preclearance will be relatively low. For example, assume that each time a jurisdiction seeks preclearance of a voting change, the cost to the jurisdiction of doing so is $500.[37] (This figure is admittedly low but will still serve to illustrate the cost-effectiveness of bailout.) A covered jurisdiction incurs the cost of bailing out by making only ten preclearance submissions. Since the preclearance requirements were recently renewed for 25 more years, the aggregate cost of preclearance submissions for a jurisdiction may make bailing out cost-effective.[38]

Regarding administrative burdens, local election officials have not found the bailout process to be administratively difficult. As discussed previously, a jurisdiction seeking bailout must simply gather data to be provided to DOJ and provide notice to the community of its decision to bail out.

3. *Minority Concerns.* Understandably, minority voters are concerned about the effect a bailout will have on their voting rights. Recently, for example, black citizens in Clarke County, Virginia, expressed opposition to a bailout there.[39] The opposition was based on the misconception that a bailout would mean that the Voting Rights Act no longer would apply, leaving minority voting rights unprotected. "We're going right back to where we were before we got these rights," one concerned minority voter in Clarke County stated.[40] Considering the critical role the VRA played in extending voting rights to minorities, combined with hearing that the jurisdiction is going to "bail out" from parts of the VRA, such a concern—though incorrect—is understandable. To resolve this concern, local officials and the jurisdiction's legal counsel should explain that bailout will not result in a diminution of voting rights and that VRA provisions prohibiting discrimination remain permanent and in effect. The jurisdiction should also explain that should any discriminatory action be taken in the future against minority voters, the bailout suit can be reactivated and the jurisdiction can once again be subject to the act's special provisions.[41]

In addition to concerns about loss of voting rights, minority voters question the need for a jurisdiction's decision to seek a bailout. "If it ain't broke," one Clarke County voter stated, referring to the status quo under preclearance, "don't fix it."[42] Here local election officials should explain how a bailout will enable local officials to make routine voting changes more expeditiously and how such changes can be of specific benefit to the minority community. For example, in Frederick County a black preacher contacted the county wanting to hold a voter registration drive at a church picnic. Because the jurisdiction was still under preclearance requirements, the County's Registrar was unable to accommodate the preacher's request because there was insufficient time to obtain preclearance, which takes up to 60 days.[43] A bailout would enable local officials to undertake such actions without waiting for preclearance. In this way, bailout gives jurisdictions that "ain't broke" (i.e., don't have any voter discrimination) the flexibility to respond to voters' needs.

Even in jurisdictions where there has been no recent history of voter discrimination, minority voters have questioned the jurisdiction's motive for bailing out as well as the potential of future voting problems if bailout is obtained. One Clarke County, Virginia, resident expressed his belief that "[t]his is something that should be left alone. I'm afraid of what could take place in the future."[44] "You may already have it in your plans to oust us," another resident stated.[45] When a jurisdiction is able to establish that it meets all requirements for bailout, including a showing that all aspects of the voting process are equally open to all citizens and have been for at least ten years, it seems highly unlikely that upon receiving a bailout local election officials will suddenly start denying the right to vote on account of race or membership in a language-minority group. Of course, mere "concerns" about future voting practices are insufficient as a matter of law to preclude bailout. Moreover, the ten-year fallback provision should provide some reassurance to concerned voters.

In addition, a jurisdiction facing concerns from minority voters over bailout can agree to provide the minority community with routine information related to future voting changes. In this way, far from hindering minority voting rights, the bailout process can actually enhance the minority community's knowledge about ongoing voting and election matters and increase the minority community's involvement in all aspects of the political process. For example, covered jurisdictions often encounter difficulty in recruiting poll officials. During the process of obtaining a bailout, local officials can inform minority community members about how to become a poll official and encourage them to serve. Here again, bailout can end up expanding the minority community's participation in the political process in ways that would not happen but for the bailout process.

4. *Choosing Not to Bail Out.* Some jurisdictions that know about the bailout option have chosen not to bail out. A jurisdiction, based on its specific circumstances, may be concerned about continuing discrimination in voting practices, either by the jurisdiction itself or governmental units that operate within it. For example, the currently ongoing case *Northwest Austin Municipal Utility District Number One v. Gonzales* involves a challenge to the VRA.[46] The case was brought by the Northwest Austin Municipal Utility District (the "MUD"), a governmental unit within the political subdivision of Travis County, Texas. The MUD argues that it should be able to bail out, and that if it can't, then the VRA is unconstitutional as applied to the MUD.[47] While the MUD seeks to bail out, it cannot do so because it does not meet the definition of "political subdivision" in the VRA.[48] Therefore, in order for the MUD to no longer be covered, Travis County would have to bail out. However, Travis County has not sought a bailout, and stated to the court that "the County actually receives benefits from the Section 5 preclearance process. The continued existence of the Act's preclearance requirements carries with it valuable educational and deterrent effects that aid Travis County and its lead election officials . . . in administering their many election-related duties, not just for themselves, but also for the more than one hundred jurisdictions whose elections the County handles and for the voters themselves."[49] Thus, Travis County serves as an example of a jurisdiction that has chosen not to bail out because of its specific circumstances.

In other cases, jurisdictions may choose not to bail out because they do not wish to disrupt racial harmony in their community or because they do not want to inflame the concerns of the minority community. Both Alexandria and Danville, Virginia, for example, held public hearings on bailout, but decided not to pursue bailout after members of the minority community raised concerns.

VI. Conclusion

Jurisdictions covered under the special provisions of the Voting Rights Act are required, among other things, to obtain preapproval—or preclearance—of all voting changes before implementing the changes. A jurisdiction that has a solid record of compliance with the act and that can show that it has taken positive steps to open up all aspects of the voting and election process can end, or "bail out" from, coverage under the special provisions. For those jurisdictions able to make such a showing, bailout can save money and reduce administrative costs and burdens. In some circumstances, bailout can actually provide opportunities to reach out to minority voters in special ways that the jurisdiction has not heretofore undertaken.

Although the VRA did not allow local jurisdictions to bail out if covered only because they were located within a state wholly covered by the VRA coverage formula, the 1982 amendments enabled local subdivisions to bail out independently of states. Bailing out most effectively takes place in three phases: gathering information; submitting this information to the Department of Justice and obtaining the Department's consent to a bailout; and filing court documents with the District Court for the District of Columbia for a declaratory judgment granting bailout. The jurisdiction must also publish notice about its intention to seek a bailout and any agreements reached with DOJ about the bailout.

The bailout provisions play an important role in the VRA by offering an incentive to covered jurisdictions to end discrimination and exempt themselves from coverage. Indeed, the first jurisdiction to obtain a bailout after the 1982 amendments, the City of Fairfax, Virginia, was motivated to do so in part by its wish to show that voting discrimination had not only had ended, but that all aspects of its voting and election procedures were equally open to all its citizens.[50]

In the years ahead, it will be interesting to see if a greater number of jurisdictions seek bailouts, particularly as the post-decennial-census redistricting process approaches. Jurisdictions fearing a racially charged or controversial redistricting process may choose to seek a bailout now and take the preclearance issue off the table. If that materializes, it will be important for DOJ to scrutinize such jurisdictions during bailout even more, to ensure that the protections of the VRA's preclearance provisions are not withdrawn when they are needed most.

Notes

1. Samuel Issacharoff, Pamela S. Karlan & Richard H. Pildes, The Law of Democracy: Legal Structure of the Political Process 546–48 (2d ed. 2001). *See also* Voting Section, Civil Rights Division, United States Department of Justice, The Voting Rights Act of 1965, http://www.usdoj.gov/crt/voting/intro/intro_b.htm (last visited July 23, 2007).

2. *See* The National Comm'n on the Voting Rights Act, Lawyers' Comm'n for Civil Rights Under Law, Protecting Minority Voters: The Voting Rights Act at Work, 1982–2005, at 3 (2006) [hereinafter Protecting Minority Voters]. The VRA protects citizens of the United States based on race, color, or membership in a language-minority group. 42 U.S.C. § 1973. The latter group, defined as citizens "from environments in which the dominant language is other than English," is protected from English-only election processes when the language minority comprises over five percent of the state or political subdivision. 42 U.S.C. § 1973b(f).

3. 42 U.S.C. § 1973b(b). The coverage formula, part of Section 4 of the original act, developed in three phases. The first phase, part of the original act, brought jurisdictions under coverage based on two general criteria, both of which had to be present on Nov. 1, 1964: (1) use of a test or device by the jurisdiction (as determined by the Attorney General); and (2) either less than 50 percent of the jurisdiction's voting-age population was registered to vote on Nov. 1, 1964, or less than 50 percent of the jurisdiction's voting-age population actually voted in the November 1964 presidential election. The second phase, part of the 1970 amendments, added to those jurisdictions already under coverage any jurisdiction that met the same criteria as in the first phase, but used Nov. 1, 1968, as the benchmark date.

The third phase, part of the 1975 amendments, added any jurisdiction meeting the same criteria using Nov. 1, 1972, as the benchmark date. The third phase also changed the meaning of "test or device" to cover jurisdictions where any language-minority group made up five percent of the population but election materials were only in English. *See* PROTECTING MINORITY VOTERS, *supra* note 2, at 27–28.

4. 42 U.S.C. § 1973c(a).

5. To obtain preclearance under Section Five, a covered jurisdiction must show that the proposed voting change is free of a racially discriminatory purpose or effect.

6. "Bailout" in this chapter refers to ending coverage under the coverage formula in Section Four of the Voting Rights Act, or § 1973b. Section 203 of the VRA, codified at 42 U.S.C. § 1973aa-1a, prescribed an entirely different coverage formula regarding jurisdictions required to provide language assistance to minority voters. This other formula, including ending coverage under the formula, is not addressed in this chapter.

7. 42 U.S.C. § 1973b. While this chapter emphasizes bailing out from preclearance requirements, this is only one effect of ending coverage under the coverage formula in 42 U.S.C. § 1973b(b). In addition to exemption from preclearance requirements, bailed-out jurisdictions are exempted from discretionary appointment of federal election observers by the Attorney General and from the automatic suspension of any test or device. 42 U.S.C. § 1973b(a)(1), 1973f.

8. PROTECTING MINORITY VOTERS, *supra* note 2, at 28. *See* City of Rome v. United States, 446 U.S. 156, 167–68 (interpreting the VRA so as to preclude bailout by political subdivisions about which a determination of coverage was not separately made).

9. South Carolina v. Katzenbach, 383 U.S. 301, 325, 327 (1966) ("The gist of the matter is that the Fifteenth Amendment supersedes contrary exertions of state power.").

10. 42 U.S.C. 1973b(b).

11. *Katzenbach,* 383 U.S. at 333.

12. "As long as the bailout option is available, there is less cause for concern that the Voting Rights Act may overreach congressional powers by imposing preclearance on a nondiscriminating government. *Without bailout, the problem of constitutional authority for preclearance becomes acute.*" *City of Rome,* 446 U.S. at 203 (1980) (Powell, J., dissenting) (emphasis added).

13. *See* The Voting Rights Act of 1965, *supra* note 1; Voting Section, Civil Rights Division, United States Department of Justice, VRA 2006, http://www.usdoj.gov/crt/voting/vra06.htm (last visited Aug. 1, 2007).

14. 42 U.S.C. §§ 1973b, 1973l(c)(2). "The term 'political subdivision' shall mean any county or parish, except that where registration for voting is not conducted under the supervision of a county or parish, the term shall include any other subdivision of a State which conducts registration for voting." 42 U.S.C. § 1973l(c)(2). *See also* PROTECTING MINORITY VOTERS, *supra* note 2, at 28.

15. PROTECTING MINORITY VOTERS, *supra* note 2, at 28. *Cf.* S. REP. No. 97-417, at 43–44, *reprinted in* 1982 U.S. CODE CONG. & AD. NEWS 177, 221–23 (*quoted in* Timothy G. O'Rourke, *Voting Rights Act Amendments of 1982: The New Bailout Provision and Virginia,* 69 VA. L. REV. 765, 783–84 (1983) ("These provisions, along with those addressing ten-year compliance

with the Voting Rights Act, aim to ensure that jurisdictions achieving bailout enjoy full minority participation in the electoral process.").

16. The coverage formula was renewed in 2006. The renewal mandates reconsideration by Congress in 2021 and expiration (barring further renewal) in 2031. *See* 42 U.S.C. §1973b(a)(8), (9).

17. "Test or device" is defined at 42 U.S.C. §1973b(c). A jurisdiction's use of a test or device in only a few instances, with prompt correction, no continuing effect, and no reasonable chance of recurrence will not bar the jurisdiction from meeting this first criteria. 42 U.S.C. §1973b(d).

18. 42 U.S.C. §1973b(a); *see also* Voting Section, Civil Rights Division, United States Department of Justice, Section 4 of the Voting Rights Act, http://www.usdoj.gov/crt/voting/misc/sec_4.htm (last visited July 17, 2007). Technically speaking, the District Court for the District of Columbia is not "objecting," but rather failing to enter a declaratory judgment in the jurisdiction's favor.

19. *Id.*

20. 42 U.S.C. §1973b(a); *see also* Section 4 of the Voting Rights Act, *supra* note 18.

21. The 1982 bailout amendments took effect on Aug. 5, 1984. *See* "CREDIT(S)," 42 U.S.C.A. §1973b.

22. Augusta, Botetourt, Essex, Frederick, Greene, Middlesex, Roanoke, Rockingham, Shenandoah, and Warren Counties in Virginia and the Cities of Fairfax, Harrisonburg, Salem, and Winchester in Virginia are the 14 political subdivisions that have bailed out. The Department of Justice Web site also lists Pulaski County, Virginia, as a jurisdiction that has been bailed out. *See* http://www.usdoj.gov/crt/voting/sec_5/covered.htm#note1 (last visited January 15, 2008). Pulaski County did seek a bailout in the District Court for the District of Columbia. However, Pulaski County failed to secure bailout approval from a *three*-judge panel, as is explicitly required by the Voting Rights Act. 42 U.S.C. §1973b(5) ("An action pursuant to this subsection shall be heard and determined by a court of three judges. . . .") Rather, Pulaski County received approval from only one judge. Consent Judgment and Decree, Pulaski County v. Gonzales, No. 05-1265 (D.D.C. filed Sept. 27, 2005).

23. 42 U.S.C. §1973b(a)(2).

24. Along these lines, the jurisdiction will need to gather data about preclearance to demonstrate that it (and all governmental units within it) has complied with VRA preclearance requirements, including preclearing all voting changes. To assist this process, the jurisdiction should obtain a Submission Tracking and Processing System (STAPS) report, which lists all past and current preclearance submissions for a given period of time. A jurisdiction can obtain a STAPS report from the Voting Section of the Civil Rights Division at the Department of Justice.

25. 42 U.S.C. §1973(a)(9).

26. Currently, both Page and Amherst Counties in Virginia are at this stage.

27. Since the 1982 amendments, not a single jurisdiction that has sought bailout has been notified by DOJ that it does not meet the bailout criteria.

28. 42 U.S.C. §1973b(a)(4) (emphasis added).

29. *Id.*

30. *See, e.g.*, Essex County v. Gonzales, No. 06-1631 (2006); Augusta County v. Gonzales, No. 05-01885 (2005). PACER, or Public Access to Court Electronic Records, is available at http://pacer.psc.uscourts.gov. An example of a consent judgment and decree is available at http://www.voterlaw.com/docs/Consent_Essex_County_Gonzales.pdf.

31. *Katzenbach*, 383 U.S. at 328.

32. S. REP. NO. 97-417, at 6, *reprinted in* 1982 U.S. CODE CONG. & AD. NEWS 177, 183 (*quoted in* Timothy G. O'Rourke, *Voting Rights Act Amendments of 1982: The New Bailout Provision and Virginia*, 69 VA. L. REV. 765, 770–71 (1983) (footnotes omitted)).

33. 42 U.S.C. § 1973b(a)(5). As with prior to bailout, all governmental units within the jurisdiction must also remain in compliance with the VRA. A discriminatory voting change by a governmental unit after bailout also brings the entire jurisdiction back under coverage.

34. Section Two of the VRA is codified at 42 U.S.C. § 1973.

35. *See* Section 5 Covered Jurisdictions, *supra* note 22.

36. For example, I spoke to the Virginia Association of Electoral Boards on March 4, 2006, in Hot Springs, Virginia, and to the Virginia Local Government Attorneys' Association on April 15, 2005, in Alexandria, Virginia.

37. The cost of a preclearance submission includes administrative costs to the county (e.g., the registrar's time) as well as attorneys' fees.

38. It is difficult to determine the average number of preclearance submissions for each jurisdiction. The Department of Justice reports receiving an average of 4,500 to 5,500 total preclearance submissions each year with between 14,000 and 20,000 proposed voting changes. Voting Section, Civil Rights Division, United States Department of Justice, About Section 5 of the Voting Rights Act, http://www.usdoj.gov/crt/voting/sec_5/about.htm (last visited Aug. 3, 2007).

39. *See* Robert Igoe, *Clark Moves Toward Voting Act Relief*, WINCHESTER STAR, May 16, 2007; Ruth Marlow, *Voting Rights Request Sparks Concern*, CLARKE TIMES-COURIER, May 23, 2007, *available at* www.timescommunity.com (search headline or author under "Archives" link); Rebecca Maynard, *Department of Justice Hears Voting Act Concerns*, CLARKE TIMES-COURIER, June 13, 2007, *available at* www.timescommunity.com (search headline or author under "Archives" link).

40. Marlow, *supra* note 39.

41. 42 U.S.C. § 1973b(a)(5). The D.C. District Court maintains jurisdiction for ten years after granting bailout. The Attorney General or an "aggrieved person" can file a complaint reopening the action, and the district court can vacate the bailout. *See supra* section IV and *supra* note 33; *see also* sample consent decree referenced in *supra* note 30.

42. Maynard, *supra* note 39.

43. 42 U.S.C. § 1973.

44. Marlow, *supra* note 39.

45. *Id.*

46. The case is currently pending before a three-judge court in the United States District Court for the District of Columbia, No. 06-01384.

47. First Amended Complaint, Northwest Austin Municipal Utility District Number One v. Gonzales, No. 06-01384 (D.D.C. filed Mar. 22, 2007).

48. *See* 42 U.S.C. § 1973l(c)(2), quoted *supra* note 14.

49. Travis County's Motion for Summary Judgment, With Accompanying Memorandum of Points and Authorities, Northwest Austin Municipal Utility District Number One v. Gonzales, No. 06-01384 (D.D.C. filed May 15, 2007). The author served as legal counsel to Travis County in this litigation.

50. J. Gerald Hebert, *City of Fairfax Obtains Voting Rights Act Bailout,* NATION'S CITIES WEEKLY, Nov. 24, 1997, at 12.

CHAPTER SEVENTEEN

HELP AMERICA VOTE ACT OF 2002:
ORIGINS AND IMPACT

LESLIE C. SCOTT*

I. Introduction

In the year 2000, the United States conducted the presidential election heard round the world. Contrary to elections of the past, the outcome of the single most significant election in our country in the course of a four-year election cycle was unknown for almost two months after the voting stopped. The delayed outcome allowed a very public examination of an electoral process in our country, and the result was not complimentary. To the contrary, the fact that the examination revealed a flawed and tortured process, culminating in the selection of the president by a United States Supreme Court edict,[1] led to monumental election reform unlike any seen since the Voting Rights and Civil Rights Acts of the 1960s.[2]

The Help America Vote Act of 2002,[3] broad in scope and accompanied by unprecedented authorized and appropriated federal funding, has now been implemented. As a result, several critical implementation issues have arisen and cries have been heard for new or revised reforms. The status of HAVA implementation, the problems that exist today as a result, and proposals for further reform are the subject of this chapter.

II. HAVA's Origins

In August 2006, some eight months after HAVA's implementation, the *New York Times* published an editorial asking whether the United States Supreme Court decision in *Bush v. Gore* had become the case "that must not be named."[4] By so doing, the editorialist suggested that the ruling that halted the 2000 Florida vote recount and handed the presidency to George W. Bush "is disappearing down the legal

---

* Butler, Snow, O'Mara, Stevens & Canada, PLLC.

world's version of the memory hole," the slot where, in Orwell's *1984*, government workers disposed of politically inconvenient records.[5]

The landmark case, handed down on December 12, 2000, held that the recount ordered by the Florida Supreme Court, the outcome of which would decide the recipient of Florida's electoral votes and the outcome of the presidential election, should be stopped because it lacked uniform standards and was thus violative of the United States Constitution's Equal Protection Clause. Finally, the Court held that to remand the case for determination of a proper remedy would endanger the state's safe harbor protection under the Election Control Act of 1887.[6]

The outcome of the presidential election hung in the balance with George Bush the certified winner prior to the outcome of the judicial appeals. In *Bush*, the Court was faced with challenges to election results based on alleged problems with the punch-card ballots used in Florida and the accuracy of the voted ballots' counting by machines. Consequently, the Florida Supreme Court ordered manual recounts to determine the intent of the voters in certain populous counties where machines had failed to detect votes for president.[7] In its opinion, the United States Supreme Court reasoned that the recounts ordered by the Florida Supreme Court were unacceptable because "intent of the voter" standards were either nonexistent or were subjective and varied from county to county. According to the Court, "Having once granted the right to vote on equal terms, the state may not, by arbitrary and disparate treatment, value one person's vote over that of another."[8]

Additionally, the Court interpreted the Election Control Act of 1887, which sets up a process for resolving electoral vote disputes in presidential elections. The Act had two major provisions: (1) the so-called "safe harbor" provision to the effect that state law procedures in place prior to the election for choosing electors are binding on Congress if they produce a definitive result at least six days prior to the meeting of presidential electors; (2) even after the safe harbor window closes, if only one set of returns from a state is submitted, it is accepted unless the United States House of Representatives and Senate, acting separately, agree to reject it on the ground that the votes were not "regularly given." If multiple returns are submitted, Congress must accept the return that conforms to the state determination under Article 2. If both houses of Congress agree to accept the same set of returns, it is accepted. If not, then the set of returns "verified by the executive of the state" is counted. The Court relied on the first of these provisions to hold that Florida's law clearly indicated it intended to take advantage of the safe harbor provision, while the "executive" provision (Florida's governor was Jeb Bush, George W. Bush's brother) loomed in the background.[9]

The *Bush v. Gore* case made legal history not just because it represented the first time a United States Supreme Court decision had effectively selected the president of the United States but also because its reasoning supported a practical conclusion that most states' electoral systems were likewise unconstitutional. Some seven years later, the case is historic for its lack of precedential value. The United States Supreme Court has not cited the case a single time since handing down the decision. Although the majority per curiam opinion in the case announced it was "limited to the present circumstances,"[10] such likely constitutes dictum and is certainly contrary to the concept of stare decisis.

In the lower federal courts, however, there is an ongoing dispute as to what *Bush v. Gore* means, if anything.[11] If the *Bush v. Gore* holding is applied in its most liberal sense, it could significantly affect future elections. If the case is relegated to the annals of history, it elected a president and birthed a sweeping piece of election reform that has changed the way elections are conducted for the foreseeable future.

III. HAVA's Critical Provisions

HAVA affects nearly every facet of elections in the United States; however, its most far-reaching and expensive reforms have to do with new election technology.

First, it authorized the appropriation of some $325 million for the replacement of old punch-card and lever-voting machines across the country.[12] These machines were in wide use across the nation when HAVA was enacted.[13] However, the *Bush v. Gore* decision had exposed at least punch-card devices as inaccurate recorders of some voters' true intentions.

A companion to the punch-card and lever-machine buy-out program was HAVA's mandatory minimum standards for voting devices used in federal elections effective January 2006. These standards required all voting devices after the law's effective date to

- Provide voters the opportunity to check for and correct ballot errors in a private and independent manner ("second chance voting");
- Have a manual audit capacity;
- Include at least one device per precinct that is accessible to the disabled;
- Provide alternative language accessibility pursuant to Section 201 of the Voting Rights Act; and
- Produce an error rate not exceeding the existing rate established by the Federal Election Commission Office of Election Administration.[14]

In addition, states were required to set standards that defined what constituted a legal vote for each type of voting device in use in the state (thus avoiding the *Bush v. Gore* standardless, equal protection defect)[15] and provide provisional or affidavit ballots to all persons not able to vote at the polls for any reason.[16]

The second major technology change mandated by HAVA was the implementation of a "single, uniform, official, centralized, interactive computerized statewide voter registration list defined, maintained, and administered at the state level."[17] This statewide voter registry (SWVR) system is required by HAVA to contain the names and registration information of every legally registered voter in the state.[18] The law's deadline for implementation of the system was 2004; however, the law allowed for, and most states received, a waiver of the deadline until January 2006.[19]

Perhaps the most controversial and contentious provision of the HAVA legislation is not related to technology but rather is its requirement that certain voters show a form of identification prior to voting a regular election day ballot.[20] While other issues addressed by HAVA were consensus issues in the area of election reform, voter identification had proven to be one of the most divisive issues in the area of election administration. At the time of HAVA's consideration by Congress, tension between voting integrity and voter access had existed in several states for some time.[21]

Prior to HAVA's enactment, some states employed no process for identifying voters other than asking for the voter's name and locating it on the registration list.[22] At the other end of the spectrum, some states required presentation of documentary identification as a pre-condition to voting. The forms of identification varied, but most of these states allowed voters to present government-issued identification cards, utility bills, credit cards, military identification, or other documents that contained a photo, birth date, address, or signature. In most such states, those without acceptable identification were required to sign an oath or affirmation concerning their identity and were allowed to vote a regular election day ballot.[23]

Although bipartisan and nonpartisan task forces making election reform recommendations after 2000 tended to sidestep the voter identification issue, as Congress moved toward enactment of major election reform, the Senate chose to address the issue. Its bill, S. 565, included language requiring first-time voters and voters who had moved to a new jurisdiction and registered to vote by mail to show evidence of their identity when voting.[24] The bill also required mail-in absentee voters to include a copy of their identification with their ballot. Finally, it also proposed that broader state identification programs be federally funded. Because these provisions in the Senate bill were so controversial, a legislative compromise was struck on HAVA's final identification requirements.[25] The new law provides certain requirements for voters who register by mail.[26] Under the HAVA compromise, if an individual registers to vote by mail and has not previously voted in a federal election, when that individual votes in person for the first time, he or she must present certain acceptable forms of identification in order to cast a regular election day ballot.[27] If this same voter votes absentee by mail, HAVA requires that he or she submit with the ballot a copy of acceptable identification.[28]

In order to address situations in which voters are required to provide these forms of identification but do not do so, HAVA mandates "provisional" or "affidavit" balloting.[29] In addition, HAVA exempts certain classes of individuals who would otherwise be required to present identification from the law. Among those exempted are those who register by mail and enclose with their application a copy of one of the forms of identification required by such individuals when voting.[30] Others exempted from the law's identification requirement include those entitled to vote under the Uniformed and Overseas Citizen Absentee Voting Act (UOCAVA) (42 U.S.C. § 1973ff-1 *et seq*), those allowed to vote other than in person under 42 U.S.C. § 1973ee-1(b)(2)(B)(ii), and those entitled to vote other than in person under any other federal law.[31]

HAVA provides that requirements, such as the voter identification mandate, are "minimum requirements." Therefore, the law allows states to enact election technology and administration requirements that are more strict than HAVA's so long as they are not inconsistent with HAVA or other federal law.[32]

HAVA enforcement is expressly limited to the institution of civil proceeding by the United States Attorney General against a state or local jurisdiction in the United States District Court for declaratory or injunctive relief as is necessary to carry out the law's mandates.[33] This federal enforcement scheme is complimented by HAVA's requirement that states establish administrative complaint procedures to address and remedy grievances as a condition of their receiving federal funds with which to pay for HAVA compliance.[34]

Finally, HAVA created a new federal agency without authority to pass rules or regulations[35] but required to issue voluntary guidelines for voting systems and other HAVA requirements, to study election issues, and to administer certain HAVA grant programs.[36] The Election Assistance Commission (EAC) consists of four members, two Democrats and two Republicans, appointed by the president with the advice and consent of the Senate.[37]

HAVA authorized the unprecedented appropriation of funds, in addition to the $325 million for punch-card and lever-machine replacement, totaling approximately $3 billion over the course of three fiscal years to fund the cost of states' expensive implementation of HAVA mandates.[38]

IV. Implementation Issues

A. DISABILITY-ACCESSIBLE VOTING DEVICES AND POLLING PLACES

In response to HAVA's mandated standards for voting devices that punch cards and lever machines could not meet,[39] and because HAVA required that at least one voting device at each precinct be disability accessible,[40] many states began to use or expanded their use of direct recording electronic (DRE) voting devices after HAVA's passage.[41] DRE devices allow voters to enter their choices on an electronic touch screen in a voting booth. The DRE machines allow voters to confirm their ballot choices before officially casting their votes, do not allow overvoting (casting more than one vote per race when not allowed to do so) and provide a notice to the voter (usually a flashing screen) when a ballot has been undervoted (a race has been skipped).

Section 301 of HAVA specifically provides that though all voting systems in place after January 2006 for use in federal elections must be completely disability accessible (voter is able to cast a private, independent vote in the precinct like any other voter), this requirement may be met by placement of at least one DRE machine in each precinct.[42] The DREs are designed to be outfitted with attachments allowing hands-free usage for paraplegic voters and headphones with audio capacity for voters who have sight or hearing impairments. Although DREs were not able to accommodate every conceivable disability at the time, HAVA's conclusion was that they were the best device available and the disability community celebrated this milestone in their electoral participation.

Nevertheless, soon questions about these "electronic" devices led to an increase in voters' skepticism as to their security.[43] These questions centered around the vendors' source code's nonaccessibility to local election officials and the possible hacking into the systems to change election outcomes in undetectable ways.[44] As these questions increased, however, states were facing HAVA's 2006 deadline for implementation of newly mandated voting devices.

Many states purchased DREs and moved forward. Others began to consider the purchase or addition of some vendors' response to the security concerns—an attachment called a voter-verified paper audit trail (VVPAT).[45] These attachments consist of paper canisters affixed to each device that print the voters' ballots and enable the voter to view that ballot, under clear plastic, prior to officially casting a vote. This is an addition to the electronic devices' summary screens that recapitulate each vote before a voter touches the "vote" or "cast ballot" button. In some cases, the paper canister is preserved as a means of recount in case of an election contest. In other cases, the paper merely provides information to the voter before he or she casts the ballot.[46]

Because this VVPAT is, by its very name, a paper record produced by DREs, it is not in a format accessible to sight-impaired voters. As a result, disability activists have questioned local and federal efforts to mandate this feature.[47] Under HAVA, one of the voting system requirements is that the system "shall . . . permit the voter to verify (in a private and independent manner) the votes selected by the voter on the ballot before the ballot is cast and counted."[48] DRE final summary screens comply with this mandate. They include an auditory component for sight-impaired and illiterate voters. The VVPAT is not required by HAVA. However, HAVA's disability accessibility requirements go further to require that voting systems be accessible to the disabled and provide "the same opportunity for access and participation as for other voters."[49] In addressing these requirements in the context of the VVPAT, the United States Department of Justice opined that even though sight-impaired voters will have no access to the contemporaneous paper records generated by the VVPATs, the addition of this feature by some states to their voting devices does not contravene HAVA.[50]

In explaining this opinion, the Justice Department's deputy assistant attorney general in the Office of Legal Counsel, Sheldon Bradshaw, wrote in October 2003 that a "voting system" under HAVA may or may not even include the paper record. According to Bradshaw, the question is not whether the paper record is accessible but rather whether the entire DRE system is accessible such that disabled voters have the same opportunity for access and participation that other voters enjoy. Taking something of a holistic approach to the issue, Bradshaw wrote that "same" does not mean "identical," because a serious disability necessarily results in a different voting experience. Therefore, so long as a disabled voter may access and participate in the essentials of the voting system (cast a ballot in private), the experience is sufficiently similar in kind, quality, quantity, or degree to that enjoyed by the non-disabled, according to the Department of Justice. So long as sight-impaired voters receive audio equipment enabling them to verify their choices before casting their ballots, the Justice Department opined that no HAVA violation is created by the generation and voter use of VVPATs.[51]

Other voting accessibility implementation issues presented themselves as HAVA deadlines approached. In March 2006, the United States Department of Justice announced it had filed suit against the State of New York alleging HAVA violations due to the state's failure to adopt disability-accessible voting systems capable of creating a permanent paper record that can be manually audited, among other grounds. The lawsuit was the culmination of an extensive effort by the Civil Rights Division of the Department of Justice to ensure timely and full HAVA implementation. Since New York State was not even close to compliance with HAVA's voting system requirements as of January 2006, suit was filed. New York had received some $221 million to assist with HAVA implementation, including $49 million to replace the state's lever-voting devices.[52]

In 2005, the secretary of state of Mississippi sought the Department of Justice's permission to sidestep HAVA's Section 301(a)(3) requirements for accessible voting systems and polling places. According to the Department of Justice's reply,[53] Mississippi sought consideration of a plan consisting of placement of at least one disability-accessible polling place with one accessible voting system in each of its 82 counties' five supervisor districts. This was proposed as a temporary plan until July 2007, after which the state proposed that all its counties' polling places would be physically accessible with accessible voting systems.

The Department of Justice rejected the Mississippi request, stating its view that under HAVA, all polling places used for federal elections must have at least one accessible system. In addition, the Department of Justice noted that without access to the polling place itself, access to the voting system is immaterial. Therefore, unless a portable system at each polling place could be taken to a voter and afford the same voting opportunity (privacy and independence), then each Mississippi polling place must be accessible and each possess at least one accessible device by January 2006 as prescribed by HAVA, according to the Justice Department.[54]

The EAC was asked in January 2007 whether a location for in-person absentee voting must comply with HAVA's requirement that each polling place be disability accessible.[55] According to the EAC, Section 301 of HAVA "was clearly intended to be applied to absentee voting." It followed that the EAC advised that Section 301 requires in-person absentee balloting be done at locations with disability-accessible voting devices.[56]

The skepticism over DRE security and the resulting cry for the VVPAT has served to pit the disability community against the civil rights community on a rare voting-rights issue.[57] How Congress chooses to resolve the issue (discussed below) and how individual states elect to shore up public confidence in DREs, which now blanket the country, are unanswered questions only two years post-HAVA implementation. However, the disability-accessible issues, and any litigation they spawn, will be worth noting.

B. STATEWIDE VOTER REGISTRY SYSTEM (SWVR)

HAVA requires the "chief state election official"[58] in each state to implement a centralized registry of all its voters that is automated and interacts with local voter registrars.[59] It is perhaps this requirement that will be HAVA's most successful and lasting legacy. However, implementation of the systems has not been without incident.

In most states, prior to HAVA, local voter registrars and other local election officials registered voters in their jurisdictions and maintained and updated the local voter registries. In this way, many states' voter registries were totally decentralized with the state having no role in maintaining voter information.[60] With HAVA, this changed radically and implementation became a tremendous, labor-intensive issue as well as a politically sensitive one, with authority shifting at least in part from local to state officials. First, in most states, there was no single software application on which voter data had previously been collected and maintained at the local level. Therefore, collecting the data and transferring it to a single centralized system meant that first, data had to be collected from many local systems that were maintained in diverse ways. Once this imposing task was complete, the process of placing data on a centralized system could begin. Loss of local control and resistance to change in system maintenance presented as many obstacles as the data transfer itself.[61]

Finally, HAVA requires that once the data is centrally collected and maintained on a going-forward basis, the data has to be coordinated in a timely way between various federal, state, and local agencies to ensure the accuracy and correctness of its information. Three forms of coordination are required: (1) coordination with registrar agencies; (2) coordination to verify voter registration information (motor vehicle offices and Social Security Administration); and (3) coordination neces-sary to perform voter-list maintenance (death and felony conviction records).[62] The coordination effort has also resulted in compliance issues.

In the course of SWVR system implementation, some voting-rights advocates expressed concerns that state record matching resulted in eligible voters' names not appearing on voter rolls. In two states, litigation over failed data matches suggests that data matching has not been reliable since, by their sheer volume and nature, such databases contain inaccurate information. Similarly, inconsistent types of data ("Will" instead of "William," for example) may result in rejected applications due to a failure to match record data based on the capability of a database to recognize the similarities. In the two states in question, plaintiffs argue database error rates of 20 to 30 percent have resulted in disqualification of a significant number of eligible voters.[63]

Since HAVA's passage, other SWVR system issues not addressed by HAVA have arisen. Variety among SWVR systems nationwide has led to confusion about HAVA's requirements and raised concerns about HAVA's lack of specificity in the area. Some states implemented HAVA's SWVR system requirement by creating a "top-down" voter registration system in which local officials supply information in real time to a state-run database. Other states implemented a "bottom-up" system in which local jurisdictions maintain their own voter rolls and submit registration data to a central system at the state level that merely compiles local voter lists at regular (not real time) intervals.[64] Critics argue that HAVA's consistent approach of mandating changes with the specific methodology for compliance being left to state and local officials[65] has led to implementation of SWVR systems ("bottom-up") that contain the same flaws that gave rise to the SWVR mandate originally. With local voter list control and mere state compilation on a periodic basis, it is argued that local main-tenance and updates to address duplications and invalid registrations is not taking place.[66]

As the deadline for HAVA's SWVR system implementation approached, some thirty-eight states were developing top-down systems, with the remainder build-ing either bottom-up or hybrid systems. Although the EAC, in interpreting HAVA, has indicated a preference for top-down systems, it has not opined that other sys-tems are noncompliant.[67] As a result, the voter registration goals implicit in HAVA's SWVR system mandate may not all be occurring.

Finally, while HAVA required SWVR systems to link to other state and federal databases to compare and match certain voter data and to update voter lists, HAVA made no requirement for interstate linking. In a mobile society, such a need exists if the goals of accurate voter rolls to prevent fraudulent voting and increase public confidence in the electoral process are to be met. Just as a statewide system con-necting local jurisdictions operates to delete duplicate registrations and address mobility of voters within a state, the same data comparison is needed between states, especially neighboring states, to address duplicate registrations caused by voter mobility across state lines.[68] A pilot project to do just this was initiated in 2006 among four states with duplications reported and valuable information generated to assist local registrars with their voter roll maintenance.[69]

As new technology is developed to register voters, new HAVA compliance issues arise as well. In August 2003, the State of Florida asked the Justice Department about its proposed paperless registration system completely integrated with its driver's license application process. The system consists of digital images and does not require an applicant to complete a paper registration form. For voter registration applications received by mail, Florida asked whether HAVA prohibited use of the digitally scanned document as the official record. In response, the Justice Department opined that no law prohibits a paperless voter registration system. However, federal retention and preservation laws pertaining to election records require that paper generated during the voter registration process be preserved for the prescribed period of 22 months.[70]

State compliance with HAVA's SWVR system deadlines has not been consistent nationwide. In several instances, the Justice Department was forced to file suit, usually followed immediately by entry of a consent order, to secure compliance with HAVA's SWVR mandate, among others.[71] In Alabama, the path to compliance was a bit rockier than most, at least insofar as public details are concerned. In 2006, the federal government sued Alabama and its then-secretary of state, Nancy Worley, for failing to meet HAVA's January 1, 2006, deadline for establishing an SWVR system.[72] Subsequently, Worley advised the federal court that she lacked the power to force state compliance (even though she was the state's chief election official). In response, the court stripped Worley of her responsibility for compliance and appointed Governor Bob Riley as a special master to resolve the state's compliance issues. Riley appointed a four-member commission to oversee this work.

By August 2007, Riley delivered a report to the federal court advising that the state would miss a court-ordered August 31, 2007, deadline for HAVA compliance but advised that Alabama was in "substantial compliance" with the court's order and would achieve full compliance within a couple of months. According to Riley, the compliance issue centered on coordination of the SWVR system with the Alabama Department of Public Safety system, because of the DPS's "complex interface." On October 24, 2007, the federal court ruled that Alabama had successfully implemented an SWVR that met federal requirements.[73]

Alabama's political and technology issues are not unique. Chief election officials are required by the SWVR system mandate to convince a large number of local election officials to release their hold on local voter registration records and depend on a new system controlled by the state. Also, the technology selected by the state undoubtedly presents user changes to many local officials who selected, used, and preferred their local software systems. Finally, coordination and interfacing of the state system with various state agencies (public safety, judicial, and vital statistics offices) requires negotiation with powerful offices not used to sharing often-confidential data with any non-law-enforcement office. While the political and technology difficulties in Alabama were publicly aired, they undoubtedly were duplicated to some degree in many states.

C. PROPOSED FEDERAL IMPLEMENTATION CHANGES

Because of complaints regarding the security of DRE voting devices, and in the face of questions from the disability community as to any changes to HAVA's DRE mandate, in 2007 Congress weighed in with new bills proposing amendments to HAVA. First, H.R. 811 (the "Holt Bill")[74] would require all electronic voting machines to produce "voter-verifiable paper records" and required that the paper version of a vote "shall serve as the vote of record in all accounts and audits." The bill would also enforce conflict-of-interest standards on laboratories that test voting systems. Finally, the bill would require that a suitable percentage of the paper ballots be audited to verify the machine tallies. Some 216 lawmakers co-sponsored this bill.[75]

In the Senate, Sen. Dianne Feinstein introduced S. 1487, the Ballot Integrity Act of 2007, and Sen. Bill Nelson introduced S. 559.[76] These parallel bills to the Holt legislation also included other reforms such as one barring secretaries of state, who certify final vote totals in many instances, from participating in partisan politics, and another requiring new and more "fair" procedures for purging voters from the rolls.

Implementation deadlines are an issue in all three bills. The Holt Bill requires implementation of voter-verifiable paper records in time for the 2008 presidential election. Some states argue that a rush to compliance with new federal mandates invites chaos. On the other hand, editorial writers assert that Congress vowed to repair the broken election systems in our country after the 2000 election and that eight years is long enough to wait on such reforms.[77] These same editorialists and other advocates seek to completely outlaw DRE systems because of the studies indicating their easy hackability and "vote flipping" technology glitch (votes for one candidate reported for the opponent).[78]

Finally, election experts have testified at length before both houses of Congress, asking them to allow local officials to get used to HAVA's mandates and give them time to come forward with their own recommended improvements based on their grass-roots familiarity with the electoral process.[79] In addition, they request that any changes Congress decides to enact not be effective in 2008 but be delayed until at least 2010 or 2012.[80]

In July 2007, talks in the House of Representatives over a possible legislative compromise on H.R. 811 hit a snag over how to guarantee easy access to voting machines for disabled voters without limiting technology improvements to everyone else. Holt has long believed that an optically scanned paper ballot system is preferable to a DRE system. However, House leaders have sided with the disabled community, who fear that optical ballots cannot be designed for their private and independent use.[81]

In the Senate, leaders of both political parties agreed that any electoral changes requiring implementation before 2010 would cause significant problems nation-wide.[82] At a late July 2007 Senate Rules Committee hearing, nearly all participants (including state election officials) agreed that changes in advance of the 2008 pres-idential election would prove chaotic to implement. Sen. Feinstein has said she will hold further hearings on S. 1487 when the State of California issues its report on a top-to-bottom review of voting machines and systems in that state.[83] As a part of that review, computer scientists hacked into voting systems manufactured by Diebold Election Systems, Hart InterCivic, and Sequoia Voting Systems.[84] Based on this preliminary information, Sen. Feinstein issued a press release calling reliance on DREs, especially those without a VVPAT, a "precarious risk" and advocating a move to optical scan machines, which use paper ballots and do not rely on a sepa-rate device (a printer) for the paper record.[85]

As states that spent the last four years working to implement HAVA mandates follow the debate on HAVA amendments, they face serious choices. Those with DRE systems without VVPATs may be inclined to retrofit their systems with this feature in anticipation of Congress's further mandate.[86] On the other hand, many experts doubt the reliability of DRE systems, even with the VVPAT, and advocate use of an optical scan/paper ballot system. The disability community, a powerful congres-sional lobby, is uncomfortable with the idea of abandoning a system that gives its members, for the first time in history, the ability to vote in person, independently, and privately like other citizens, at least not until alternative systems have been thoroughly adapted for the same type of disability accessibility.

V. Conclusion

Although enormously significant standing alone, one of HAVA's greatest legacies is the fact that its passage invited an atmosphere of electoral innovation and creativ-ity nationwide. Some states have used the HAVA mandates as an opportunity to improve and modernize the electoral process in ways not originally contemplated when HAVA was enacted, and that will spark other innovations over time.

On issues such as early voting, election-day voter registration, and electronic poll books, HAVA's imprint is felt. At present, only fifteen states lack some form of con-venience or no-excuse voting, with early results showing the promise of increased participation.[87] To eliminate new resident disenfranchisement, more states have adopted election-day registration with the hoped-for result being that last-minute voters, many of whom are younger voters, will vote in greater numbers.[88] The elec-tronic poll book is perhaps the innovation most directly triggered by HAVA reforms.

The SWVR system mandate is a natural first step toward having electronic polling place capability to access such systems and obviates the need for hard-copy poll books. The vast capacity of such systems to address any number of polling place issues has made these devices popular with poll workers and voters alike.[89]

Finally, some states, such as Mississippi, have used HAVA mandates and federal funds to completely overhaul their entire statewide election management systems with local election officials being linked electronically not just to the state's SWVR system, but also to a centralized system of management of every aspect of the electoral process—from precinct lists and jurisdictional boundary lines for state and local elected offices to generating ballot forms and reporting election returns, there is consistency and the convenience of a centralized system statewide.[90]

Truly HAVA has served to change the electoral landscape for the foreseeable future. As states continue to innovate as a result of HAVA's impetus, only time will tell us how significant its impact will be.

Notes

1. Bush v. Gore, 531 U.S. 98 (2000).
2. electionline.org "The Help America Vote Act at 5," November 2007, at 1, 5.
3. Pub. L. No. 107-252 (2002), 42 U.S.C. §§ 15301–15545.
4. Adam Cohen, *Has Bush v. Gore Become the Case That Must Not Be Named?*, N.Y. TIMES, Aug. 15, 2006.
5. *Id.*
6. *Supra* note 1 at 121, 122; 3 U.S.C. §§ 5, 15.
7. Palm Beach County Canvassing Board v. Harris, 772 So. 2d 1243 (2000).
8. *Supra* note 1 at 104, 105.
9. *Id.* at 109.
10. *Id.*
11. Common Cause S. Christian Leadership Conference of Greater La. v. Jones, 213 F. Supp. 2d 1006, 1007–08 (C.D. Cal. 2001); Black v. McGuffage, 209 F. Supp. 889 (P. Ill. 2002) (this case settled after the district court ruling); Stewart v. Blackwell, 444 F.3d 843 (6th Cir. 2006).
12. 42 U.S.C. §§ 15302, 15304(a)(2).
13. Election Data Services' survey of voting equipment changes from November 2000 to November 2006 indicates that in November 2000, some 566 counties nationwide used punch-card voting systems, with 454 counties still using them in November 2002. Some 434 counties nationwide used level voting systems in November 2000, with 287 counties still using them in November 2002. All totaled, according to the survey, some 1000 of the 3113 counties in the country (32 percent) used punch-card and lever machines in 2000, with 741 counties (24 percent) still using these devices at the time of HAVA's enactment in 2002. Election Data Services, Voting Equipment Studies (February 6 and October 2, 2006), *available at* http://www.edssurvey.com.

14. 42 U.S.C. § 15481(a).

15. *Id.* § 15481(a)(6).

16. *Id.* § 15482. *See also* Sandusky County Democratic Party v. Blackwell, 387 F.3d 565 (6th Cir. 2004) (affirming injunctive relief against Ohio Secretary of State directive in violation of HAVA provisional voting requirement); Florida Democratic Party v. Hood, 342 F. Supp. 2d 1073 (N.D. Fla. 2004) (issuing injunction against enforcement of state interpretation of HAVA provisional voting provision.).

17. 42 U.S.C. § 15483.

18. *Id.*

19. *Id.* § 15483(d).

20. *Id.* § 15483.

21. Attorney General Opinion, State of Michigan, No. 6930 (January 29, 1997); electionline.org, "Election Reform Briefing: Voter Identification," April 2002, at 9.

22. Nine states employed this method of identification prior to HAVA. They were North Dakota, South Dakota, Wyoming, Utah, North Carolina, Vermont, New Hampshire, Maine, and Rhode Island. electionline.org, "Election Reform Briefing: Voter Identification," April 2002, at 10–14.

23. Identification was required in eleven states in 2002, pre-HAVA. Those states were Alaska, Connecticut, Delaware, Florida, Georgia, Kentucky, Louisiana, Missouri, South Carolina, Texas, and Virginia. In another four states (Arkansas, Hawaii, Massachusetts, and Wisconsin), identification was optional pre-HAVA, with poll workers being authorized to ask for the documentation or localities being authorized to set their own rules. Eighteen states pre-HAVA (a majority) only required the voter to sign a poll book in order to be eligible to vote. Those states were Alabama, Arizona, California, Colorado, D.C., Idaho, Indiana, Iowa, Kansas, Maryland, Michigan, Minnesota, Mississippi, Montana, Nebraska, New Mexico, Oklahoma, and Washington. Nine states performed signature matches pre-HAVA by comparing the signature at the polls with the signature either on file with election officials or on a form of identification provided by the voter. Those states were Illinois, Nevada, New Jersey, New York, Ohio, Oregon, Pennsylvania, Tennessee, and West Virginia. electionline.org, "Election Reform Briefing: Voter Identification," April 2002, at 10–14.

24. S. 565, 110th Cong. (2002).

25. *See* D. Rogers, *Bill to Overhaul Voting System Clears Hurdles for Senate Passage,* WALL STREET JOURNAL, March 25, 2002.

26. 42 U.S.C. § 15483(b).

27. *Id.* § 15483(b)(2)(A)(i). The types of identification required to be presented are "a copy of a current utility bill, bank statement, government check, paycheck, or other government document that shows the name and address of the voter. . . ."

28. *Id.* The forms of acceptable identification that may be submitted along with a mail-in absentee ballot are "a copy of a current and valid photo identification . . . or a copy of a current utility bill, bank statement, government check, paycheck, or other government document that shows the name and address of the voter."

29. *Id.* § 15483(b)(2)(B)(i)(ii). See 42 U.S.C. § 15482(a) for requirements for provisional voting.

30. *Id.* § 15483(b)(3).

31. *Id.* § 15484. Since HAVA's adoption of its compromise identification requirement, battles in state legislatures and the courts have resulted as states attempt to take advantage of HAVA's "minimum requirements" language to expand their state identification requirements. See Weinschenk v. Missouri, 203 S.W.3d 301 (Mo. 2006); Indiana Democratic Party v. Rokita, 458 F. Supp. 2d 775 (S.D. Ind. 2006), *consolidated with* Crawford v. Marion County Election Board, *aff'd*, 472 F.3d 949 (7th Cir. 2007), *certiorari granted*, 128 S. Ct. 34 (2007); and Common Cause/Georgia League of Women Voters of Georgia, Inc. v. Billups, 439 F. Supp. 2d 1294 (N.D. Ga. 2006). The partisan debate on the issue has continued to rage at the national level as well. *See* Press Release, The Democratic Party, DNC Statement on Court Ruling to Block Georgia's Voter Identification Law, (July 10, 2006); and Press Release, Office of Senator Mitch McConnell, R-Ky. McConnell: Voting Is the Cornerstone of Our Democracy," (June 5, 2007). Since 2000, and aided by HAVA's passage of an identification requirement, the number of states requesting or requiring all voters to present some form of identification before casting votes in the polling place increased from eleven to twenty-four in 2007. electionline.org, "The Help America Vote Act at 5," November 2007, at 32.

32. 42 U.S.C. § 15484.

33. *Id.* § 15511.

34. *Id.* § 15512. However, the Sixth Circuit Court of Appeals has held that a private cause of action brought under 42 U.S.C. § 1983 does exist for enforcement of HAVA's "unambiguously conferred" rights. Sandusky County Democratic Party v. Blackwell, 387 F.3d 565 (6th Cir. 2004).

35. *Id.* § 15329.

36. *Id.* §§ 15322, 15501.

37. *Id.* § 15323.

38. *Id.* §§ 15304, 15407, 15424, 15443, 15453, 15462, 15472. The exact amount of federal HAVA funding spent by states since 2002 is $3,012,610,958. electionline.org "The Help America Vote Act at 5," November 2007, at 10–11.

39. *Id.* § 15481.

40. *Id.* § 15481(a)(3)(B).

41. A national survey indicated that in November 2006, some 1050 counties (33.72 percent) used electronic (DRE) voting devices as opposed to only 320 counties (10 percent) in November 2000. Election Data Services, Voting Equipment Studies (February 6 and October 2, 2006), *available at* http://www.edssurvey.com.

42. 42 U.S.C.. § 15481 (a)(3).

43. Daniel P. Tokaji, *Voting Technology: Beyond HAVA, Beyond Paper,* ELECTION LAW @ MORITZ, Mar. 14, 2006, http://moritzlaw.osu.edu/electionlaw/comments/2006/060314 .php.

44. *Id. See also* electionline.org, "The Help America Vote Act at 5," November 2007, at 15.

45. *Id. See also* electionline.org, "The Help America Vote Act at 5," November 2007, at 14, which surveyed states and found that, as of late 2007, seventeen states use DREs requiring VVPATs; two states use DREs with VVPATs, although they are not required to; eighteen states use and/or require paper-based voting systems; and fourteen states use DREs without VVPATs.

46. *Id. See also* electionline.org "Recounts: from Punch Cards to Paper Trails" October 2005, at 7–9.

47. Am. Ass'n of People with Disabilities v. Shelley, 324 F. Supp. 2d 1120, 1125 (C.D. Cal. 2004); National Council on Independent Living, Voting Rights Working Group, Voting Rights Guiding Statement (Mar. 10, 2007), http://www.ncil.org/news/ VotingPositionStatement.html; electionline.org "Recounts: from Punch Cards to Paper Trails" October 2005, at 9.

48. 42 U.S.C. § 15481(a)(1)(A)(i).

49. *Id.* § 15481(a)(3)(A).

50. Memorandum Op. of Deputy Assistant Att'y Gen., Civil Rights Division, *Whether Certain Direct Recording Electronic Voting Systems Comply with the Help America Vote Act and the Americans with Disabilities Act* (Oct. 10, 2003), www.usdoj.gov/olc/2003opinions.htm.

51. *Id.* The Paralyzed Veterans of America filed suit on August 1, 2006, against California election officials challenging, among other things, the inaccessibility of DREs using VVPATs in the state to those with visual disabilities. www.moritzlaw.osu.edu/blogs/tokaj/2006/08/ disability-rights-suit-over-Calif.html and pleadings filed in Paralyzed Veterans of America v. McPherson, C:06-4670 (N.D. Calif.).

52. New York state has still not complied with HAVA's accessible voting machine requirement, with the parties expected in court on the issue in late 2007. With the February 2008 presidential primary election fast approaching, voters are presently set to use non-compliant machines. *New York Won't Meet HAVA Requirements by Presidential Primary,* Nov. 25, 2007, http://www.newsday.com. A similar DOJ suit was filed against Maine (Press Release, Department of Justice, Justice Department Announces Agreement to Protect Voting Rights in Maine (July 28, 2006), *available at* http://www.usdoj.gov/opa/pr/2006/July/06_crt_475.html.

53. Letter from Hans. A. von Spakovsky, Counsel to the Assistant Att'y Gen., U.S. Department of Justice, to John Eads, Mississippi Assistant Sec'y of State for Elections (Mar. 4, 2005), *available at* http://www.usdoj.gov/crt/voting/hava/msdisability.htm.

54. *Id.*

55. U.S. Election Assistance Comm'n, EAC Advisory 2007-001: Accessible Voting Systems for In-Person Absentee Voting, (Jan. 24, 2007), www.eac.gov/election/advisories %20and%20guidance.

56. *Id.*

57. *Supra* note 51.

58. 42 U.S.C. §15483(a)(A).

59. *Id.* § 15483.

60. *Supra* note 2 at 23, 24.

61. *Id.*

62. *Id.* § 15483(a)(5)(B).

63. *Supra* note 2, at 28, *citing* The Brennan Center for Justice at NYU School of Law, Using Databases to Keep Eligible Voters Off Roles, September 2006.

64. Report of the Commissioner on Federal Election Reform, Building Confidence in United States Elections (September 2005) at 10–11.

65. 42 U.S.C. § 15485.

66. *Id. See* note 64 above.

67. *Id. See also* U.S. Election Assistance Commission, Voluntary Guidance on Implementation of Statewide Voter Registration Lists (July 2005) at 6.

68. *Supra* note 2 at 27–28.

69. *Id.*

70. Letter from Hans A. von Spakovsky, Counsel to the Assistant Att'y Gen., U.S. Dept. of Justice, to Paul W. Craft, Division of Elections, Fla. Dept. of State (August 12, 2003), *available at* http://www.usdoj.gov/crt/voting/hava/florida_ltr.htm.

71. Press Release, Department of Justice, Justice Department Agreement Will Help Protect Voting Rights of New Jersey Citizens in 2006 Federal Election (Oct. 12, 2006), *available at* http://www.usdoj.gov/opa/pr/2006/October/06_crt_698.html; Press Release, Department of Justice, Justice Department Sues Alabama Over Voting Rights (May 1, 2006), *available at* http://www.usdoj.gov/opa/pr/2006/May/06_crt_265.html; United States of America v. State of Alabama, Case No. 2:06-cv-392-WKW (N.D. Ala. 2006), *available at* http://www.moritzlaw.osu.edu/electionlaw/litigation/alabama.php.

72. Press Release, Department of Justice, Federal Court Rules Alabama in Compliance with Help America Vote Act (Oct. 25, 2007), *available at* http://www.usdoj.gov/opa/pr/2007/October/07_crt_848.html; Sebastian Kitchen, *Riley: State Will Miss August 31 Deadline*, PRESS-REGISTER (Mobile, Ala.), Aug. 9, 2007, *available at* http://www.al.com/press-register/stories/index.ssf?/base/news/118665137124250.xml&coll=3.

73. *See* Justice Department Sues Alabama Over Voting Rights, *supra* note 71; *see also* Sebastian Kitchen, *Governor: State in Compliance*, PRESS-REGISTER (Mobile, Ala.), Oct. 24, 2007, *available at* http://www.al.com/press-register/stories/index.ssf?/base/news/119321789482250.xml&coll=3.

74. H.R. 811, 110th Cong. (2007).

75. *Id.*

76. S. 1487 and S. 559, 110th Cong. (2007).

77. Christopher Drew, *Overhaul Plan for Vote System Will Be Delayed*, N.Y. TIMES, July 20, 2007, *available at* http://www.nytimes.com/2007/07/20/washington/20vote.html; Editorial, *A Chance to Make Votes Count*, N.Y. TIMES, Sept. 6, 2007, *available at* http://www.nytimes.com/2007/09/06/opinion/06thu1.html.

78. *Id.*

79. Testimony of R. Doug Lewis, Executive Director, CERA National Association of Election Officials (Election Center), before the U.S. Senate Rules Committee (July 25, 2007), *available at* http://www.electioncenter.org/Testimony/Senate/SenateTestimony7-2007Lewis.pdf; Testimony of R. Doug Lewis, Executive Director, CERA National Association of Election Officials (Election Center), before the U.S. House Administration Elections Hearing (Mar. 20, 2007).

80. *Id.*

81. Drew, *supra* note 48; *A Chance to Make Votes Count*, *supra* note 77.

82. *Id.*

83. *Id.*

84. *Id.*

85. *Id.*

86. Predicting future congressional action can prove expensive. In advance of HAVA, attention focused on the problems with punch-card and lever-voting machines. Consequently, some jurisdictions invested in OMR devices (paper ballots read by optical mark readers) to replace these devices. HAVA's mandates regarding disability accessibility, leading many states later to purchase DREs, meant those jurisdictions predicted wrongly.

87. *Supra* note 2 at 38.

88. *Id.* at 39.

89. *Id.* at 40.

90. Miss. Code Ann. §§ 23-15-33 et seq., 23-15-113, 23-15-165, 23-15-531.10 (1972).

Table of Cases

Index